COPELAND'S
TREASURY FOR BOOKLOVERS

THE BLESSED DAMOSEL

From a painting by Dante Gabriel Rossetti

COPELAND'S TREASURY FOR BOOKLOVERS

A PANORAMA OF ENGLISH
AND AMERICAN POETRY AND PROSE FROM THE
EARLIEST TIMES TO THE PRESENT

SELECTED AND EDITED

BY

CHARLES TOWNSEND COPELAND

BOYLSTON PROFESSOR OF
ORATORY AND RHETORIC AT HARVARD UNIVERSITY

VOLUME III

NEW YORK
CHARLES SCRIBNER'S SONS
1930

CONTENTS

CONTENTS

Whole Duty of Children 223
Foreign Lands 223
The Land of Counterpane 223
System 224
Good and Bad Children 224
The Unseen Playmate 224
From Underwoods
Requiem 224
The Celestial Surgeon 225
Say not of me that weakly I declined 225
From The Manse
Probably Arboreal 225
A Lodging for the Night 227
Will o' the Mill 244
Markheim 265

WILLIAM ERNEST HENLEY
From Hospital Sketches
Before 279
Operation 279
Apparition 279

JOSEPH CONRAD
Youth 280

SIR WILLIAM WATSON
Wordsworth's Grave 306

KENNETH GRAHAME
From The Golden Age
The Roman Road 310
The Burglars 316

SIR JAMES MATTHEW BARRIE
From My Lady Nicotine
Matrimony and Smoking Compared 321
My First Cigar 325
The Arcadia Mixture 327
From Sentimental Tommy
The Essay-Writing Contest 331
From Margaret Ogilvy
My Heroine 334
R. L. S. 340
From The Little White Bird
The Inconsiderate Waiter 346

FRANCIS THOMPSON
Daisy 354
The Poppy 354
The Hound of Heaven 356

WILLIAM BUTLER YEATS
The Lake Isle of Innisfree 358
From Kathleen ni Hoolihan 359

RUDYARD KIPLING
The Last Chantey 365
The Truce of the Bear 366
The Bell Buoy 367
Mandalay 368
The 'Eathen 369
Chant-Pagan 371

LIONEL JOHNSON
By the Statue of King Charles at Charing Cross 372

ILLUSTRATIONS

COPELAND'S
TREASURY FOR BOOKLOVERS

COPELAND'S
TREASURY FOR BOOKLOVERS

CHARLES DICKENS (1812-1870)

From THE POSTHUMOUS PAPERS OF THE PICKWICK CLUB

The first Day's Journey and the first Evening's Adventures; with their Consequences

THAT punctual servant of all work, the sun, had just risen, and begun to strike a light on the morning of the thirteenth of May, one thousand eight hundred and twenty-seven, when Mr. Samuel Pickwick burst like another sun from his slumbers, threw open his chamber window, and looked out upon the world beneath. Goswell street was at his feet, Goswell street was on his right hand—as far as the eye could reach, Goswell street extended on his left; and the opposite side of Goswell street was over the way. "Such," thought Mr. Pickwick, "are the narrow views of those philosophers who, content with examining the things that lie before them, look not to the truths which are hidden beyond. As well might I be content to gaze on Goswell street forever, without one effort to penetrate to the hidden countries which on every side surround it." And having given vent to this beautiful reflection, Mr. Pickwick proceeded to put himself into his clothes; and his clothes into his portmanteau. Great men are seldom over-scrupulous in the arrangement of their attire; the operation of shaving, dressing, and coffee-imbibing was soon performed: and, in another hour, Mr. Pickwick, with his portmanteau in his hand, his telescope in his great-coat pocket, and his note-book in his waistcoat, ready for the reception of any discoveries worthy of being noted down, had arrived at the coach stand in St. Martin's-le-Grand.

"Cab!" said Mr. Pickwick.

"Here you are, sir," shouted a strange specimen of the human race in a sackcloth coat, and apron of the same, who with a brass label and number round his neck, looked as if he were catalogued in some collection of rarities. This was the waterman. "Here you are, sir. Now, then, fust cab!" And the first cab having been fetched from the public-house, where he had been smoking his first pipe, Mr. Pickwick and his portmanteau were thrown into the vehicle.

"Golden Cross," said Mr. Pickwick.

"Only a bob's vorth, Tommy," cried the driver, sulkily, for the information of his friend the waterman, as the cab drove off.

"How old is that horse, my friend?" inquired Mr. Pickwick, rubbing his nose with the shilling he had reserved for the fare.

"Forty-two," replied the driver, eying him askant.

"What!" ejaculated Mr. Pickwick, laying his hand upon his note-book. The driver reiterated his former statement. Mr. Pickwick looked very hard at the man's face, but his features were immovable, so he noted down the fact forthwith.

"And how long do you keep him out at a time?" inquired Mr. Pickwick, searching for further information.

"Two or three veeks," replied the man.

"Weeks!" said Mr. Pickwick in astonishment—and out came the note-book again.

"He lives at Pentonwil when he's at home," observed the driver, coolly, "but we seldom takes him home, on account of his veakness."

"On account of his weakness," reiterated the perplexed Mr. Pickwick.

"He always falls down, when he's took out o' the cab," continued the driver, "but when he's in it we bears him up werry tight, and takes him in werry short, so as he can't werry well fall down, and we've got a pair o' precious large wheels on; so ven he *does* move, they run after him, and he must go on—he can't help it."

Mr. Pickwick entered every word of this statement in his note-book, with the view of communicating it to the club as a singular instance of the tenacity of life in horses, under trying circumstances. The entry was scarcely completed when they reached the Golden Cross. Down jumped the driver, and out got Mr. Pickwick. Mr. Tupman, Mr. Snodgrass, and Mr. Winkle, who had been anxiously waiting the arrival of their illustrious leader, crowded to welcome him.

"Here's your fare," said Mr. Pickwick, holding out the shilling to the driver.

What was the learned man's astonishment, when that unaccountable person flung the money on the pavement, and requested in figurative terms to be allowed the pleasure of fighting him (Mr. Pickwick) for the amount!

"You are mad," said Mr. Snodgrass.

"Or drunk," said Mr. Winkle.

"Or both," said Mr. Tupman.

"Come on," said the cab-driver, sparring away like clockwork. "Come on—all four on you."

"Here's a lark!" shouted half a dozen hackney coachmen. "Go to vork, Sam,"—and they crowded with great glee round the party.

"What's the row, Sam?" inquired one gentleman in black calico sleeves.

"Row!" replied the cabman, "what did he want my number for?"

"I didn't want your number," said the astonished Mr. Pickwick.

"What did you take it for, then?" inquired the cabman.

"I didn't take it," said Mr. Pickwick, indignantly.

"Would anybody believe," continued the cab-driver, appealing to the crowd,—"would anybody believe as an informer 'ud go about in a man's cab, not only takin' down his number, but ev'ry word he says into the bargain?" (a light flashed upon Mr. Pickwick—it was the note-book).

"Did he though?" inquired another cabman.

"Yes, did he," replied the first—"and then arter aggerawatin' me to assault him, gets three witnesses here to prove it. But I'll give it him, if I've six months for it. Come on," and the cabman dashed his hat upon the ground, with a reckless disregard of his own private property, and knocked Mr. Pickwick's spectacles off, and followed up the attack with a blow on Mr. Pickwick's nose, and another on Mr. Pickwick's chest, and a third in Mr. Snodgrass's eye, and a fourth, by way of variety, in Mr. Tupman's waistcoat, and then danced into the road, and then back again to the pavement, and finally dashed the whole temporary supply of breath out of Mr. Winkle's body; and all in half a dozen seconds.

"Where's an officer?" said Mr. Snodgrass.

"Put 'em under the pump," suggested a hot-pie man.

"You shall smart for this," gasped Mr. Pickwick.

"Informers," shouted the crowd.

"Come on," cried the cabman, who had been sparring without cessation the whole time.

The mob had hitherto been passive spectators of the scene, but as the intelligence of the Pickwickians being informers was spread among them, they began to canvass with considerable vivacity the propriety of enforcing the heated pastry-vender's proposition: and there is no saying what acts of personal aggression they might have committed, had not the affray been unexpectedly terminated by the interposition of a new-comer.

"What's the fun?" said a rather tall thin young man, in a green coat, emerging suddenly from the coach-yard.

"Informers!" shouted the crowd again.

"We are not," roared Mr. Pickwick, in a tone which, to any dispassionate listener, carried conviction with it.

"Ain't you, though,—ain't you?" said the young man, appealing to Mr. Pickwick, and making his way through the crowd, by the infallible process of elbowing the countenances of its component members.

That learned man in a few hurried words explained the real state of the case.

"Come along, then," said he of the green coat, lugging Mr. Pickwick after him by main force, and talking the whole way. "Here, No. 924, take your fare, and take yourself off—respectable gentleman,—know him well—none of your nonsense—this way, sir—where's your friends? —all a mistake, I see—never mind—accidents will happen—best regulated families—never say die—down upon your luck—pull him up— put that in his pipe—like the flavor—damned rascals." And with a lengthened string of similar broken sentences, delivered with extraordinary volubility, the stranger led the way to the travellers' waiting-room, whither he was closely followed by Mr. Pickwick and his disciples.

"Here, waiter," shouted the stranger, ringing the bell with tremendous violence, "glasses round,—brandy-and-water, hot and strong, and sweet, and plenty,—eye damaged, sir? Waiter; raw beef-steak for the gentleman's eye,—nothing like raw beef-steak for a bruise, sir; cold lamp-post very good, but lamp-post inconvenient—damned odd standing in the open street half an hour, with your eye against a lamp-post,— eh—very good—ha! ha!" And the stranger, without stopping to take breath, swallowed at a draught full half a pint of the reeking brandy-and-water, and flung himself into a chair with as much ease as if nothing uncommon had occurred.

While his three companions were busily engaged in proffering their thanks to their new acquaintance, Mr. Pickwick had leisure to examine his costume and appearance.

He was about the middle height, but the thinness of his body, and the length of his legs, gave him the appearance of being much taller. The green coat had been a smart dress garment in the days of swallow-tails, but had evidently in those times adorned a much shorter man than the stranger, for the soiled and faded sleeves scarcely reached to his wrists. It was buttoned closely up to his chin, at the imminent hazard of splitting the back; and an old stock, without a vestige of shirt collar, ornamented his neck. His scanty black trousers displayed here and there those shiny patches which bespeak long service, and were strapped very tightly over a pair of patched and mended shoes, as if to conceal the dirty white stockings, which were nevertheless distinctly visible. His long black hair escaped in negligent waves from beneath each side of his old pinched-up hat; and glimpses of his bare wrist might be observed, between the tops of his gloves, and the cuffs of his coat sleeves. His face was thin and haggard; but an indescribable air of jaunty impudence and perfect self-possession pervaded the whole man.

Such was the individual, on whom Mr. Pickwick gazed through his spectacles (which he had fortunately recovered), and to whom he proceeded, when his friends had exhausted themselves, to return, in chosen terms, his warmest thanks for his recent assistance.

"Never mind," said the stranger, cutting the address very short, "said enough,—no more; smart chap that cabman—handled his fives well; but if I'd been your friend in the green jemmy—damn me—punch his head—'cod I would,—pig's whisper,—pieman too,—no gammon."

This coherent speech was interrupted by the entrance of the Rochester coachman, to announce that "The Commodore" was on the point of starting.

"Commodore!" said the stranger, starting up, "my coach,—place booked,—one outside—leave you to pay for the brandy-and-water,—want change for a five,—bad silver—Brummagem buttons—won't do—no go—eh?" and he shook his head most knowingly.

Now it so happened that Mr. Pickwick and his three companions had resolved to make Rochester their first halting place too; and having intimated to their new-found acquaintance that they were journeying to the same city, they agreed to occupy the seat at the back of the coach, where they could all sit together.

"Up with you," said the stranger, assisting Mr. Pickwick on to the roof with so much precipitation, as to impair the gravity of that gentleman's deportment very materially.

"Any luggage, sir?" inquired the coachman.

"Who—I? Brown paper parcel here, that's all, other luggage gone by water,—packing cases, nailed up—big as houses—heavy, heavy, damned heavy," replied the stranger, as he forced into his pocket as much as he could of the brown paper parcel, which presented most suspicious indications of containing one shirt and a handkerchief.

"Heads, heads, take care of your heads," cried the loquacious stranger, as they came out under the low archway, which in those days formed the entrance to the coach-yard. "Terrible place—dangerous work—other day—five children—mother—tall lady, eating sandwiches—forgot the arch—crash—knock—children look round—mother's head off —sandwich in her hand—no mouth to put it in—head of a family off—shocking, shocking. Looking at Whitehall, sir,—fine place—little window—somebody else's head off there, eh, sir?—he didn't keep a sharp look-out enough either—eh, sir, eh?"

"I was ruminating," said Mr. Pickwick, "on the strange mutability of human affairs."

"Ah! I see—in at the palace door one day, out at the window the next. Philosopher, sir?"

"An observer of human nature, sir," said Mr. Pickwick.

"Ah, so am I. Most people are when they've little to do, and less to get. Poet, sir?"

"My friend Mr. Snodgrass has a strong poetic turn," said Mr. Pickwick.

"So have I," said the stranger. "Epic poem,—ten thousand lines—revolution of July—composed it on the spot—Mars by day, Apollo by night,—bang the field-piece, twang the lyre."

"You were present at that glorious scene, sir?" said Mr. Snodgrass.

"Present! think I was;[1] fired a musket,—fired with an idea,—rushed into wine shop—wrote it down—back again—whiz, bang—another idea—wine shop again—pen and ink—back again—cut and slash —noble time, sir. Sportsman, sir?" abruptly turning to Mr. Winkle.

"A little, sir," replied that gentleman.

"Fine pursuit, sir,—fine pursuit.—Dogs, sir?"

"Not just now," said Mr. Winkle.

"Ah! you should keep dogs—fine animals—sagacious creatures— dog of my own once—Pointer—surprising instinct—out shooting one day — entering enclosure — whistled — dog stopped — whistled again— Ponto—no go: stock-still—called him—Ponto, Ponto—wouldn't move —dog transfixed—staring at a board—looked up, saw an inscription— 'Gamekeeper has orders to shoot all dogs found in this enclosure'— wouldn't pass it—wonderful dog—valuable dog that—very."

"Singular circumstance that," said Mr. Pickwick. "Will you allow me to make a note of it?"

"Certainly, sir, certainly—hundred more anecdotes of the same animal.—Fine girl, sir" (to Mr. Tracy Tupman, who had been bestowing sundry anti-Pickwickian glances on a young lady by the roadside).

"Very!" said Mr. Tupman.

"English girls not so fine as Spanish—noble creatures—jet hair— black eyes—lovely forms—sweet creatures—beautiful."

"You have been in Spain, sir?" said Mr. Tracy Tupman.

"Lived there—ages."

[1] A remarkable instance of the prophetic force of Mr. Jingle's imagination; this dialogue occurred in the year 1827: and the Revolution in 1830.

"Many conquests, sir?" inquired Mr. Tupman.

"Conquests! Thousands. Don Bolaro Fizzgig — Grande — only daughter—Donna Christina—splendïd creature—loved me to distraction —jealous father—high-souled daughter—handsome Englishman—Donna Christina in despair—prussic acid—stomach pump in my portmanteau— operation performed—old Bolaro in ecstasies—consent to our union— join hands and floods of tears—romantic story—very."

"Is the lady in England now, sir?" inquired Mr. Tupman, on whom the description of her charms had produced a powerful impression.

"Dead, sir—dead," said the stranger, applying to his right eye the brief remnant of a very old cambric handkerchief. "Never recovered the stomach pump—undermined constitution—fell a victim."

"And her father?" inquired the poetic Snodgrass.

"Remorse and misery," replied the stranger. "Sudden disappearance —talk of the whole city—search made everywhere—without success— public fountain in the great square suddenly ceased playing—weeks elapsed—still a stoppage—workmen employed to clean it—water drawn off—father-in-law discovered sticking head first in the main pipe with a full confession in his right boot—took him out, and the fountain played away again, as well as ever."

"Will you allow me to note that little romance down, sir?" said Mr. Snodgrass, deeply affected.

"Certainly, sir, certainly,—fifty more if you like to hear 'em— strange life mine—rather curious history—not extraordinary, but singular."

In this strain, with an occasional glass of ale, by way of parenthesis, when the coach changed horses, did the stranger proceed, until they reached Rochester Bridge, by which time the note-books, both of Mr. Pickwick and Mr. Snodgrass, were completely filled with selections from his adventures.

"Magnificent ruin!" said Mr. Augustus Snodgrass, with all the poetic fervor that distinguished him, when they came in sight of the fine old castle.

"What a study for an antiquarian," were the very words which fell from Mr. Pickwick's mouth, as he applied his telescope to his eye.

"Ah! fine place," said the stranger, "glorious pile—frowning walls— tottering arches—dark nooks—crumbling staircases—old cathedral too —earthy smell—pilgrims' feet worn away the old steps—little Saxon doors—confessionals like money-takers' boxes at theatres—queer customers those monks—Popes, and Lord Treasurers, and all sorts of old fellows, with great red faces, and broken noses, turning up every day

—buff jerkins too—matchlocks—Sarcophagus—fine place—old legends too—strange stories: capital;" and the stranger continued to soliloquize until they reached the Bull Inn, in the High street, where the coach stopped.

"Do you remain here, sir?" inquired Mr. Nathaniel Winkle.

"Here—not I—but you'd better—good house—nice beds—Wright's next house, dear—very dear—half a crown in the bill, if you look at the waiter—charge you more if you dine at a friend's than they would if you dined in the coffee-room—rum fellows—very."

Mr. Winkle turned to Mr. Pickwick, and murmured a few words; a whisper passed from Mr. Pickwick to Mr. Snodgrass, from Mr. Snodgrass to Mr. Tupman, and nods of assent were exchanged. Mr. Pickwick addressed the stranger.

"You rendered us a very important service, this morning, sir," said he; "will you allow us to offer a slight mark of our gratitude by begging the favor of your company at dinner?"

"Great pleasure—not presume to dictate, but broiled fowl and mushrooms—capital thing! What time?"

"Let me see," replied Mr. Pickwick, referring to his watch. "It is now nearly three. Shall we say five?"

"Suit me excellently," said the stranger, "five precisely—till then—care of yourselves;" and lifting the pinched-up hat a few inches from his head, and carelessly replacing it very much on one side, the stranger, with half the brown paper parcel sticking out of his pocket, walked briskly up the yard, and turned into the High street.

"Evidently a traveller in many countries, and a close observer of men and things," said Mr. Pickwick.

"I should like to see his poem," said Mr. Snodgrass.

"I should like to have seen that dog," said Mr. Winkle.

Mr. Tupman said nothing; but he thought of Donna Christina, the stomach pump, and the fountain; and his eyes filled with tears.

A private sitting-room having been engaged, bedrooms inspected, and dinner ordered, the party walked out to view the city and adjoining neighborhood.

We do not find, from a careful perusal of Mr. Pickwick's notes on the four towns, Stroud, Rochester, Chatham, and Brompton, that his impressions of their appearance differ in any material point, from those of other travellers who have gone over the same ground. His general description is easily abridged.

"The principal productions of these towns," says Mr. Pickwick, "appear to be soldiers, sailors, Jews, chalk, shrimps, officers, and dock-yard men. The commodities chiefly exposed for sale in the public streets, are marine stores, hard-bake, apples, flat-fish and oysters. The streets present a lively and animated appearance, occasioned chiefly by the conviviality of the military. It is truly delightful to a philanthropic mind, to see these gallant men, staggering along under the influence of an overflow, both of animal and ardent spirits; more especially when we remember that the following them about, and jesting with them, affords a cheap and innocent amusement for the boy population. Nothing (adds Mr. Pickwick) can exceed their good humor. It was but the day before my arrival, that one of them had been most grossly insulted in the house of a publican. The barmaid had positively refused to draw him any more liquor; in return for which, he had (merely in playfulness) drawn his bayonet, and wounded the girl in the shoulder. And yet this fine fellow was the very first to go down to the house next morning, and express his readiness to overlook the matter, and forget what had occurred!

"The consumption of tobacco in these towns (continues Mr. Pickwick) must be very great: and the smell which pervades the streets must be exceedingly delicious to those who are extremely fond of smoking. A superficial traveller might object to the dirt which is their leading characteristic; but to those who view it as an indication of traffic, and commercial prosperity, it is truly gratifying."

Punctual to five o'clock came the stranger, and shortly afterwards the dinner. He had divested himself of his brown paper parcel, but had made no alteration in his attire; and was, if possible, more loquacious than ever.

"What's that?" he inquired, as the waiter removed one of the covers.

"Soles, sir."

"Soles—ah!—capital fish—all come from London—stage-coach proprietors get up political dinners—carriage of soles—dozens of baskets—cunning fellows. Glass of wine, sir?"

"With pleasure," said Mr. Pickwick—and the stranger took wine; first with him, and then with Mr. Snodgrass, and then with Mr. Tupman, and then with Mr. Winkle, and then with the whole party together, almost as rapidly as he talked.

"Devil of a mess on the staircase, waiter," said the stranger. "Forms going up—carpenters coming down—lamps, glasses, harps. What's going forward?"

"Ball, sir," said the waiter.

"Assembly—eh?"

"No, sir, not Assembly, sir. Ball for the benefit of a charity, sir."

"Many fine women in this town, do you know, sir?" inquired Mr.
Tupman, with great interest.

"Splendid—capital. Kent, sir—everybody knows Kent—apples, cherries, hops, and women. Glass of wine, sir?"

"With great pleasure," replied Mr. Tupman. The stranger filled and
emptied.

"I should very much like to go," said Mr. Tupman, resuming the
subject of the ball, "very much."

"Tickets at the bar, sir," interposed the waiter, "half a guinea each,
sir."

Mr. Tupman again expressed an earnest wish to be present at the
festivity; but meeting with no response in the darkened eye of Mr.
Snodgrass or the abstracted gaze of Mr. Pickwick, he applied himself
with great interest to the port wine and dessert which had just been
placed on the table. The waiter withdrew, and the party were left to
enjoy the cosey couple of hours succeeding dinner.

"Beg your pardon, sir," said the stranger, "bottle stands—pass it
round—way of the sun—through the button-hole—no heeltaps," and he
emptied his glass, which he had filled about two minutes before; and
poured out another, with the air of a man who was used to it.

The wine was passed, and a fresh supply ordered. The visitor talked,
the Pickwickians listened. Mr. Tupman felt every moment more disposed for the ball. Mr. Pickwick's countenance glowed with an expression of universal philanthropy; and Mr. Winkle, and Mr. Snodgrass,
fell fast asleep.

"They're beginning up-stairs," said the stranger—"hear the company—fiddles tuning—now the harp—there they go." The various
sounds which found their way down-stairs, announced the commence-
ment of the first quadrille.

"How I should like to go," said Mr. Tupman, again.

"So should I," said the stranger,—"confounded luggage—heavy
smacks—nothing to go in—odd, ain't it?"

Now general benevolence was one of the leading features of the
Pickwickian theory, and no one was more remarkable for the zealous
manner in which he observed so noble a principle, than Mr. Tracy
Tupman. The number of instances, recorded on the Transactions of the
Society, in which that excellent man referred objects of charity to the
houses of other members for left-off garments, or pecuniary relief, is
almost incredible.

"I should be very happy to lend you a change of apparel for the
purpose," said Mr. Tracy Tupman, "but you are rather slim, and I am"—

"Rather fat—grown-up Bacchus—cut the leaves—dismounted from the tub, and adopted kersey, eh?—not double distilled, but double milled —ha! ha!—pass the wine."

Whether Mr. Tupman was somewhat indignant at the peremptory tone in which he was desired to pass the wine which the stranger passed so quickly away; or whether he felt very properly scandalized, at an influential member of the Pickwick Club being ignominiously compared to a dismounted Bacchus, is a fact not yet completely ascertained. He passed the wine, coughed twice, and looked at the stranger for several seconds with a stern intensity; as that individual, however, appeared perfectly collected, and quite calm under his searching glance, he gradually relaxed, and reverted to the subject of the ball.

"I was about to observe, sir," he said, "that though my apparel would be too large, a suit of my friend Mr. Winkle's would, perhaps, fit you better."

The stranger took Mr. Winkle's measure with his eye; and that feature glistened with satisfaction as he said—"Just the thing!"

Mr. Tupman looked round him. The wine which had exerted its somniferous influence over Mr. Snodgrass, and Mr. Winkle, had stolen upon the senses of Mr. Pickwick. That gentleman had gradually passed through the various stages which precede the lethargy produced by dinner, and its consequences. He had undergone the ordinary transitions from the height of conviviality, to the depth of misery, and from the depth of misery to the height of conviviality. Like a gas lamp in the street, with the wind in the pipe, he had exhibited for a moment an unnatural brilliancy: then sunk so low as to be scarcely discernible: after a short interval, he had burst out again, to enlighten for a moment, then flickered with an uncertain, staggering sort of light, and then gone out altogether. His head was sunk upon his bosom; and perpetual snoring, with a partial choke, occasionally, were the only audible indications of the great man's presence.

The temptation to be present at the ball, and to form his first impressions of the beauty of the Kentish ladies, was strong upon Mr. Tupman. The temptation to take the stranger with him, was equally great. He was wholly unacquainted with the place, and its inhabitants; and the stranger seemed to possess as great a knowledge of both as if he had lived there from his infancy. Mr. Winkle was asleep, and Mr. Tupman had had sufficient experience in such matters to know, that the moment he awoke, he would, in the ordinary course of nature, roll heavily to bed. He was undecided. "Fill your glass, and pass the wine," said the indefatigable visitor.

Mr. Tupman did as he was requested; and the additional stimulus of the last glass settled his determination.

"Winkle's bedroom is inside mine," said Mr. Tupman; "I couldn't make him understand what I wanted, if I woke him now, but I know he has a dress suit, in a carpet bag; and supposing you wore it to the ball, and took it off when we returned, I could replace it without troubling him at all about the matter."

"Capital," said the stranger, "famous plan—damned odd situation—fourteen coats in the packing cases, and obliged to wear another man's—very good notion, that—very."

"We must purchase our tickets," said Mr. Tupman.

"Not worth while splitting a guinea," said the stranger, "toss who shall pay for both—I call; you spin—first time—woman—woman—bewitching woman," and down came the sovereign, with the Dragon (called by courtesy a woman) uppermost.

Mr. Tupman rang the bell, purchased the tickets, and ordered chamber candlesticks. In another quarter of an hour the stranger was completely arrayed in a full suit of Mr. Nathaniel Winkle's.

"It's a new coat," said Mr. Tupman, as the stranger surveyed himself with great complacency in a cheval glass. "The first that's been made with our club button,"—and he called his companion's attention to the large gilt button which displayed a bust of Mr. Pickwick in the centre, and the letters "P. C." on either side.

"P. C.," said the stranger,—"queer set out—old fellow's likeness, and 'P. C.'—What does 'P. C.' stand for—Peculiar Coat, eh?" Mr. Tupman, with rising indignation, and great importance, explained the mystic device.

"Rather short in the waist, ain't it?" said the stranger, screwing himself round, to catch a glimpse in the glass of the waist buttons which were half-way up his back. "Like a general postman's coat—queer coats those—made by contract—no measuring—mysterious dispensations of Providence—all the short men get long coats—all the long men short ones." Running on in this way, Mr. Tupman's new companion adjusted his dress, or rather the dress of Mr. Winkle; and accompanied by Mr. Tupman, ascended the staircase leading to the ball-room.

"What names, sir?" said the man at the door. Mr. Tracy Tupman was stepping forward to announce his own titles, when the stranger prevented him.

"No names at all,"—and then he whispered Mr. Tupman, "Names won't do—not known—very good names in their way, but not great ones—capital names for a small party, but won't make an impression in public assemblies—*incog.* the thing—Gentlemen from London—distinguished foreigners—anything." The door was thrown open; and Mr. Tracy Tupman and the stranger entered the ball-room.

It was a long room, with crimson-covered benches, and wax candles in glass chandeliers. The musicians were securely confined in an elevated den, and quadrilles were being systematically got through by two or three sets of dancers. Two card-tables were made up in the adjoining card-room, and two pairs of old ladies, and a corresponding number of stout gentlemen, were executing whist therein.

The finale concluded, the dancers promenaded the room, and Mr. Tupman and his companion stationed themselves in a corner, to observe the company.

"Charming women," said Mr. Tupman.

"Wait a minute," said the stranger, "fun presently—nobs not come yet—queer place—Dock-yard people of upper rank don't know Dock-yard people of lower rank—Dock-yard people of lower rank don't know small gentry—small gentry don't know tradespeople—Commissioner don't know anybody."

"Who's that little boy with the light hair and pink eyes, in a fancy dress?" inquired Mr. Tupman.

"Hush, pray—pink eyes—fancy dress—little boy—nonsense—Ensign Ninety-seventh—Honorable Wilmot Snipe—great family—Snipes—very."

"Sir Thomas Clubber, Lady Clubber, and the Miss Clubbers!" shouted the man at the door in a stentorian voice. A great sensation was created throughout the room, by the entrance of a tall gentleman in a blue coat and bright buttons, a large lady in blue satin, and two young ladies on a similar scale, in fashionably made dresses of the same hue.

"Commissioner—head of the yard—great man—remarkably great man," whispered the stranger in Mr. Tupman's ear, as the charitable committee ushered Sir Thomas Clubber and family to the top of the room. The Honorable Wilmot Snipe and other distinguished gentlemen crowded to render homage to the Miss Clubbers; and Sir Thomas Clubber stood bolt-upright, and looked majestically over his black neckerchief at the assembled company.

"Mr. Smithie, Mrs. Smithie, and the Misses Smithie," was the next announcement.

"What's Mr. Smithie?" inquired Mr. Tracy Tupman.

"Something in the yard," replied the stranger. Mr. Smithie bowed deferentially to Sir Thomas Clubber; and Sir Thomas Clubber acknowledged the salute with conscious condescension. Lady Clubber took a telescopic view of Mrs. Smithie and family through her eyeglass, and Mrs. Smithie stared, in her turn, at Mrs. Somebody else, whose husband was not in the dock-yard at all.

"Colonel Bulder, Mrs. Colonel Bulder, and Miss Bulder," were the next arrivals.

"Head of the garrison," said the stranger, in reply to Mr. Tupman's inquiring look.

Miss Bulder was warmly welcomed by the Miss Clubbers; the greeting between Mrs. Colonel Bulder and Lady Clubber was of the most affectionate description; Colonel Bulder and Sir Thomas Clubber exchanged snuff-boxes, and looked very much like a pair of Alexander Selkirks;—"Monarchs of all they surveyed."

While the aristocracy of the place—the Bulders, and Clubbers, and Snipes—were thus preserving their dignity at the upper end of the room, the other classes of society were imitating their example in other parts of it. The less aristocratic officers of the Ninety-seventh devoted themselves to the families of the less important functionaries from the dockyard. The solicitors' wives, and the wine-merchant's wife, headed another grade (the brewer's wife visited the Bulders) ; and Mrs. Tomlinson, the postoffice keeper, seemed by mutual consent to have been chosen the leader of the trade party.

One of the most popular personages, in his own circle, present, was a little fat man, with a ring of upright black hair round his head, and an extensive bald plain on the top of it—Doctor Slammer, surgeon to the Ninety-seventh. The doctor took snuff with everybody, chatted with everybody, laughed, danced, made jokes, played whist, did everything, and was everywhere. To these pursuits, multifarious as they were, the little doctor added a more important one than any—he was indefatigable in paying the most unremitting and devoted attention to a little old widow whose rich dress and profusion of ornament bespoke her a most desirable addition to a limited income.

Upon the doctor and the widow, the eyes of both Mr. Tupman and his companion had been fixed for some time, when the stranger broke silence.

"Lots of money—old girl—pompous doctor—not a bad idea—good fun," were the intelligible sentences which issued from his lips. Mr. Tupman looked inquisitively in his face.

"I'll dance with the widow," said the stranger.

"Who is she?" inquired Mr. Tupman.

"Don't know—never saw her in all my life—cut out the doctor—

here goes." And the stranger forthwith crossed the room; and, leaning against a mantel-piece, commenced gazing with an air of respectful and melancholy admiration on the fat countenance of the little old lady. Mr. Tupman looked on, in mute astonishment. The stranger progressed rapidly, the little doctor danced with another lady—the widow dropped her fan; the stranger picked it up, and presented it,—a smile—a bow— a courtesy—a few words of conversation. The stranger walked boldly up to, and returned with, the master of the ceremonies; a little intro- ductory pantomime; and the stranger and Mrs. Budger took their places in a quadrille.

The surprise of Mr. Tupman at this summary proceeding, great as it was, was immeasurably exceeded by the astonishment of the doctor. The stranger was young, and the widow was flattered. The doctor's attentions were unheeded by the widow; and the doctor's indignation was wholly lost on his imperturbable rival. Doctor Slammer was par- alyzed. He, Doctor Slammer of the Ninety-seventh, to be extinguished in a moment, by a man whom nobody had ever seen before, and whom nobody knew even now! Doctor Slammer—Doctor Slammer of the Ninety-seventh rejected! Impossible! It could not be! Yes, it was; there they were. What! introducing his friend! Could he believe his eyes! He looked again, and was under the painful necessity of admitting the veracity of his optics; Mrs. Budger was dancing with Mr. Tracy Tupman, there was no mistaking the fact. There was the widow before him, bouncing bodily here and there, with unwonted vigor; and Mr. Tracy Tupman hopping about, with a face expressive of the most intense solemnity, dancing (as a good many people do) as if a quadrille were not a thing to be laughed at, but a severe trial to the feelings, which it requires inflexible resolution to encounter.

Silently and patiently did the doctor bear all this, and all the hand- ings of negus, and watching for glasses, and darting for biscuits, and coquetting, that ensued; but, a few seconds after the stranger had dis- appeared to lead Mrs. Budger to her carriage, he darted swiftly from the room with every particle of his hitherto-bottled-up indignation effer- vescing from all parts of his countenance, in a perspiration of passion.

The stranger was returning, and Mr. Tupman was beside him. He spoke in a low tone, and laughed. The little doctor thirsted for his life. He was exulting. He had triumphed.

"Sir!" said the doctor in an awful voice, producing a card, and retiring into an angle of the passage, "my name is Slammer, Doctor Slammer, sir—Ninety-seventh regiment—Chatham Barracks—my card, sir, my card." He would have added more, but his indignation choked him.

"Ah!" replied the stranger, coolly, "Slammer—much obliged—polite attention—not ill now, Slammer—but when I am—knock you up."

"You—you're a shuffler, sir," gasped the furious doctor, "a poltroon —a coward—a liar—a—a—will nothing induce you to give me your card, sir?"

"Oh! I see," said the stranger, half aside, "negus too strong here —liberal landlord—very foolish—very—lemonade much better—hot rooms—elderly gentleman—suffer for it in the morning—cruel—cruel;" and he moved on a step or two.

"You are stopping in this house, sir," said the indignant little man; "you are intoxicated now, sir; you shall hear from me in the morning, sir. I shall find you out, sir; I shall find you out."

"Rather you found me out than found me at home," replied the unmoved stranger.

Doctor Slammer looked unutterable ferocity, as he fixed his hat on his head with an indignant knock: and the stranger and Mr. Tupman ascended to the bedroom of the latter to restore the borrowed plumage to the unconscious Winkle.

That gentleman was fast asleep; the restoration was soon made; the stranger was extremely jocose; and Mr. Tracy Tupman, being quite bewildered with wine, negus, lights, and ladies, thought the whole affair an exquisite joke. His new friend departed; and, after experiencing some slight difficulty in finding the orifice in his nightcap, originally intended for the reception of his head, and finally overturning his candlestick in his struggles to put it on, Mr. Tracy Tupman managed to get into bed, by a series of complicated evolutions, and shortly afterwards sank into repose.

Seven o'clock had hardly ceased striking on the following morning, when Mr. Pickwick's comprehensive mind was aroused from the state of unconsciousness, in which slumber had plunged it, by a loud knocking at his chamber door.

"Who's there?" said Mr. Pickwick, starting up in bed.

"Boots, sir."

"What do you want?"

"Please, sir, can you tell me which gentleman of your party wears a bright blue dress coat, with a gilt button with P. C. on it?"

"It's been given out to brush," thought Mr. Pickwick; "and the man has forgotten whom it belongs to—Mr. Winkle," he called out, "next room but two, on the right hand."

"Thank'ee, sir," said the Boots, and away he went.

"What's the matter?" cried Mr. Tupman, as a loud knocking at *his* door roused *him* from his oblivious repose.

"Can I speak to Mr. Winkle, sir?" replied the Boots, from the outside.

"Winkle—Winkle," shouted Mr. Tupman, calling into the inner room.

"Hallo!" replied a faint voice from within the bed-clothes.

"You're wanted—some one at the door—" and having exerted himself to articulate thus much, Mr. Tracy Tupman turned round and fell fast asleep again.

"Wanted!" said Mr. Winkle, hastily jumping out of bed, and putting on a few articles of clothing: "wanted! at this distance from town —who on earth can want me!"

"Gentleman in the coffee-room, sir," replied the Boots, as Mr. Winkle opened the door, and confronted him; "gentleman says he'll not detain you a moment, sir, but he can take no denial."

"Very odd!" said Mr. Winkle; "I'll be down directly."

He hurriedly wrapped himself in a travelling-shawl and dressing-gown, and proceeded down-stairs. An old woman and a couple of waiters were cleaning the coffee-room, and an officer in undress uniform was looking out of the window. He turned round as Mr. Winkle entered, and made a stiff inclination of the head. Having ordered the attendants to retire, and closed the door very carefully, he said, "Mr. Winkle, I presume?"

"My name *is* Winkle, sir."

"You will not be surprised, sir, when I inform you, that I have called here this morning on behalf of my friend, Dr. Slammer, of the Ninety-seventh."

"Doctor Slammer!" said Mr. Winkle.

"Doctor Slammer. He begged me to express his opinion that your conduct of last evening was of a description which no gentleman could endure: and (he added) which no one gentleman would pursue towards another."

Mr. Winkle's astonishment was too real, and too evident, to escape the observation of Doctor Slammer's friend; he therefore proceeded: "My friend, Doctor Slammer, requested me to add, that he is firmly persuaded you were intoxicated during a portion of the evening, and possibly unconscious of the extent of the insult you were guilty of. He commissioned me to say, that should this be pleaded as an excuse for your behavior, he will consent to accept a written apology, to be penned by you from my dictation."

"A written apology!" repeated Mr. Winkle, in the most emphatic tone of amazement possible.

"Of course you know the alternative," replied the visitor, coolly.

"Were you intrusted with this message to me, by name?" inquired Mr. Winkle, whose intellects were hopelessly confused by this extraordinary conversation.

"I was not present myself," replied the visitor, "and, in consequence of your firm refusal to give your card to Doctor Slammer, I was desired by that gentleman to identify the wearer of a very uncommon coat—a bright blue dress coat, with a gilt button, displaying a bust, and the letters 'P. C.' "

Mr. Winkle actually staggered with astonishment, as he heard his own costume thus minutely described. Doctor Slammer's friend proceeded:—

"From the inquiries I made at the bar, just now, I was convinced that the owner of the coat in question arrived here, with three gentlemen, yesterday afternoon. I immediately sent up to the gentleman who was described as appearing the head of the party; and he at once referred me to you."

If the principal tower of Rochester Castle had suddenly walked from its foundation, and stationed itself opposite the coffee-room window, Mr. Winkle's surprise would have been as nothing, compared with the profound astonishment with which he had heard this address. His first impression was, that his coat had been stolen. "Will you allow me to detain you one moment?" said he.

"Certainly," replied the unwelcome visitor.

Mr. Winkle ran hastily up-stairs, and, with a trembling hand, opened the bag. There was the coat in its usual place, but exhibiting, on a close inspection, evident tokens of having been worn on the preceding night.

"It must be so," said Mr. Winkle, letting the coat fall from his hands. "I took too much wine after dinner, and have a very vague recollection of walking about the streets, and smoking a cigar afterwards. The fact is, I was very drunk;—I must have changed my coat—gone somewhere—and insulted somebody—I have no doubt of it; and this message is the terrible consequence." Saying which, Mr. Winkle retraced his steps in the direction of the coffee-room, with the gloomy and dreadful resolve of accepting the challenge of the warlike Doctor Slammer, and abiding by the worst consequences that might ensue.

To this determination Mr. Winkle was urged by a variety of consideration, the first of which was, his reputation with the club. He had always been looked up to as a high authority on all matters of amusement and dexterity, whether offensive, defensive, or inoffensive; and if, on this very first occasion of being put to the test, he shrunk back from the trial, beneath his leader's eye, his name and standing were lost forever. Besides, he remembered to have heard it frequently surmised by the uninitiated in such matters, that by an understood arrangement between the seconds, the pistols were seldom loaded with ball; and, furthermore, he reflected that if he applied to Mr. Snodgrass to act as his second, and depicted the danger in glowing terms, that gentleman might possibly communicate the intelligence to Mr. Pickwick, who would certainly lose no time in transmitting it to the local authorities, and thus prevent the killing or maiming of his follower.

Such were his thoughts when he returned to the coffee-room, and intimated his intention of accepting the doctor's challenge.

"Will you refer me to a friend, to arrange the time and place of meeting?" said the officer.

"Quite unnecessary," replied Mr. Winkle; "name them to me, and I can procure the attendance of a friend afterwards."

"Shall we say—sunset this evening?" inquired the officer, in a careless tone.

"Very good," replied Mr. Winkle; thinking in his heart it was very bad.

"You know Fort Pitt?"

"Yes; I saw it yesterday."

"If you will take the trouble to turn into the field which borders the trench, take the foot-path to the left, when you arrive at an angle of the fortification; and keep straight on till you see me; I will precede you to a secluded place, where the affair can be conducted without fear of interruption."

"*Fear* of interruption!" thought Mr. Winkle.

"Nothing more to arrange, I think," said the officer.

"I am not aware of anything more," replied Mr. Winkle.

"Good-morning."

"Good-morning." And the officer whistled a lively air, as he strode away.

That morning's breakfast passed heavily off. Mr. Tupman was not in a condition to rise, after the unwonted dissipation of the previous night; Mr. Snodgrass appeared to labor under a poetical depression of spirits; and even Mr. Pickwick evinced an unusual attachment to silence and soda-water. Mr. Winkle eagerly watched his opportunity. It was not long wanting. Mr. Snodgrass proposed a visit to the castle, and as Mr. Winkle was the only other member of the party disposed to walk, they went out together.

"Snodgrass," said Mr. Winkle, when they had turned out of the public street; "Snodgrass, my dear fellow, can I rely upon your secrecy?" as he said this, he most devoutly and earnestly hoped he could not.

"You can," replied Mr. Snodgrass. "Hear me swear—"

"No, no," interrupted Winkle, terrified at the idea of his companion's unconsciously pledging himself not to give information; "don't swear, don't swear; it's quite unnecessary."

Mr. Snodgrass dropped the hand which he had, in the spirit of poesy, raised toward the clouds as he made the above appeal, and assumed an attitude of attention.

"I want your assistance, my dear fellow, in an affair of honor," said Mr. Winkle.

"You shall have it," replied Mr. Snodgrass, clasping his friend's hand.

"With a doctor—Doctor Slammer, of the Ninety-seventh," said Mr. Winkle, wishing to make the matter appear as solemn as possible; "an affair with an officer, seconded by another officer, at sunset this evening, in a lonely field beyond Fort Pitt."

"I will attend you," said Mr. Snodgrass.

He was astonished, but by no means dismayed. It is extraordinary how cool any party but the principal can be in such cases. Mr. Winkle had forgotten this. He had judged of his friend's feelings by his own.

"The consequences may be dreadful," said Mr. Winkle.

"I hope not," said Mr. Snodgrass.

"The doctor, I believe, is a very good shot," said Mr. Winkle.

"Most of these military men are," observed Mr. Snodgrass calmly, "but so are you, ain't you?"

Mr. Winkle replied in the affirmative; and perceiving that he had not alarmed his companion sufficiently, changed his ground.

"Snodgrass," he said, in a voice tremulous with emotion, "if I fall, you will find in a packet which I shall place in your hands a note for my—for my father."

This attack was a failure also. Mr. Snodgrass was affected, but he undertook the delivery of the note, as readily as if he had been a Twopenny Postman.

"If I fall," said Mr. Winkle, "or if the doctor falls, you, my dear friend, will be tried as an accessory before the fact. Shall I involve my friend in transportation—possibly for life!"

Mr. Snodgrass winced a little at this, but his heroism was invincible. "In the cause of friendship," he fervently exclaimed, "I would brave all dangers."

How Mr. Winkle cursed his companion's devoted friendship internally, as they walked silently along, side by side, for some minutes, each immersed in his own meditations! The morning was wearing away; he grew desperate.

"Snodgrass," he said, stopping suddenly, "do *not* let me be balked in this matter—do *not* give information to the local authorities—do *not* obtain the assistance of several peace officers, to take either me or Doctor Slammer, of the Ninety-seventh regiment, at present quartered in Chatham Barracks, into custody, and thus prevent this duel;—I say, do *not*."

Mr. Snodgrass seized his friend's hand warmly, as he enthusiastically replied, "Not for worlds!"

A thrill passed over Mr. Winkle's frame, as the conviction, that he had nothing to hope from his friend's fears, and that he was destined to become an animated target, rushed forcibly upon him.

The state of the case having been formally explained to Mr. Snodgrass, and a case of satisfaction pistols, with the satisfactory accompaniments of powder, ball and caps, having been hired from a manufacturer in Rochester, the two friends returned to their inn: Mr. Winkle, to ruminate on the approaching struggle; and Mr. Snodgrass, to arrange the weapons of war, and put them into proper order for immediate use.

It was a dull and heavy evening, when they again sallied forth on their awkward errand. Mr. Winkle was muffled up in a huge cloak to escape observation; and Mr. Snodgrass bore under his the instruments of destruction.

"Have you got everything?" said Mr. Winkle, in an agitated tone.

"Ev'rything," replied Mr. Snodgrass; "plenty of ammunition, in case the shots don't take effect. There's a quarter of a pound of powder in the case, and I have got two newspapers in my pocket, for the loadings."

These were instances of friendship, for which any man might reasonably feel most grateful. The presumption is, that the gratitude of Mr. Winkle was too powerful for utterance, as he said nothing, but continued to walk on—rather slowly.

"We are in excellent time," said Mr. Snodgrass, as they climbed the fence of the first field; "the sun is just going down." Mr. Winkle looked up at the declining orb, and painfully thought of the probability of his "going down" himself, before long.

"There's the officer," exclaimed Mr. Winkle, after a few minutes' walking.

"Where?" said Mr. Snodgrass.

"There;—the gentleman in the blue cloak." Mr. Snodgrass looked in the direction indicated by the forefinger of his friend, and observed a figure, muffled up, as he had described. The officer evinced his consciousness of their presence by slightly beckoning with his hand; and the two friends followed him, at a little distance, as he walked away.

The evening grew more dull every moment, and a melancholy wind sounded through the deserted fields, like a distant giant whistling for his house-dog. The sadness of the scene imparted a sombre tinge to the feelings of Mr. Winkle. He started, as they passed the angle of the trench—it looked like a colossal grave.

The officer turned suddenly from the path; and after climbing a paling, and scaling a hedge, entered a secluded field. Two gentlemen were waiting in it; one was a little fat man, with black hair; and the other—a portly personage in a braided surtout—was sitting with perfect equanimity on a camp-stool.

"The other party, and a surgeon, I suppose," said Mr. Snodgrass; "take a drop of brandy." Mr. Winkle seized the wicker bottle, which his friend proffered, and took a lengthened pull at the exhilarating liquid.

"My friend, sir, Mr. Snodgrass," said Mr. Winkle, as the officer approached. Doctor Slammer's friend bowed, and produced a case similar to that which Mr. Snodgrass carried.

"We have nothing further to say, sir, I think," he coldly remarked, as he opened the case; "an apology has been resolutely declined."

"Nothing, sir," said Mr. Snodgrass, who began to feel rather uncomfortable himself.

"Will you step forward?" said the officer.

"Certainly," replied Mr. Snodgrass. The ground was measured, and preliminaries arranged.

"You will find these better than your own," said the opposite second, producing his pistols. "You saw me load them. Do you object to use them?"

"Certainly not," replied Mr. Snodgrass. The offer relieved him from considerable embarrassment; for his previous notions of loading a pistol were rather vague and undefined.

"We may place our men, then, I think," observed the officer, with as much indifference as if the principals were chess-men, and the seconds players.

"I think we may," replied Mr. Snodgrass; who would have assented to any proposition, because he knew nothing about the matter. The officer crossed to Doctor Slammer, and Mr. Snodgrass went up to Mr. Winkle.

"It's all ready," he said, offering the pistol. "Give me your cloak."

"You have got the packet, my dear fellow," said poor Winkle.

"All right," said Mr. Snodgrass. "Be steady and wing him."

It occurred to Mr. Winkle that this advice was very like that which bystanders invariably give to the smallest boy in a street fight; namely, "Go in, and win:"—an admirable thing to recommend, if you only know how to do it. He took off his cloak, however, in silence—it always took a long time to undo that cloak—and accepted the pistol. The seconds retired, the gentleman on the camp-stool did the same, and the belligerents approached each other.

Mr. Winkle was always remarkable for extreme humanity. It is conjectured that his unwillingness to hurt a fellow-creature intentionally, was the cause of his shutting his eyes when he arrived at the fatal spot; and that the circumstance of his eyes being closed, prevented his observing the very extraordinary and unaccountable demeanor of Doctor Slammer. That gentleman started, stared, retreated, rubbed his eyes, stared again; and, finally, shouted "Stop, stop!"

"What's all this?" said Doctor Slammer, as his friend and Mr. Snodgrass came running up—"That's not the man."

"Not the man!" said Doctor Slammer's second.

"Not the man!" said Mr. Snodgrass.

"Not the man!" said the gentleman with the camp-stool in his hand.

"Certainly not," replied the little doctor. "That's not the person who insulted me last night."

"Very extraordinary!" exclaimed the officer.

"Very," said the gentleman with the camp-stool. "The only question is, whether the gentleman, being on the ground, must not be considered, as a matter of form, to be the individual who insulted our friend, Doctor Slammer, yesterday evening, whether he is really that individual or not." And having delivered this suggestion with a very sage and mysterious air, the man with the camp-stool took a large pinch of snuff, and looked profoundly round with the air of an authority in such matters.

Now Mr. Winkle had opened his eyes, and his ears too, when he heard his adversary call out for a cessation of hostilities; and perceiving by what he had afterward said, that there was beyond all question some mistake in the matter, he at once foresaw the increase of reputation he should inevitably acquire, by concealing the real motive of his coming out; he therefore stepped boldly forward, and said,—

"I am not the person. I know it."

"Then, that," said the man with the camp-stool, "is an affront to Doctor Slammer, and a sufficient reason for proceeding immediately."

"Pray be quiet, Payne," said the doctor's second. "Why did you not communicate this fact to me this morning, sir?"

"To be sure—to be sure," said the man with the camp-stool, indignantly.

"I entreat you to be quiet, Payne," said the other. "May I repeat my question, sir?"

"Because, sir," replied Mr. Winkle, who had had time to deliberate upon his answer—"because, sir, you described an intoxicated and ungentlemanly person as wearing a coat, which I have the honor, not only to wear, but to have invented—the proposed uniform, sir, of the Pickwick Club in London. The honor of that uniform I feel bound to maintain, and I therefore, without inquiry, accepted the challenge which you offered me."

"My dear sir," said the good-humored little doctor, advancing with extended hand, "I honor your gallantry. Permit me to say, sir, that I highly admire your conduct, and extremely regret having caused you the inconvenience of this meeting, to no purpose."

"I beg you won't mention it, sir," said Mr. Winkle.

"I shall feel proud of your acquaintance, sir," said the little doctor.

"It will afford me the greatest pleasure to know you, sir," replied Mr. Winkle. Thereupon the doctor and Mr. Winkle shook hands, and then Mr. Winkle and Lieutenant Tappleton (the doctor's second), and then Mr. Winkle and the man with the camp-stool, and finally, Mr. Winkle and Mr. Snodgrass: the last-named gentleman in an excess of admiration at the noble conduct of his heroic friend.

"I think we may adjourn," said Lieutenant Tappleton.

"Certainly," added the doctor.

"Unless," interposed the man with the camp-stool; "unless Mr. Winkle feels himself aggrieved by the challenge; in which case, I submit, he has a right to satisfaction."

Mr. Winkle, with great self-denial, expressed himself quite satisfied already.

"Or possibly," said the man with the camp-stool, "the gentleman's second may feel himself affronted with some observations which fell from me at an early period of this meeting: if so I shall be happy to give *him* satisfaction immediately."

Mr. Snodgrass hastily professed himself very much obliged with the handsome offer of the gentleman who had spoken last, which he was only induced to decline, by his entire contentment with the whole proceedings. The two seconds adjusted the cases, and the whole party left the ground in a much more lively manner than they had proceeded to it.

"Do you remain long here?" inquired Doctor Slammer of Mr. Winkle, as they walked on most amicably together.

"I think we shall leave here the day after to-morrow," was the reply.

"I trust I shall have the pleasure of seeing you and your friend at my rooms, and of spending a pleasant evening with you, after this awkward mistake," said the little doctor; "are you disengaged this evening?"

"We have some friends here," replied Mr. Winkle, "and I should not like to leave them to-night. Perhaps you and your friend will join us at the Bull."

"With great pleasure," said the little doctor; "will ten o'clock be too late to look in for half an hour?"

"Oh dear, no," said Mr. Winkle. "I shall be most happy to introduce you to my friends, Mr. Pickwick and Mr. Tupman."

"It will give me great pleasure, I am sure," replied Doctor Slammer, little suspecting who Mr. Tupman was.

"You will be sure to come?" said Mr. Snodgrass.

"Oh, certainly."

By this time they had reached the road. Cordial farewells were exchanged, and the party separated. Doctor Slammer and his friends repaired to the barracks, and Mr. Winkle, accompanied by his friend, Mr. Snodgrass, returned to their inn.

Mr. Pickwick on the Ice

"Now," said Wardle, after a substantial lunch, with the agreeable items of strong beer and cherry-brandy, had been done ample justice to, "what say you to an hour on the ice? We shall have plenty of time."

"Capital!" said Mr. Benjamin Allen.

"Prime!" ejaculated Mr. Bob Sawyer.

"You skate, of course, Winkle?" said Wardle.

"Ye—yes; oh, yes," replied Mr. Winkle. "I—I—am *rather* out of practice."

"Oh, *do* skate, Mr. Winkle," said Arabella. "I like to see it so much."

"Oh, it is *so* graceful," said another young lady.

A third young lady said it was elegant, and a fourth expressed her opinion that it was "swan-like."

"I should be very happy, I'm sure," said Mr. Winkle, reddening; "but I have no skates."

This objection was at once overruled. Trundle had a couple of pair, and the fat boy announced that there were half a dozen more downstairs; whereat Mr. Winkle expressed exquisite delight, and looked exquisitely uncomfortable.

Old Wardle led the way to a pretty large sheet of ice; and the fat boy and Mr. Weller, having shovelled and swept away the snow which had fallen on it during the night, Mr. Bob Sawyer adjusted his skates with a dexterity which to Mr. Winkle was perfectly marvellous, and described circles with his left leg, and cut figures of eight, and inscribed upon the ice, without once stopping for breath, a great many other pleasant and astonishing devices, to the excessive satisfaction of Mr. Pickwick, Mr. Tupman, and the ladies; which reached a pitch of positive enthusiasm, when old Wardle and Benjamin Allen, assisted by the aforesaid Bob Sawyer, performed some mystic evolutions, which they called a reel.

All this time, Mr. Winkle, with his face and hands blue with the cold, had been forcing a gimlet into the soles of his feet, and putting his skates on, with the points behind, and getting the straps into a very complicated and entangled state, with the assistance of Mr. Snodgrass, who knew rather less about skates than a Hindoo. At length, however, with the assistance of Mr. Weller, the unfortunate skates were firmly screwed and buckled on, and Mr. Winkle was raised to his feet.

"Now, then, sir," said Sam, in an encouraging tone; "off vith you, and show 'em how to do it."

"Stop, Sam, stop!" said Mr. Winkle, trembling violently, and clutching hold of Sam's arms with the grasp of a drowning man. "How slippery it is, Sam!"

"Not an uncommon thing upon ice, sir," replied Mr. Weller. "Hold up, sir!"

This last observation of Mr. Weller's bore reference to a demonstration Mr. Winkle made at the instant, of a frantic desire to throw his feet in the air, and dash the back of his head on the ice.

"These—these—are very awkward skates; ain't they, Sam?" inquired Mr. Winkle, staggering.

"I'm afeerd there's a orkard gen'l'm'n in 'em, sir," replied Sam.

"Now, Winkle," cried Mr. Pickwick, quite unconscious that there was anything the matter. "Come; the ladies are all anxiety."

"Yes, yes," replied Mr. Winkle, with a ghastly smile. "I'm coming."

"Just a-goin' to begin," said Sam, endeavouring to disengage himself. "Now, sir, start off!"

"Stop an instant, Sam," gasped Mr. Winkle, clinging most affectionately to Mr. Weller. "I find I've got a couple of coats at home that I don't want, Sam. You may have them, Sam."

"Thank'ee, sir," replied Mr. Weller.

"Never mind touching your hat, Sam," said Mr. Winkle hastily. "You needn't take your hand away to do that. I meant to have given you five shillings this morning for a Christmas box, Sam. I'll give it you this afternoon, Sam."

"You're wery good, sir," replied Mr. Weller.

"Just hold me at first, Sam! will you?" said Mr. Winkle. "There—that's right. I shall soon get in the way of it, Sam. Not too fast, Sam; not too fast."

Mr. Winkle, stooping forward, with his body half doubled up, was being assisted over the ice by Mr. Weller, in a very singular and unswan-like manner, when Mr. Pickwick most innocently shouted from the opposite bank—

"Sam!"

"Sir?"

"Here. I want you."

"Let go, sir," said Sam. "Don't you hear the governor a-callin'? Let go, sir."

With a violent effort, Mr. Weller disengaged himself from the grasp of the agonised Pickwickian, and, in so doing, administered a considerable impetus to the unhappy Mr. Winkle. With an accuracy which no degree of dexterity or practice could have insured, that unfortunate gentleman bore swiftly down into the centre of the reel, at the very moment when Mr. Bob Sawyer was performing a flourish of unparalleled beauty. Mr. Winkle struck wildly against him, and with a loud crash they both fell heavily down. Mr. Pickwick ran to the spot. Bob Sawyer had risen to his feet, but Mr. Winkle was far too wise to do anything of the kind, in skates. He was seated on the ice, making spasmodic efforts to smile; but anguish was depicted on every lineament of his countenance.

"Are you hurt?" inquired Mr. Benjamin Allen, with great anxiety.

"Not much," said Mr. Winkle, rubbing his back very hard.

"I wish you'd let me bleed you," said Mr. Benjamin, with great eagerness.

"No, thank you," replied Mr. Winkle hurriedly.

"I really think you had better," said Allen.

"Thank you," replied Mr. Winkle; "I'd rather not."

"What do *you* think, Mr. Pickwick?" inquired Bob Sawyer.

Mr. Pickwick was excited and indignant. He beckoned to Mr. Weller, and said in a stern voice, "Take his skates off."

"No; but really I had scarcely begun," remonstrated Mr. Winkle.

"Take his skates off," repeated Mr. Pickwick firmly.

The command was not to be resisted. Mr. Winkle allowed Sam to obey it, in silence.

"Lift him up," said Mr. Pickwick. Sam assisted him to rise.

Mr. Pickwick retired a few paces apart from the bystanders; and, beckoning his friend to approach, fixed a searching look upon him, and uttered in a low, but distinct and emphatic tone, these remarkable words—

"You're a humbug, sir."

"A what?" said Mr. Winkle, starting.

"A humbug, sir. I will speak plainer, if you wish it. An impostor, sir."

With these words, Mr. Pickwick turned slowly on his heel, and rejoined his friends.

While Mr. Pickwick was delivering himself of the sentiment just recorded, Mr. Weller and the fat boy, having by their joint endeavours cut out a slide, were exercising themselves thereupon, in a very masterly and brilliant manner. Sam Weller, in particular, was displaying that beautiful feat of fancy-sliding which is currently denominated "knocking at the cobbler's door," and which is achieved by skimming over the ice on one foot, and occasionally giving a postman's knock upon it with the other. It was a good long slide, and there was something in the motion which Mr. Pickwick, who was very cold with standing still, could not help envying.

"It looks a nice warm exercise that, doesn't it?" he inquired of Wardle, when that gentleman was thoroughly out of breath, by reason of the indefatigable manner in which he had converted his legs into a pair of compasses, and drawn complicated problems on the ice.

"Ah, it does, indeed," replied Wardle. "Do you slide?"

"I used to do so, on the gutters, when I was a boy," replied Mr. Pickwick.

"Try it now," said Wardle.

"Oh, do, please, Mr. Pickwick!" cried all the ladies.

"I should be very happy to afford you any amusement," replied Mr. Pickwick, "but I haven't done such a thing these thirty years."

"Pooh! pooh! Nonsense!" said Wardle, dragging off his skates with the impetuosity which characterised all his proceedings. "Here; I'll keep you company; come along!" And away went the good-tempered old fellow down the slide, with a rapidity which came very close upon Mr. Weller, and beat the fat boy all to nothing.

Mr. Pickwick paused, considered, pulled off his gloves and put them in his hat; took two or three short runs, balked himself as often, and at last took another run, and went slowly and gravely down the slide, with his feet about a yard and a quarter apart, amidst the gratified shouts of all the spectators.

"Keep the pot a-bilin', sir!" said Sam; and down went Wardle again, and then Mr. Pickwick, and then Sam, and then Mr. Winkle, and then Mr. Bob Sawyer, and then the fat boy, and then Mr. Snodgrass, following closely upon each other's heels, and running after each other with as much eagerness as if their future prospects in life depended on their expedition.

It was the most intensely interesting thing, to observe the manner in which Mr. Pickwick performed his share in the ceremony; to watch the torture of anxiety with which he viewed the person behind, gaining upon him at the imminent hazard of tripping him up; to see him gradually expend the painful force he had put on at first, and turn slowly round on the slide, with his face towards the point from which he had started; to contemplate the playful smile which mantled on his face when he had accomplished the distance, and the eagerness with which he turned round when he had done so, and ran after his predecessor, his black gaiters tripping pleasantly through the snow, and his eyes beaming cheerfulness and gladness through his spectacles. And when he was knocked down (which happened upon the average every third round), it was the most invigorating sight that can possibly be imagined, to behold him gather up his hat, gloves, and handkerchief, with a glowing countenance, and resume his station in the rank, with an ardour and enthusiasm that nothing could abate.

The sport was at its height, the sliding was at the quickest, the laughter was at the loudest, when a sharp smart crack was heard. There was a quick rush towards the bank, a wild scream from the ladies, and a shout from Mr. Tupman. A large mass of ice disappeared; the water bubbled up over it; Mr. Pickwick's hat, gloves, and handkerchief were floating on the surface; and this was all of Mr. Pickwick that anybody could see.

Dismay and anguish were depicted on every countenance; the males turned pale, and the females fainted; Mr. Snodgrass and Mr. Winkle grasped each other by the hand, and gazed at the spot where their leader had gone down, with frenzied eagerness; while Mr. Tupman, by way of rendering the promptest assistance, and at the same time conveying to any persons who might be within hearing, the clearest possible notion of the catastrophe, ran off across the country at his utmost speed, screaming "Fire!" with all his might.

It was at this moment, when old Wardle and Sam Weller were approaching the hole with cautious steps, and Mr. Benjamin Allen was holding a hurried consultation with Mr. Bob Sawyer on the advisability of bleeding the company generally, as an improving little bit of professional practice—it was at this very moment, that a face, head, and shoulders, emerged from beneath the water, and disclosed the features and spectacles of Mr. Pickwick.

"Keep yourself up for an instant—for only one instant!" bawled Mr. Snodgrass.

"Yes, do; let me implore you—for my sake!" roared Mr. Winkle, deeply affected. The adjuration was rather unnecessary; the probability being, that if Mr. Pickwick had declined to keep himself up for anybody else's sake, it would have occurred to him that he might as well do so, for his own.

"Do you feel the bottom there, old fellow?" said Wardle.

"Yes, certainly," replied Mr. Pickwick, wringing the water from his head and face, and gasping for breath. "I fell upon my back. I couldn't get on my feet at first."

The clay upon so much of Mr. Pickwick's coat as was yet visible, bore testimony to the accuracy of this statement; and as the fears of the spectators were still further relieved by the fat boy's suddenly recollecting that the water was nowhere more than five feet deep, prodigies of valour were performed to get him out. After a vast quantity of splashing, and cracking, and struggling, Mr. Pickwick was at length fairly extricated from his unpleasant position, and once more stood on dry land.

"Oh, he'll catch his death of cold," said Emily.

"Dear old thing!" said Arabella. "Let me wrap this shawl round you, Mr. Pickwick."

"Ah, that's the best thing you can do," said Wardle; "and when you've got it on, run home as fast as your legs can carry you, and jump into bed directly."

A dozen shawls were offered on the instant. Three or four of the thickest having been selected, Mr. Pickwick was wrapped up, and started off, under the guidance of Mr. Weller; presenting the singular phenomenon of an elderly gentleman, dripping wet, and without a hat, with his arms bound down to his sides, skimming over the ground, without any clearly-defined purpose, at the rate of six good English miles an hour.

But Mr. Pickwick cared not for appearances in such an extreme case, and urged on by Sam Weller, he kept at the very top of his speed until he reached the door of Manor Farm, where Mr. Tupman had arrived some five minutes before, and had frightened the old lady into palpitations of the heart by impressing her with the unalterable conviction that the kitchen chimney was on fire—a calamity which always presented itself in glowing colours to the old lady's mind, when anybody about her evinced the smallest agitation.

Mr. Pickwick paused not an instant until he was snug in bed. Sam Weller lighted a blazing fire in the room, and took up his dinner; a bowl of punch was carried up afterwards, and a grand carouse held in honour of his safety. Old Wardle would not hear of his rising, so they made the bed the chair, and Mr. Pickwick presided. A second and a third bowl were ordered in; and when Mr. Pickwick awoke next morning, there was not a symptom of rheumatism about him; which proves, as Mr. Bob Sawyer very justly observed, that there is nothing like hot punch in such cases; and that if ever hot punch did fail to act as a preventive, it was merely because the patient fell into the vulgar error of not taking enough of it.

Bob Sawyer's Party

MR. BOB SAWYER embellished one side of the fire, in his first-floor front, early on the evening for which he had invited Mr. Pickwick, and Mr. Ben Allen the other. The preparations for the reception of visitors appeared to be completed. The umbrellas in the passage had been heaped into the little corner outside the back-parlour door; the bonnet and shawl of the landlady's servant had been removed from the banisters; there were not more than two pairs of pattens on the street-door mat; and a kitchen candle, with a very long snuff, burned cheerfully on the ledge of the staircase window. Mr. Bob Sawyer had himself purchased the spirits at a wine vault in High Street, and had returned home preceding the bearer thereof, to preclude the possibility of their delivery at the wrong house. The punch was ready-made in a red pan in the bedroom; a little table, covered with a green baize cloth, had been borrowed from the parlour, to play at cards on; and the glasses of the establishment, together with those which had been borrowed for the occasion from the public-house, were all drawn up in a tray, which was deposited on the landing outside the door.

Notwithstanding the highly satisfactory nature of all these arrangements, there was a cloud on the countenance of Mr. Bob Sawyer, as he sat by the fireside. There was a sympathising expression, too, in the features of Mr. Ben Allen, as he gazed intently on the coals, and a tone of melancholy in his voice, as he said, after a long silence—

"Well, it *is* unlucky she should have taken it into her head to turn sour, just on this occasion. She might at least have waited till tomorrow."

"That's her malevolence—that's her malevolence," returned Mr. Bob Sawyer vehemently. "She says that if I can afford to give a party I ought to be able to pay her confounded 'little bill.'"

"How long has it been running?" inquired Mr. Ben Allen. A bill, by the bye, is the most extraordinary locomotive engine that the genius of man ever produced. It would keep on running during the longest lifetime, without ever once stopping of its own accord.

"Only a quarter, and a month or so," replied Mr. Bob Sawyer.

Ben Allen coughed hopelessly, and directed a searching look between the two top bars of the stove.

"It'll be a deuced unpleasant thing if she takes it into her head to let out, when those fellows are here, won't it?" said Mr. Ben Allen at length.

"Horrible," replied Bob Sawyer, "horrible."

A low tap was heard at the room door. Mr. Bob Sawyer looked expressively at his friend, and bade the tapper come in; whereupon a dirty, slipshod girl in black cotton stockings, who might have passed for the neglected daughter of a superannuated dustman in very reduced circumstances, thrust in her head, and said —

"Please, Mr. Sawyer, Mrs. Raddle wants to speak to *you.*"

Before Mr. Bob Sawyer could return any answer, the girl suddenly disappeared with a jerk, as if somebody had given her a violent pull behind; this mysterious exit was no sooner accomplished, than there was another tap at the door—a smart, pointed tap, which seemed to say, "Here I am, and in I'm coming."

Mr. Bob Sawyer glanced at his friend with a look of abject apprehension, and once more cried, "Come in."

The permission was not at all necessary, for, before Mr. Bob Sawyer had uttered the words, a little, fierce woman bounced into the room, all in a tremble with passion, and pale with rage.

"Now, Mr. Sawyer," said the little, fierce woman, trying to appear very calm, "if you'll have the kindness to settle that little bill of mine

I'll thank you, because I've got my rent to pay this afternoon, and my landlord's a-waiting below now." Here the little woman rubbed her hands, and looked steadily over Mr. Bob Sawyer's head, at the wall behind him.

"I am very sorry to put you to any inconvenience, Mrs. Raddle," said Bob Sawyer deferentially, "but——"

"Oh, it isn't any inconvenience," replied the little woman, with a shrill titter. "I didn't want it particular before to-day; leastways, as it has to go to my landlord directly, it was as well for you to keep it as me. You promised me this afternoon, Mr. Sawyer, and every gentleman as has ever lived here, has kept his word, sir, as of course anybody as calls himself a gentleman does." Mrs. Raddle tossed her head, bit her lips, rubbed her hands harder, and looked at the wall more steadily than ever. It was plain to see, as Mr. Bob Sawyer remarked in a style of Eastern allegory on a subsequent occasion, that she was "getting the steam up."

"I am very sorry, Mrs. Raddle," said Bob Sawyer, with all imaginable humility, "but the fact is, that I have been disappointed in the city to-day."—Extraordinary place that city. An astonishing number of men always *are* getting disappointed there.

"Well, Mr. Sawyer," said Mrs. Raddle, planting herself firmly on a purple cauliflower in the Kidderminster carpet, "and what's that to me, sir?"

"I—I—have no doubt, Mrs. Raddle," said Bob Sawyer, blinking this last question, "that before the middle of next week we shall be able to set ourselves quite square, and go on, on a better system, afterwards."

This was all Mrs. Raddle wanted. She had bustled up to the apartment of the unlucky Bob Sawyer, so bent upon going into a passion, that, in all probability, payment would have rather disappointed her than otherwise. She was in excellent order for a little relaxation of the kind, having just exchanged a few introductory compliments with Mr. R. in the front kitchen.

"Do you suppose, Mr. Sawyer," said Mrs. Raddle, elevating her voice for the information of the neighbours—"do you suppose that I'm a-going day after day to let a fellar occupy my lodgings as never thinks of paying his rent, nor even the very money laid out for the fresh butter and lump sugar that's bought for his breakfast, and the very milk that's took in, at the street door? Do you suppose a hard-working and industrious woman as has lived in this street for twenty year (ten year over the way, and nine year and three-quarters in this very house) has nothing else to do but to work herself to death after a parcel of lazy idle fellars, that are always smoking and drinking, and lounging, when they ought to be glad to turn their hands to anything that would help 'em to pay their bills? Do you——"

"My good soul," interposed Mr. Benjamin Allen soothingly.

"Have the goodness to keep your observashuns to yourself, sir, I beg," said Mrs. Raddle, suddenly arresting the rapid torrent of her speech, and addressing the third party with impressive slowness and solemnity. "I am not aweer, sir, that you have any right to address your conversation to me. I don't think I let these apartments to you, sir."

"No, you certainly did not," said Mr. Benjamin Allen.

"Very good, sir," responded Mrs. Raddle, with lofty politeness. "Then p'raps, sir, you'll confine yourself to breaking the arms and legs of the poor people in the hospitals, and keep yourself to yourself, sir, or there may be some persons here as will make you, sir."

"But you are such an unreasonable woman," remonstrated Mr. Benjamin Allen.

"I beg your parding, young man," said Mrs. Raddle, in a cold perspiration of anger. "But will you have the goodness just to call me that again, sir?"

"I didn't make use of the word in any invidious sense, ma'am," replied Mr. Benjamin Allen, growing somewhat uneasy on his own account.

"I beg your parding, young man," demanded Mrs. Raddle, in a louder and more imperative tone. "But who do you call a woman? Did you make that remark to me, sir?"

"Why, bless my heart!" said Mr. Benjamin Allen.

"Did you apply that name to me, I ask of you, sir?" interrupted Mrs. Raddle, with intense fierceness, throwing the door wide open.

"Why, of course I did," replied Mr. Benjamin Allen.

"Yes, of course you did," said Mrs. Raddle, backing gradually to the door, and raising her voice to its loudest pitch, for the special behoof of Mr. Raddle in the kitchen. "Yes, of course you did! And everybody knows that they may safely insult me in my own 'ouse while my husband sits sleeping downstairs, and taking no more notice than if I was a dog in the streets. He ought to be ashamed of himself (here Mrs. Raddle sobbed) to allow his wife to be treated in this way by a parcel of young cutters and carvers of live people's bodies, that disgraces the lodgings (another sob), and leaving her exposed to all manner of abuse; a base, faint-hearted, timorous wretch, that's afraid to come upstairs, and face the ruffinly creatures—that's afraid—that's afraid to come!" Mrs. Raddle paused to listen whether the repetition of the taunt had roused her better half; and finding that it had not been successful, proceeded to descend the stairs with sobs innumerable; when there came a loud double knock at the street door; whereupon she burst into an hysterical fit of weeping, accompanied with dismal moans, which was prolonged until the knock had been repeated six times, when, in an uncontrollable burst of mental agony, she threw down all the umbrellas, and disappeared into the back parlour, closing the door after her with an awful crash.

"Does Mr. Sawyer live here?" said Mr. Pickwick, when the door was opened.

"Yes," said the girl, "first floor. It's the door straight afore you, when you gets to the top of the stairs." Having given this instruction, the handmaid, who had been brought up among the aboriginal inhabitants of Southwark, disappeared, with the candle in her hand, down the kitchen stairs, perfectly satisfied that she had done everything that could possibly be required of her under the circumstances.

Mr. Snodgrass, who entered last, secured the street door, after several ineffectual efforts, by putting up the chain; and the friends stumbled upstairs, where they were received by Mr. Bob Sawyer, who had been afraid to go down, lest he should be waylaid by Mrs. Raddle.

"How are you?" said the discomfited student. "Glad to see you— take care of the glasses." This caution was addressed to Mr. Pickwick, who had put his hat in the tray.

"Dear me," said Mr. Pickwick, "I beg your pardon."

"Don't mention it, don't mention it," said Bob Sawyer. "I'm rather confined for room here, but you must put up with all that, when you come to see a young bachelor. Walk in. You've seen this gentleman before, I think?" Mr. Pickwick shook hands with Mr. Benjamin Allen, and his friends followed his example. They had scarcely taken their seats when there was another double knock.

"I hope that's Jack Hopkins!" said Mr. Bob Sawyer. "Hush. Yes, it is. Come up, Jack; come up."

A heavy footstep was heard upon the stairs, and Jack Hopkins presented himself. He wore a black velvet waistcoat, with thunder-and-lightning buttons; and a blue striped shirt, with a white false collar.

"You're late, Jack?" said Mr. Benjamin Allen.

"Been detained at Bartholomew's," replied Hopkins.

"Anything new?"

"No, nothing particular. Rather a good accident brought into the casualty ward."

"What was that, sir?" inquired Mr. Pickwick.

"Only a man fallen out of a four pair of stairs' window; but it's a very fair case indeed."

"Do you mean that the patient is in a fair way to recover?" inquired Mr. Pickwick.

"No," replied Mr. Hopkins carelessly. "No, I should rather say he wouldn't. There must be a splendid operation, though, to-morrow—magnificent sight if Slasher does it."

"You consider Mr. Slasher a good operator?" said Mr. Pickwick.

"Best alive," replied Hopkins. "Took a boy's leg out of the socket last week—boy ate five apples and a gingerbread cake—exactly two minutes after it was all over, boy said he wouldn't lie there to be made game of, and he'd tell his mother if they didn't begin."

"Dear me!" said Mr. Pickwick, astonished.

"Pooh! That's nothing, that ain't," said Jack Hopkins. "Is it, Bob?"

"Nothing at all," replied Mr. Bob Sawyer.

"By the bye, Bob," said Hopkins, with a scarcely perceptible glance at Mr. Pickwick's attentive face, "we had a curious accident last night. A child was brought in, who had swallowed a necklace."

"Swallowed what, sir?" interrupted Mr. Pickwick.

"A necklace," replied Jack Hopkins. "Not all at once, you know, that would be too much—*you* couldn't swallow that, if the child did—eh, Mr. Pickwick? ha, ha!" Mr. Hopkins appeared highly gratified with his own pleasantry, and continued—"No, the way was this. Child's parents were poor people who lived in a court. Child's eldest sister bought a necklace—common necklace, made of large black wooden beads. Child being fond of toys, cribbed the necklace, hid it, played with it, cut the string, and swallowed a bead. Child thought it capital fun, went back next day, and swallowed another bead."

"Bless my heart," said Mr. Pickwick, "what a dreadful thing! I beg your pardon, sir. Go on."

"Next day, child swallowed two beads; the day after that, he treated himself to three, and so on, till in a week's time he had got through the necklace—five-and-twenty beads in all. The sister, who was an industrious girl, and seldom treated herself to a bit of finery, cried her eyes out, at the loss of the necklace; looked high and low for it; but, I needn't say, didn't find it. A few days afterwards, the family were at dinner—baked shoulder of mutton, and potatoes under it—the child, who wasn't hungry, was playing about the room, when suddenly there was heard a devil of a noise, like a small hail-storm. 'Don't do that, my boy,' said the father. 'I ain't a-doin' nothing,' said the child. 'Well, don't do it again,' said the father. There was a short silence, and then the noise began again, worse than ever. 'If you don't mind what I say, my boy,' said the father, 'you'll find yourself in bed, in something less than a pig's whisper.' He gave the child a shake to make him obedient, and such a rattling ensued as nobody ever heard before. 'Why, damme, it's *in* the child!' said the father, 'he's got the croup in the wrong place!' 'No, I haven't, father,' said the child, beginning to cry, 'it's the necklace; I swallowed it, father.'—The father caught the child up, and ran with him to the hospital; the beads in the boy's stomach rattling all the way with the jolting; and the people looking up in the air, and down in the cellars, to see where the unusual sound came from. He's in the hospital now," said Jack Hopkins, "and he makes such a devil of a noise when he walks about, that they're obliged to muffle him in a watchman's coat, for fear he should wake the patients."

"That's the most extraordinary case I ever heard of," said Mr. Pickwick, with an emphatic blow on the table.

"Oh, that's nothing," said Jack Hopkins. "Is it, Bob?"

"Certainly not," replied Mr. Bob Sawyer.

"Very singular things occur in our profession, I can assure you, sir," said Hopkins.

"So I should be disposed to imagine," replied Mr. Pickwick.

Another knock at the door announced a large-headed young man in a black wig, who brought with him a scorbutic youth in a long stock. The next comer was a gentleman in a shirt emblazoned with pink anchors, who was closely followed by a pale youth with a plated watchguard. The arrival of a prim personage in clean linen and cloth boots rendered the party complete. The little table with the green baize cover was wheeled out; the first instalment of punch was brought in, in a white jug; and the succeeding three hours were devoted to *vingt-et-un* at sixpence a dozen, which was only once interrupted by a slight dispute between the scorbutic youth and the gentleman with the pink anchors; in the course of which, the scorbutic youth intimated a burning desire to pull the nose of the gentleman with the emblems of hope; in reply to which, that individual expressed his decided unwillingness to accept of any "sauce" on gratuitous terms, either from the irascible young gentleman with the scorbutic countenance, or any other person who was ornamented with a head.

When the last "natural" had been declared, and the profit and loss account of fish and sixpences adjusted, to the satisfaction of all parties, Mr. Bob Sawyer rang for supper, and the visitors squeezed themselves into corners while it was getting ready.

It was not so easily got ready as some people may imagine. First of all, it was necessary to awaken the girl, who had fallen asleep with her face on the kitchen table; this took a little time, and, even when she did answer the bell, another quarter of an hour was consumed in fruitless endeavours to impart to her a faint and distant glimmering of reason. The man to whom the order for the oysters had been sent, had not been told to open them; it is a very difficult thing to open an oyster with a limp knife and a two-pronged fork; and very little was done in this way. Very little of the beef was done either; and the ham (which was also from the German-sausage shop round the corner) was in a similar predicament. However, there was plenty of porter in a tin can; and the cheese went a great way, for it was very strong. So upon the whole, perhaps, the supper was quite as good as such matters usually are.

After supper, another jug of punch was put upon the table, together with a paper of cigars, and a couple of bottles of spirits. Then there was an awful pause; and this awful pause was occasioned by a very common occurrence in this sort of place, but a very embarrassing one notwithstanding.

The fact is, the girl was washing the glasses. The establishment boasted four: we do not record the circumstance as at all derogatory to Mrs. Raddle, for there never was a lodging-house yet, that was not short of glasses. The landlady's glasses were little, thin, blown-glass tumblers, and those which had been borrowed from the public-house were great, dropsical, bloated articles, each supported on a huge gouty leg. This would have been in itself sufficient to have possessed the company with the real state of affairs; but the young woman of all work had prevented the possibility of any misconception arising in the mind of any gentleman upon the subject, by forcibly dragging every man's glass away, long before he had finished his beer, and audibly stating, despite the winks and interruptions of Mr. Bob Sawyer, that it was to be conveyed downstairs, and washed forthwith.

It is a very ill wind that blows nobody any good. The prim man in the cloth boots, who had been unsuccessfully attempting to make a joke during the whole time the round game lasted, saw his opportunity, and availed himself of it. The instant the glasses disappeared, he commenced a long story about a great public character, whose name he had forgotten, making a particularly happy reply to another eminent and illustrious individual whom he had never been able to identify. He enlarged at some length and with great minuteness upon divers collateral circumstances, distantly connected with the anecdote in hand, but for the life of him he couldn't recollect at that precise moment what the anecdote was, although he had been in the habit of telling the story with great applause for the last ten years.

"Dear me," said the prim man in the cloth boots, "it is a very extraordinary circumstance."

"I am sorry you have forgotten it," said Mr. Bob Sawyer, glancing eagerly at the door, as he thought he heard the noise of glasses jingling; "very sorry."

"So am I," responded the prim man, "because I know it would have afforded so much amusement. Never mind; I dare say I shall manage to recollect it, in the course of half an hour or so."

The prim man arrived at this point just as the glasses came back, when Mr. Bob Sawyer, who had been absorbed in attention during the whole time, said he should very much like to hear the end of it, for, so far as it went, it was, without exception, the very best story he had ever heard.

The sight of the tumblers restored Bob Sawyer to a degree of equanimity which he had not possessed since his interview with his landlady. His face brightened up, and he began to feel quite convivial.

"Now, Betsy," said Mr. Bob Sawyer, with great suavity, and dispersing, at the same time, the tumultuous little mob of glasses the girl had collected in the centre of the table—"now, Betsy, the warm water; be brisk, there's a good girl."

"You can't have no warm water," replied Betsy.

"No warm water!" exclaimed Mr. Bob Sawyer.

"No," said the girl, with a shake of the head which expressed a more decided negative than the most copious language could have conveyed. "Mrs. Raddle said you warn't to have none."

The surprise depicted on the countenances of his guests imparted new courage to the host.

"Bring up the warm water instantly—instantly!" said Mr. Bob Sawyer, with desperate sternness.

"No. I can't," replied the girl, "Mrs. Raddle raked out the kitchen fire afore she went to bed, and locked up the kittle."

"Oh, never mind; never mind. Pray don't disturb yourself about such a trifle," said Mr. Pickwick, observing the conflict of Bob Sawyer's passions, as depicted in his countenance, "cold water will do very well."

"Oh, admirably," said Mr. Benjamin Allen.

"My landlady is subject to some slight attacks of mental derangement," remarked Bob Sawyer, with a ghastly smile; "I fear I must give her warning."

"No, don't," said Ben Allen.

"I fear I must," said Bob, with heroic firmness. "I'll pay her what I owe her, and give her warning to-morrow morning." Poor fellow! how devoutly he wished he could!

Mr. Bob Sawyer's heart-sickening attempts to rally under this last blow, communicated a dispiriting influence to the company, the greater part of whom, with the view of raising their spirits, attached themselves with extra cordiality to the cold brandy-and-water, the first perceptible effects of which were displayed in a renewal of hostilities between the scorbutic youth and the gentleman in the shirt. The belligerents vented their feelings of mutual contempt, for some time, in a variety of frownings and snortings, until at last the scorbutic youth felt it necessary to come to a more explicit understanding on the matter; when the following clear understanding took place.

"Sawyer," said the scorbutic youth, in a loud voice.

"Well, Noddy," replied Mr. Bob Sawyer.

"I should be very sorry, Sawyer," said Mr. Noddy, "to create any unpleasantness at any friend's table, and much less at yours, Sawyer—very; but I must take this opportunity of informing Mr. Gunter that he is no gentleman."

"And *I* should be very sorry, Sawyer, to create any disturbance in the street in which you reside," said Mr. Gunter, "but I'm afraid I shall be under the necessity of alarming the neighbours by throwing the person who has just spoken, out o' window."

"What do you mean by that, sir?" inquired Mr. Noddy.

"What I say, sir," replied Mr. Gunter.

"I should like to see you do it, sir," said Mr. Noddy.

"You shall *feel* me do it in half a minute, sir," replied Mr. Gunter.

"I request that you'll favour me with your card, sir," said Mr. Noddy.

"I'll do nothing of the kind, sir," replied Mr. Gunter.

"Why not, sir?" inquired Mr. Noddy.

"Because you'll stick it up over your chimney-piece, and delude your visitors into the false belief that a gentleman has been to see you, sir," replied Mr. Gunter.

"Sir, a friend of mine shall wait on you in the morning," said Mr. Noddy.

"Sir, I'm very much obliged to you for the caution, and I'll leave particular directions with the servant to lock up the spoons," replied Mr. Gunter.

At this point the remainder of the guests interposed, and remonstrated with both parties on the impropriety of their conduct; on which Mr. Noddy begged to state that his father was quite as respectable as Mr. Gunter's father; to which Mr. Gunter replied that his father was to the full as respectable as Mr. Noddy's father, and that his father's son was as good a man as Mr. Noddy, any day in the week. As this announcement seemed the prelude to a recommencement of the dispute, there was another interference on the part of the company; and a vast quantity of talking and clamouring ensued, in the course of which Mr. Noddy gradually allowed his feelings to overpower him, and professed that he had ever entertained a devoted personal attachment towards Mr. Gunter. To this Mr. Gunter replied that, upon the whole, he rather preferred Mr. Noddy to his own brother; on hearing which admission, Mr. Noddy magnanimously rose from his seat, and proffered his hand to Mr. Gunter. Mr. Gunter grasped it with affecting fervour; and everybody said that the whole dispute had been conducted in a manner which was highly honourable to both parties concerned.

"Now," said Jack Hopkins, "just to set us going again, Bob, I don't mind singing a song." And Hopkins, incited thereto by tumultuous applause, plunged himself at once into "The King, God bless him," which he sang as loud as he could, to a novel air, compounded of the "Bay of Biscay," and "A Frog he would." The chorus was the essence of the song; and, as each gentleman sang it to the tune he knew best, the effect was very striking indeed.

It was at the end of the chorus to the first verse, that Mr. Pickwick held up his hand in a listening attitude, and said, as soon as silence was restored—

"Hush! I beg your pardon. I thought I heard somebody calling from upstairs."

A profound silence immediately ensued; and Mr. Bob Sawyer was observed to turn pale.

"I think I hear it now," said Mr. Pickwick. "Have the goodness to open the door."

The door was no sooner opened than all doubt on the subject was removed.

"Mr. Sawyer! Mr. Sawyer!" screamed a voice from the two-pair landing.

"It's my landlady," said Bob Sawyer, looking round him with great dismay. "Yes, Mrs. Raddle."

"What do you mean by this, Mr. Sawyer?" replied the voice, with great shrillness and rapidity of utterance. "Ain't it enough to be swindled out of one's rent, and money lent out of pocket besides, and abused and insulted by your friends that dares to call themselves men, without having the house turned out of window, and noise enough made to bring the fire-engines here, at two o'clock in the morning?—Turn them wretches away."

"You ought to be ashamed of yourselves," said the voice of Mr. Raddle, which appeared to proceed from beneath some distant bed-clothes.

"Ashamed of themselves!" said Mrs. Raddle. "Why don't you go down and knock 'em every one downstairs? You would if you was a man."

"I should if I was a dozen men, my dear," replied Mr. Raddle pacifically, "but they have the advantage of me in numbers, my dear."

"Ugh, you coward!" replied Mrs. Raddle, with supreme contempt. "*Do* you mean to turn them wretches out, or not, Mr. Sawyer?"

"They're going, Mrs. Raddle, they're going," said the miserable Bob. "I am afraid you'd better go," said Mr. Bob Sawyer to his friends. "I *thought* you were making too much noise."

"It's a very unfortunate thing," said the prim man. "Just as we were getting so comfortable too!" The prim man was just beginning to have a dawning recollection of the story he had forgotten.

"It's hardly to be borne," said the prim man, looking round. "Hardly to be borne, is it?"

"Not to be endured," replied Jack Hopkins; "let's have the other verse, Bob. Come, here goes!"

"No, no, Jack, don't," interposed Bob Sawyer; "it's a capital song, but I am afraid we had better not have the other verse. They are very violent people, the people of the house."

"Shall I step upstairs, and pitch into the landlord?" inquired Hopkins, "or keep on ringing the bell, or go and groan on the staircase? You may command me, Bob."

"I am very much indebted to you for your friendship and good-nature, Hopkins," said the wretched Mr. Bob Sawyer, "but I think the best plan to avoid any further dispute is for us to break up at once."

"Now, Mr. Sawyer," screamed the shrill voice of Mrs. Raddle, "*are* them brutes going?"

"They're only looking for their hats, Mrs. Raddle," said Bob; "they are going directly."

"Going!" said Mrs. Raddle, thrusting her nightcap over the banisters just as Mr. Pickwick, followed by Mr. Tupman, emerged from the sitting-room. "Going! what did they ever come for?"

"My dear ma'am," remonstrated Mr. Pickwick, looking up.

"Get along with you, old wretch!" replied Mrs. Raddle, hastily withdrawing the nightcap. "Old enough to be his grandfather, you willin! You're worse than any of 'em."

Mr. Pickwick found it in vain to protest his innocence, so hurried downstairs into the street, whither he was closely followed by Mr. Tupman, Mr. Winkle, and Mr. Snodgrass. Mr. Ben Allen, who was dismally depressed with spirits and agitation, accompanied them as far as London Bridge, and in the course of the walk confided to Mr. Winkle, as an especially eligible person to intrust the secret to, that he was resolved to cut the throat of any gentleman, except Mr. Bob Sawyer, who should aspire to the affections of his sister Arabella. Having expressed his determination to perform this painful duty of a brother with proper firmness, he burst into tears, knocked his hat over his eyes, and, making the best of his way back, knocked double knocks at the door of the Borough Market office, and took short naps on the steps alternately, until daybreak, under the firm impression that he lived there, and had forgotten the key.

The visitors having all departed, in compliance with the rather pressing request of Mrs. Raddle, the luckless Mr. Bob Sawyer was left alone, to meditate on the probable events of to-morrow, and the pleasures of the evening.

From MARTIN CHUZZLEWIT

The first Appearance of Mrs. Gamp

MR. PECKSNIFF was in a hackney cabriolet, for Jonas Chuzzlewit had said "Spare no expense." Mankind is evil in its thoughts and in its base constructions, and Jonas was resolved it should not have an inch to stretch into an ell against him. It never should be charged upon his father's son that he had grudged the money for his father's funeral. Hence, until the obsequies should be concluded, Jonas had taken for his motto "Spend, and spare not!"

Mr. Pecksniff had been to the undertaker, and was now upon his way to another officer in the train of mourning: a female functionary, a nurse, and watcher, and performer of nameless offices about the persons of the dead: whom he had recommended. Her name, as Mr. Pecksniff gathered from a scrap of writing in his hand, was Gamp; her residence in Kingsgate Street, High Holborn. So Mr. Pecksniff, in a hackney cab, was rattling over Holborn stones, in quest of Mrs. Gamp.

This lady lodged at a bird-fancier's, next door but one to the celebrated mutton-pie shop, and directly opposite to the original cat's-meat warehouse; the renown of which establishments was duly heralded on their respective fronts. It was a little house, and this was the more convenient; for Mrs. Gamp being, in her highest walk of art, a monthly nurse, or, as her sign-board boldly had it, "Midwife," and lodging in the first-floor front, was easily assailable at night by pebbles, walking-sticks, and fragments of tobacco-pipe: all much more efficacious than the street-door knocker, which was so constructed as to wake the street with ease, and even spread alarms of fire in Holborn, without making the smallest impression on the premises to which it was addressed.

It chanced on this particular occasion, that Mrs. Gamp had been up all the previous night, in attendance upon a ceremony to which the usage of gossips has given that name which expresses, in two syllables, the curse pronounced on Adam. It chanced that Mrs. Gamp had not been regularly engaged, but had been called in at a crisis, in conse-quence of her great repute, to assist another professional lady with her advice; and thus it happened that, all points of interest in the case being over, Mrs. Gamp had come home again to the bird-fancier's, and gone to bed. So, when Mr. Pecksniff drove up in the hackney cab, Mrs. Gamp's curtains were drawn close, and Mrs. Gamp was fast asleep behind them.

If the bird-fancier had been at home, as he ought to have been, there would have been no great harm in this; but he was out, and his shop was closed. The shutters were down certainly; and in every pane of glass there was at least one tiny bird in a tiny bird-cage, twittering and hopping his little ballet of despair, and knocking his head against the roof: while one unhappy goldfinch who lived outside a red villa with his name on the door, drew the water for his own drinking, and mutely appealed to some good man to drop a farthing's worth of poison in it. Still, the door was shut. Mr. Pecksniff tried the latch, and shook it, causing a cracked bell inside to ring most mournfully; but no one came. The bird-fancier was an easy shaver also, and a fashionable hair-dresser also; and perhaps he had been sent for, express, from the court end of the town, to trim a lord, or cut and curl a lady; but however that might be, there, upon his own ground, he was not; nor was there any more distinct trace of him to assist the imagination of an inquirer, than a professional print or emblem of his calling (much favoured in the trade), representing a hair-dresser of easy manners curling a lady of distinguished fashion, in the presence of a patent upright grand pianoforte.

Noting these circumstances, Mr. Pecksniff, in the innocence of his heart, applied himself to the knocker; but at the first double knock, every window in the street became alive with female heads; and before he could repeat the performance, whole troops of married ladies (some about to trouble Mrs. Gamp themselves, very shortly) came flocking round the steps, all crying out with one accord, and with uncommon interest, "Knock at the winder, sir, knock at the winder. Lord bless you, don't lose no more time than you can help; knock at the winder!"

Acting upon this suggestion, and borrowing the driver's whip for the purpose, Mr. Pecksniff soon made a commotion among the first-floor flower-pots, and roused Mrs. Gamp, whose voice—to the great satisfaction of the matrons—was heard to say, "I'm coming."

"He's as pale as a muffin," said one lady, in allusion to Mr. Pecksniff.

"So he ought to be, if he's the feelings of a man," observed another.

A third lady (with her arms folded) said she wished he had chosen any other time for fetching Mrs. Gamp, but it always happened so with *her*.

It gave Mr. Pecksniff much uneasiness to find, from these remarks, that he was supposed to have come to Mrs. Gamp upon an errand touching—not the close of life, but the other end. Mrs. Gamp herself was under the same impression, for, throwing open the window, she cried behind the curtains, as she hastily attired herself:

"Is it Mrs. Perkins?"

"No!" returned Mr. Pecksniff, sharply. "Nothing of the sort."

"What, Mr. Whilks!" cried Mrs. Gamp. "Don't say it's you, Mr. Whilks, and that poor creetur Mrs. Whilks with not even a pincushion ready. Don't say it's you, Mr. Whilks!"

"It isn't Mr. Whilks," said Pecksniff. "I don't know the man. Nothing of the kind. A gentleman is dead; and some person being wanted in the house, you have been recommended by Mr. Mould the undertaker."

As she was by this time in a condition to appear, Mrs. Gamp, who had a face for all occasions, looked out of the window with her mourning countenance, and said she would be down directly. But the matrons took it very ill, that Mr. Pecksniff's mission was of so unimportant a kind; and the lady with her arms folded rated him in good round terms, signifying that she would be glad to know what he meant by terrifying delicate females "with his corpses;" and giving it as her opinion that he was quite ugly enough to know better. The other ladies were not at all behind-hand in expressing similar sentiments; and the children, of whom some scores had now collected, hooted and defied Mr. Pecksniff quite savagely. So, when Mrs. Gamp appeared, the unoffending gentleman was glad to hustle her with very little ceremony into the cabriolet, and drive off, overwhelmed with popular execration.

Mrs. Gamp had a large bundle with her, a pair of pattens, and a species of gig umbrella; the latter article in colour like a faded leaf, except where a circular patch of a lively blue had been dexterously let in at the top. She was much flurried by the haste she had made, and laboured under the most erroneous views of cabriolets, which she appeared to confound with mail-coaches or stage-waggons, inasmuch as she was constantly endeavouring for the first half mile to force her luggage through the little front window, and clamouring to the driver to "put it in the boot." When she was disabused of this idea, her whole being resolved itself into an absorbing anxiety about her pattens, with which she played innumerable games at quoits, on Mr. Pecksniff's legs. It was not until they were close upon the house of mourning that she had enough composure to observe:

"And so the gentleman's dead, sir! Ah! The more's the pity." She didn't even know his name. "But it's what we must all come to. It's as certain as being born, except that we can't make our calculations as exact. Ah! Poor dear!"

She was a fat old woman, this Mrs. Gamp, with a husky voice and a moist eye, which she had a remarkable power of turning up, and only showing the white of it. Having very little neck, it cost her some trouble to look over herself, if one may say so, at those to whom she talked. She wore a very rusty black gown, rather the worse for snuff, and a shawl and bonnet to correspond. In these dilapidated articles of dress she had, on principle, arrayed herself, time out of mind, on such occasions as the present; for this at once expressed a decent amount of veneration for the deceased, and invited the next of kin to present her with a fresher suit of weeds: an appeal so frequently successful, that the very fetch and ghost of Mrs. Gamp, bonnet and all, might be seen hanging up, any hour in the day, in at least a dozen of the second-hand clothes shops about Holborn. The face of Mrs. Gamp—the nose in particular—was somewhat red and swollen, and it was difficult to enjoy her society without becoming conscious of a smell of spirits. Like most persons who have attained to great eminence in their profession, she took to hers very kindly; insomuch, that setting aside her natural pre-dilections as a woman, she went to a lying-in or a laying-out with equal zest and relish.

"Ah!" repeated Mrs. Gamp; for it was always a safe sentiment in cases of mourning. "Ah dear! When Gamp was summoned to his long home, and I see him a lying in Guy's Hospital with a penny-piece on each eye, and his wooden leg under his left arm, I thought I should have fainted away. But I bore up."

If certain whispers current in the Kingsgate Street circles had any truth in them, she had indeed borne up surprisingly; and had exerted such uncommon fortitude, as to dispose of Mr. Gamp's remains for the benefit of science. But it should be added, in fairness, that this had happened twenty years before; and that Mr. and Mrs. Gamp had long been separated, on the ground of incompatibility of temper in their drink.

"You have become indifferent since then, I suppose?" said Mr. Pecksniff. "Use is second nature, Mrs. Gamp."

"You may well say second nater, sir," returned that lady. "One's first ways is to find sich things a trial to the feelings, and so is one's lasting custom. If it wasn't for the nerve a little sip of liquor gives me (I never was able to do more than taste it), I never could go through with what I sometimes has to do. 'Mrs. Harris,' I says, at the very last case as ever I acted in, which it was but a young person, 'Mrs. Harris,' I says, 'leave the bottle on the chimley-piece, and don't ask me to take none, but let me put my lips to it when I am so dispoged, and then I will do what I'm engaged to do, according to the best of my ability.' 'Mrs. Gamp,' she says, in answer, 'if ever there was a sober creetur to be got at eighteen pence a day for working people, and three and six for gentlefolks—night watching,'" said Mrs. Gamp, with emphasis, "'being a extra charge — you are that inwallable person.' 'Mrs. Harris,' I says to her, 'don't name the charge, for if I could afford to lay all my feller creeturs out for nothink, I would gladly do it, sich is the love I bears 'em. But what I always says to them as has the management of matters, Mrs. Harris:'" here she kept her eye on Mr. Pecksniff: "'be they gents or be they ladies, is, don't ask me whether I won't take none, or whether I will, but leave the bottle on the chimley-piece, and let me put my lips to it when I am so dispoged.'"

From A CHRISTMAS CAROL

The Cratchits' Dinner

THEN up rose Mrs. Cratchit, Cratchit's wife, dressed out but poorly in a twice-turned gown, but brave in ribbons, which are cheap and make a goodly show for sixpence; and she laid the cloth, assisted by Belinda Cratchit, second of her daughters, also brave in ribbons; while Master Peter Cratchit plunged a fork into the saucepan of potatoes, and getting the corners of his monstrous shirt collar (Bob's private property, conferred upon his son and heir in honor of the day) into his mouth, rejoiced to find himself so gallantly attired, and yearned to show his linen in the fashionable Parks. And now two smaller Cratchits, boy and girl, came tearing in, screaming that outside the baker's they had smelt the goose, and known it for their own; and basking in luxurious thoughts of sage and onion, these young Cratchits danced about the table, and exalted Master Peter Cratchit to the skies, while he (not proud, although his collar near choked him) blew the fire, until the slow potatoes bubbling up, knocked loudly at the saucepan-lid to be let out and peeled.

"What has ever got your precious father then?" said Mrs. Cratchit. "And your brother, Tiny Tim! And Martha warn't as late last Christmas Day by half an hour!"

"Here's Martha, mother," said a girl appearing as she spoke.

"Here's Martha, mother!" cried the two young Cratchits. "Hurrah! There's *such* a goose, Martha!"

"Why, bless your heart alive, my dear, how late you are!" said Mrs. Cratchit, kissing her a dozen times, and taking off her shawl and bonnet for her with officious zeal.

"We'd a deal of work to finish up last night," replied the girl, "and had to clear away this morning, mother!"

"Well! never mind so long as you are come," said Mrs. Cratchit. "Sit ye down before the fire, my dear, and have a warm, Lord bless ye!"

"No no! There's father coming," cried the two young Cratchits, who were everywhere at once. "Hide, Martha, hide!"

So Martha hid herself, and in came little Bob, the father, with at least three feet of comforter exclusive of the fringe hanging down before him; and his threadbare clothes darned up and brushed, to look seasonable; and Tiny Tim upon his shoulder. Alas for Tiny Tim, he bore a little crutch, and had his limbs supported by an iron frame.

"Why, where's our Martha?" cried Bob Cratchit looking round.

"Not coming," said Mrs. Cratchit.

"Not coming!" said Bob, with a sudden declension in his high spirits; for he had been Tim's blood horse all the way from church, and had come home rampant. "Not coming upon Christmas Day!"

Martha didn't like to see him disappointed, if it were only a joke; so she came out prematurely from behind the closet door, and ran into his arms, while the two young Cratchits hustled Tiny Tim, and bore him off into the washhouse, that he might hear the pudding singing in the copper.

"And how did little Tim behave?" asked Mrs. Cratchit, when she had

TINY TIM AND BOB CRATCHIT ON CHRISTMAS DAY

From a painting by Jessie Willcox Smith

rallied Bob on his credulity, and Bob had hugged his daughter to his heart's content.

"As good as gold," said Bob, "and better. Somehow he gets thoughtful, sitting by himself so much, and thinks the strangest things you ever heard. He told me coming home, that he hoped the people saw him in the church, because he was a cripple, and it might be pleasant to them to remember upon Christmas Day, who made lame beggars walk and blind men see."

Bob's voice was tremulous when he told them this, and trembled more when he said that Tiny Tim was growing strong and hearty.

His active little crutch was heard upon the floor, and back came Tiny Tim before another word was spoken, escorted by his brother and sister to his stool beside the fire; and while Bob, turning up his cuffs—as if, poor fellow, they were capable of being made more shabby—compounded some hot mixture in a jug with gin and lemons, and stirred it round and round and put it on the hob to simmer; Master Peter and the two ubiquitous young Cratchits went to fetch the goose, with which they soon returned in high procession.

Such a bustle ensued that you might have thought a goose the rarest of all birds; a feathered phenomenon, to which a black swan was a matter of course—and in truth it was something very like it in that house. Mrs. Cratchit made the gravy (ready beforehand in a little saucepan) hissing hot: Master Peter mashed the potatoes with incredible vigor; Miss Belinda sweetened up the apple-sauce; Martha dusted the hot plates; Bob took Tiny Tim beside him in a tiny corner at the table; the two young Cratchits set chairs for everybody, not forgetting themselves, and mounting guard upon their posts, crammed spoons into their mouths, lest they should shriek for goose before their turn came to be helped. At last the dishes were set on, and grace was said. It was succeeded by a breathless pause, as Mrs. Cratchit, looking slowly all along the carving-knife, prepared to plunge it in the breast; but when she did, and when the long-expected gush of stuffing issued forth, one murmur of delight arose all round the board, and even Tiny Tim, excited by the two young Cratchits, beat on the table with the handle of his knife, and feebly cried Hurrah!

There never was such a goose. Bob said he didn't believe there ever was such a goose cooked. Its tenderness and flavor, size and cheapness, were the themes of universal admiration. Eked out by apple-sauce and mashed potatoes, it was a sufficient dinner for the whole family; indeed, as Mrs. Cratchit said with great delight (surveying one small atom of a bone upon the dish), they hadn't ate it all at last! Yet every one had had enough, and the youngest Cratchits in particular, were steeped in sage and onion to the eyebrows! But now the plates being changed by Miss Belinda, Mrs. Cratchit left the room alone—too nervous to bear witness—to take the pudding up, and bring it in.

Suppose it should not be done enough! Suppose it should break in turning out! Suppose somebody should have got over the wall of the backyard, and stolen it, while they were merry with the goose—a supposition at which the two young Cratchits became livid! All sorts of horrors were supposed.

Hallo! A great deal of steam! The pudding was out of the copper. A smell like a washing-day! That was the cloth. A smell like an eating-house and a pastrycook's next door to each other, with a laundress's next door to that! That was the pudding! In half a minute Mrs. Cratchit entered—flushed, but smiling proudly—with the pudding, like a speckled cannon-ball, so hard and firm, blazing in half of half a quartern of ignited brandy, and bedight with Christmas holly stuck into the top.

Oh, a wonderful pudding! Bob Cratchit said, and calmly too, that he regarded it as the greatest success achieved by Mrs. Cratchit since their marriage. Mrs. Cratchit said that now the weight was off her mind, she would confess she had her doubts about the quantity of flour. Everybody had something to say about it, but nobody said or thought it was at all a small pudding for a large family. It would have been flat heresy to do so. Any Cratchit would have blushed to hint at such a thing.

At last the dinner was all done, the cloth was cleared, the hearth swept, and the fire made up. The compound in the jug being tasted, and considered perfect, apples and oranges were put upon the table, and a shovel full of chestnuts on the fire. Then all the Cratchit family drew round the hearth, in what Bob Cratchit called a circle, meaning half a one; and at Bob Cratchit's elbow stood the family display of glass. Two tumblers and a custard-cup without a handle.

These held the hot stuff from the jug, however, as well as golden goblets would have done; and Bob served it out with beaming looks, while the chestnuts on the fire sputtered and cracked noisily. Then Bob proposed,—

"A Merry Christmas to us all, my dears. God bless us!"

Which all the family re-echoed.

"God bless us every one!" said Tiny Tim, the last of all.

From DAVID COPPERFIELD

My first Dissipation

Miss Betsey Trotwood, David Copperfield's great-aunt, wished him to become a proctor and, upon securing the young man's assent to her proposal, arranged at once to place him with Spenlow and Jorkins. He was to have a month's probation. Miss Trotwood secured bachelor's lodgings for him with Mrs. Crupp, in Buckingham Street in the Adelphi. The furniture had belonged to the last occupant, who, according to Mrs. Crupp, had died of drink and smoke. The young lady in the box is Agnes Wickfield, daughter of an attorney at Dover, in whose house David had lived while attending school. David had come to regard her as tenderly as a sister.

IT was a wonderfully fine thing to have that lofty castle to myself, and to feel, when I shut my outer door, like Robinson Crusoe, when he had got into his fortification, and pulled his ladder up after him. It was a wonderfully fine thing to walk about town with the key of my house in my pocket, and to know that I could ask any fellow to come home, and make quite sure of its being inconvenient to nobody, if it were not so to me. It was a wonderfully fine thing to let myself in and out, and to come and go without a word to any one, and to ring Mrs. Crupp up, gasping, from the depths of the earth, when I wanted her—and when she was disposed to come. All this, I say, was wonderfully fine; but I must say, too, that there were times when it was very dreary.

It was fine in the morning, particularly in the fine mornings. It looked a very fresh, free life, by daylight: still fresher, and more free, by sunlight. But as the day declined, the life seemed to go down too. I don't know how it was; it seldom looked well by candle-light. I wanted somebody to talk to, then. I missed Agnes. I found a tremendous blank, in the place of that smiling repository of my confidence. Mrs. Crupp appeared to be a long way off. I thought about my predecessor, who had died of drink and smoke: and I could have wished he had been so good as to live, and not bother me with his decease.

After two days and nights, I felt as if I had lived there for a year, and yet I was not an hour older, but was quite as much tormented by my own youthfulness as ever.

Steerforth not yet appearing, which induced me to apprehend that he must be ill, I left the Commons early on the third day, and walked out to Highgate. Mrs. Steerforth was very glad to see me, and said that he had gone away with one of his Oxford friends to see another who lived near St. Alban's, but that she expected him to return to-morrow. I was so fond of him, that I felt quite jealous of his Oxford friends.

As she pressed me to stay to dinner, I remained, and I believe we talked about nothing but him all day. I told her how much the people liked him at Yarmouth, and what a delightful companion he had been. Miss Dartle was full of hints and mysterious questions, but took a great interest in all our proceedings there, and said, "was it really though?" and so forth, so often, that she got everything out of me she wanted to know. Her appearance was exactly what I have described it, when I first saw her; but the society of the two ladies was so agreeable, and came so natural to me, that I felt myself falling a little in love with her. I could not help thinking, several times in the course of the evening, and particularly when I walked home at night, what delightful company she would be in Buckingham Street.

I was taking my coffee and roll in the morning, before going to the Commons—and I may observe in this place that it is surprising how much coffee Mrs. Crupp used, and how weak it was, considering—when Steerforth himself walked in, to my unbounded joy.

"My dear Steerforth," cried I, "I began to think I should never see you again!"

"I was carried off, by force of arms," said Steerforth, "the very next morning after I got home. Why, Daisy, what a rare old bachelor you are here!"

I showed him over the establishment, not omitting the pantry, with no little pride, and he commended it highly. "I tell you what, old boy," he added, "I shall make quite a town-house of this place, unless you give me notice to quit."

This was a delightful hearing. I told him if he waited for that, he would have to wait till doomsday.

"But you shall have some breakfast!" said I, with my hand on the bell-rope, "and Mrs. Crupp shall make you some fresh coffee, and I'll toast you some bacon in a bachelor's Dutch-oven that I have got here."

"No, no!" said Steerforth. "Don't ring! I can't! I am going to breakfast with one of these fellows who is at the Piazza Hotel, in Covent Garden."

"But you'll come back to dinner?" said I.

"I can't, upon my life. There's nothing I should like better, but I must remain with these two fellows. We are all three off together to-morrow morning."

"Then bring them here to dinner," I returned. "Do you think they would come?"

"Oh! they would come fast enough," said Steerforth; "but we should inconvenience you. You had better come and dine with us somewhere."

I would not by any means consent to this, for it occurred to me that I really ought to have a little housewarming, and that there never could be a better opportunity. I had a new pride in my rooms after his approval of them, and burned with a desire to develop their utmost resources. I therefore made him promise positively in the names of his two friends, and we appointed six o'clock as the dinner-hour.

When he was gone, I rang for Mrs. Crupp, and acquainted her with my desperate design. Mrs. Crupp said, in the first place, of course it was well known she couldn't be expected to wait, but she knew a handy young man, who she thought could be prevailed upon to do it, and whose terms would be five shillings, and what I pleased. I said, certainly we would have him. Next, Mrs. Crupp said it was clear she couldn't be in two places at once (which I felt to be reasonable), and that "a young gal" stationed in the pantry with a bed-room candle, there never to desist from washing plates, would be indispensable. I said, what would be the expense of this young female, and Mrs. Crupp said she supposed eighteen-pence would neither make me nor break me. I said I supposed not; and *that* was settled. Then Mrs. Crupp said, Now about the dinner.

It was a remarkable instance of want of forethought on the part of the ironmonger who had made Mrs. Crupp's kitchen fire-place, that it was capable of cooking nothing but chops and mashed potatoes. As to a fish-kittle, Mrs. Crupp said, well! would I only come and look at the range. She couldn't say fairer than that. Would I come and look at it? As I should not have been much the wiser if I *had* looked at it, I declined, and said, "Never mind fish." But Mrs. Crupp said, "Don't say that; oysters was in, and why not them?" So *that* was settled. Mrs. Crupp then said what she would recommend would be this. A pair of hot roast fowls—from the pastry-cook's; a dish of stewed beef, with vegetables—from the pastry-cook's; two little corner things, as a raised pie and a dish of kidneys—from the pastry-cook's; a tart, and (if I liked) a shape of jelly —from the pastry-cook's. This, Mrs. Crupp said, would leave her at full liberty to concentrate her mind on the potatoes, and to serve up the cheese and celery as she could wish to see it done.

I acted on Mrs. Crupp's opinion, and gave the order at the pastry-cook's myself. Walking along the Strand, afterwards, and observing a hard mottled substance in the window of a ham and beef shop, which resembled marble, but was labelled "Mock Turtle," I went in and bought a slab of it, which I have since seen reason to believe would have sufficed for fifteen people. This preparation, Mrs. Crupp, after some difficulty, consented to warm up; and it shrunk so much in a liquid state, that we found it what Steerforth called "rather a tight fit" for four.

These preparations happily completed, I bought a little dessert in Covent Garden Market, and gave a rather extensive order at a retail wine-merchant's in that vicinity. When I came home in the afternoon, and saw the bottles drawn up in a square on the pantry-floor, they looked so numerous (though there were two missing, which made Mrs. Crupp very uncomfortable), that I was absolutely frightened at them.

One of Steerforth's friends was named Grainger, and the other Markham. They were both very gay and lively fellows; Grainger, something older than Steerforth; Markham, youthful-looking, and I should say not more than twenty. I observed that the latter always spoke of himself indefinitely, as "a man," and seldom or never in the first person singular.

"A man might get on very well here, Mr. Copperfield," said Markham —meaning himself.

"It's not a bad situation," said I, "and the rooms are really commodious."

"I hope you have both brought appetites with you?" said Steerforth.

"Upon my honor," returned Markham, "town seems to sharpen a man's appetite. A man is hungry all day long. A man is perpetually eating."

Being a little embarrassed at first, and feeling much too young to preside, I made Steerforth take the head of the table when dinner was announced, and seated myself opposite to him. Everything was very good; we did not spare the wine; and he exerted himself so brilliantly to make the thing pass off well, that there was no pause in our festivity. I was not quite such good company during dinner, as I could have wished to be, for my chair was opposite the door, and my attention was distracted by observing that the handy young man went out of the room very often, and that his shadow always presented itself, immediately afterwards, on the wall of the entry, with a bottle at his mouth. The "young gal" likewise occasioned me some uneasiness: not so much by neglecting to wash the plates, as by breaking them. For being of an inquisitive disposition, and unable to confine herself (as her positive instructions were) to the pantry, she was constantly peering in at us, and constantly imagining herself detected; in which belief, she several times retired upon the plates (with which she had carefully paved the floor), and did a great deal of destruction.

These, however, were small drawbacks, and easily forgotten when the cloth was cleared, and the dessert put on the table; at which period of the entertainment the handy young man was discovered to be speechless. Giving him private directions to seek the society of Mrs. Crupp, and to remove the "young gal" to the basement also, I abandoned myself to enjoyment.

I began by being singularly cheerful and light-hearted; all sorts of half-forgotten things to talk about came rushing into my mind, and made me hold forth in a most unwonted manner. I laughed heartily at my own jokes, and everybody else's; called Steerforth to order for not passing the wine; made several engagements to go to Oxford; announced that I meant to have a dinner party exactly like that, once a week until further notice; and madly took so much snuff out of Grainger's box, that I was obliged to go into the pantry, and have a private fit of sneezing ten minutes long.

I went on, by passing the wine faster and faster yet, and continually starting up with a corkscrew to open more wine, long before any was needed. I proposed Steerforth's health. I said he was my dearest friend, the protector of my boyhood, and the companion of my prime. I said I was delighted to propose his health. I said I owed him more obligations than I could ever repay, and held him in a higher admiration than I could ever express. I finished by saying, "I'll give you Steerforth! God bless him! Hurrah!" We gave him three times three, and another, and a good one to finish with. I broke my glass in going round the table to shake hands with him, and I said (in two words) "Steerforth, you're-theguidingstarofmyexistence."

I went on, by finding suddenly that somebody was in the middle of a song. Markham was the singer, and he sang "When the heart of a man is depressed with care." He said, when he had sung it, he would give us "Woman!" I took objection to that, and I couldn't allow it. I said it was not a respectful way of proposing the toast, and I would never permit that toast to be drunk in my house otherwise than as "The Ladies!" I was very high with him, mainly I think because I saw Steerforth and Grainger laughing at me—or at him—or at both of us. He said a man was not to be dictated to. I said a man *was*. He said a man was not to be insulted, then. I said he was right there—never under my roof, where the Lares were sacred, and the laws of hospitality paramount. He said it was no derogation from a man's dignity to confess that I was a devilish good fellow. I instantly proposed his health.

Somebody was smoking. We were all smoking. *I* was smoking, and trying to suppress a rising tendency to shudder. Steerforth had made a speech about me, in the course of which I had been affected almost to tears. I returned thanks, and hoped the present company would dine with me to-morrow, and the day after—each day at five o'clock, that we might enjoy the pleasures of conversation and society through a long evening. I felt called upon to propose an individual. I would give them my aunt. Miss Betsey Trotwood, the best of her sex!

Somebody was leaning out of my bed-room window, refreshing his forehead against the cool stone of the parapet, and feeling the air upon his face. It was myself. I was addressing myself as "Copperfield," and saying, "Why did you try to smoke? You might have known you couldn't do it." Now, somebody was unsteadily contemplating his features in the looking-glass. That was I too. I was very pale in the looking-glass; my eyes had a vacant appearance; and my hair—only my hair, nothing else—looked drunk.

Somebody said to me, "Let us go to the theatre, Copperfield!" There was no bed-room before me, but again the jingling table covered with glasses; the lamp; Grainger on my right hand, Markham on my left, and Steerforth opposite—all sitting in a mist, and a long way off. The theatre? To be sure. The very thing. Come along! But they must excuse me if I saw everybody out first, and turned the lamp off—in case of fire.

Owing to some confusion in the dark, the door was gone. I was feeling for it in the window-curtains, when Steerforth laughing, took me by the arm and led me out. We went down stairs, one behind another. Near the bottom, somebody fell, and rolled down. Somebody else said it was Copperfield. I was angry at that false report, until, finding myself on my back in the passage, I began to think there might be some foundation for it.

A very foggy night, with great rings round the lamps in the streets! There was an indistinct talk of its being wet. *I* considered it frosty. Steerforth dusted me under a lamp-post, and put my hat into shape, which somebody produced from somewhere in a most extraordinary manner, for I hadn't had it on before. Steerforth then said, "You are all right, Copperfield, are you not?" and I told him, "Neverberrer."

A man, sitting in a pigeon-hole-place, looked out of the fog, and took money from somebody, inquiring if I was one of the gentlemen paid for, and appearing rather doubtful (as I remember in the glimpse I had of him) whether to take the money for me or not. Shortly afterwards, we were very high up in a very hot theatre, looking down into a large pit, that seemed to me to smoke; the people with whom it was crammed were so indistinct. There was a great stage, too, looking very clean and smooth after the streets; and there were people upon it, talking about something or other, but not at all intelligibly. There was an abundance of bright lights, and there was music, and there were ladies down in the boxes, and I don't know what more. The whole building looked to me, as if it were learning to swim; it conducted itself in such an unaccountable manner, when I tried to steady it.

On somebody's motion, we resolved to go down stairs to the dress-boxes, where the ladies were. A gentleman lounging, full dressed, on a sofa, with an opera-glass in his hand, passed before my view, and also my own figure at full length in a glass. Then I was being ushered into one of these boxes, and found myself saying something as I sat down, and people about me crying "Silence!" to somebody, and ladies casting indignant glances at me, and—what! yes!—Agnes, sitting on the seat before me, in the same box, with a lady and gentleman beside her whom I didn't know. I see her face now, better than I did then, I dare say, with its indelible look of regret and wonder turned upon me.

"Agnes!" I said, thickly, "Lorblessmer! Agnes!"

"Hush! Pray!" she answered, I could not conceive why. "You disturb the company. Look at the stage!"

I tried, on her injunction, to fix it, and to hear something of what was going on there, but quite in vain. I looked at her again by and by, and saw her shrink into her corner, and put her gloved hand to her forehead.

"Agnes!" I said. "I'mafraidyou'renorwell."

"Yes, yes. Do not mind me, Trotwood," she returned. "Listen! Are you going away soon?"

"Amigoarawaysoo?" I repeated.

"Yes."

I had a stupid intention of replying that I was going to wait, to hand her down stairs. I suppose I expressed it somehow; for after she had looked at me attentively for a little while, she appeared to understand, and replied in a low tone:

"I know you will do as I ask you, if I tell you I am very earnest in it. Go away now, Trotwood, for my sake, and ask your friends to take you home."

She had so far improved me, for the time, that though I was angry with her, I felt ashamed, and with a short "Goori!" (which I intended for "Good night!") got up and went away. They followed, and I stepped at once out of the box-door into my bed-room, where only Steerforth was with me, helping me to undress, and where I was by turns telling him that Agnes was my sister, and adjuring him to bring the corkscrew, that I might open another bottle of wine.

How somebody, lying in my bed, lay saying and doing all this over again, at cross purposes, in a feverish dream all night—the bed a rocking sea, that was never still! How, as that somebody slowly settled down into myself, did I begin to parch, and feel as if my outer covering of skin were a hard board; my tongue the bottom of an empty kettle, furred with long service, and burning up over a slow fire; the palms of my hands, hot plates of metal which no ice could cool!

But the agony of mind, the remorse and shame I felt, when I became conscious next day! My horror of having committed a thousand offences I had forgotten, and which nothing could ever expiate—my recollection of that indelible look which Agnes had given me—the torturing impossibility of communicating with her, not knowing, beast that I was, how she came to be in London, or where she stayed—my disgust of the very sight of the room where the revel had been held—my racking head—the smell of smoke, the sight of glasses, the impossibility of going out, or even getting up! Oh, what a day it was!

Oh, what an evening, when I sat down by my fire to a basin of mutton broth, dimpled all over with fat, and thought I was going the way of my predecessor, and should succeed to his dismal story as well as to his chambers, and had half a mind to rush express to Dover and reveal all! What an evening, when Mrs. Crupp, coming in to take away the broth-basin, produced one kidney on a cheese-plate as the entire remains of yesterday's feast, and I was really inclined to fall upon her nankeen breast, and say, in heartfelt penitence, "Oh, Mrs. Crupp, Mrs. Crupp, never mind the broken meats! I am very miserable!"—only that I doubted, even at that pass, if Mrs. Crupp were quite the sort of woman to confide in!

The Seven Poor Travellers

STRICTLY speaking, there were only six Poor Travellers, but, being a Traveller myself, though an idle one, and being withal as poor as I hope to be, I brought the number up to seven. This word of explanation is due at once, for what says the inscription over the quaint old door?

RICHARD WATTS, Esq.
by his Will, dated 22 Aug. 1579,
founded this Charity
for Six poor Travellers,
who not being ROGUES, or PROCTORS,
May receive gratis for one Night,
Lodging, Entertainment,
and Fourpence each.

It was in the ancient little city of Rochester in Kent, of all the good days in the year upon a Christmas-eve, that I stood reading this inscription over the quaint old door in question. I had been wandering about the neighboring Cathedral, and had seen the tomb of Richard Watts, with the effigy of worthy Master Richard starting out of it like a ship's figure-head; and I had felt that I could do no less, as I gave the Verger his fee, than inquire the way to Watts's Charity. The way being very short and very plain, I had come prosperously to the inscription and the quaint old door.

"Now," said I to myself, as I looked at the knocker, "I know *I* am not a Proctor; I wonder whether I am a Rogue!"

Upon the whole, though Conscience reproduced two or three pretty faces which might have had smaller attraction for a moral Goliath than they had had for me, who am but a Tom Thumb in that way, I came to the conclusion that I was not a Rogue. So, beginning to regard the establishment as in some sort my property, bequeathed to me and divers co-legatees, share and share alike, by the Worshipful Master Richard Watts, I stepped backward into the road to survey my inheritance.

I found it to be a clean white house, of a staid and venerable air, with the quaint old door already three times mentioned (an arched door), choice little long low lattice-windows, and a roof of three gables. The silent High-street of Rochester is full of gables, with old beams and timbers carved into strange faces. It is oddly garnished with a queer old clock that projects over the pavement out of a grave red-brick building, as if Time carried on business there, and hung out his sign. Sooth to say, he did an active stroke of work in Rochester, in the old days of the Romans, and the Saxons, and the Normans; and down to the times of King John, when the rugged castle—I will not undertake to say how many hundreds of years old then—was abandoned to the centuries of weather which have so defaced the dark apertures in its walls, that the ruin looks as if the rooks and daws had picked its eyes out.

I was very well pleased, both with my property and its situation. While I was yet surveying it with growing content, I espied, at one of the upper lattices which stood open, a decent body, of a wholesome matronly appearance, whose eyes I caught inquiringly addressed to mine. They said so plainly, "Do you wish to see the house?" that I answered aloud, "Yes, if you please." And within a minute the old door opened, and I bent my head, and went down two steps into the entry.

"This," said the matronly presence, ushering me into a low room on the right, "is where the Travellers sit by the fire, and cook what bits of suppers they buy with their fourpences."

"O! Then they have no Entertainment?" said I. For the inscription over the outer door was still running in my head, and I was mentally repeating, in a kind of tune, "Lodging, entertainment, and fourpence each."

"They have a fire provided for 'em," returned the matron,—a mighty civil person, not, as I could make out, overpaid; "and these cooking utensils. And this what's painted on a board is the rules for their behavior. They have their fourpences when they get their tickets from the steward over the way,—for I don't admit 'em myself, they must get their tickets first,—and sometimes one buys a rasher of bacon, and another a herring, and another a pound of potatoes, or what not. Sometimes two or three of 'em will club their fourpences together, and make a supper that way. But not much of anything is to be got for fourpence, at present, when provisions is so dear."

"True indeed," I remarked. I had been looking about the room, admiring its snug fireside at the upper end, its glimpse of the street through the low mullioned window, and its beams overhead. "It is very comfortable," said I.

"Ill-conwenient," observed the matronly presence.

I liked to hear her say so; for it showed a commendable anxiety to execute in no niggardly spirit the intentions of Master Richard Watts. But the room was really so well adapted to its purpose that I protested, quite enthusiastically, against her disparagement.

"Nay, ma'am," said I, "I am sure it is warm in winter and cool in summer. It has a look of homely welcome and soothing rest. It has a remarkably cosey fireside, the very blink of which, gleaming out into the street upon a winter night, is enough to warm all Rochester's heart. And as to the convenience of the six Poor Travellers—"

"I don't mean them," returned the presence. "I speak of its being an ill-conwenience to myself and my daughter, having no other room to sit in of a night."

This was true enough, but there was another quaint room of corresponding dimensions on the opposite side of the entry: so I stepped across to it, through the open doors of both rooms, and asked what this chamber was for.

"This," returned the presence, "is the Board Room. Where the gentlemen meet when they come here."

Let me see. I had counted from the street six upper windows besides these on the ground-story. Making a perplexed calculation in my mind, I rejoined, "Then the six Poor Travellers sleep up stairs?"

My new friend shook her head. "They sleep," she answered "in two little outer galleries at the back, where their beds has always been, ever since the Charity was founded. It being so very ill-conwenient to me as things is at present, the gentlemen are going to take off a bit of the back yard, and make a slip of a room for 'em there, to sit in before they go to bed."

"And then the six Poor Travellers," said I, "will be entirely out of the house?"

"Entirely out of the house," assented the presence, comfortably smoothing her hands. "Which is considered much better for all parties, and much more conwenient."

I had been a little startled, in the Cathedral, by the emphasis with which the effigy of Master Richard Watts was bursting out of his tomb; but I began to think, now, that it might be expected to come across the High-street some stormy night, and make a disturbance here.

Howbeit, I kept my thoughts to myself, and accompanied the presence to the little galleries at the back. I found them on a tiny scale, like the galleries in old inn-yards; and they were very clean. While I was looking at them, the matron gave me to understand that the prescribed number of Poor Travellers were forthcoming every night from year's end to year's end; and that the beds were always occupied. My questions upon this, and her replies, brought us back to the Board Room so essential to the dignity of "the gentlemen," where she showed me the printed accounts of the Charity hanging up by the window. From them I gathered that the greater part of the property bequeathed by the Worshipful Master Richard Watts for the maintenance of this foundation was, at the period of his death, mere marsh-land; but that, in course of time, it had been reclaimed and built upon, and was very considerably increased in value. I found, too, that about a thirtieth part of the annual revenue was now expended on the purposes commemorated in the inscription over the door; the rest being handsomely laid out in Chancery, law expenses, collectorship, receivership, poundage, and other appendages of management, highly complimentary to the importance of the six Poor Travellers. In short, I made the not entirely new discovery that it may be said of an establishment like this, in dear old England, as of the fat oyster in the American story, that it takes a good many men to swallow it whole.

"And pray, ma'am," said I, sensible that the blankness of my face began to brighten as a thought occurred to me, "could one see these Travellers?"

"Well!" she returned dubiously, "no!"

"Not to-night, for instance?" said I.

"Well!" she returned more positively, "no. Nobody ever asked to see them, and nobody ever did see them."

As I am not easily balked in a design when I am set upon it, I urged to the good lady that this was Christmas-eve; that Christmas comes but once a year,—which is unhappily too true, for when it begins to stay with us the whole year round we shall make this earth a very different place; that I was possessed by the desire to treat the Travellers to a supper and a temperate glass of hot Wassail; that the voice of Fame had been heard in that land, declaring my ability to make hot Wassail; that if I were permitted to hold the feast, I should be found conformable to reason, sobriety, and good hours; in a word, that I could be merry and wise myself, and had been even known at a pinch to keep others so, although I was decorated with no badge or medal, and was not a Brother, Orator, Apostle, Saint, or Prophet of any denomination whatever. In the end I prevailed, to my great joy. It was settled that at nine o'clock that night a Turkey and a piece of Roast Beef should smoke upon the board; and that I, faint and unworthy minister for once of Master Richard Watts, should preside as the Christmas-supper host of the six Poor Travellers.

I went back to my inn to give the necessary directions for the Turkey and Roast Beef, and, during the remainder of the day, could settle to nothing for thinking of the Poor Travellers. When the wind blew hard against the windows,—it was a cold day, with dark gusts of sleet alternating with periods of wild brightness, as if the year were dying fitfully,— I pictured them advancing towards their resting-place along various cold roads, and felt delighted to think how little they foresaw the supper that awaited them. I painted their portraits in my mind, and indulged in little heightening touches. I made them footsore; I made them weary; I made them carry packs and bundles; I made them stop by finger-posts and milestones, leaning on their bent sticks, and looking wistfully at what was written there; I made them lose their way, and filled their five wits with apprehensions of lying out all night, and being frozen to death. I took up my hat, and went out, climbed to the top of the Old Castle, and looked over the windy hills that slope down to the Medway, almost believing that I could descry some of my Travellers in the distance. After it fell dark, and the Cathedral bell was heard in the invisible steeple— quite a bower of frosty rime when I had last seen it—striking five, six, seven, I became so full of my Travellers that I could eat no dinner, and felt constrained to watch them still in the red coals of my fire. They were all arrived by this time, I thought, had got their tickets, and were gone in.—There my pleasure was dashed by the reflection that probably some Travellers had come too late and were shut out.

After the Cathedral bell had struck eight, I could smell a delicious savor of Turkey and Roast Beef rising to the window of my adjoining bed-room, which looked down into the inn-yard just where the lights of the kitchen reddened a massive fragment of the Castle Wall. It was high time to make the Wassail now; therefore I had up the materials (which, together with their proportions and combinations, I must decline to impart, as the only secret of my own I was ever known to keep), and made a glorious jorum. Not in a bowl; for a bowl anywhere but on a shelf is a low superstition, fraught with cooling and slopping; but in a brown earthenware pitcher, tenderly suffocated, when full, with a coarse cloth. It being now upon the stroke of nine, I set out for Watts's Charity, carrying my brown beauty in my arms. I would trust Ben, the waiter, with untold gold; but there are strings in the human heart which must never be sounded by another, and drinks that I make myself are those strings in mine.

The Travellers were all assembled, the cloth was laid, and Ben had brought a great billet of wood, and had laid it artfully on the top of the fire, so that a touch or two of the poker after supper should make a roaring blaze. Having deposited my brown beauty in a red nook of the hearth, inside the fender, where she soon began to sing like an ethereal cricket, diffusing at the same time odors as of ripe vineyards, spice forests, and orange groves—I say, having stationed my beauty in a place of security and improvement, I introduced myself to my guests by shaking hands all round, and giving them a hearty welcome.

I found the party to be thus composed. Firstly, myself. Secondly, a very decent man indeed, with his right arm in a sling, who had a certain clean agreeable smell of wood about him, from which I judged him to have something to do with ship-building. Thirdly, a little sailor-boy, a mere child, with a profusion of rich dark brown hair, and deep womanly-looking eyes. Fourthly, a shabby-genteel personage in a thread-bare black suit, and apparently in very bad circumstances, with a dry suspicious look; the absent buttons on his waistcoat eked out with red tape; and a bundle of extraordinarily tattered papers sticking out of an inner breast-pocket. Fifthly, a foreigner by birth, but an Englishman in speech, who carried his pipe in the band of his hat, and lost no time in telling me, in an easy, simple, engaging way, that he was a watch-maker from Geneva, and travelled all about the Continent, mostly on foot, working as a journeyman, and seeing new countries,—possibly (I thought) also smuggling a watch or so, now and then. Sixthly, a little widow, who had been very pretty and was still very young, but whose beauty had been wrecked in some great misfortune, and whose manner was remarkably timid, scared, and solitary. Seventhly and lastly, a Traveller of a kind familiar to my boyhood, but now almost obsolete,

—a Book-Pedler, who had a quantity of Pamphlets and Numbers with him, and who presently boasted that he could repeat more verses in an evening than he could sell in a twelvemonth.

All these I have mentioned in the order in which they sat at table. I presided, and the matronly presence faced me. We were not long in taking our places, for the supper had arrived with me, in the following procession:

Myself with the pitcher.
Ben with Beer.
Inattentive Boy with hot plates. Inattentive Boy with hot plates.
THE TURKEY.
Female carrying sauces to be heated on the spot.
THE BEEF.
Man with Tray on his head, containing Vegetables and Sundries.
Volunteer Hostler from Hotel, grinning,
And rendering no assistance.

As we passed along the High-street, comet-like, we left a long tail of fragrance behind us which caused the public to stop, sniffing in wonder. We had previously left at the corner of the inn-yard a wall-eyed young man connected with the Fly department, and well accustomed to the sound of a railway whistle which Ben always carries in his pocket, whose instructions were, so soon as he should hear the whistle blown, to dash into the kitchen, seize the hot plum-pudding and mince-pies, and speed with them to Watts's Charity, where they would be received (he was further instructed) by the sauce-female, who would be provided with brandy in a blue state of combustion.

All these arrangements were executed in the most exact and punctual manner. I never saw a finer turkey, finer beef, or greater prodigality of sauce and gravy; and my Travellers did wonderful justice to everything set before them. It made my heart rejoice to observe how their wind and frost hardened faces softened in the clatter of plates and knives and forks, and mellowed in the fire and supper heat. While their hats and caps and wrappers, hanging up, a few small bundles on the ground in a corner, and in another corner three or four old walking-sticks, worn down at the end to mere fringe, linked this snug interior with the bleak outside in a golden chain.

When supper was done, and my brown beauty had been elevated on the table, there was a general requisition to me to "take the corner"; which suggested to me comfortably enough how much my friends here made of a fire,—for when had *I* ever thought so highly of the corner, since the days when I connected it with Jack Horner? However, as I declined, Ben, whose touch on all convivial instruments is perfect,

drew the table apart, and instructing my Travellers to open right and
left on either side of me, and form round the fire, closed up the centre
with myself and my chair, and preserved the order we had kept at table.
He had already, in a tranquil manner, boxed the ears of the inattentive
boys until they had been by imperceptible degrees boxed out of the
room; and he now rapidly skirmished the sauce-female into the High-
street, disappeared, and softly closed the door.

This was the time for bringing the poker to bear on the billet of
wood. I tapped it three times, like an enchanted talisman, and a brilliant host of merry-makers burst out of it, and sported off by the
chimney,—rushing up the middle in a fiery country dance, and never
coming down again. Meanwhile, by their sparkling light, which threw
our lamp into the shade, I filled the glasses, and gave my Travellers,
CHRISTMAS!—CHRISTMAS-EVE, my friends, when the shepherds, who
were Poor Travellers, too, in their way, heard the Angels sing, "On
earth, peace. Good-will towards men!"

I don't know who was the first among us to think that we ought
to take hands as we sat, in deference to the toast, or whether any of
us anticipated the others, but at any rate we all did it. We then drank
to the memory of the good Master Richard Watts. And I wish his
Ghost may never have had worse usage under that roof than it had
from us.

It was the witching time for Story-telling. "Our whole life, Travellers," said I, "is a story more or less intelligible,—generally less; but we
shall read it by a clearer light when it is ended. I, for one, am so
divided this night between fact and fiction, that I scarce know which
is which. Shall I beguile the time by telling you a story as we sit here?"

They all answered, yes. I had little to tell them, but I was bound
by my own proposal. Therefore, after looking for a while at the spiral
column of smoke wreathing up from my brown beauty, through which
I could have almost sworn I saw the effigy of Master Richard Watts
less startled than usual, I fired away.

[The story was about a relative of the narrator's, named Richard. As a lad,
he had given his sweetheart, Mary Marshall, cause to dismiss him. Assuming the
name of Richard Doubledick, he enlisted in a regiment of the line, acting at first
like the despicable, drunken scapegrace he was. Under the good influence of
Captain Taunton, he changed from the worst of soldiers to the best, and in the
course of the Peninsular War in India, rose to the rank of Ensign. Captain
Taunton likewise rose, to the rank of Major; and the tattered colors of their
regiment, carried by Ensign Doubledick, became the center of glorious legend
throughout the British Army. Major Taunton was killed in action. Doubledick
rose to the rank of Lieutenant, was severely wounded at the battle of Toulouse,
and at Midsummer-time in 1814, was sent home invalided. To Taunton's mother,
at her home in Somersetshire, he disclosed his story. Her little garden became
the boundary of his home; and when, in the spring, he was able to rejoin his

regiment, it was "the first time that he had ever turned his face toward the old colours with a woman's blessing."

At Waterloo, in June, he was wounded again. After many days of total unconsciousness, he awoke to find himself in a hospital in Brussels, with Mrs. Taunton ministering to him. Then one day he found another at his bedside—one whom he had last known, years before, as Mary Marshall. She is now Mrs. Captain Doubledick. While he was unconscious and expected momentarily to die, she had been married to him.

The story ends with his encountering in France the officer who had commanded the enemy under whose fire Captain Taunton had fallen. The man was now the host of Mrs. Taunton and of Doubledick's own family. And Doubledick discovered the Spirit of Forgiveness in time to make him feel that the memory of Major Taunton was the better for his letting the tragedies of war lie buried in the past. He never disclosed to any one, least of all to Mrs. Taunton, the identity of the kindly Frenchman, and renounced in fact and in spirit his long-cherished purpose of taking vengeance on the slayer of Major Taunton.]

My story being finished, and the Wassail too, we broke up as the Cathedral bell struck Twelve. I did not take leave of my Travellers that night; for it had come into my head to reappear, in conjunction with some hot coffee, at seven in the morning.

As I passed along the High-street, I heard the Waits at a distance, and struck off to find them. They were playing near one of the old gates of the City, at the corner of a wonderfully quaint row of red-brick tenements, which the clarionet obligingly informed me were inhabited by the Minor-Canons. They had odd little porches over the doors, like sounding-boards over old pulpits; and I thought I should like to see one of the Minor-Canons come out upon his top step, and favor us with a little Christmas discourse about the poor scholars of Rochester; taking for his text the words of his Master, relative to the devouring of Widows' houses.

The clarionet was so communicative, and my inclinations were (as they generally are) of so vagabond a tendency, that I accompanied the Waits across an open green called the Vines, and assisted—in the French sense—at the performance of two waltzes, two polkas, and three Irish melodies, before I thought of my inn any more. However, I returned to it then, and found a fiddle in the kitchen, and Ben, the wall-eyed young man, and two chamber-maids, circling round the great deal table with the utmost animation.

I had a very bad night. It cannot have been owing to the turkey or the beef,—and the Wassail is out of the question,—but in every endeavor that I made to get to sleep I failed most dismally. I was never asleep; and in whatsoever unreasonable direction my mind rambled, the effigy of Master Richard Watts perpetually embarrassed it.

In a word, I only got out of the Worshipful Master Richard Watts's way by getting out of bed in the dark at six o'clock, and tumbling, as my custom is, into all the cold water that could be accumulated for the purpose. The outer air was dull and cold enough in the street, when I came down there; and the one candle in our supper-room at Watts's Charity looked as pale in the burning as if it had had a bad night too. But my Travellers had all slept soundly, and they took to the hot coffee, and the piles of bread-and-butter, which Ben had arranged like deals in a timber-yard, as kindly as I could desire.

While it was yet scarcely daylight, we all came out into the street together, and there shook hands. The widow took the little sailor towards Chatham, where he was to find a steamboat for Sheerness; the lawyer, with an extremely knowing look, went his own way, without committing himself by announcing his intentions; two more struck off by the cathedral and old castle for Maidstone; and the book-pedler accompanied me over the bridge. As for me, I was going to walk by Cobham Woods, as far upon my way to London as I fancied.

When I came to the stile and footpath by which I was to diverge from the main road, I bade farewell to my last remaining Poor Traveller, and pursued my way alone. And now the mists began to rise in the most beautiful manner, and the sun to shine; and as I went on through the bracing air, seeing the hoar-frost sparkle everywhere, I felt as if all Nature shared in the joy of the great Birthday.

Going through the woods, the softness of my tread upon the mossy ground and among the brown leaves enhanced the Christmas sacredness by which I felt surrounded. As the whitened stems environed me, I thought how the Founder of the time had never raised his benignant hand, save to bless and heal, except in the case of one unconscious tree. By Cobham Hall, I came to the village, and the churchyard where the dead had been quietly buried, "in the sure and certain hope" which Christmas time inspired. What children could I see at play, and not be loving of, recalling who had loved them! No garden that I passed was out of unison with the day, for I remembered that the tomb was in a garden, and that "she supposing him to be the gardener," had said, "Sir, if thou have borne him hence, tell me where thou hast laid him, and I will take him away." In time, the distant river with the ships came full in view, and with it pictures of the poor fishermen, mending their nets, who arose and followed him,—of the teaching of the people from a ship pushed off a little way from shore, by reason of the multitude,—of a majestic figure walking on the water, in the loneliness of night. My very shadow on the ground was eloquent of Christmas; for did not the people lay their sick where the mere shadows of the men who had heard and seen him might fall as they passed along?

Thus Christmas begirt me, far and near, until I had come to Blackheath, and had walked down the long vista of gnarled old trees in Greenwich Park, and was being steam-rattled through the mists now closing in once more, towards the lights of London. Brightly they shone, but not so brightly as my own fire, and the brighter faces around it, when we came together to celebrate the day. And there I told of worthy Master Richard Watts, and of my supper with the Six Poor Travellers who were neither Rogues nor Proctors, and from that hour to this I have never seen one of them again.

From THE HOLLY-TREE

The Boots

The narrator of the following selection, a very bashful man, was snowed up in the Holly-Tree inn, somewhere on a Yorkshire moor, on the Great North Road. Installed in a very large and solitary sitting-room, screened in alone beside a blazing fire, he beguiled the hours with memories of inns he had known in many lands and of stories connected with them. But at length his memories ended. "A desperate idea came into my head. Under any other circumstances I should have rejected it; but, in the strait at which I was, I held it fast. Could I so far overcome the inherent bashfulness which withheld me from the landlord's table and the company which I might find there, as to call up the Boots, and ask him to take a chair,—and something in a liquid form,—and talk to me? I could. I would. I did."

WHERE had he been in his time? he repeated, when I asked him the question. Lord, he had been everywhere! And what had he been? Bless you, he had been everything you could mention a'most!

Seen a good deal? Why, of course he had. I should say so, he could assure me, if I only knew about a twentieth part of what had come in *his* way. Why, it would be easier for him, he expected, to tell what he hadn't seen than what he had. Ah! A deal, it would.

What was the curiousest thing he had seen? Well! He didn't know. He couldn't momently name what was the curiousest thing he had seen,— unless it was a Unicorn,—and he see *him* once at a Fair. But sup- posing a young gentleman not eight year old was to run away with a fine young woman of seven, might I think *that* a queer start? Certainly. Then that was a start as he himself had had his blessed eyes on, and he had cleaned the shoes they run away in—and they was so little that he couldn't get his hand into 'em.

Master Harry Walmer's father, you see, he lived at the Elmses, down away by Shooter's Hill there, six or seven miles from Lunnon. He was a gentleman of spirit, and good-looking, and held his head up when he walked, and had what you may call Fire about him. He wrote poetry, and he rode, and he ran, and he cricketed, and he danced, and he acted, and he done it all equally beautiful. He was uncommon proud of Master Harry as was his only child; but he didn't spoil him neither. He was a gentleman that had a will of his own and a eye of his own, and that would be minded. Consequently, though he made quite a companion of the fine bright boy, and was delighted to see him so fond of reading his fairy books, and was never tired of hearing him say my name in Norval, or hearing him sing his songs about Young May Moons is beaming love, and When he as adores thee has left but the name, and that; still he kept the command over the child, and the child *was* a child, and it's to be wished more of 'em was!

How did Boots happen to know all this? Why, through being under-gardener. Of course he couldn't be under-gardener, and be always about, in the summer-time, near the windows on the lawn, a mowing, and sweeping, and weeding, and pruning, and this and that, without getting acquainted with the ways of the family. Even supposing Master Harry hadn't come to him one morning early, and said, "Cobbs, how should you spell Norah, if you was asked?" and then began cutting it in print all over the fence.

He couldn't say he had taken particular notice of children before that; but really it was pretty to see them two mites a going about the place together, deep in love. And the courage of the boy! Bless your soul, he'd have throwed off his little hat, and tucked up his little sleeves, and gone in at a Lion, he would, if they had happened to meet one, and she had been frightened of him. One day he stops, along with her, where Boots was hoeing weeds in the gravel, and says, speaking up, "Cobbs," he says, "I like *you*." "Do you, sir? I'm proud to hear it." "Yes, I do, Cobbs. Why do I like you, do you think, Cobbs?" "Don't know, Master Harry, I am sure." "Because Norah likes you, Cobbs." "Indeed, sir? That's very gratifying." "Gratifying, Cobbs? It's better than millions of the brightest diamonds to be liked by Norah." "Certainly, sir." "You're going away, ain't you, Cobbs?" "Yes, sir." "Would you like another situation, Cobbs?" "Well, sir, I shouldn't object, if it was a good 'un." "Then, Cobbs," says he, "you shall be our Head Gardener when we are married." And he tucks her, in her little sky-blue mantle, under his arm, and walks away.

Boots could assure me that it was better than a picter, and equal to a play, to see them babies, with their long, bright, curling hair, their sparkling eyes, and their beautiful light tread, a rambling about the garden, deep in love. Boots was of opinion that the birds believed they was birds, and kept up with 'em, singing to please 'em. Sometimes they would creep under the Tulip-tree, and would sit there with their arms round one another's necks, and their soft cheeks touching, a reading about the Prince and the Dragon, and the good and bad enchanters, and the king's fair daughter. Sometimes he would hear them planning about having a house in a forest, keeping bees and a cow, and living entirely on milk and honey. Once he came upon them by the pond, and heard Master Harry say, "Adorable Norah, kiss me, and say you love me to distraction, or I'll jump in head-foremost." And Boots made no question he would have done it if she hadn't complied. On the whole, Boots said it had a tendency to make him feel as if he was in love himself—only he didn't exactly know who with.

"Cobbs," said Master Harry, one evening, when Cobbs was watering the flowers, "I am going on a visit, this present Mid-summer, to my grandmamma's at York."

"Are you indeed, sir? I hope you'll have a pleasant time. I am going into Yorkshire, myself, when I leave here."

"Are you going to your grandmamma's, Cobbs?"

"No, sir. I haven't got such a thing."

"Not as a grandmamma, Cobbs?"

"No, sir."

The boy looked on at the watering of the flowers for a little while, and then said, "I shall be very glad indeed to go, Cobbs,—Norah's going."

"You'll be all right then, sir," says Cobbs, "with your beautiful sweetheart by your side."

"Cobbs," returned the boy, flushing, "I never let anybody joke about it, when I can prevent them."

"It wasn't a joke, sir," says Cobbs, with humility,—"wasn't so meant."

"I am glad of that, Cobbs, because I like you, you know, and you're going to live with us.—Cobbs!"

"Sir."

"What do you think my grandmamma gives me when I go down there?"

"I couldn't so much as make a guess, sir."

"A Bank of England five-pound note, Cobbs."

"Whew!" says Cobbs, "that's a spanking sum of money, Master Harry."

"A person could do a good deal with such a sum of money as that,— couldn't a person, Cobbs?"

"I believe you, sir!"

"Cobbs," said the boy, "I'll tell you a secret. At Norah's house, they have been joking her about me, and pretending to laugh at our being engaged,—pretending to make game of it, Cobbs!"

"Such, sir," said Cobbs, "is the depravity of human natur."

The boy, looking exactly like his father, stood for a few minutes with his glowing face towards the sunset, and then departed with, "Good night, Cobbs. I'm going in."

If I was to ask Boots how it happened that he was a going to leave that place just at that present time, well, he couldn't rightly answer me. He did suppose he might have stayed there till now if he had been anyways inclined. But, you see, he was younger then, and he wanted change. That's what he wanted,—change. Mr. Walmers, he said to him when he gave him notice of his intentions to leave, "Cobbs," he says, "have you anythink to complain of? I make the inquiry because if I find that any of my people really has anythink to complain of, I wish to make it right if I can." "No, sir," says Cobbs; "thanking you, sir, I find myself as well sitiwated here as I could hope to be any-wheres. The truth is, sir, that I'm a going to seek my fortun." "O, indeed, Cobbs!" he says; "I hope you may find it." And Boots could assure me—which he did, touching his hair with his bootjack, as a salute in the way of his present calling—that he hadn't found it yet.

Well, sir! Boots left the Elmses when his time was up, and Master Harry, he went down to the old lady's at York, which old lady would have given that child the teeth out of her head (if she had had any), she was so wrapped up in him. What does that Infant do,—for Infant you may call him and be within the mark,—but cut away from that old lady's with his Norah, on a expedition to go to Gretna Green and be married!

Sir, Boots was at this identical Holly-Tree Inn (having left it several times since to better himself, but always come back through one thing or another), when, one summer afternoon, the coach drives up, and out of the coach gets them two children. The Guard says to our Governor, "I don't quite make out these little passengers, but the young gentleman's words was, that they was to be brought here." The young gentleman gets out; hands his lady out; gives the Guard something for himself; says to our Governor, "We're to stop here to-night, please. Sitting-room and two bedrooms will be required. Chops and cherry-pudding for two!" and tucks her, in her little sky-blue mantle, under his arm, and walks into the house much bolder than Brass.

Boots leaves me to judge what the amazement of that establishment was, when these two tiny creatures all alone by themselves was marched into the Angel,—much more so, when he, who had seen them without their seeing him, give the Governor his views of the expedition they was upon. "Cobbs," says the Governor, "if this is so, I must set off myself to York, and quiet their friends' minds. In which case you must keep your eye upon 'em, and humor 'em, till I come back. But before I take these measures, Cobbs, I should wish you to find from themselves whether your opinions is correct." "Sir, to you," says Cobbs, "that shall be done directly."

So Boots goes up stairs to the Angel, and there he finds Master Harry, on a e-normous sofa,—immense at any time, but looking like the Great Bed of Ware, compared with him,—a drying the eyes of Miss Norah with his pocket-hankercher. Their little legs was entirely off the ground, of course, and it really is not possible for Boots to express to me how small them children looked.

"It's Cobbs! It's Cobbs!" cries Master Harry, and comes running to him, and catching hold of his hand. Miss Norah comes running to him on t'other side and catching hold of his t'other hand, and they both jump for joy.

"I see you a getting out, sir," says Cobbs. "I thought it was you. I thought I couldn't be mistaken in your height and figure. What's the object of your journey, sir?—Matrimonial?"

"We are going to be married, Cobbs, at Gretna Green," returned the boy. "We have run away on purpose. Norah has been in rather low spirits, Cobbs; but she'll be happy, now we have found you to be our friend."

"Thank you, sir, and thank *you,* miss," says Cobbs, "for your good opinion. *Did* you bring any luggage with you, sir?"

If I will believe Boots when he gives me his word and honor upon it, the lady had got a parasol, a smelling-bottle, a round and a half of cold buttered toast, eight peppermint drops, and a hair-brush,—seemingly a doll's. The gentleman had got about half a dozen yards of string, a knife, three or four sheets of writing-paper folded up surprisingly small, an orange, and a Chaney mug with his name upon it.

"What may be the exact natur of your plans, sir?" says Cobbs.

"To go on," replied the boy,—which the courage of that boy was something wonderful!—"in the morning, and be married to-morrow."

"Just so, sir," says Cobbs. "Would it meet your views, sir, if I was to accompany you?"

When Cobbs said this, they both jumped for joy again, and cried out, "O yes, yes, Cobbs! Yes!"

"Well, sir," says Cobbs. "If you will excuse my having the freedom to give an opinion, what I should recommend would be this. I'm acquainted with a pony, sir, which, put in a pheayton that I could borrow, would take you and Mrs. Harry Walmers, Junior, (myself driving, if you approved,) to the end of your journey in a very short space of time. I am not altogether sure, sir, that this pony will be at liberty to-morrow, but even if you had to wait over to-morrow for him, it might be worth your while. As to the small account here, sir, in case you was to find yourself running at all short, that don't signify; because I'm a part proprietor of this inn, and it could stand over."

Boots assures me that when they clapped their hands, and jumped for joy again, and called him "Good Cobbs!" and "Dear Cobbs!" and bent across him to kiss one another in the delight of their confiding hearts, he felt himself the meanest rascal for deceiving 'em that ever was born.

"Is there anything you want just at present, sir?" says Cobbs, mortally ashamed of himself.

"We should like some cakes after dinner," answered Master Harry, folding his arms, putting out one leg, and looking straight at him, "and two apples,—and jam. With dinner we should like to have toast-and-water. But Norah has always been accustomed to half a glass of currant wine at dessert. And so have I."

"It shall be ordered at the bar, sir," says Cobbs; and away he went.

Boots has the feeling as fresh upon him at this minute of speaking as he had then, that he would far rather have had it out in half a dozen rounds with the Governor than have combined with him; and that he wished with all his heart there was any impossible place where those two babies could make an impossible marriage, and live impossibly happy ever afterwards. However, as it couldn't be, he went into the Governor's plans, and the Governor set off for York in half an hour.

The way in which the women of that house—without exception—every one of 'em—married *and* single—took to that boy when they heard the story, Boots considers surprising. It was as much as he could do to keep 'em from dashing into the room and kissing him. They climbed up all sorts of places, at the risk of their lives, to look at him through a pane of glass. They was seven deep at the keyhole. They was out of their minds about him and his bold spirit.

In the evening, Boots went into the room to see how the runaway couple was getting on. The gentleman was on the window-seat, supporting the lady in his arms. She had tears upon her face, and was lying, very tired and half asleep, with her head upon his shoulder.

"Mrs. Harry Walmers, Junior, fatigued, sir?" says Cobbs.

"Yes, she is tired, Cobbs; but she is not used to be away from home, and she has been in low spirits again. Cobbs, do you think you could bring a biffin, please?"

"I ask your pardon, sir," says Cobbs. "What was it you——?"

"I think a Norfolk biffin would rouse her, Cobbs. She is very fond of them."

Boots withdrew in search of the required restorative, and, when he brought it in, the gentleman handed it to the lady, and fed her with a spoon, and took a little himself; the lady being heavy with sleep, and rather cross. "What should you think, sir," says Cobbs, "of a chamber candlestick?" The gentleman approved; the chambermaid went first, up the great staircase; the lady, in her sky-blue mantle, followed, gallantly escorted by the gentleman; the gentleman embraced her at her door, and retired to his own apartment, where Boots softly locked him up.

Boots couldn't but feel with increased acuteness what a base deceiver he was, when they consulted him at breakfast (they had ordered sweet milk-and-water, and toast and currant jelly, over-night) about the pony. It really was as much as he could do, he don't mind confessing to me, to look them two young things in the face, and think what a wicked old father of lies he had grown up to be. Howsomever, he went on a lying like a Trojan about the pony. He told 'em that it did so unfort'nately happen that the pony was half clipped, you see, and that he couldn't be taken out in that state, for fear it should strike to his inside. But that he'd be finished clipping in the course of the day, and that to-morrow morning at eight o'clock the pheayton would be ready. Boots's view of the whole case, looking back on it in my room, is, that Mrs. Harry Walmers, Junior, was beginning to give in. She hadn't had her hair curled when she went to bed, and she didn't seem quite up to brushing it herself, and its getting in her eyes put her out. But nothing put out Master Harry. He sat behind his breakfast-cup, a tearing away at the jelly, as if he had been his own father.

After breakfast, Boots is inclined to consider that they drawed soldiers,—at least, he knows that many such was found in the fireplace, all on horseback. In the course of the morning, Master Harry rang the bell,—it was surprising how that there boy did carry on,—and said, in a sprightly way, "Cobbs, is there any good walks in this neighborhood?"

"Yes, sir," says Cobbs. "There's Love-lane."

"Get out with you, Cobbs!"—that was that there boy's expression,—"you're joking."

"Begging your pardon, sir," says Cobbs, "there really is Love-lane.

And a pleasant walk it is, and proud shall I be to show it to yourself and Mrs. Harry Walmers, Junior."

"Norah, dear," said Master Harry, "this is curious. We really ought to see Love-lane. Put on your bonnet, my sweetest darling, and we will go there with Cobbs."

Boots leaves me to judge what a Beast he felt himself to be, when that young pair told him, as they all three jogged along together, that they had made up their minds to give him two thousand guineas a year as head-gardener, on accounts of his being so true a friend to 'em. Boots could have wished at the moment that the earth would have opened and swallowed him up, he felt so mean, with their beaming eyes a looking at him, and believing him. Well, sir, he turned the conversation as well as he could, and he took 'em down Love-lane to the water-meadows, and there Master Harry would have drowned himself in half a moment more, a getting out a water-lily for her,—but nothing daunted that boy. Well, sir, they was tired out. All being so new and strange to 'em, they was tired as tired could be. And they laid down on a bank of daisies, like the children in the wood, leastways meadows, and fell asleep.

Boots don't know—perhaps I do,—but never mind, it don't signify either way—why it made a man fit to make a fool of himself to see them two pretty babies a lying there in the clear still sunny day, not dreaming half so hard when they was asleep as they done when they was awake. But, Lord! when you come to think of yourself, you know, and what a game you have been up to ever since you was in your own cradle, and what a poor sort of a chap you are, and how it's always either Yesterday with you, or else To-morrow, and never To-day, that's where it is!

Well, sir, they woke up at last, and then one thing was getting pretty clear to Boots, namely, that Mrs. Harry Walmers's, Junior's, temper was on the move. When Master Harry took her round the waist, she said he "teased her so;" and when he says, "Norah, my young May Moon, your Harry tease you?" she tells him, "Yes; and I want to go home!"

A biled fowl, and baked bread-and-butter pudding, brought Mrs. Walmers up a little; but Boots could have wished, he must privately own to me, to have seen her more sensible of the woice of love, and less abandoning of herself to currants. However, Master Harry, he kept up, and his noble heart was as fond as ever. Mrs. Walmers turned very sleepy about dusk, and began to cry. Therefore, Mrs. Walmers went off to bed as per yesterday; and Master Harry ditto repeated.

About eleven or twelve at night comes back the Governor in a chaise, along with Mr. Walmers and a elderly lady. Mr. Walmers looks amused and very serious, both at once, and says to our missis, "We are much indebted to you, ma'am, for your kind care of our little children, which we can never sufficiently acknowledge. Pray, ma'am, where is my boy?" Our missis says, "Cobbs has the dear child in charge, sir. Cobbs, show Forty!" Then he says to Cobbs, "Ah, Cobbs, I am glad to see *you!* I understood you was here!" And Cobbs says, "Yes, sir. Your most obedient, sir."

I may be surprised to hear Boots say it, perhaps; but Boots assures me that his heart beat like a hammer, going up stairs. "I beg your pardon, sir," says he, while unlocking the door; "I hope you are not angry with Master Harry. For Master Harry is a fine boy, sir, and will do you credit and honor." And Boots signifies to me, that, if the fine boy's father had contradicted him in the daring state of mind in which he then was, he thinks he should have "fetched him a crack," and taken the consequences.

But Mr. Walmers only says, "No, Cobbs. No, my good fellow. Thank you!" And, the door being opened, goes in.

Boots goes in too, holding the light, and he sees Mr. Walmers go up to the bedside, bend gently down, and kiss the little sleeping face. Then he stands looking at it for a minute, looking wonderfully like it (they do say he ran away with Mrs. Walmers); and then he gently shakes the little shoulder.

"Harry, my dear boy! Harry!"

Master Harry starts up and looks at him. Looks at Cobbs too. Such is the honor of that mite, that he looks at Cobbs, to see whether he has brought him into trouble.

"I am not angry, my child. I only want you to dress yourself and come home."

"Yes, pa."

Master Harry dresses himself quickly. His breast begins to swell when he has nearly finished, and it swells more and more as he stands, at last, a looking at his father: his father standing a looking at him, the quiet image of him.

"Please may I"—the spirit of that little creatur, and the way he kept his rising tears down!—"please, dear pa—may I—kiss Norah before I go?"

"You may, my child."

So he takes Master Harry in his hand, and Boots leads the way with the candle, and they come to that other bed-room, where the elder lady is seated by the bed, and poor little Mrs. Harry Walmers, Junior, is fast asleep. There the father lifts the child up to the pillow, and he lays his little face down for an instant by the little warm face of poor unconscious little Mrs. Harry Walmers, Junior, and gently draws it to him,— a sight so touching to the chambermaids who are peeping through the door, that one of them calls out, "It's a shame to part 'em!" But this chambermaid was always, as Boots informs me, a soft-hearted one. Not that there was any harm in that girl. Far from it.

Finally, Boots says, that's all about it. Mr. Walmers drove away in the chaise, having hold of Master Harry's hand. The elderly lady and Mrs. Harry Walmers, Junior, that was never to be (she married a Captain long afterwards, and died in India), went off next day. In conclusion, Boots put it to me whether I hold with him in two opinions: firstly, that there are not many couples on their way to be married who are half as innocent of guile as those two children; secondly, that it would be a jolly good thing for a great many couples on their way to be married, if they could only be stopped in time, and brought back separately.

From A TALE OF TWO CITIES

The Last Scene

Sydney Carton, law student and idler, had led a dissipated, careless life; but he did many noble and courageous things. He remained loyal in his love for Lucy Manette, after she had married Charles Darnay. And later, in France, when Darnay, or St. Evrémonde, was caught in the toils of the Revolution of 1792, Sydney Carton came to the prison, obtained entrance by threatening to betray a turnkey whom he recognized as a spy, drugged Darnay, exchanged clothes with him, and effected Darnay's rescue by remaining to face La Guillotine in place of the young Frenchman, whom he strangely resembled. Dickens attributes to him a final thought—if he had chosen to express his thoughts—"It is a far, far better thing that I do, than I have ever done; it is a far, far better rest that I go to, than I have ever known."

ALONG the Paris streets, the death-carts rumble, hollow and harsh. Six tumbrils carry the day's wine to La Guillotine. All the devouring and insatiate Monsters imagined since imagination could record itself, are fused in the one realization, Guillotine. And yet there is not in France, with its rich variety of soil and climate, a blade, a leaf, a root, a sprig, a peppercorn which will grow to maturity under conditions more certain than those that have produced this horror. Crush humanity out of shape once more, under similar hammers, and it will twist itself into the same tortured forms. Sow the same seeds of rapacious license and oppression ever again, and it will surely yield the same fruit according to its kind.

Six tumbrils roll along the streets. Change these back again to what they were, thou powerful enchanter, Time, and they shall be seen to be the carriages of absolute monarchs, the equipages of feudal nobles, the toilets of flaring Jezebels, the churches that are not my father's house but dens of thieves, the huts of millions of starving peasants! No; the great magician who majestically works out the appointed order of the Creator, never reverses his transformations. "If thou be changed into this shape by the will of God," say the seers to the enchanted, in the wise Arabian stories, "then remain so! But, if thou wear this form through mere passing conjuration, then resume thy former aspect!" Changeless and hopeless, the tumbrils roll along.

As the sombre wheels of the six carts go round, they seem to plough up a long crooked furrow among the populace in the streets. Ridges of faces are thrown to this side and to that, and the ploughs go steadily onward. So used are the regular inhabitants of the houses to the spectacle, that in many windows there are no people, and in some the occupation of the hands is not so much as suspended, while the eyes survey the faces in the tumbrils. Here and there, the inmate has visitors to see the sight; then he points his finger, with something of the complacency of a curator or authorized exponent, to this cart and to this, and seems to tell who sat here yesterday, and who there the day before.

Of the riders in the tumbrils, some observe these things, and all things on their last roadside, with an impassive stare; others, with a lingering interest in the ways of life and men. Some, seated with drooping heads, are sunk in silent despair; again, there are some so heedful of their looks that they cast upon the multitude such glances as they have seen in theatres, and in pictures. Several close their eyes, and think, or try to get their straying thoughts together. Only one, and he a miserable creature of a crazed aspect, is so shattered and made drunk by horror that he sings, and tries to dance. Not one of the whole number appeals, by look or gesture, to the pity of the people.

There is a guard of sundry horsemen riding abreast of the tumbrils, and faces are often turned up to some of them and they are asked some question. It would seem to be always the same question, for, it is always followed by a press of people towards the third cart. The horsemen abreast of that cart, frequently point out one man in it with their swords. The leading curiosity is, to know which is he; he stands at the back of the tumbril with his head bent down, to converse with a mere girl who sits on the side of the cart, and holds his hand. He has no curiosity or care for the scene about him, and always speaks to the girl. Here and there in a long Street of St. Honoré, cries are raised against him. If they move him at all, it is only to a quiet smile, as he shakes his hair a little more loosely about his face. He cannot easily touch his face, his arms being bound.

On the steps of a church, awaiting the coming-up of the tumbrils, stands the Spy and prison-sheep. He looks into the first of them: not there. He looks into the second: not there. He already asks himself, "Has he sacrificed me?" when his face clears, as he looks into the third.

"Which is Evrémonde?" said a man behind him.

"That. At the back there."

"With his hand in the girl's?"

"Yes."

The man cries, "Down, Evrémonde! To the Guillotine all aristocrats! Down, Evrémonde!"

"Hush, hush!" the Spy entreats him, timidly.

"And why not, citizen?"

"He is going to pay the forfeit; it will be paid in five minutes more. Let him be at peace."

But, the man continuing to exclaim, "Down, Evrémonde!" the face of Evrémonde is for a moment turned towards him. Evrémonde then sees the Spy, and looks attentively at him, and goes his way.

The clocks are on the stroke of three, and the furrow ploughed among the populace is turning round, to come on into the place of execution, and end. The ridges thrown to this side and to that, now crumble in and close behind the last plough as it passes on, for all are following to the Guillotine. In front of it, seated in chairs as in a garden of public diversion, are a number of women, busily knitting. On one of the foremost chairs, stands The Vengeance, looking about for her friend.

"Thérèse!" she cries, in her shrill tones. "Who has seen her? Thérèse Defarge!"

"She never missed before," says a knitting-woman of the sisterhood.

"No; nor will she miss now," cries The Vengeance, petulantly. "Thérèse!"

"Louder," the woman recommends.

Ay! Louder, Vengeance, much louder, and still she will scarcely hear thee. Louder yet, Vengeance, with a little oath or so added, and yet it will hardly bring her. Send other women up and down to seek her, lingering somewhere; and yet, although the messengers have done dread deeds, it is questionable whether of their own wills they will go far enough to find her.

"Bad Fortune!" cries The Vengeance, stamping her foot in the chair, "and here are the tumbrils! And Evrémonde will be despatched in a wink, and she not here! See her knitting in my hand, and her empty chair ready for her. I cry with vexation and disappointment!"

As The Vengeance descends from her elevation to do it, the tumbrils begin to discharge their loads. The ministers of Sainte Guillotine are robed and ready. Crash!—A head is held up, and the knitting-women who scarcely lifted their eyes to look at it a moment ago when it could think and speak, count One.

The second tumbril empties and moves on; the third comes up. Crash!—And the knitting-women, never faltering or pausing in their work, count Two.

The supposed Evrémonde descends, and the seamstress is lifted out next after him. He has not relinquished her patient hand in getting out, but still holds it as he promised. He gently places her with her back to the crashing engine that constantly whirs up and falls, and she looks into his face and thanks him.

"But for you, dear stranger, I should not be so composed, for I am naturally a poor little thing, faint of heart; nor should I have been able to raise my thoughts to Him who was put to death, that we might have hope and comfort here to-day. I think you were sent to me by Heaven."

"Or you to me," says Sydney Carton. "Keep your eyes upon me, dear child, and mind no other object."

"I mind nothing while I hold your hand. I shall mind nothing when I let it go, if they are rapid."

"They will be rapid. Fear not!"

The two stand in the fast-thinning throng of victims, but they speak as if they were alone. Eye to eye, voice to voice, hand to hand, heart to heart, these two children of the Universal Mother, else so wide apart and differing, have come together on the dark highway, to repair home together and to rest in her bosom.

"Brave and generous friend, will you let me ask you one last question? I am very ignorant, and it troubles me—just a little."

"Tell me what it is."

"I have a cousin, an only relative and an orphan, like myself, whom I love very dearly. She is five years younger than I, and she lives in a farmer's house in the south country. Poverty parted us, and she knows nothing of my fate—for I cannot write—and if I could, how should I tell her! It is better as it is."

"Yes, yes: better as it is."

"What I have been thinking as we came along, and what I am still thinking now, as I look into your kind strong face which gives me so much support, is this:—If the Republic really does good to the poor, and they come to be less hungry, and in all ways to suffer less, she may live a long time; she may even live to be old."

"What then, my gentle sister?"

"Do you think:" the uncomplaining eyes in which there is so much endurance, fill with tears, and the lips part a little more and tremble: "that it will seem long to me, while I wait for her in the better land where I trust both you and I will be mercifully sheltered?"

"It cannot be, my child; there is no Time there, and no trouble there."

"You comfort me so much! I am so ignorant. Am I to kiss you now? Is the moment come?"

"Yes."

She kisses his lips; he kisses hers; they solemnly bless each other. The spare hand does not tremble as he releases it; nothing worse than a sweet, bright constancy is in the patient face. She goes next before him—is gone; the knitting-women count Twenty-Two.

"I am the Resurrection and the Life, saith the Lord: he that believeth in me, though he were dead, yet shall he live: and whosoever liveth and believeth in me, shall never die."

The murmuring of many voices, the upturning of many faces, the pressing on of many footsteps in the outskirts of the crowd, so that it swells forward in a mass, like one great heave of water, all flashes away. Twenty-Three.

From GREAT EXPECTATIONS

Chapters I and III

CHAPTER I

My father's family name being Pirrip, and my christian name Philip, my infant tongue could make of both names nothing longer or more explicit than Pip. So, I called myself Pip, and came to be called Pip.

I give Pirrip as my father's family name, on the authority of his tombstone and my sister—Mrs. Joe Gargery, who married the blacksmith. As I never saw my father or my mother, and never saw any likeness of either of them (for their days were long before the days of photographs), my first fancies regarding what they were like, were unreasonably derived from their tombstones. The shape of the letters on my father's, gave me an odd idea that he was a square, stout, dark man, with curly black hair. From the character and turn of the inscription, *"Also Georgiana Wife of the Above,"* I drew a childish conclusion that my mother was freckled and sickly. To five little stone lozenges, each about a foot and a half long, which were arranged in a neat row beside their grave, and were sacred to the memory of five little brothers of mine—who gave up trying to get a living exceedingly early in that universal struggle—I am indebted for a belief I religiously entertained that they had all been born on their backs with their hands in their trousers-pockets, and had never taken them out in this state of existence.

Ours was the marsh country, down by the river, within, as the river wound, twenty miles of the sea. My first most vivid and broad impression of the identity of things, seems to me to have been gained on a memorable raw afternoon towards evening. At such a time I found out for certain, that this bleak place overgrown with nettles was the churchyard; and that Philip Pirrip, late of this parish, and also Georgiana wife of the above, were dead and buried; and that Alexander, Bartholomew, Abraham, Tobias, and Roger, infant children of the aforesaid, were also dead and buried; and that the dark flat wilderness beyond the churchyard, intersected with dykes and mounds and gates, with scattered cattle feeding on it, was the marshes; and that the low leaden line beyond, was the river: and that the distant savage lair from which the wind was rushing, was the sea; and that the small bundle of shivers growing afraid of it all and beginning to cry, was Pip.

"Hold your noise!" cried a terrible voice, as a man started up from among the graves at the side of the church porch. "Keep still, you little devil, or I'll cut your throat!"

A fearful man, all in coarse gray, with a great iron on his leg. A man with no hat, and with broken shoes, and with an old rag tied round his head. A man who had been soaked in water, and smothered in mud, and lamed by stones, and cut by flints, and stung by nettles, and torn by briars; who limped, and shivered, and glared and growled; and whose teeth chattered in his head as he seized me by the chin.

"O! Don't cut my throat, sir," I pleaded in terror. "Pray don't do it, sir."

"Tell us your name!" said the man. "Quick!"

"Pip, sir."

"Once more," said the man, staring at me. "Give it mouth!"

"Pip. Pip, sir."

"Show us where you live," said the man. "Pint out the place!"

I pointed to where our village lay, on the flat in-shore among the alder-trees and pollards, a mile or more from the church.

The man, after looking at me for a moment, turned me upside-down, and emptied my pockets. There was nothing in them but a piece of bread. When the church came to itself—for he was so sudden and strong that he made it go head-over-heels before me, and I saw the steeple under my feet—when the church came to itself, I say, I was seated on a high tombstone, trembling, while he ate the bread ravenously.

"You young dog," said the man, licking his lips, "what fat cheeks you ha' got."

I believe they were fat, though I was at that time under-sized for my years, and not strong.

"Darn me if I couldn't eat 'em," said the man, with a threatening shake of his head, "and if I han't half a mind to't!"

I earnestly expressed my hope that he wouldn't, and held tighter to the tombstone on which he had put me; partly, to keep myself upon it; partly, to keep myself from crying.

"Now lookee here!" said the man. "Where's your mother?"

"There, sir!" said I.

He started, made a short run, and stopped and looked over his shoulder.

"There, sir!" I timidly explained. "Also Georgiana. That's my mother."

"Oh!" said he, coming back. "And is that your father alonger your mother?"

"Yes, sir," said I; "him too; late of this parish."

"Ha!" he muttered then, considering. "Who d'ye live with—supposin' you're kindly let to live, which I han't made up my mind about?"

"My sister, sir—Mrs. Joe Gargery—wife of Joe Gargery, the blacksmith, sir."

"Blacksmith, eh?" said he. And looked down at his leg.

After darkly looking at his leg and at me several times, he came closer to my tombstone, took me by both arms, and tilted me back as far as he could hold me; so that his eyes looked most powerfully down into mine, and mine looked most helplessly up into his.

"Now lookee here," he said, "the question being whether you're to be let to live. You know what a file is?"

"Yes, sir."

"And you know what wittles is?"

"Yes, sir."

After each question he tilted me over a little more, so as to give me a greater sense of helplessness and danger.

"You get me a file." He tilted me again. "And you get me wittles." He tilted me again. "You bring 'em both to me." He tilted me again. "Or I'll have your heart and liver out." He tilted me again.

I was dreadfully frightened, and so giddy that I clung to him with both hands, and said, "If you would kindly please to let me keep upright, sir, perhaps I shouldn't be sick, and perhaps I could attend more."

He gave me a most tremendous dip and roll, so that the church jumped over its own weather-cock. Then, he held me by the arms, in an upright position on the top of the stone, and went on in these fearful terms:

"You bring me, to-morrow morning early, that file and them wittles. You bring the lot to me, at that old Battery over yonder. You do it, and you never dare to say a word or dare to make a sign concerning your having seen such a person as me, or any person sumever, and you shall be let to live. You fail, or you go from my words in any partickler, no matter how small it is, and your heart and your liver shall be tore out, roasted and ate. Now, I ain't alone, as you may think I am. There's a young man hid with me, in comparison with which young man I am a Angel. That young man hears the words I speak. That young man has a secret way pecooliar to himself, of getting at a boy, and at his heart, and at his liver. It is in wain for a boy to attempt to hide himself from that young man. A boy may lock his door, may be warm in bed, may tuck himself up, may draw the clothes over his head, may think himself comfortable and safe, but that young man will softly creep and creep his way to him and tear him open. I am a keeping that young man from harming of you at the present moment, with great difficulty. I find it wery hard to hold that young man off of your inside. Now, what do you say?"

I said that I would get him the file, and I would get him what broken bits of food I could, and I would come to him at the Battery, early in the morning.

"Say Lord strike you dead if you don't!" said the man.

I said so, and he took me down.

"Now," he pursued, "you remember what you've undertook, and you remember that young man, and you get home!"

"Goo-good night, sir," I faltered.

"Much of that!" said he, glancing about him over the cold wet flat. "I wish I was a frog. Or a eel!"

At the same time, he hugged his shuddering body in both his arms—

clasping himself, as if to hold himself together—and limped towards the low church wall. As I saw him go, picking his way among the nettles, and among the brambles that bound the green mounds, he looked in my young eyes as if he were eluding the hands of the dead people, stretching up cautiously out of their graves, to get a twist upon his ankle and pull him in.

When he came to the low church wall, he got over it, like a man whose legs were numbed and stiff, and then turned round to look for me. When I saw him turning, I set my face towards home, and made the best use of my legs. But presently I looked over my shoulder, and saw him going on again towards the river, still hugging himself in both arms, and picking his way with his sore feet among the great stones dropped into the marshes here and there, for stepping-places when the rains were heavy, or the tide was in.

The marshes were just a long black horizontal line then, as I stopped to look after him; and the river was just another horizontal line, not nearly so broad nor yet so black; and the sky was just a row of long angry red lines and dense black lines intermixed. On the edge of the river I could faintly make out the only two black things in all the prospect that seemed to be standing upright; one of these was the beacon by which the sailors steered—like an unhooped cask upon a pole—an ugly thing when you were near it; the other a gibbet, with some chains hanging to it which had once held a pirate. The man was limping on towards this latter, as if he were the pirate come to life, and come down, and going back to hook himself up again. It gave me a terrible turn when I thought so; and as I saw the cattle lifting their heads to gaze after him, I wondered whether they thought so too. I looked all round for the horrible young man, and could see no signs of him. But, now I was frightened again, and ran home without stopping.

[Pip spent a most wretched night, in childish terror at his plight. Very early in the morning, he raided Mrs. Joe Gargery's pantry, in fear and trembling, and stole a file from among Joe Gargery's tools, and ran for the misty meadows.]

CHAPTER III

It was a rimy morning, and very damp. I had seen the damp lying on the outside of my little window, as if some goblin had been crying there all night, and using the window for a pocket-handkerchief. Now I saw the damp lying on the bare hedges and spare grass, like a coarser sort of spiders' webs; hanging itself from twig to twig and blade to blade. On every rail and gate, wet lay clammy, and the marsh-mist was so thick, that the wooden finger on the post directing people to our village—a direction which they never accepted, for they never came there—was invisible to me until I was quite close under it. Then, as I looked up at it, while it dripped, it seemed to my oppressed conscience like a phantom devoting me to the Hulks.

The mist was heavier yet when I got out upon the marshes, so that instead of my running at everything, everything seemed to run at me. This was very disagreeable to a guilty mind. The gates and dykes and banks came bursting at me through the mist, as if they cried as plainly as could be, "A boy with Somebody-else's pork pie! Stop him!" The cattle came upon me with like suddenness, staring out of their eyes, and steaming out of their nostrils, "Holloa, young thief!" One black ox, with a white cravat on—who even had to my awakened conscience something of a clerical air—fixed me so obstinately with his eyes, and moved his blunt head round in such an accusatory manner as I moved round, that I blubbered out to him, "I couldn't help it, sir! It wasn't for myself I took it!" Upon which he put down his head, blew a cloud of smoke out of his nose, and vanished with a kick-up of his hind-legs and a flourish of his tail.

All this time, I was getting on towards the river; but however fast I went, I couldn't warm my feet, to which the damp cold seemed riveted, as the iron was riveted to the leg of the man I was running to meet. I knew my way to the Battery pretty straight, for I had been down there on a Sunday with Joe, and Joe, sitting on an old gun, had told me that when I was 'prentice to him, regularly bound, we would have such Larks there! However, in the confusion of the mist, I found myself at last too far to the right, and consequently had to try back along the river-side, on the bank of loose stones above the mud and the stakes that staked the tide out. Making my way along here with all despatch, I had just crossed a ditch which I knew to be very near the Battery, and had just scrambled up the mound beyond the ditch, when I saw the man sitting before me. His back was towards me, and he had his arms folded, and was nodding forward, heavy with sleep.

I thought he would be more glad if I came upon him with his breakfast, in that unexpected manner, so I went forward softly and touched him on the shoulder. He instantly jumped up, and it was not the same man but another man!

And yet this man was dressed in coarse gray, too, and had a great iron on his leg, and was lame, and hoarse, and cold, and was everything that the other man was; except that he had not the same face, and had a flat, broad-brimmed, low-crowned felt hat on. All this I saw in a moment, for I had only a moment to see it in: he swore an oath at me, made a hit at me—it was a round, weak blow that missed me and almost knocked himself down, for it made him stumble—and then he ran into the mist stumbling twice as he went, and I lost him.

"It's the young man!" I thought, feeling my heart shoot as I identified him. I dare say I should have felt a pain in my liver, too, if I had known where it was.

I was soon at the Battery, after that, and there was the right man—hugging himself and limping to and fro, as if he had never all night left off hugging and limping—waiting for me. He was awfully cold, to be sure. I half expected to see him drop down before my face and die of deadly cold. His eyes looked so awfully hungry, too, that when I handed him the file and he laid it down on the grass, it occurred to me he would have tried to eat it, if he had not seen my bundle. He did not turn me upside down, this time, to get at what I had, but left me right side upwards while I opened the bundle and emptied my pockets.

"What's in the bottle, boy?" said he.

"Brandy," said I.

He was already handing mincemeat down his throat in the most curious manner—more like a man who was putting it away somewhere in a violent hurry, than a man who was eating it—but he left off to take some of the liquor. He shivered all the while, so violently, that it was quite as much as he could do to keep the neck of the bottle between his teeth, without biting it off.

"I think you have got the ague," said I.

"I'm much of your opinion, boy," said he.

"It's bad about here," I told him. "You've been lying out on the meshes, and they're dreadful aguish. Rheumatic too."

"I'll eat my breakfast afore they're the death of me," said he, "I'd do that, if I was going to be strung up to that there gallows as there is over there, directly arterwards. I'll beat the shivers so far, I'll bet you."

He was gobbling mincemeat, meat-bone, bread, cheese, and pork pie, all at once: staring distrustfully while he did so at the mist all round us, and often stopping—even stopping his jaws—to listen. Some real or fancied sound, some clink upon the river or breathing of beast upon the marsh, now gave him a start, and he said, suddenly:

"You're not a deceiving imp? You brought no one with you?"

"No, sir! No!"

"Nor giv' no one the office to follow you?"

"No!"

"Well," said he, "I believe you. You'd be but a fierce young hound indeed, if at your time of life you could help to hunt a wretched warmint, hunted as near death and dunghill as this poor wretched warmint is!"

Something clicked in his throat as if he had works in him like a clock, and was going to strike. And he smeared his ragged rough sleeve over his eyes.

Pitying his desolation, and watching him as he gradually settled down upon the pie, I made bold to say, "I am glad you enjoy it."

"Did you speak?"

"I said I was glad you enjoyed it."

"Thankee, my boy. I do."

I had often watched a large dog of ours eating his food; and I now noticed a decided similarity between the dog's way of eating, and the man's. The man took strong, sharp, sudden bites, just like the dog. He swallowed, or rather snapped up, every mouthful, too soon and too fast; and he looked sideways here and there while he ate, as if he thought there was danger in every direction, of somebody's coming to take the pie away. He was altogether too unsettled in his mind over it, to appreciate it comfortably, I thought, or to have anybody to dine with him, without making a chop with his jaws at the visitor. In all of which particulars he was very like the dog.

"I am afraid you won't leave any of it for him," said I timidly; after a silence during which I had hesitated as to the politeness of making the remark. "There's no more to be got where that came from." It was the certainty of this fact that impelled me to offer the hint.

"Leave any for him? Who's him?" said my friend, stopping in his crunching of pie-crust.

"The young man. That you spoke of. That was hid with you."

"Oh ah!" he returned, with something like a gruff laugh. "Him? Yes, yes! *He* don't want no wittles."

"I thought he looked as if he did," said I.

The man stopped eating, and regarded me with the keenest scrutiny and the greatest surprise.

"Looked? When?"

"Just now."

"Where?"

"Yonder," said I, pointing; "over there, where I found him nodding asleep, and thought it was you."

He held me by the collar and stared at me so, that I began to think his first idea about cutting my throat had revived.

"Dressed like you, you know, only with a hat," I explained, trembling; "and—and"—I was very anxious to put this delicately—"and with—the same reason for wanting to borrow a file. Didn't you hear the cannon last night?"

"Then, there *was* firing!" he said to himself.

"I wonder you shouldn't have been sure of that," I returned, "for we heard it up at home, and that's further away, and we were shut in besides."

"Why, see now!" said he. "When a man's alone on these flats, with a light head and a light stomach, perishing of cold and want, he hears nothin' all night, but guns firing, and voices calling. Hears? He sees the soldiers, with their red coats lighted up by the torches carried afore, closing in round him. He hears his number called, hears himself challenged, hears the rattle of the muskets, hears the orders 'Make ready! Present! Cover him steady, men!' and is laid hands on— and there's nothin'! Why, if I see one pursuing party last night—coming up in order, Damn 'em, with their tramp, tramp—I see a hundred. And as to firing! Why, I see the mist shake with the cannon, arter it was broad day.—But this man;" he had said all the rest as if he had forgotten my being there; "did you notice anything in him?"

"He had a badly bruised face," said I, recalling what I hardly knew I knew.

"Not here?" exclaimed the man, striking his left cheek mercilessly, with the flat of his hand.

"Yes, there!"

"Where is he?" He crammed what little food was left, into the breast of his gray jacket. "Show me the way he went. I'll pull him down, like a bloodhound. Curse this iron on my sore leg! Give us hold of the file, boy."

I indicated in what direction the mist had shrouded the other man, and he looked up at it for an instant. But he was down on the rank wet grass, filing at his iron like a madman, and not minding me or minding his own leg, which had an old chafe upon it and was bloody, but which he handled as roughly as if it had no more feeling in it than the file. I was very much afraid of him again, now that he had worked himself into this fierce hurry, and I was likewise very much afraid of keeping away from home any longer. I told him I must go, but he took no notice, so I thought the best thing I could do was to slip off. The last I saw of him, his head was bent over his knee and he was working hard at his fetter, muttering impatient imprecations at it and at his leg. The last I heard of him, I stopped in the mist to listen, and the file was still going.

ROBERT BROWNING (1812-1889)

Cavalier Tunes

I. MARCHING ALONG

KENTISH Sir Byng stood for his King,
Bidding the crop-headed Parliament
  swing:
And, pressing a troop unable to stoop
And see the rogues flourish and honest
  folk droop,
Marched them along, fifty-score strong,
Great-hearted gentlemen, singing this
  song.

God for King Charles! Pym and such
  carles
To the Devil that prompts 'em their
  treasonous parles!
Cavaliers, up! Lips from the cup,
Hands from the pastry, nor bite take nor
  sup
Till you're—
  (*Chorus*) *Marching along, fifty-score*
      strong,
        Great-hearted gentlemen,
        singing this song.

Hampden to Hell, and his obsequies'
  knell
Serve Hazelrig, Fiennes, and young
  Harry as well!
England, good cheer! Rupert is near!
Kentish and loyalists, keep we not here
  (*Chorus*) *Marching along, fifty-score*
      strong,
        Great-hearted gentlemen,
        singing this song?

Then, God for King Charles! Pym and
  his snarls
To the Devil that pricks on such pesti-
  lent carles!
Hold by the right, you double your
  might;
So, onward to Nottingham, fresh for the
  fight,
  (*Chorus*) *March we along, fifty-score*
      strong,
        Great-hearted gentlemen,
        singing this song!

II. GIVE A ROUSE

King Charles, and who'll do him right
  now?
King Charles, and who's ripe for fight
  now?
Give a rouse: here's, in Hell's despite
  now,
King Charles!

Who gave me the goods that went since?
Who raised me the house that sank
  once?
Who helped me to gold I spent since?
Who found me in wine you drank once?
  (*Chorus*) *King Charles, and who'll do*
      him right now?
      King Charles, and who's
        ripe for fight now?
      Give a rouse: here's, in
        Hell's despite now,
      King Charles!

To whom used my boy George quaff else,
By the old fool's side that begot him?
For whom did he cheer and laugh else,
While Noll's damned troopers shot him?
  (*Chorus*) *King Charles, and who'll do*
      him right now?
      King Charles, and who's
        ripe for fight now?
      Give a rouse: here's, in
        Hell's despite now,
      King Charles!

III. BOOT AND SADDLE

Boot, saddle, to horse, and away!
Rescue my Castle, before the hot day
Brightens to blue from its silvery grey,
  (*Chorus*) *Boot, saddle, to horse, and*
      away!

Ride past the suburbs, asleep as you'd
  say;
Many's the friend there, will listen and
  pray
"God's luck to gallants that strike up
  the lay—
  (*Chorus*) *Boot, saddle, to horse, and*
      away!"

Forty miles off, like a roebuck at bay,
Flouts Castle Brancepeth the Round-
heads' array:
Who laughs, "Good fellows ere this, by
my fay,
(*Chorus*) *Boot, saddle, to horse, and
away?*"

Who? My wife Gertrude; that, honest
and gay,
Laughs when you talk of surrendering,
"Nay!
I've better counsellors; what counsel
they?
(*Chorus*) *Boot, saddle, to horse, and
away!*"

"How they brought the Good News from Ghent to Aix"

I SPRANG to the stirrup, and Joris, and
he;
I galloped, Dirck galloped, we galloped
all three;
"Good speed!" cried the watch, as the
gate-bolts undrew;
"Speed!" echoed the wall to us galloping
through;
Behind shut the postern, the lights sank
to rest,
And into the midnight we galloped
abreast.

Not a word to each other; we kept the
great pace
Neck by neck, stride by stride, never
changing our place;
I turned in my saddle and made its girths
tight,
Then shortened each stirrup, and set the
pique right,
Rebuckled the cheek-strap, chained
slacker the bit,
Nor galloped less steadily Roland a whit.

'Twas moonset at starting; but while we
drew near
Lokeren, the cocks crew and twilight
dawned clear;

At Boom, a great yellow star came out to
see;
At Düffeld, 'twas morning as plain as
could be;
And from Mecheln church-steeple we
heard the half-chime,
So Joris broke silence with, "Yet there is
time!"

At Aershot, up leaped of a sudden the
sun,
And against him the cattle stood black
every one,
To stare through the mist at us galloping
past,
And I saw my stout galloper Roland at
last,
With resolute shoulders, each butting
away
The haze, as some bluff river headland
its spray:

And his low head and crest, just one
sharp ear bent back
For my voice, and the other pricked out
on his track;
And one eye's black intelligence,—ever
that glance
O'er its white edge at me, his own master, askance!
And the thick heavy spume-flakes which
aye and anon
His fierce lips shook upwards in galloping on.

By Hasselt, Dirck groaned; and cried
Joris, "Stay, spur!
Your Roos galloped bravely, the fault's
not in her.
We'll remember at Aix"—for one heard
the quick wheeze
Of her chest, saw the stretched neck and
staggering knees,
And sunk tail, and horrible heave of the
flank,
As down on her haunches she shuddered
and sank.

So, we were left galloping, Joris and I,
Past Looz and past Tongres, no cloud in
the sky;
The broad sun above laughed a pitiless
laugh,
'Neath our feet broke the brittle bright
stubble like chaff;
Till over by Dalhem a dome-spire sprang
white,
And "Gallop," gasped Joris, "for Aix is
in sight!"

"How they'll greet us!"—and all in a
moment his roan
Rolled neck and croup over, lay dead as
a stone;
And there was my Roland to bear the
whole weight
Of the news which alone could save Aix
from her fate,
With his nostrils like pits full of blood to
the brim,
And with circles of red for his eye-
sockets' rim.

Then I cast loose my buffcoat, each hol-
ster let fall,
Shook off both my jack-boots, let go belt
and all,
Stood up in the stirrup, leaned, patted his
ear,
Called my Roland his pet-name, my horse
without peer;
Clapped my hands, laughed and sang, any
noise, bad or good,
Till at length into Aix Roland galloped
and stood.

And all I remember is—friends flocking
round
As I sat with his head 'twixt my knees
on the ground;
And no voice but was praising this Roland of mine,
As I poured down his throat our last
measure of wine,
Which (the burgesses voted by common
consent)
Was no more than his due who brought
good news from Ghent.

The Laboratory

[ANCIEN RÉGIME]

Now that I, tying thy glass mask tightly,
May gaze thro' these faint smokes curling whitely,
As thou pliest thy trade in this devil's-
smithy—
Which is the poison to poison her,
prithee?

He is with her; and they know that I
know
Where they are, what they do: they
believe my tears flow
While they laugh, laugh at me, at me
fled to the drear
Empty church, to pray God in, for
them!—I am here.

Grind away, moisten and mash up thy
paste,
Pound at thy powder,—I am not in
haste!
Better sit thus, and observe thy strange
things,
Than go where men wait me and dance
at the King's.

That in the mortar—you call it a gum?
Ah, the brave tree whence such gold
oozings come!
And yonder soft phial, the exquisite
blue,
Sure to taste sweetly,—is that poison
too?

Had I but all of them, thee and thy
treasures,
What a wild crowd of invisible pleasures!
To carry pure death in an earring, a
casket,
A signet, a fan-mount, a filigree-basket!

Soon, at the King's, a mere lozenge to
give
And Pauline should have just thirty
minutes to live!

But to light a pastille, and Elise, with
her head
And her breast and her arms and her
hands, should drop dead!

Quick—is it finished? The colour's too
grim!
Why not soft like the phial's, enticing
and dim?
Let it brighten her drink, let her turn
it and stir,
And try it and taste, ere she fix and
prefer!

What a drop! She's not little, no
minion like me—
That's why she ensnared him: this never
will free
The soul from those masculine eyes,—
say, "no!"
To that pulse's magnificent come-and-go.

For only last night, as they whispered,
I brought
My own eyes to bear on her so, that I
thought
Could I keep them one half minute fixed,
she would fall,
Shrivelled; she fell not; yet this does
it all!

Not that I bid you spare her the pain!
Let death be felt and the proof remain;
Brand, burn up, bite into its grace—
He is sure to remember her dying face!

Is it done? Take my mask off! Nay,
be not morose;
It kills her, and this prevents seeing it
close:
The delicate droplet, my whole fortune's fee—
If it hurts her, beside, can it ever hurt
me?

Now, take all my jewels, gorge gold to
your fill,
You may kiss me, old man, on my mouth
if you will!

But brush this dust off me, lest horror
it brings
Ere I know it—next moment I dance at
the King's!

Up at a Villa—Down in the City

*(As Distinguished by an Italian Person
of Quality)*

Had I but plenty of money, money
enough and to spare,
The house for me, no doubt, were a
house in the city-square;
Ah, such a life, such a life, as one leads
at the window there!

Something to see, by Bacchus, something
to hear, at least!
There, the whole day long, one's life is a
perfect feast;
While up at a villa one lives, I maintain
it, no more than a beast.

Well now, look at our villa! stuck like
the horn of a bull
Just on a mountain-edge as bare as the
creature's skull,
Save a mere shag of a bush with hardly
a leaf to pull!
—I scratch my own, sometimes, to see if
the hair's turned wool.

But the city, oh the city—the square with
the houses! Why?
They are stone-faced, white as a curd,
there's something to take the eye!
Houses in four straight lines, not a single
front awry;
You watch who crosses and gossips, who
saunters, who hurries by;
Green blinds, as a matter of course, to
draw when the sun gets high;
And the shops with fanciful signs which
are painted properly.

What of a villa? Though winter be over
in March by rights,
'Tis May perhaps ere the snow shall
have withered well off the heights:

You've the brown ploughed land before,
    where the oxen steam and wheeze,
And the hills over-smoked behind by the
    faint gray olive-trees.

Is it better in May, I ask you? You've
    summer all at once;
In a day he leaps complete with a few
    strong April suns.
'Mid the sharp short emerald wheat,
    scarce risen three fingers well,
The wild tulip, at end of its tube, blows
    out its great red bell
Like a thin clear bubble of blood, for the
    children to pick and sell.

Is it ever hot in the square? There's a
    fountain to spout and splash!
In the shade it sings and springs: in the
    shine such foambows flash
On the horses with curling fish-tails, that
    prance and paddle and pash
Round the lady atop in her conch—fifty
    gazers do not abash,
Though all that she wears is some weeds
    round her waist in a sort of sash.

All the year long at the villa, nothing to
    see though you linger,
Except yon cypress that points like
    death's lean lifted forefinger.
Some think fireflies pretty, when they
    mix i' the corn and mingle,
Or thrid the stinking hemp till the stalks
    of it seem a-tingle.
Late August or early September, the
    stunning cicala is shrill,
And the bees keep their tiresome whine
    round the resinous firs on the hill.
Enough of the seasons,—I spare you the
    months of the fever and chill.

Ere you open your eyes in the city, the
    blessed church-bells begin:
No sooner the bells leave off than the
    diligence rattles in:
You get the pick of the news, and it
    costs you never a pin.

By and by there's the travelling doctor
    gives pills, lets blood, draws teeth;
Or the Pulcinello-trumpet breaks up the
    market beneath.
At the post-office such a scene-picture—
    the new play, piping hot!
And a notice how, only this morning,
    three liberal thieves were shot.
Above it, behold the Archbishop's most
    fatherly of rebukes,
And beneath, with his crown and his lion,
    some little new law of the Duke's!
Or a sonnet with flowery marge, to the
    Reverend Don So-and-so,
Who is Dante, Boccaccio, Petrarca, Saint
    Jerome, and Cicero,
"And moreover" (the sonnet goes rhym-
    ing), "the skirts of Saint Paul has
    reached,
Having preached us those six Lent-lec-
    tures more unctuous than ever he
    preached."
Noon strikes,—here sweeps the proces-
    sion! our Lady borne smiling and
    smart
With a pink gauze gown all spangles,
    and seven swords stuck in her heart!
Bang-whang-whang goes the drum,
    tootle-te-tootle the fife;
No keeping one's haunches still: it's the
    greatest pleasure in life.

But bless you, it's dear—it's dear! fowls,
    wine, at double the rate.
They have clapped a new tax upon salt,
    and what oil pays passing the gate
It's a horror to think of. And so, the
    villa for me, not the city!
Beggars can scarcely be choosers: but
    still—ah, the pity, the pity!
Look, two and two go the priests, then
    the monks with cowls and sandals,
And the penitents dressed in white shirts,
    a-holding the yellow candles;
One, he carries a flag up straight, and
    another a cross with handles,
And the Duke's guard brings up the rear,
    for the better prevention of scandals;

Bang-whang-whang goes the drum,
   tootle-te-tootle the fife.
Oh, a day in the city-square, there is no
   such pleasure in life!

A Toccata of Galuppi's

OH Galuppi, Baldassare, this is very sad
   to find!
I can hardly misconceive you; it would
   prove me deaf and blind;
But although I take your meaning, 'tis
   with such a heavy mind!

Here you come with your old music,
   and here's all the good it brings.
What, they lived once thus at Venice
   where the merchants were the kings,
Where St. Mark's is, where the Doges
   used to wed the sea with rings?

Ay, because the sea's the street there;
   and 'tis arched by . . . what you
   call
. . . Shylock's bridge with houses on it,
   where they kept the carnival:
I was never out of England—it's as if
   I saw it all.

Did young people take their pleasure
   when the sea was warm in May?
Balls and masks begun at midnight,
   burning ever to mid-day,
When they made up fresh adventures for
   the morrow, do you say?

Was a lady such a lady, cheeks so round
   and lips so red,—
On her neck the small face buoyant, like
   a bell-flower on its bed,
O'er the breast's superb abundance where
   a man might base his head?

Well, and it was graceful of them—
   they'd break talk off and afford
—She, to bite her mask's black velvet—
   he, to finger on his sword,
While you sat and played Toccatas,
   stately at the clavichord?

What? Those lesser thirds so plaintive,
   sixths diminished, sigh on sigh,
Told them something? Those suspen-
   sions, those solutions—"Must we
   die?"
Those commiserating sevenths—"Life
   might last! we can but try!"

"Were you happy?"—"Yes."—"And are
   you still as happy?"—"Yes. And
   you?"
—"Then, more kisses!"—"Did *I* stop
   them, when a million seemed so
   few?"
Hark, the dominant's persistence till it
   must be answered to!

So, an octave struck the answer. Oh,
   they praised you, I dare say!
"Brave Galuppi! that was music! good
   alike at grave and gay!
I can always leave off talking when I
   hear a master play!"

Then they left you for their pleasure:
   till in due time, one by one,
Some with lives that came to nothing,
   some with deeds as well undone,
Death stepped tacitly and took them
   where they never see the sun.

But when I sit down to reason, think to
   take my stand nor swerve,
While I triumph o'er a secret wrung
   from nature's close reserve,
In you come with your cold music till
   I creep through every nerve.

Yes, you, like a ghostly cricket, creaking
   where a house was burned:
"Dust and ashes, dead and done with,
   Venice spent what Venice earned.
The soul, doubtless, is immortal—where
   a soul can be discerned.

"Yours for instance: you know physics,
   something of geology,
Mathematics are your pastime; souls
   shall rise in their degree;
Butterflies may dread extinction,—you'll
   not die, it cannot be!

"As for Venice and her people, merely
  born to bloom and drop,
Here on earth they bore their fruitage,
  mirth and folly were the crop:
What of soul was left, I wonder, when
  the kissing had to stop?

"Dust and ashes!" So you creak it, and
  I want the heart to scold.
Dear dead women, with such hair, too—
  what's become of all the gold
Used to hang and brush their bosoms? I
  feel chilly and grown old.

Home-Thoughts, from Abroad

OH, to be in England
Now that April's there,
And whoever wakes in England
Sees, some morning, unaware,
That the lowest boughs and the brush-
  wood sheaf
Round the elm-tree bole are in tiny leaf,
While the chaffinch sings on the orchard
  bough
In England—now!

And after April, when May follows,
And the whitethroat builds, and all the
  swallows!
Hark, where my blossomed pear-tree in
  the hedge
Leans to the field and scatters on the
  clover
Blossoms and dewdrops—at the bent
  spray's edge—
That's the wise thrush; he sings each song
  twice over,
Lest you should think he never could re-
  capture
The first fine careless rapture!
And though the fields look rough with
  hoary dew,
All will be gay when noontide wakes anew
The buttercups, the little children's
  dower—
Far brighter than this gaudy melon-
flower.

The Patriot

IT was roses, roses, all the way,
  With myrtle mixed in my path like
    mad:
The house-roofs seemed to heave and
    sway,
  The church-spires flamed, such flags
    they had,
A year ago on this very day.

The air broke into a mist with bells,
  The old walls rocked with the crowd
    and cries.
Had I said, "Good folk, mere noise re-
    pels—
  But give me your sun from yonder
    skies!"
They had answered, "And afterward,
    what else?"

Alack, it was I who leaped at the sun
  To give it my loving friends to keep!
Naught man could do, have I left
    undone:
  And you see my harvest, what I reap
This very day, now a year is run.

There's nobody on the house-tops now—
  Just a palsied few at the windows
    set;
For the best of the sight is, all allow,
  At the Shambles' Gate—or, better yet,
By the very scaffold's foot, I trow.

I go in the rain, and, more than needs,
  A rope cuts both my wrists behind;
And I think, by the feel, my forehead
    bleeds,
  For they fling, whoever has a mind,
Stones at me for my year's misdeeds.

Thus I entered, and thus I go!
  In triumphs, people have dropped down
    dead.
"Paid by the world, what dost thou owe
  Me?"—God might question; now in-
    stead,
'Tis God shall repay: I am safer so.

My Last Duchess

FERRARA

THAT'S my last Duchess painted on the
    wall,
Looking as if she were alive. I call
That piece a wonder, now: Fra Pandolf's
    hands
Worked busily a day, and there she
    stands.
Will't please you sit and look at her? I
    said
"Fra Pandolf" by design, for never read
Strangers like you that pictured counte-
    nance,
The depth and passion of its earnest
    glance,
But to myself they turned (since none
    puts by
The curtain I have drawn for you, but I)
And seemed as they would ask me, if they
    durst,
How such a glance came there; so, not the
    first
Are you to turn and ask thus. Sir, 'twas
    not
Her husband's presence only, called that
    spot
Of joy into the Duchess' cheek: perhaps
Fra Pandolf chanced to say, "Her mantle
    laps
Over my lady's wrist too much," or
    "Paint
Must never hope to reproduce the faint
Half-flush that dies along her throat:"
    such stuff
Was courtesy, she thought, and cause
    enough
For calling up that spot of joy. She had
A heart—how shall I say?—too soon
    made glad,
Too easily impressed: she liked whate'er
She looked on, and her looks went every-
    where.
Sir, 'twas all one! My favour at her
    breast,
The dropping of the daylight in the West,
The bough of cherries some officious fool

Broke in the orchard for her, the white
    mule
She rode with round the terrace—all and
    each
Would draw from her alike the approv-
    ing speech,
Or blush, at least. She thanked men,—
    good! but thanked
Somehow—I know not how—as if she
    ranked
My gift of a nine-hundred-years-old name
With anybody's gift. Who'd stoop to
    blame
This sort of trifling? Even had you skill
In speech—(which I have not)—to make
    your will
Quite clear to such an one, and say, "Just
    this
Or that in you disgusts me; here you miss,
Or there exceed the mark"—and if she let
Herself be lessoned so, nor plainly set
Her wits to yours, forsooth, and made
    excuse,
—E'en then would be some stooping; and
    I choose
Never to stoop. Oh sir, she smiled, no
    doubt,
Whene'er I passed her; but who passed
    without
Much the same smile? This grew; I
    gave commands;
Then all smiles stopped together. There
    she stands
As if alive. Will't please you rise? We'll
    meet
The company below, then. I repeat,
The Count your master's known munifi-
    cence
Is ample warrant that no just pretence
Of mine for dowry will be disallowed;
Though his fair daughter's self, as I
    avowed
At starting, is my object. Nay, we'll go
Together down, sir. Notice Neptune,
    though,
Taming a sea-horse, thought a rarity,
Which Claus of Innsbruck cast in bronze
    for me!

A Grammarian's Funeral, shortly after the Revival of Learning in Europe.

LET us begin and carry up this corpse,
Singing together.
Leave we the common crofts, the vulgar thorpes,
Each in its tether
Sleeping safe on the bosom of the plain,
Cared-for till cock-crow:
Look out if yonder be not day again
Rimming the rock-row!
That's the appropriate country; there, man's thought,
Rarer, intenser,
Self-gathered for an outbreak, as it ought,
Chafes in the censer!
Leave we the unlettered plain its herd and crop;
Seek we sepulture
On a tall mountain, cited to the top,
Ⴎwded with culture!
All the peaks soar, but one the rest excels;
Clouds overcome it;
No, yonder sparkle is the citadel's
Circling its summit!
Thither our path lies; wind we up the heights:
Wait ye the warning?
Our low life was the level's and the night's;
He's for the morning!
Step to a tune, square chests, erect the head,
'Ware the beholders!
This is our master, famous, calm, and dead,
Borne on our shoulders.

Sleep, crop and herd! sleep, darkling thorpe and croft,
Safe from the weather!
He, whom we convoy to his grave aloft,
Singing together,
He was a man born with thy face and throat,
Lyric Apollo!

Long he lived nameless: how should spring take note
Winter would follow?
Till lo, the little touch, and youth was gone!
Cramped and diminished,
Moaned he, "New measures, other feet anon!
My dance is finished?"
No, that's the world's way! (keep the mountain-side,
Make for the city,)
He knew the signal, and stepped on with pride
Over men's pity;
Left play for work, and grappled with the world
Bent on escaping:
"What's in the scroll," quoth he, "thou keepest furled?
Show me their shaping,
Theirs, who most studied man, the bard and sage,—
Give!"—So he gowned him,
Straight got by heart that book to its last page:
Learned, we found him!
Yea, but we found him bald too—eyes like lead,
Accents uncertain:
"Time to taste life," another would have said,
"Up with the curtain!"—
This man said rather, "Actual life comes next?
Patience a moment!
Grant I have mastered learning's crabbed text,
Still, there's the comment.
Let me know all! Prate not of most or least,
Painful or easy:
Even to the crumbs I'd fain eat up the feast,
Ay, nor feel queasy!"
Oh, such a life as he resolved to live,
When he had learned it,
When he had gathered all books had to give!

Sooner, he spurned it.
Image the whole, then execute the parts—
  Fancy the fabric
Quite, ere you build, ere steel strike fire
    from quartz,
  Ere mortar dab brick!

(Here's the town-gate reached: there's
    the market-place
  Gaping before us.)
Yea, this in him was the peculiar grace
  (Hearten our chorus)
That before living he'd learn how to
    live—
  No end to learning:
Earn the means first—God surely will
    contrive
  Use for our earning.
Others mistrust and say—"But time es-
    capes!
  Live now or never!"
He said, "What's time? leave Now for
    dogs and apes!
  Man has Forever."
Back to his book then: deeper drooped
    his head:
  Calculus racked him:
Leaden before, his eyes grew dross of
    lead:
  Tussis attacked him.
"Now, Master, take a little rest!"—not
    he!
  (Caution redoubled!
Step two a-breast, the way winds nar-
    rowly)
  Not a whit troubled,
Back to his studies, fresher than at first,
  Fierce as a dragon
He (soul-hydroptic with a sacred thirst)
  Sucked at the flagon.
Oh, if we draw a circle premature,
  Heedless of far gain,
Greedy for quick returns of profit, sure,
  Bad is our bargain!
Was it not great? did not he throw on
    God,
  (He loves the burthen)—
God's task to make the heavenly period
  Perfect the earthen?

Did not he magnify the mind, show clear
  Just what it all meant?
He would not discount life, as fools do
    here,
  Paid by instalment!
He ventured neck or nothing—Heaven's
    success
  Found, or earth's failure:
"Wilt thou trust death or not?" He
    answered "Yes!
  Hence with life's pale lure!"
That low man seeks a little thing to do,
  Sees it and does it:
This high man, with a great thing to
    pursue,
  Dies ere he knows it.
That low man goes on adding one to one,
  His hundred's soon hit:
This high man, aiming at a million,
  Misses an unit.
That, has the world here—should he need
    the next,
  Let the world mind him!
This, throws himself on God, and un-
    perplext
  Seeking shall find Him,
So, with the throttling hands of Death at
    strife,
  Ground he at grammar;
Still, thro' the rattle, parts of speech were
    rife:
  While he could stammer
He settled *Hoti's* business—let it be!—
  Properly based *Oun*—
Gave us the doctrine of the enclitic *De*,
  Dead from the waist down.
Well, here's the platform, here's the
    proper place.
  Hail to your purlieus,
All ye highfliers of the feathered race,
  Swallows and curlews!
Here's the top-peak! the multitude
    below
  Live, for they can, there.
This man decided not to Live but Know—
  Bury this man there?
Here—here's his place, where meteors
    shoot, clouds form,
  Lightnings are loosened,

Stars come and go! let joy break with
the storm,
Peace let the dew send!
Lofty designs must close in like effects:
Loftily lying,
Leave him—still loftier than the world
suspects,
Living and dying.

The Statue and the Bust

THERE'S a palace in Florence, the world
knows well,
And a statue watches it from the square,
And this story of both do our townsmen
tell.

Ages ago, a lady there,
At the farthest window facing the East
Asked, "Who rides by with the royal air?"

The brides-maids' prattle around her
ceased;
She leaned forth, one on either hand;
They saw how the blush of the bride increased—

They felt by its beats her heart expand—
As one at each ear and both in a breath
Whispered, "The Great-Duke Ferdi-
nand."

That selfsame instant, underneath,
The Duke rode past in his idle way,
Empty and fine like a swordless sheath.

Gay he rode, with a friend as gay,
Till he threw his head back—"Who is
she?"
—"A bride the Riccardi brings home
to-day."

Hair in heaps lay heavily
Over a pale brow spirit-pure—
Carved like the heart of the coal-black
tree,

Crisped like a war-steed's encolure—
And vainly sought to dissemble her eyes
Of the blackest black our eyes endure.

And lo, a blade for a knight's emprise
Filled the fine empty sheath of a man,—
The Duke grew straightway brave and
wise.

He looked at her, as a lover can;
She looked at him, as one who awakes,—
The past was a sleep, and her life began.

Now, love so ordered for both their sakes,
A feast was held that selfsame night
In the pile which the mighty shadow
makes.

(For Via Larga is three-parts light,
But the palace overshadows one,
Because of a crime which may God
requite!

To Florence and God the wrong was
done,
Through the first republic's murder there
By Cosimo and his cursed son.)

The Duke (with the statue's face in the
square)
Turned in the midst of his multitude
At the bright approach of the bridal pair.

Face to face the lovers stood
A single minute and no more,
While the bridegroom bent as a man
subdued—

Bowed till his bonnet brushed the floor—
For the Duke on the lady a kiss conferred,
As the courtly custom was of yore.

In a minute can lovers exchange a word?
If a word did pass, which I do not think,
Only one out of the thousand heard.

That was the bridegroom. At day's brink
He and his bride were alone at last
In a bed-chamber by a taper's blink.

Calmly he said that her lot was cast,
That the door she had passed was shut
on her
Till the final catafalque repassed.

The world meanwhile, its noise and stir,
Through a certain window facing the
    East
She could watch like a convent's chron-
    icler.

Since passing the door might lead to a
    feast,
And a feast might lead to so much beside,
He, of many evils, chose the least.

"Freely I choose too," said the bride—
"Your window and its world suffice,"
Replied the tongue, while the heart
    replied—

"If I spend the night with that devil twice,
May his window serve as my loop of hell
Whence a damned soul looks on Paradise!

"I fly to the Duke who loves me well,
Sit by his side and laugh at sorrow
Ere I count another ave-bell.

" 'Tis only the coat of a page to borrow,
And tie my hair in a horse-boy's trim,
And I save my soul—but not to-
    morrow"—

(She checked herself and her eye grew
    dim)—
"My father tarries to bless my state:
I must keep it one day more for him.

"Is one day more so long to wait?
Moreover the Duke rides past, I know;
We shall see each other, sure as fate."

She turned on her side and slept. Just so!
So we resolve on a thing and sleep:
So did the lady, ages ago.

That night the Duke said, "Dear or cheap
As the cost of this cup of bliss may prove
To body or soul, I will drain it deep."

And on the morrow, bold with love,
He beckoned the bridegroom (close on
    call,
As his duty bade, by the Duke's alcove)

And smiled " 'Twas a very funeral,
Your lady will think, this feast of ours,—
A shame to efface, whate'er befall!

"What if we break from the Arno bowers,
And try if Petraja, cool and green,
Cure last night's fault with this morn-
    ing's flowers?"

The bridegroom, not a thought to be seen
On his steady brow and quiet mouth,
Said, "Too much favour for me so mean!

"But, alas! my lady leaves the South;
Each wind that comes from the Apennine
Is a menace to her tender youth:

"Nor a way exists, the wise opine,
If she quits her palace twice this year,
To avert the flower of life's decline."

Quoth the Duke, "A sage and a kindly
    fear.
Moreover Petraja is cold this spring:
Be our feast to-night as usual here!"

And then to himself—"Which night shall
    bring
Thy bride to her lover's embraces, fool—
Or I am the fool, and thou art the king!

"Yet my passion must wait a night, nor
    cool—
For to-night the Envoy arrives from
    France,
Whose heart I unlock with thyself, my
    tool.

"I need thee still and might miss per-
    chance.
To-day is not wholly lost, beside,
With its hope of my lady's countenance:

"For I ride—what should I do but ride?
And passing her palace, if I list,
May glance at its window—well betide!"

So said, so done: nor the lady missed
One ray that broke from the ardent brow,
Nor a curl of the lips where the spirit
    kissed.

Be sure that each renewed the vow,
No morrow's sun should arise and set
And leave them then as it left them now.

But next day passed, and next day yet,
With still fresh cause to wait one day
     more
Ere each leaped over the parapet.

And still, as love's brief morning wore,
With a gentle start, half smile, half sigh,
They found love not as it seemed before.

They thought it would work infallibly,
But not in despite of heaven and earth—
The rose would blow when the storm
     passed by.

Meantime they could profit in winter's
     dearth
By winter's fruits that supplant the rose:
The world and its ways have a certain
     worth!

And to press a point while these oppose
Were a simple policy; better wait:
We lose no friends and we gain no foes.

Meantime, worse fates than a lover's fate,
Who daily may ride and pass and look
Where his lady watches behind the grate!

And she—she watched the square like a
     book
Holding one picture and only one,
Which daily to find she undertook:

When the picture was reached the book
     was done,
And she turned from the picture at night
     to scheme
Of tearing it out for herself next sun.

So weeks grew months, years—gleam by
     gleam
The glory dropped from their youth and
     love,
And both perceived they had dreamed a
     dream;

Which hovered as dreams do, still
     above,—
But who can take a dream for a truth?
Oh, hide our eyes from the next remove!

One day as the lady saw her youth
Depart, and the silver thread that
     streaked
Her hair, and, worn by the serpent's
     tooth,

The brow so puckered, the chin so
     peaked,—
And wondered who the woman was,
Hollow-eyed and haggard-cheeked,

Fronting her silent in the glass—
"Summon here," she suddenly said,
"Before the rest of my old self pass,

"Him, the Carver, a hand to aid,
Who fashions the clay no love will change,
And fixes a beauty never to fade.

"Let Robbia's craft so apt and strange
Arrest the remains of young and fair,
And rivet them while the seasons range.

"Make me a face on the window there,
Waiting as ever, mute the while,
My love to pass below in the square!

"And let me think that it may beguile
Dreary days which the dead must spend
Down in their darkness under the aisle,

"To say, 'What matters it at the end?
I did no more while my heart was warm
Than does that image, my pale-faced
     friend.'

"Where is the use of the lip's red charm,
The heaven of hair, the pride of the brow,
And the blood that blues the inside arm—

"Unless we turn, as the soul knows how,
The earthly gift to an end divine?
A lady of clay is as good, I trow."

But long ere Robbia's cornice, fine
With flowers and fruits which leaves
     enlace,
Was set where now is the empty shrine—

(And, leaning out of a bright blue space,
As a ghost might lean from a chink of sky,
The passionate pale lady's face—

Eyeing ever with earnest eye
And quick-turned neck at its breathless
  stretch,
Some one who ever is passing by—)

The Duke had sighed like the simplest
  wretch
In Florence, "Youth—my dream escapes!
Will its record stay?" And he bade them
  fetch

Some subtle moulder of brazen shapes—
"Can the soul, the will, die out of a man
Ere his body find the grave that gapes?

"John of Douay shall effect my plan,
Set me on horseback here aloft,
Alive, as the crafty sculptor can,

"In the very square I have crossed so oft!
That men may admire, when future suns
Shall touch the eyes to a purpose soft,

"While the mouth and the brow stay
  brave in bronze—
Admire and say, 'When he was alive,
How he would take his pleasure once!'

"And it shall go hard but I contrive
To listen the while and laugh in my tomb
At idleness which aspires to strive."

So! while these wait the trump of doom,
How do their spirits pass, I wonder,
Nights and days in the narrow room?

Still, I suppose, they sit and ponder
What a gift life was, ages ago,
Six steps out of the chapel yonder.

Only they see not God, I know,
Nor all that chivalry of His,
The soldier-saints who, row on row,

Burn upward each to his point of bliss—
Since, the end of life being manifest,
He had burned his way thro' the world
  to this.

I hear you reproach, "But delay was best,
For their end was a crime."—Oh, a crime
  will do
As well, I reply, to serve for a test,

As a virtue golden through and through,
Sufficient to vindicate itself
And prove its worth at a moment's view!

Must a game be played for the sake of
  pelf?
Where a button goes, 'twere an epigram
To offer the stamp of the very Guelph.

The true has no value beyond the sham:
As well the counter as coin, I submit,
When your table's a hat, and your prize,
  a dram.

Stake your counter as boldly every whit,
Venture as truly, use the same skill,
Do your best, whether winning or losing
  it,

If you choose to play!—is my principle.
Let a man contend to the uttermost
For his life's set prize, be it what it will!

The counter our lovers staked was lost
As surely as if it were lawful coin:
And the sin I impute to each frustrate
  ghost

Is, the unlit lamp and the ungirt loin,
Though the end in sight was a vice, I say.
You of the virtue, (we issue join)
How strive you? *De te, fabula!*

"Childe Roland to the Dark Tower Came"

My first thought was, he lied in every
  word,
  That hoary cripple, with malicious eye
  Askance to watch the working of his lie
On mine, and mouth scarce able to afford
Suppression of the glee that pursed and
  scored
  Its edge at one more victim gained
    thereby.

What else should he be set for, with his
staff?
  What, save to waylay with his lies,
  ensnare
  All travellers that might find him
  posted there,
And ask the road? I guessed what skull-
like laugh
Would break, what crutch 'gin write my
epitaph
  For pastime in the dusty thoroughfare,

If at his counsel I should turn aside
  Into that ominous tract which, all
  agree,
  Hides the Dark Tower. Yet acquies-
  cingly
I did turn as he pointed; neither pride
Nor hope rekindling at the end descried,
  So much as gladness that some end
  might be.

For, what with my whole world-wide
wandering,
  What with my search drawn out
  through years, my hope
  Dwindled into a ghost not fit to cope
With that obstreperous joy success would
bring,—
I hardly tried now to rebuke the spring
  My heart made, finding failure in its
  scope.

As when a sick man very near to death
  Seems dead indeed, and feels begin and
  end
  The tears and takes the farewell of
  each friend,
And hears one bid the other go, draw
breath
Freelier outside, ("since all is o'er," he
saith,
  "And the blow fallen no grieving can
  amend;")

While some discuss if near the other
graves
  Be room enough for this, and when a
  day
Suits best for carrying the corpse away,

With care about the banners, scarves and
staves,—
And still the man hears all, and only
craves
  He may not shame such tender love and
  stay.

Thus, I had so long suffered in this quest,
  Heard failure prophesied so oft, been
  writ
  So many times among "The Band"—
  to wit,
The knights who to the Dark Tower's
search addressed
Their steps—that just to fail as they,
seemed best,
  And all the doubt was now—should I
  be fit.

So, quiet as despair, I turned from him,
  That hateful cripple, out of his high-
  way
  Into the path he pointed. All the day
Had been a dreary one at best, and dim
Was settling to its close, yet shot one grim
  Red leer to see the plain catch its estray.

For mark! no sooner was I fairly found
  Pledged to the plain, after a pace or
  two,
  Than, pausing to throw backward a
  last view
To the safe road, 'twas gone; grey plain
all round:
Nothing but plain to the horizon's bound.
  I might go on; nought else remained
  to do.

So, on I went. I think I never saw
  Such starved ignoble nature; nothing
  throve;
  For flowers—as well expect a cedar
  grove!
But cockle, spurge, according to their law
Might propagate their kind, with none to
awe,
  You'd think; a burr had been a treas-
  ure-trove.

No! penury, inertness and grimace,
  In some strange sort, were the land's
    portion. "See
Or shut your eyes," said Nature
    peevishly,
"It nothing skills: I cannot help my case:
'Tis the Last Judgment's fire must cure
    this place,
  Calcine its clods and set my prisoners
    free."

If there pushed any ragged thistle-stalk
  Above its mates, the head was chopped
    —the bents
  Were jealous else. What made those
    holes and rents
In the dock's harsh swarth leaves—
    bruised as to baulk
All hope of greenness? 'tis a brute must
    walk
  Pashing their life out, with a brute's
    intents.

As for the grass, it grew as scant as hair
  In leprosy; thin dry blades pricked the
    mud
  Which underneath looked kneaded up
    with blood.
One stiff blind horse, his every bone
    a-stare,
Stood stupefied, however he came there:
  Thrust out past service from the devil's
    stud!

Alive? he might be dead for aught I know,
  With that red, gaunt and colloped neck
    a-strain,
  And shut eyes underneath the rusty
    mane;
Seldom went such grotesqueness with
    such woe;
I never saw a brute I hated so;
  He must be wicked to deserve such
    pain.

I shut my eyes and turned them on my
    heart.
  As a man calls for wine before he fights,
  I asked one draught of earlier, happier
    sights,

Ere fitly I could hope to play my part.
Think first, fight afterwards—the sol-
    dier's art:
  One taste of the old time sets all to
    rights!

Not it! I fancied Cuthbert's reddening
    face
  Beneath its garniture of curly gold,
  Dear fellow, till I almost felt him fold
An arm in mine to fix me to the place,
That way he used. Alas, one night's
    disgrace!
  Out went my heart's new fire and left
    it cold.

Giles, then, the soul of honour—there he
    stands
  Frank as ten years ago when knighted
    first.
  What honest men should dare (he said)
    he durst.
Good—but the scene shifts—faugh! what
    hangman's hands
Pin to his breast a parchment? his own
    bands
  Read it. Poor traitor, spit upon and
    curst!

Better this present than a past like that;
  Back therefore to my darkening path
    again.
  No sound, no sight as far as eye could
    strain.
Will the night send a howlet or a bat?
I asked: when something on the dismal
    flat
  Came to arrest my thoughts and change
    their train.

A sudden little river crossed my path
  As unexpected as a serpent comes.
  No sluggish tide congenial to the
    glooms—
This, as it frothed by, might have been a
    bath
For the fiend's glowing hoof—to see the
    wrath
  Of its black eddy bespate with flakes
    and spumes.

So petty yet so spiteful! all along,
　　Low scrubby alders kneeled down over
　　　it;
　　Drenched willows flung them headlong
　　　in a fit
Of mute despair, a suicidal throng:
The river which had done them all the
　　wrong,
　　Whate'er that was, rolled by, deterred
　　　no whit.

Which, while I forded,—good saints, how
　　I feared
　　To set my foot upon a dead man's
　　　cheek,
　　Each step, or feel the spear I thrust to
　　　seek
For hollows, tangled in his hair or beard!
—It may have been a water-rat I speared,
　　But, ugh! it sounded like a baby's
　　　shriek.

Glad was I when I reached the other
　　bank.
　　Now for a better country. Vain
　　　presage!
　　Who were the strugglers, what war did
　　　they wage
Whose savage trample thus could pad the
　　dank
Soil to a plash? toads in a poisoned tank,
　　Or wild cats in a red-hot iron cage—

The fight must so have seemed in that fell
　　cirque.
　　What penned them there, with all the
　　　plain to choose?
　　No foot-print leading to that horrid
　　　mews,
None out of it. Mad brewage set to
　　work
Their brains, no doubt, like galley-slaves
　　the Turk
　　Pits for his pastime, Christians against
　　　Jews.

And more than that—a furlong on—why,
　　there!
　　What bad use was that engine for, that
　　　wheel,

Or brake, not wheel—that harrow fit
　　to reel
Men's bodies out like silk? with all the
　　air
Of Tophet's tool, on earth left unaware,
　　Or brought to sharpen its rusty teeth
　　　of steel.

Then came a bit of stubbed ground, once
　　a wood,
　　Next a marsh, it would seem, and now
　　　mere earth
　　Desperate and done with; (so a fool
　　　finds mirth,
Makes a thing and then mars it, till his
　　mood
Changes and off he goes!) within a
　　rood—
　　Bog, clay and rubble, sand and stark
　　　black dearth.

Now blotches rankling, coloured gay and
　　grim,
　　Now patches where some leanness of
　　　the soil's
　　Broke into moss or substances like
　　　boils;
Then came some palsied oak, a cleft in
　　him
Like a distorted mouth that splits its rim
　　Gaping at death, and dies while it re-
　　　coils.

And just as far as ever from the end!
　　Nought in the distance but the evening,
　　　nought
　　To point my footstep further! At the
　　　thought,
A great black bird, Apollyon's bosom-
　　friend,
Sailed past, nor beat his wide wing
　　dragon-penned
　　That brushed my cap—perchance the
　　　guide I sought.

For, looking up, aware I somehow grew,
　　'Spite of the dusk, the plain had given
　　　place
　　All round to mountains—with such
　　　name to grace

Mere ugly heights and heaps now stolen
    in view.
How thus they had surprised me,—solve
    it, you!
How to get from them was no clearer
    case.

Yet half I seemed to recognise some trick
    Of mischief happened to me, God
    knows when—
    In a bad dream perhaps. Here ended,
    then,
Progress this way. When, in the very
    nick
Of giving up, one time more, came a click
    As when a trap shuts—you're inside
    the den!

Burningly it came on me all at once,
    This was the place! those two hills on
    the right,
    Crouched like two bulls locked horn in
    horn in fight;
While to the left, a tall scalped moun-
    tain . . . Dunce,
Fool, to be dozing at the very nonce,
    After a life spent training for the sight!

What in the midst lay but the Tower
    itself?
    The round squat turret, blind as the
    fool's heart,
    Built of brown stone, without a coun-
    terpart
In the whole world. The tempest's mock-
    ing elf
Points to the shipman thus the unseen
    shelf
    He strikes on, only when the timbers
    start.

Not see? because of night perhaps?—
    Why, day
    Came back again for that! before it
    left,
    The dying sunset kindled through a
    cleft:
The hills, like giants at a hunting, lay,

Chin upon hand, to see the game at bay,—
    "Now stab and end the creature—to
    the heft!"

Not hear? when noise was everywhere! it
    tolled
    Increasing like a bell. Names in my
    ears,
    Of all the lost adventurers my peers,—
How such a one was strong, and such was
    bold,
And such was fortunate, yet each of old
    Lost, lost! one moment knelled the woe
    of years.

There they stood, ranged along the hill-
    sides, met
    To view the last of me, a living frame
    For one more picture! in a sheet of
    flame
I saw them and I knew them all. And yet
Dauntless the slug-horn to my lips I set,
    And blew. *"Childe Roland to the Dark
    Tower came."*

An Epistle containing the Strange Medical Experience of Karshish, the Arab Physician

KARSHISH, the picker-up of learning's
    crumbs,
The not-incurious in God's handiwork
(This man's-flesh He hath admirably
    made,
Blown like a bubble, kneaded like a paste,
To coop up and keep down on earth a
    space
That puff of vapour from His mouth,
    man's soul)
—To Abib, all-sagacious in our art,
Breeder in me of what poor skill I boast,
Like me inquisitive how pricks and cracks
Befall the flesh through too much stress
    and strain,
Whereby the wily vapour fain would slip
Back and rejoin its source before the
    term,—
And aptest in contrivance, under God,

To baffle it by deftly stopping such:—
The vagrant Scholar to his Sage at home
Sends greeting (health and knowledge, fame with peace)
Three samples of true snake-stone—rarer still,
One of the other sort, the melon-shaped,
(But fitter, pounded fine, for charms than drugs)
And writeth now the twenty-second time.

My journeyings were brought to Jericho:
Thus I resume. Who studious in our art
Shall count a little labour unrepaid?
I have shed sweat enough, left flesh and bone
On many a flinty furlong of this land.
Also, the country-side is all on fire
With rumours of a marching hitherward:
Some say Vespasian cometh, some, his son.
A black lynx snarled and pricked a tufted ear;
Lust of my blood inflamed his yellow balls:
I cried and threw my staff and he was gone.
Twice have the robbers stripped and beaten me,
And once a town declared me for a spy,
But at the end, I reach Jerusalem,
Since this poor covert where I pass the night,
This Bethany, lies scarce the distance thence
A man with plague-sores at the third degree
Runs till he drops down dead. Thou laughest here!
'Sooth, it elates me, thus reposed and safe,
To void the stuffing of my travel-scrip
And share with thee whatever Jewry yields.
A viscid choler is observable
In tertians, I was nearly bold to say,
And falling-sickness hath a happier cure
Than our school wots of: there's a spider here

Weaves no web, watches on the ledge of tombs,
Sprinkled with mottles on an ash-grey back;
Take five and drop them . . . but who knows his mind,
The Syrian run-a-gate I trust this to?
His service payeth me a sublimate
Blown up his nose to help the ailing eye.
Best wait: I reach Jerusalem at morn,
There set in order my experiences,
Gather what most deserves, and give thee all—
Or I might add, Judæa's gum-tragacanth
Scales off in purer flakes, shines clearer-grained,
Cracks 'twixt the pestle and the porphyry,
In fine exceeds our produce. Scalp-disease
Confounds me, crossing so with leprosy—
Thou hadst admired one sort I gained at Zoar—
But zeal outruns discretion. Here I end.

Yet stay: my Syrian blinketh gratefully,
Protesteth his devotion is my price—
Suppose I write what harms not, though he steal?
I half resolve to tell thee, yet I blush,
What set me off a-writing first of all.
An itch I had, a sting to write, a tang
For, be it this town's barrenness—or else
The Man had something in the look of him—
His case has struck me far more than 'tis worth.
So, pardon if—(less presently I lose
In the great press of novelty at hand
The care and pains this somehow stole from me)
I bid thee take the thing while fresh in mind,
Almost in sight—for, wilt thou have the truth?
The very man is gone from me but now,
Whose ailment is the subject of discourse.
Thus then, and let thy better wit help all.

'Tis but a case of mania—subinduced
By epilepsy, at the turning-point
Of trance prolonged unduly some three
    days,
When, by the exhibition of some drug
Or spell, exorcization, stroke of art
Unknown to me and which 'twere well to
    know,
The evil thing out-breaking all at once
Left the man whole and sound of body
    indeed,—
But, flinging, so to speak, life's gates too
    wide,
Making a clear house of it too suddenly,
The first conceit that entered might in-
    scribe
Whatever it was minded on the wall
So plainly at that vantage, as it were,
(First come, first served) that nothing
    subsequent
Attaineth to erase those fancy-scrawls
The just-returned and new-established
    soul
Hath gotten now so thoroughly by heart
That henceforth she will read or these or
    none.
And first—the man's own firm conviction
    rests
That he was dead (in fact they buried
    him)
—That he was dead and then restored to
    life
By a Nazarene physician of his tribe:
—'Sayeth, the same bade "Rise," and he
    did rise.
"Such cases are diurnal," thou wilt cry.
Not so this figment!—not, that such a
    fume,
Instead of giving way to time and health,
Should eat itself into the life of life,
As saffron tingeth flesh, blood, bones and
    all!
For see, how he takes up the after-life.
The man—it is one Lazarus a Jew,
Sanguine, proportioned, fifty years of age,
The body's habit wholly laudable,
As much, indeed, beyond the common
    health
As he were made and put aside to show.

Think, could we penetrate by any drug
And bathe the wearied soul and worried
    flesh,
And bring it clear and fair, by three days'
    sleep!
Whence has the man the balm that
    brightens all?
This grown man eyes the world now like
    a child.
Some elders of his tribe, I should premise,
Led in their friend, obedient as a sheep,
To bear my inquisition. While they spoke,
Now sharply, now with sorrow,—told the
    case,—
He listened not except I spoke to him,
But folded his two hands and let them
    talk,
Watching the flies that buzzed: and yet
    no fool.
And that's a sample how his years must
    go.
Look if a beggar, in fixed middle-life,
Should find a treasure, can he use the
    same
With straitened habits and with tastes
    starved small,
And take at once to his impoverished
    brain
The sudden element that changes things,
That sets the undreamed-of rapture at
    his hand,
And puts the cheap old joy in the scorned
    dust?
Is he not such an one as moves to mirth—
Warily parsimonious, when no need,
Wasteful as drunkenness at undue times?
All prudent counsel as to what befits
The golden mean, is lost on such an one:
The man's fantastic will is the man's law.
So here—we'll call the treasure knowl-
    edge, say,
Increased beyond the fleshly faculty—
Heaven opened to a soul while yet on
    earth,
Earth forced on a soul's use while seeing
    Heaven.
The man is witless of the size, the sum,
The value in proportion of all things,
Or whether it be little or be much.

Discourse to him of prodigious arma-
    ments
Assembled to besiege his city now,
And of the passing of a mule with
    gourds—
'Tis one! Then take it on the other side,
Speak of some trifling fact—he will gaze
    rapt
With stupor at its very littleness,
(Far as I see)—as if in that indeed
He caught prodigious import, whole re-
    sults;
And so will turn to us the bystanders
In ever the same stupor (note this point)
That we too see not with his opened eyes.
Wonder and doubt come wrongly into
    play,
Preposterously, at cross purposes.
Should his child sicken unto death,—why,
    look
For scarce abatement of his cheerfulness,
Or pretermission of his daily craft—
While a word, gesture, glance, from that
    same child
At play or in the school or laid asleep,
Will startle him to an agony of fear,
Exasperation, just as like! demand
The reason why—"'tis but a word,"
    object—
"A gesture"—he regards thee as our lord
Who lived there in the pyramid alone,
Looked at us, dost thou mind?—when
    being young
We both would unadvisedly recite
Some charm's beginning, from that book
    of his,
Able to bid the sun throb wide and burst
All into stars, as suns grown old are wont.
Thou and the child have each a veil alike
Thrown o'er your heads, from under
    which ye both
Stretch your blind hands and trifle with
    a match
Over a mine of Greek fire, did ye know!
He holds on firmly to some thread of
    life—
(It is the life to lead perforcedly)
Which runs across some vast distracting
    orb

Of glory on either side that meagre
    thread,
Which, conscious of, he must not enter
    yet—
The spiritual life around the earthly life!
The law of that is known to him as this—
His heart and brain move there, his feet
    stay here.
So is the man perplext with impulses
Sudden to start off crosswise, not straight
    on,
Proclaiming what is right and wrong
    across,
And not along, this black thread through
    the blaze—
"It should be" balked by "here it cannot
    be"
And oft the man's soul springs into his
    face
As if he saw again and heard again
His sage that bade him "Rise" and he did
    rise.
Something, a word, a tick of the blood
    within
Admonishes—then back he sinks at once
To ashes, that was very fire before,
In sedulous recurrence to his trade
Whereby he earneth him the daily bread;
And studiously the humbler for that pride,
Professedly the faultier that he knows
God's secret, while he holds the thread
    of life.
Indeed the especial marking of the man
Is prone submission to the Heavenly
    will—
Seeing it, what it is, and why it is.
'Sayeth, he will wait patient to the last
For that same death which must restore
    his being
To equilibrium, body loosening soul
Divorced even now by premature full
    growth:
He will live, nay, it pleaseth him to live
So long as God please, and just how God
    please.
He even seeketh not to please God more
(Which meaneth, otherwise) than as God
    please.
Hence I perceive not he affects to preach

The doctrine of his sect whate'er it be,
Make proselytes as madmen thirst to do:
How can he give his neighbour the real
    ground,
His own conviction? ardent as he is—
Call his great truth a lie, why, still the
    old
"Be it as God please" reassureth him.
I probed the sore as thy disciple should—
"How, beast," said I, "this stolid care-
    lessness
Sufficeth thee, when Rome is on her march
To stamp out like a little spark thy town,
Thy tribe, thy crazy tale and thee at
    once?"
He merely looked with his large eyes on
    me.
The man is apathetic, you deduce?
Contrariwise he loves both old and young,
Able and weak—affects the very brutes
And birds—how say I? flowers of the
    field—
As a wise workman recognises tools
In a master's workshop, loving what they
    make.
Thus is the man as harmless as a lamb:
Only impatient, let him do his best,
At ignorance and carelessness and sin—
An indignation which is promptly curbed:
As when in certain travels I have feigned
To be an ignoramus in our art
According to some preconceived design,
And happed to hear the land's prac-
    titioners
Steeped in conceit sublimed by ignorance,
Prattle fantastically on disease,
Its cause and cure—and I must hold my
    peace!

Thou wilt object—why have I not ere
    this
Sought out the sage himself, the Nazarene
Who wrought this cure, inquiring at the
    source,
Conferring with the frankness that befits?
Alas! it grieveth me, the learned leech
Perished in a tumult many years ago,
Accused,—our learning's fate,—of wiz-
    ardry,

Rebellion, to the setting up a rule
And creed prodigious as described to me.
His death which happened when the
    earthquake fell
(Prefiguring, as soon appeared, the loss
To occult learning in our lord the sage
Who lived there in the pyramid alone)
Was wrought by the mad people—that's
    their wont—
On vain recourse, as I conjecture it,
To his tried virtue, for miraculous help—
How could he stop the earthquake?
    That's their way!
The other imputations must be lies:
But take one—though I loathe to give it
    thee,
In mere respect to any good man's fame!
(And after all, our patient Lazarus
Is stark mad; should we count on what
    he says?
Perhaps not: though in writing to a
    leech
'Tis well to keep back nothing of a case.)
This man so cured regards the curer
    then,
As—God forgive me—who but God him-
    self,
Creator and Sustainer of the world,
That came and dwelt in flesh on it
    awhile!
—'Sayeth that such an One was born and
    lived,
Taught, healed the sick, broke bread at
    his own house,
Then died, with Lazarus by, for aught I
    know,
And yet was . . . what I said nor choose
    repeat,
And must have so avouched himself, in
    fact,
In hearing of this very Lazarus
Who saith—but why all this of what he
    saith?
Why write of trivial matters, things of
    price
Calling at every moment for remark?
I noticed on the margin of a pool
Blue-flowering borage, the Aleppo sort,
Aboundeth, very nitrous. It is strange!

Thy pardon for this long and tedious
case,
Which, now that I review it, needs must
seem
Unduly dwelt on, prolixly set forth!
Nor I myself discern in what is writ
Good cause for the peculiar interest
And awe indeed this man has touched me
with.
Perhaps the journey's end, the weariness
Had wrought upon me first. I met him
thus:
I crossed a ridge of short sharp broken
hills
Like an old lion's cheek-teeth. Out there
came
A moon made like a face with certain
spots
Multiform, manifold and menacing:
Then a wind rose behind me. So we
met
In this old sleepy town at unaware,
The man and I. I send thee what is writ.
Regard it as a chance, a matter risked
To this ambiguous Syrian—he may lose,
Or steal, or give it thee with equal good.
Jerusalem's repose shall make amends
For time this letter wastes, thy time and
mine;
Till when, once more thy pardon and
farewell!

The very God! think, Abib; dost thou
think?
So, the All-Great, were the All-Loving
too—
So, through the thunder comes a human
voice
Saying, "O heart I made, a heart beats
here!
Face, My hands fashioned, see it in
Myself.
Thou hast no power nor may'st conceive
of Mine,
But love I gave thee, with Myself to love,
And thou must love Me who have died
for thee!"
The madman saith He said so: it is
strange.

Fra Lippo Lippi

I AM poor brother Lippo, by your leave!
You need not clap your torches to my
face.
Zooks, what's to blame? you think you
see a monk!
What, it's past midnight, and you go the
rounds,
And here you catch me at an alley's end
Where sportive ladies leave their doors
ajar?
The Carmine's my cloister: hunt it up,
Do,—harry out, if you must show your
zeal,
Whatever rat, there, haps on his wrong
hole,
And nip each softling of a wee white
mouse,
Weke, weke, that's crept to keep him
company!
Aha, you know your betters? Then,
you'll take
Your hand away that's fiddling on my
throat,
And please to know me likewise. Who
am I?
Why, one, sir, who is lodging with a
friend
Three streets off—he's a certain . . .
how d'ye call?
Master—a . . . Cosimo of the Medici,
In the house that caps the corner. Boh!
you were best!
Remember and tell me, the day you're
hanged,
How you affected such a gullet's-gripe!
But you, sir, it concerns you that your
knaves
Pick up a manner nor discredit you.
Zooks, are we pilchards, that they sweep
the streets
And count fair prize what comes into
their net?
He's Judas to a tittle, that man is!
Just such a face! why, sir, you make
amends.
Lord, I'm not angry! Bid your hang-
dogs go

Drink out this quarter-florin to the health
Of the munificent House that harbours
    me
(And many more beside, lads! more
    beside!)
And all's come square again. I'd like his
    face—
His, elbowing on his comrade in the door
With the pike and lantern,—for the slave
    that holds
John Baptist's head a-dangle by the hair
With one hand ("look you, now," as who
    should say)
And his weapon in the other, yet un-
    wiped!
It's not your chance to have a bit of chalk,
A wood-coal or the like? or you should
    see!
Yes, I'm the painter, since you style me so.
What, brother Lippo's doings, up and
    down,
You know them and they take you? like
    enough!
I saw the proper twinkle in your eye—
'Tell you, I liked your looks at very first.
Let's sit and set things straight now, hip
    to haunch.
Here's spring come, and the nights one
    makes up bands
To roam the town and sing out carnival,
And I've been three weeks shut within my
    mew,
A-painting for the great man, saints and
    saints
And saints again. I could not paint all
    night—
Ouf! I leaned out of window for fresh
    air.
There came a hurry of feet and little
    feet,
A sweep of lute-strings, laughs, and
    whiffs of song,—
Flower o' the broom,
Take away love, and our earth is a tomb!
Flower o' the quince,
*I let Lisa go, and what good's in life
    since?*
Flower o' the thyme—and so on. Round
    they went.

Scarce had they turned the corner when
    a titter
Like the skipping of rabbits by moonlight,
    —three slim shapes—
And a face that looked up . . . zooks, sir,
    flesh and blood,
That's all I'm made of! Into shreds it
    went,
Curtain and counterpane and coverlet,
All the bed-furniture—a dozen knots,
There was a ladder! down I let myself,
Hands and feet, scrambling somehow, and
    so dropped,
And after them. I came up with the fun
Hard by Saint Laurence, hail fellow, well
    met,—
Flower o' the rose,
*If I've been merry, what matter who
    knows?*
And so as I was stealing back again
To get to bed and have a bit of sleep
Ere I rise up to-morrow and go work
On Jerome knocking at his poor old
    breast
With his great round stone to subdue the
    flesh,
You snap me of the sudden. Ah, I see!
Though your eye twinkles still, you shake
    your head—
Mine's shaved,—a monk, you say—the
    sting's in that!
If Master Cosimo announced himself,
Mum's the word naturally; but a monk!
Come, what am I a beast for? tell us,
    now!
I was a baby when my mother died
And father died and left me in the street.
I starved there, God knows how, a year
    or two
On fig skins, melon-parings, rinds and
    shucks,
Refuse and rubbish. One fine frosty day
My stomach being empty as your hat,
The wind doubled me up and down I
    went.
Old Aunt Lapaccia trussed me with one
    hand,
(Its fellow was a stinger as I knew)
And so along the wall, over the bridge,

By the straight cut to the convent. Six
    words, there,
While I stood munching my first bread
    that month:
"So, boy, you're minded," quoth the good
    fat father
Wiping his own mouth, 'twas refection-
    time,—
"To quit this very miserable world?
Will you renounce" . . . The mouthful
    of bread? thought I;
By no means! Brief, they made a monk
    of me;
I did renounce the world, its pride and
    greed,
Palace, farm, villa, shop and banking-
    house,
Trash, such as these poor devils of Medici
Have given their hearts to—all at eight
    years old.
Well, sir, I found in time, you may be
    sure,
'Twas not for nothing—the good bellyful,
The warm serge and the rope that goes all
    round,
And day-long blessed idleness beside!
"Let's see what the urchin's fit for"—
    that came next.
Not overmuch their way, I must confess.
Such a to-do! they tried me with their
    books.
Lord, they'd have taught me Latin in
    pure waste!
Flower o' the clove,
All the Latin I construe is, "amo" I love!
But, mind you, when a boy starves in the
    streets
Eight years together, as my fortune was,
Watching folk's faces to know who will
    fling
The bit of half-stripped grape-bunch he
    desires,
And who will curse or kick him for his
    pains—
Which gentleman processional and fine,
Holding a candle to the Sacrament
Will wink and let him lift a plate and
    catch
The droppings of the wax to sell again,

Or holla for the Eight and have him
    whipped,—
How say I?—nay, which dog bites, which
    lets drop
His bone from the heap of offal in the
    street,—
Why, soul and sense of him grow sharp
    alike,
He learns the look of things, and none
    the less
For admonitions from the hunger-pinch.
I had a store of such remarks, be sure,
Which, after I found leisure, turned to
    use:
I drew men's faces on my copy-books,
Scrawled them within the antiphonary's
    marge,
Joined legs and arms to the long music-
    notes,
Found nose and eyes and chin for A's and
    B's,
And made a string of pictures of the
    world
Betwixt the ins and outs of verb and noun,
On the wall, the bench, the door. The
    monks looked black.
"Nay," quoth the Prior, "turn him out,
    d'ye say?
In no wise. Lose a crow and catch a lark.
What if at last we get our man of parts,
We Carmelites, like those Camaldolese
And Preaching Friars, to do our church
    up fine
And put the front on it that ought to
    be!"
And hereupon they bade me daub away.
Thank you! my head being crammed,
    their walls a blank,
Never was such prompt disemburdening.
First, every sort of monk, the black and
    white,
I drew them, fat and lean: then, folks
    at church,
From good old gossips waiting to confess
Their cribs of barrel-droppings, candle-
    ends,—
To the breathless fellow at the altar-foot,
Fresh from his murder, safe and sitting
    there

With the little children round him in a
row
Of admiration, half for his beard and half
For that white anger of his victim's son
Shaking a fist at him with one fierce arm,
Signing himself with the other because of
Christ
(Whose sad face on the cross sees only
this
After the passion of a thousand years)
Till some poor girl, her apron o'er her
head
Which the intense eyes looked through,
came at eve
On tip-toe, said a word, dropped in a loaf,
Her pair of earrings and a bunch of
flowers
The brute took growling, prayed, and
then was gone.
I painted all, then cried " 'tis ask and
have—
Choose, for more's ready!"—laid the
ladder flat,
And showed my covered bit of cloister-
wall.
The monks closed in a circle and praised
loud
Till checked,—taught what to see and not
to see,
Being simple bodies,—"that's the very
man!
Look at the boy who stoops to pat the
dog!
That woman's like the Prior's niece who
comes
To care about his asthma: it's the life!"
But there my triumph's straw-fire flared
and funked—
Their betters took their turn to see and
say:
The Prior and the learned pulled a face
And stopped all that in no time. "How?
what's here?
Quite from the mark of painting, bless us
all!
Faces, arms, legs and bodies like the
true
As much as pea and pea! it's devil's-
game!

Your business is not to catch men with
show,
With homage to the perishable clay,
But lift them over it, ignore it all,
Make them forget there's such a thing as
flesh.
Your business is to paint the souls of
men—
Man's soul, and it's a fire, smoke . . . no
it's not . . .
It's vapour done up like a new-born
babe—
(In that shape when you die it leaves your
mouth)
It's . . . well, what matters talking, it's
the soul!
Give us no more of body than shows soul!
Here's Giotto, with his Saint a-praising
God,
That sets you praising,—why not stop
with him?
Why put all thoughts of praise out of our
heads
With wonder at lines, colours, and what
not?
Paint the soul, never mind the legs and
arms!
Rub all out, try at it a second time.
Oh, that white smallish female with the
breasts,
She's just my niece . . . Herodias, I
would say,—
Who went and danced and got men's
heads cut off—
Have it all out!" Now, is this sense, I
ask?
A fine way to paint soul, by painting body
So ill, the eye can't stop there, must go
further
And can't fare worse! Thus, yellow does
for white
When what you put for yellow's simply
black,
And any sort of meaning looks intense
When all beside itself means and looks
naught.
Why can't a painter lift each foot in turn,
Left foot and right foot, go a double
step,

Make his flesh liker and his soul more
like,
Both in their order? Take the prettiest
face,
The Prior's niece . . . patron-saint—is it
so pretty
You can't discover if it means hope,
fear,
Sorrow or joy? won't beauty go with
these?
Suppose I've made her eyes all right and
blue,
Can't I take breath and try to add life's
flash,
And then add soul and heighten them
threefold?
Or say there's beauty with no soul at
all—
(I never saw it—put the case the
same—)
If you get simple beauty and naught
else,
You get about the best thing God in-
vents,—
That's somewhat. And you'll find the
soul you have missed,
Within yourself when you return Him
thanks,
"Rub all out!" Well, well, there's my
life, in short.
And so the thing has gone on ever since.
I'm grown a man no doubt, I've broken
bounds—
You should not take a fellow eight years
old
And make him swear to never kiss the
girls.
I'm my own master, paint now as I
please—
Having a friend, you see, in the Corner-
house!
Lord, it's fast holding by the rings in
front—
Those great rings serve more purposes
than just
To plant a flag in, or tie up a horse!
And yet the old schooling sticks, the old
grave eyes
Are peeping o'er my shoulder as I work,

The heads shake still—"It's art's decline,
my son!
You're not of the true painters, great and
old;
Brother Angelico's the man, you'll find;
Brother Lorenzo stands his single peer:
Fag on at flesh, you'll never make the
third!"
Flower o' the pine,
You keep your mistr . . . manners, and
I'll stick to mine!
I'm not the third, then: bless us, they
must know!
Don't you think they're the likeliest to
know,
They with their Latin? so, I swallow my
rage,
Clench my teeth, suck my lips in tight,
and paint
To please them—sometimes do, and
sometimes don't,
For, doing most, there's pretty sure to
come
A turn, some warm eve finds me at my
saints—
A laugh, a cry, the business of the world—
(*Flower o' the peach,*
Death for us all, and his own life for
each!)
And my whole soul revolves, the cup runs
over,
The world and life's too big to pass for
a dream,
And I do these wild things in sheer
despite,
And play the fooleries you catch me at,
In pure rage! the old mill-horse, out at
grass
After hard years, throws up his stiff heels
so,
Although the miller does not preach to
him
The only good of grass is to make chaff.
What would men have? Do they like
grass or no—
May they or mayn't they? all I want's
the thing
Settled for ever one way: as it is,
You tell too many lies and hurt yourself.

You don't like what you only like too
    much,
You do like what, if given you at your
    word,
You find abundantly detestable.
For me, I think I speak as I was taught—
I always see the garden and God there
A-making man's wife—and, my lesson
    learned,
The value and significance of flesh,
I can't unlearn ten minutes afterwards.

    You understand me: I'm a beast, I
    know.
But see, now—why, I see as certainly
As that the morning-star's about to shine,
What will hap some day. We've a
    youngster here
Comes to our convent, studies what I do,
Slouches and stares and lets no atom
    drop—
His name is Guidi—he'll not mind the
    monks—
They call him Hulking Tom, he lets them
    talk—
He picks my practice up—he'll paint
    apace,
I hope so—though I never live so long,
I know what's sure to follow. You be
    judge!
You speak no Latin more than I, belike—
However, you're my man, you've seen the
    world
—The beauty and the wonder and the
    power,
The shapes of things, their colours, lights
    and shades,
Changes, surprises,—and God made it
    all!
—For what? do you feel thankful, ay or
    no,
For this fair town's face, yonder river's
    line,
The mountain round it and the sky
    above,
Much more the figures of man, woman,
    child,
These are the frame to? What's it all
    about?

To be passed over, despised? or dwelt
    upon,
Wondered at? oh, this last of course!—
    you say.
But why not do as well as say,—paint
    these
Just as they are, careless what comes of
    it?
God's works—paint any one, and count
    it crime
To let a truth slip. Don't object, "His
    works
Are here already—nature is complete:
Suppose you reproduce her—(which you
    can't)
There's no advantage! you must beat her,
    then."
For, don't you mark, we're made so that
    we love
First when we see them painted, things we
    have passed
Perhaps a hundred times nor cared to see;
And so they are better, painted—better
    to us,
Which is the same thing. Art was given
    for that—
God uses us to help each other so,
Lending our minds out. Have you
    noticed, now,
Your cullion's hanging face? A bit of
    chalk,
And trust me but you should, though!
    How much more,
If I drew higher things with the same
    truth!
That were to take the Prior's pulpit-
    place,
Interpret God to all of you! oh, oh,
It makes me mad to see what men shall do
And we in our graves! This world's no
    blot for us,
Nor blank—it means intensely, and
    means good:
To find its meaning is my meat and drink.
"Ay, but you don't so instigate to prayer!"
Strikes in the Prior: "when your mean-
    ing's plain
It does not say to folks—remember
    matins,

Or, mind you fast next Friday." Why,
    for this
What need of art at all? A skull and
    bones,
Two bits of stick nailed cross-wise, or,
    what's best,
A bell to chime the hour with, does as
    well.
I painted a Saint Laurence six months
    since
At Prato, splashed the fresco in fine style:
"How looks my painting, now the scaf-
    fold's down?"
I ask a brother: "Hugely," he returns—
"Already not one phiz of your three slaves
That turn the Deacon off his toasted side,
But's scratched and prodded to our
    heart's content,
The pious people have so eased their own
When coming to say prayers there in a
    rage:
We get on fast to see the bricks beneath.
Expect another job this time next year,
For pity and religion grow i' the crowd—
Your painting serves its purpose!" Hang
    the fools!

—That is—you'll not mistake an idle
    word
Spoke in a huff by a poor monk, God wot,
Tasting the air this spicy night which
    turns
The unaccustomed head like Chianti
    wine!
Oh, the church knows! don't misreport
    me, now!
It's natural a poor monk out of bounds
Should have his apt word to excuse him-
    self:
And hearken how I plot to make amends.
I have bethought me: I shall paint a piece
. . . There's for you! Give me six
    months, then go, see
Something in Sant' Ambrogio's! Bless
    the nuns!
They want a cast of my office. I shall
    paint
God in the midst, Madonna and her babe,
Ringed by a bowery, flowery angel-brood,

Lilies and vestments and white faces,
    sweet
As puff on puff of grated orris-root
When ladies crowd to church at mid-
    summer.
And then in the front, of course a saint
    or two—
Saint John, because he saves the Floren-
    tines,
Saint Ambrose, who puts down in black
    and white
The convent's friends and gives them a
    long day,
And Job, I must have him there past mis-
    take,
The man of Uz, (and Us without the z,
Painters who need his patience.) Well,
    all these
Secured at their devotions, up shall come
Out of a corner when you least expect,
As one by a dark stair into a great light,
Music and talking, who but Lippo! I!—
Mazed, motionless and moon-struck—
    I'm the man!
Back I shrink—what is this I see and
    hear?
I, caught up with my monk's things by
    mistake,
My old serge gown and rope that goes all
    round,
I, in this presence, this pure company!
Where's a hole, where's a corner for
    escape?
Then steps a sweet angelic slip of a
    thing
Forward, puts out a soft palm—"Not so
    fast!"
—Addresses the celestial presence, "nay—
He made you and devised you, after all,
Though he's none of you! Could Saint
    John there, draw—
His camel-hair make up a painting-
    brush?
We come to brother Lippo for all that,
Iste perfecit opus!" So, all smile—
I shuffle sideways with my blushing face
Under the cover of a hundred wings
Thrown like a spread of kirtles when
    you're gay

And play hot cockles, all the doors being
    shut,
Till, wholly unexpected, in there pops
The hothead husband! Thus I scuttle off
To some safe bench behind, not letting go
The palm of her, the little lily thing
That spoke the good word for me in the
    nick,
Like the Prior's niece . . . Saint Lucy, I
    would say.
And so all's saved for me, and for the
    church
A pretty picture gained. Go, six months
    hence!
Your hand, sir, and good-bye: no lights,
    no lights!
The street's hushed, and I know my own
    way back,
Don't fear me! There's the grey begin-
    ning. Zooks!

The Bishop orders his Tomb at Saint Praxed's Church

[ROME, 15—.]

VANITY, saith the preacher, vanity!
Draw round my bed: is Anselm keeping
    back?
Nephews—sons mine . . . ah God, I
    know not! Well—
She, men would have to be your mother
    once,
Old Gandolf envied me, so fair she was!
What's done is done, and she is dead
    beside,
Dead long ago, and I am Bishop since,
And as she died so must we die ourselves,
And thence ye may perceive the world's a
    dream.
Life, how and what is it? As here I lie
In this state-chamber, dying by degrees,
Hours and long hours in the dead night,
    I ask
"Do I live, am I dead?" Peace, peace
    seems all.
Saint Praxed's ever was the church for
    peace;

And so, about this tomb of mine. I
    fought
With tooth and nail to save my niche, ye
    know:
—Old Gandolf cozened me, despite my
    care;
Shrewd was that snatch from out the
    corner South
He graced his carrion with, God curse the
    same!
Yet still my niche is not so cramped but
    thence
One sees the pulpit o' the epistle-side,
And somewhat of the choir, those silent
    seats,
And up into the aery dome where live
The angels, and a sunbeam's sure to
    lurk:
And I shall fill my slab of basalt there,
And 'neath my tabernacle take my rest,
With those nine columns round me, two
    and two,
The odd one at my feet where Anselm
    stands:
Peach-blossom marble all, the rare, the
    ripe
As fresh-poured red wine of a mighty
    pulse
—Old Gandolf with his paltry onion-
    stone,
Put me where I may look at him! True
    peach,
Rosy and flawless: how I earned the
    prize!
Draw close: that conflagration of my
    church
—What then? So much was saved if
    aught were missed!
My sons, ye would not be my death? Go
    dig
The white-grape vineyard where the oil-
    press stood,
Drop water gently till the surface sinks,
And if ye find . . . Ah, God I know not,
    I! . . .
Bedded in store of rotten figleaves soft,
And corded up in a tight olive-frail,
Some lump, ah God, of *lapis lazuli*,
Big as a Jew's head cut off at the nape,

Blue as a vein o'er the Madonna's
  breast . . .
Sons, all have I bequeathed you, villas, all,
That brave Frascati villa with its bath,
So, let the blue lump poise between my
  knees,
Like God the Father's globe on both His
  hands
Ye worship in the Jesu Church so gay,
For Gandolf shall not choose but see and
  burst!
Swift as a weaver's shuttle fleet our
  years:
Man goeth to the grave, and where is he?
Did I say basalt for my slab, sons?
  Black—
'Twas ever antique-black I meant! How
  else
Shall ye contrast my frieze to come be-
  neath?
The bas-relief in bronze ye promised me,
Those Pans and Nymphs ye wot of, and
  perchance
Some tripod, thyrsus, with a vase or so,
The Saviour at his sermon on the mount,
Saint Praxed in a glory, and one Pan
Ready to twitch the Nymph's last gar-
  ment off,
And Moses with the tables . . . but I
  know
Ye mark me not! What do they whisper
  thee,
Child of my bowels, Anselm? Ah, ye
  hope
To revel down my villas while I gasp
Bricked o'er with beggar's mouldy traver-
  tine
Which Gandolf from his tomb-top
  chuckles at!
Nay, boys, ye love me—all of jasper, then!
'Tis jasper ye stand pledged to, lest I
  grieve
My bath must needs be left behind, alas!
One block, pure green as a pistachio-nut,
There's plenty jasper somewhere in the
  world—
And have I not Saint Praxed's ear to pray
Horses for ye, and brown Greek manu-
  scripts,

And mistresses with great smooth marbly
  limbs?
—That's if ye carve my epitaph aright,
Choice Latin, picked phrase, Tully's every
  word,
No gaudy ware like Gandolf's second
  line—
Tully, my masters? Ulpian serves his
  need!
And then how I shall lie through cen-
  turies,
And hear the blessed mutter of the mass,
And see God made and eaten all day long,
And feel the steady candle-flame, and
  taste
Good strong thick stupefying incense-
  smoke!
For as I lie here, hours of the dead night,
Dying in state and by such slow degrees,
I fold my arms as if they clasped a
  crook,
And stretch my feet forth straight as
  stone can point,
And let the bedclothes for a mortcloth
  drop
Into great laps and folds of sculptor's-
  work:
And as yon tapers dwindle, and strange
  thoughts
Grow, with a certain humming in my
  ears,
About the life before I lived this life,
And this life too, popes, cardinals and
  priests,
Saint Praxed at his sermon on the mount,
Your tall pale mother with her talking
  eyes,
And new-found agate urns as fresh as
  day,
And marble's language, Latin pure, dis-
  creet,
—Aha, ELUCESCEBAT quoth our friend?
No Tully, said I, Ulpian at the best!
Evil and brief hath been my pilgrimage.
All *lapis,* all, sons! Else I give the Pope
My villas: will ye ever eat my heart?
Ever your eyes were as a lizard's quick,
They glitter like your mother's for my
  soul,

Or ye would heighten my impoverished
frieze,
Piece out its starved design, and fill my
vase
With grapes, and add a vizor and a Term,
And to the tripod ye would tie a lynx
That in his struggle throws the thyrsus
down,
To comfort me on my entablature
Whereon I am to lie till I must ask
"Do I live, am I dead?" There, leave me,
there!
For ye have stabbed me with ingratitude
To death—ye wish it—God, ye wish it!
Stone—
Gritstone, a-crumble! Clammy squares
which sweat
As if the corpse they keep were oozing
through—
And no more *lapis* to delight the world!
Well, go! I bless ye. Fewer tapers there,
But in a row: and, going, turn your backs
—Ay, like departing altar-ministrants,
And leave me in my church, the church
for peace,
That I may watch at leisure if he leers—
Old Gandolf, at me, from his onion-stone,
As still he envied me, so fair she was!

Bishop Blougram's Apology

No more wine? then we'll push back
chairs and talk.
A final glass for me, though: cool, i' faith!
We ought to have our Abbey back, you
see.
It's different, preaching in basilicas,
And doing duty in some masterpiece
Like this of brother Pugin's, bless his
heart!
I doubt if they're half baked, those chalk
rosettes,
Ciphers and stucco-twiddlings every-
where;
It's just like breathing in a lime-kiln: eh?
These hot long ceremonies of our church
Cost us a little—oh, they pay the price,
You take me—amply pay it! Now, we'll
talk.

So, you despise me, Mr. Gigadibs.
No deprecation,—nay, I beg you, sir!
Beside 'tis our engagement: don't you
know,
I promised, if you'd watch a dinner out,
We'd see truth dawn together?—truth
that peeps
Over the glass's edge when dinner's done,
And body gets its sop and holds its
noise
And leaves soul free a little. Now's the
time—
'Tis break of day! You do despise me
then.
And if I say, "despise me,"—never fear—
I know you do not in a certain sense—
Not in my arm-chair for example: here,
I well imagine you respect my place
(Status, *entourage*, worldly circum-
stance)
Quite to its value—very much indeed
—Are up to the protesting eyes of you
In pride at being seated here for once—
You'll turn it to such capital account!
When somebody, through years and years
to come,
Hints of the bishop,—names me—that's
enough—
"Blougram? I knew him"—(into it you
slide)
"Dined with him once, a Corpus Christi
Day,
All alone, we two—he's a clever man—
And after dinner,—why, the wine you
know,—
Oh, there was wine, and good!—what
with the wine . . .
'Faith, we began upon all sorts of talk!
He's no bad fellow, Blougram—he had
seen
Something of mine he relished—some re-
view—
He's quite above their humbug in his
heart,
Half-said as much, indeed—the thing's
his trade—
I warrant, Blougram's sceptical at
times—
How otherwise? I liked him, I confess!"

Che che, my dear sir, as we say at Rome,
Don't you protest now! It's fair give
    and take;
You have had your turn and spoken your
    home-truths:
The hand's mine now, and here you fol-
    low suit.

    Thus much conceded, still the first fact
      stays—
You do despise me; your ideal of life
Is not the bishop's—you would not be I—
You would like better to be Goethe,
    now,
Or Buonaparte—or, bless me, lower still,
Count D'Orsay,—so you did what you
    preferred,
Spoke as you thought, and, as you cannot
    help,
Believed or disbelieved, no matter what,
So long as on that point, whate'er it was,
You loosed your mind, were whole and
    sole yourself.
—That, my ideal never can include,
Upon that element of truth and worth
Never be based! for say they make me
    Pope
(They can't—suppose it for our argu-
    ment)
Why, there I'm at my tether's end—I've
    reached
My height, and not a height which pleases
    you.
An unbelieving Pope won't do, you say.
It's like those eerie stories nurses tell,
Of how some actor on a stage played
    Death,
With pasteboard crown, sham orb and
    tinselled dart,
And called himself the monarch of the
    world,
Then, going in the tire-room afterward
Because the play was done, to shift him-
    self,
Got touched upon the sleeve familiarly
The moment he had shut the closet door
By Death himself. Thus God might
    touch a Pope
At unawares, ask what his baubles mean,

And whose part he presumed to play just
    now?
Best be yourself, imperial, plain and true!

So, drawing comfortable breath again,
You weigh and find, whatever more or
    less
I boast of my ideal realized
Is nothing in the balance when opposed
To your ideal, your grand simple life,
Of which you will not realize one jot.
I am much, you are nothing; you would
    be all,
I would be merely much—you beat me
    there.

No, friend, you do not beat me,—hearken
    why.
The common problem, yours, mine, every
    one's,
Is not to fancy what were fair in life
Provided it could be,—but, finding first
What may be, then find how to make it
    fair
Up to our means—a very different thing!
No abstract intellectual plan of life
Quite irrespective of life's plainest laws,
But one, a man, who is man and nothing
    more,
May lead within a world which (by your
    leave)
Is Rome or London—not Fool's-paradise.
Embellish Rome, idealize away,
Make paradise of London if you can,
You're welcome, nay, you're wise.

               A simile!
  We mortals cross the ocean of this
    world
Each in his average cabin of a life—
The best's not big, the worst yields elbow-
    room.
Now for our six months' voyage—how
    prepare?
You come on shipboard with a landsman's
    list
Of things he calls convenient—so they
    are!
An India screen is pretty furniture,

A piano-forte is a fine resource,
All Balzac's novels occupy one shelf,
The new edition fifty volumes long;
And little Greek books, with the funny
    type
They get up well at Leipsic, fill the next—
Go on! slabbed marble, what a bath it
    makes!
And Parma's pride, the Jerome, let us
    add!
'Twere pleasant could Correggio's fleet-
    ing glow
Hang full in face of one where'er one
    roams,
Since he more than the others brings with
    him
Italy's self,—the marvellous Moden-
    ese!—
Yet was not on your list before, perhaps.

—Alas! friend, here's the agent . . . is't
    the name?
The captain, or whoever's master here—
You see him screw his face up; what's his
    cry
Ere you set foot on shipboard? "Six feet
    square!"
If you won't understand what six feet
    mean,
Compute and purchase stores accord-
    ingly—
And if in pique because he overhauls
Your Jerome, piano, bath, you come on
    board
Bare—why, you cut a figure at the first
While sympathetic landsmen see you off;
Not afterwards, when, long ere half seas
    over,
You peep up from your utterly naked
    boards
Into some snug and well-appointed berth,
Like mine, for instance (try the cooler
    jug—
Put back the other, but don't jog the ice)
And mortified you mutter, "Well and
    good—
He sits enjoying his sea-furniture—
'Tis stout and proper, and there's store
    of it,

Though I've the better notion, all agree,
Of fitting rooms up! Hang the carpenter,
Neat ship-shape fixings and contriv-
    ances—
I would have brought my Jerome, frame
    and all!"
And meantime you bring nothing: never
    mind—
You've proved your artist-nature: what
    you don't,
You might bring, so despise me, as I say.

    Now come, let's backward to the
      starting-place.
See my way: we're two college friends,
    suppose—
Prepare together for our voyage, then,
Each note and check the other in his
    work,—
Here's mine, a bishop's outfit; criticize!
What's wrong? why won't you be a bishop
    too?

    Why, first, you don't believe, you don't
      and can't,
(Not statedly, that is, and fixedly
And absolutely and exclusively)
In any revelation called divine.
No dogmas nail your faith—and what
    remains
But say so, like the honest man you are?
First, therefore, overhaul theology!
Nay, I too, not a fool, you please to think,
Must find believing every whit as hard,
And if I do not frankly say as much,
The ugly consequence is clear enough.

    Now, wait, my friend: well, I do not
      believe—
If you'll accept no faith that is not fixed,
Absolute and exclusive, as you say.
You're wrong—I mean to prove it in due
    time.
Meanwhile, I know where difficulties lie
I could not, cannot solve, nor ever shall,
So give up hope accordingly to solve—
(To you, and over the wine). Our dog-
    mas then
With both of us, though in unlike degree,

Missing full credence—overboard with
  them!
I mean to meet you on your own
  premise—
Good, there go mine in company with
  yours!

And now what are we? unbelievers
  both,
Calm and complete, determinately fixed
To-day, to-morrow, and for ever, pray?
You'll guarantee me that? Not so, I
  think!
In no wise! all we've gained is, that be-
  lief,
As unbelief before, shakes us by fits,
Confounds us like its predecessor.
  Where's
The gain? how can we guard our un-
  belief,
Make it bear fruit to us?—the problem
  here.
Just when we are safest, there's a sunset-
  touch,
A fancy from a flower-bell, some one's
  death,
A chorus-ending from Euripides,—
And that's enough for fifty hopes and
  fears
As old and new at once as Nature's self,
To rap and knock and enter in our soul,
Take hands and dance there, a fantastic
  ring,
Round the ancient idol, on his base
  again,—
The grand Perhaps! We look on help-
  lessly,—
There the old misgivings, crooked ques-
  tions are—
This good God,—what he could do, if
  he would,
Would, if he could—then must have done
  long since:
If so, when, where, and how? some way
  must be,—
Once feel about, and soon or late you hit
Some sense, in which it might be, after all.
Why not, "The Way, the Truth, the
  Life?"

—That way
Over the mountain, which who stands
  upon
Is apt to doubt if it be indeed a road;
While if he views it from the waste itself,
Up goes the line there, plain from base to
  brow,
Not vague, mistakeable! what's a break
  or two
Seen from the unbroken desert either
  side?
And then (to bring in fresh philosophy)
What if the breaks themselves should
  prove at last
The most consummate of contrivances
To train a man's eye, teach him what is
  faith?
And so we stumble at truth's very test!
All we have gained then by our unbelief
Is a life of doubt diversified by faith,
For one of faith diversified by doubt:
We called the chess-board white,—we call
  it black.

"Well," you rejoin, "the end's no
  worse, at least;
We've reason for both colours on the
  board:
Why not confess, then, where I drop the
  faith
And you the doubt, that I'm as right as
  you?"

Because, friend, in the next place, this
  being so,
And both things even,—faith and unbelief
Left to a man's choice,—we'll proceed a
  step,
Returning to our image, which I like.

A man's choice, yes—but a cabin-
  passenger's—
The man made for the special life of the
  world—
Do you forget him? I remember though!
Consult our ship's conditions and you
  find
One and but one choice suitable to all,
The choice, that you unluckily prefer,

Turning things topsy-turvy—they or it
Going to the ground. Belief or unbelief
Bears upon life, determines its whole
    course,
Begins at its beginning. See the world
Such as it is,—you made it not, nor I;
I mean to take it as it is,—and you
Not so you'll take it,—though you get
    nought else.
I know the special kind of life I like,
What suits the most my idiosyncrasy,
Brings out the best of me and bears me
    fruit
In power, peace, pleasantness and length
    of days.
I find that positive belief does this
For me, and unbelief, no whit of this.
—For you, it does, however?—that we'll
    try!
'Tis clear, I cannot lead my life, at least,
Induce the world to let me peaceably,
Without declaring at the outset, "Friends,
I absolutely and peremptorily
Believe!"—I say, faith is my waking life.
One sleeps, indeed, and dreams at in-
    tervals,
We know, but waking's the main point
    with us,
And my provision's for life's waking
    part.
Accordingly, I use heart, head and hands
All day, I build, scheme, study and make
    friends;
And when night overtakes me, down I lie,
Sleep, dream a little, and get done with it,
The sooner the better, to begin afresh.
What's midnight's doubt before the day-
    spring's faith?
You, the philosopher, that disbelieve,
That recognize the night, give dreams
    their weight—
To be consistent you should keep your
    bed,
Abstain from healthy acts that prove you
    a man,
For fear you drowse perhaps at un-
    awares!
And certainly at night you'll sleep and
    dream,

Live through the day and bustle as you
    please.
And so you live to sleep as I to wake,
To unbelieve as I to still believe?
Well, and the common sense o' the world
    calls you
Bed-ridden,—and its good things come
    to me.
Its estimation, which is half the fight,
That's the first cabin-comfort I secure—
The next . . . but you perceive with half
    an eye!
Come, come, it's best believing, if we
    may—
You can't but own that!

             Next, concede again—
If once we choose belief, on all accounts
We can't be too decisive in our faith,
Conclusive and exclusive in its terms,
To suit the world which gives us the good
    things.
In every man's career are certain points
Whereon he dares not be indifferent;
The world detects him clearly, if he dare,
As baffled at the game, and losing life.
He may care little or he may care much
For riches, honour, pleasure, work, re-
    pose,
Since various theories of life and life's
Success are extant which might easily
Comport with either estimate of these;
And whoso chooses wealth or poverty,
Labour or quiet, is not judged a fool
Because his fellows would choose other-
    wise:
We let him choose upon his own account
So long as he's consistent with his choice.
But certain points, left wholly to himself,
When once a man has arbitrated on,
We say he must succeed there or go
    hang.
Thus, he should wed the woman he loves
    most
Or needs most, whatsoe'er the love or
    need—
For he can't wed twice. Then, he must
    avouch
Or follow, at the least, sufficiently,

The form of faith his conscience holds the
    best,
Whate'er the process of conviction was:
For nothing can compensate his mistake
On such a point, the man himself being
    judge—
He cannot wed twice, nor twice lose his
    soul.

    Well now, there's one great form of
    Christian faith
I happened to be born in—which to teach
Was given me as I grew up, on all hands,
As best and readiest means of living by;
The same on examination being proved
The most pronounced moreover, fixed,
    precise
And absolute form of faith in the whole
    world—
Accordingly, most potent of all forms
For working on the world. Observe, my
    friend,
Such as you know me, I am free to say,
In these hard latter days which hamper
    one,
Myself, by no immoderate exercise
Of intellect and learning, and the tact
To let external forces work for me,
—Bid the street's stones be bread and they
    are bread,
Bid Peter's creed, or, rather, Hilde-
    brand's,
Exalt me o'er my fellows in the world
And make my life an ease and joy and
    pride,
It does so,—which for me's a great point
    gained,
Who have a soul and body that exact
A comfortable care in many ways.
There's power in me and will to dom-
    inate
Which I must exercise, they hurt me else:
In many ways I need mankind's respect,
Obedience, and the love that's born of
    fear:
While at the same time, there's a taste
    I have,
A toy of soul, a titillating thing,
Refuses to digest these dainties crude.

The naked life is gross till clothed upon:
I must take what men offer, with a grace
As though I would not, could I help it,
    take!
An uniform I wear though over-rich—
Something imposed on me, no choice of
    mine;
No fancy-dress worn for pure fancy's sake
And despicable therefore! now folk kneel
And kiss my hand—of course the
    Church's hand.
Thus I am made, thus life is best for
    me,
And thus that it should be I have pro-
    cured;
And thus it could not be another way,
I venture to imagine.

                    You'll reply,
So far my choice, no doubt, is a success;
But were I made of better elements,
With nobler instincts, purer tastes, like
    you,
I hardly would account the thing success
Though it did all for me I say.

                    But, friend,
We speak of what is—not of what might
    be,
And how 'twere better if 'twere other-
    wise.
I am the man you see here plain enough:
Grant I'm a beast, why, beasts must lead
    beasts' lives!
Suppose I own at once to tail and claws;
The tailless man exceeds me: but being
    tailed
I'll lash out lion-fashion, and leave apes
To dock their stump and dress their
    haunches up.
My business is not to remake myself,
But make the absolute best of what God
    made.
Or—our first simile—though you proved
    me doomed
To a viler berth still, to the steerage-hole,
The sheep-pen or the pig-sty, I should
    strive
To make what use of each were possible;

And as this cabin gets upholstery,
That hutch should rustle with sufficient
straw.

But, friend, I don't acknowledge quite
so fast
I fail of all your manhood's lofty tastes
Enumerated so complacently,
On the mere ground that you forsooth
can find
In this particular life I choose to lead
No fit provision for them. Can you not?
Say you, my fault is I address myself
To grosser estimators than should judge?
And that's no way of holding up the
soul—
Which, nobler, needs men's praise per-
haps, yet knows
One wise man's verdict outweighs all the
fools',—
Would like the two, but, forced to choose,
takes that.
I pine among my million imbeciles
(You think) aware some dozen men of
sense
Eye me and know me, whether I believe
In the last winking Virgin, as I vow,
And am a fool, or disbelieve in her
And am a knave,—approve in neither
case,
Withhold their voices though I look their
way:
Like Verdi when, at his worst opera's end
(The thing they gave at Florence,—
what's its name?)
While the mad houseful's plaudits near
out-bang
His orchestra of salt-box, tongs and
bones,
He looks through all the roaring and the
wreaths
Where sits Rossini patient in his stall.

Nay, friend, I meet you with an answer
here—
That even your prime men who appraise
their kind
Are men still, catch a wheel within a
wheel,

See more in a truth than the truth's sim-
ple self,
Confuse themselves. You see lads walk
the street
Sixty the minute; what's to note in that?
You see one lad o'erstride a chimney-
stack;
Him you must watch—he's sure to fall,
yet stands!
Our interest's on the dangerous edge of
things.
The honest thief, the tender murderer,
The superstitious atheist, demirep
That loves and saves her soul in new
French books—
We watch while these in equilibrium keep
The giddy line midway: one step aside,
They're classed and done with. I, then,
keep the line
Before your sages,—just the men to
shrink
From the gross weights, coarse scales, and
labels broad
You offer their refinement. Fool or
knave?
Why needs a bishop be a fool or knave
When there's a thousand diamond weights
between?
So I enlist them. Your picked twelve,
you'll find,
Profess themselves indignant, scandalized
At thus being held unable to explain
How a superior man who disbelieves
May not believe as well: that's Schel-
ling's way!
It's through my coming in the tail of time,
Nicking the minute with a happy tact.
Had I been born three hundred years
ago
They'd say, "What's strange? Blougram
of course believes;"
And, seventy years since, "disbelieves of
course."
But now, "He may believe; and yet, and
yet
How can he?"—All eyes turn with in-
terest.
Whereas, step off the line on either side—
You, for example, clever to a fault,

The rough and ready man who write
    apace,
Read somewhat seldomer, think perhaps
    even less—
You disbelieve! Who wonders and who
    cares?
Lord So-and-so—his coat bedropt with
    wax,
All Peter's chains about his waist, his
    back
Brave with the needlework of Noodle-
    dom,
Believes! Again, who wonders and who
    cares?
But I, the man of sense and learning
    too,
The able to think yet act, the this, the
    that,
I, to believe at this late time of day!
Enough; you see, I need not fear con-
    tempt.

—Except it's yours! admire me as these
    may,
You don't. But whom at least do you
    admire?
Present your own perfections, your ideal,
Your pattern man for a minute—oh,
    make haste!
Is it Napoleon you would have us grow?
Concede the means; allow his head and
    hand,
(A large concession, clever as you are)
Good!—In our common primal element
Of unbelief (we can't believe, you know—
We're still at that admission, recollect!)
Where do you find—apart from, tower-
    ing o'er
The secondary temporary aims
Which satisfy the gross tastes you de-
    spise—
Where do you find his star?—his crazy
    trust
God knows through what or in what?
    it's alive
And shines and leads him and that's all
    we want.
Have we aught in our sober night shall
    point

Such ends as his were, and direct the
    means
Of working out our purpose straight as
    his,
Nor bring a moment's trouble on success
With after-care to justify the same?
—Be a Napoleon and yet disbelieve—
Why, the man's mad, friend, take his light
    away!
What's the vague good of the world for
    which you'd dare
With comfort to yourself blow millions
    up?
We neither of us see it! we do see
The blown-up millions—spatter of their
    brains
And writhing of their bowels and so forth,
In that bewildering entanglement
Of horrible eventualities
Past calculation to the end of time!
Can I mistake for some clear word of
    God
(Which were my ample warrant for it
    all)
His puff of hazy instincts, idle talk,
"The State, that's I," quack-nonsense
    about crowns,
And (when one beats the man to his last
    hold)
A vague idea of setting things to rights,
Policing people efficaciously,
More to their profit, most of all to his
    own;
The whole to end that dismallest of
    ends
By an Austrian marriage, cant to us the
    Church,
And resurrection of the old règime.
Would I, who hope to live a dozen years,
Fight Austerlitz for reasons such and
    such?
No: for, concede me but the merest
    chance
Doubt may be wrong—there's judgment,
    life to come!
With just that chance, I dare not. Doubt
    proves right?
This present life is all?—you offer me
Its dozen noisy years without a chance

That wedding an archduchess, wearing lace,
And getting called by divers new-coined names,
Will drive off ugly thoughts and let me dine,
Sleep, read and chat in quiet as I like!
Therefore, I will not.

                Take another case;
Fit up the cabin yet another way.
What say you to the poets? shall we write
Hamlet, Othello—make the world our own,
Without a risk to run of either sort?
I can't!—to put the strongest reason first.
"But try," you urge, "the trying shall suffice;
The aim, if reached or not, makes great the life:
Try to be Shakespeare, leave the rest to fate!"
Spare my self-knowledge—there's no fooling me!
If I prefer remaining my poor self,
I say so not in self-dispraise but praise.
If I'm a Shakespeare, let the well alone—
Why should I try to be what now I am?
If I'm no Shakespeare, as too probable,—
His power and consciousness and self-delight
And all we want in common, shall I find—
Trying for ever? while on points of taste
Wherewith, to speak it humbly, he and I
Are dowered alike—I'll ask you, I or he,
Which in our two lives realizes most?
Much, he imagined—somewhat, I possess.
He had the imagination; stick to that!
Let him say "In the face of my soul's works
Your world is worthless and I touch it not
Lest I should wrong them"—I'll withdraw my plea.
But does he say so? look upon his life!
Himself, who only can, gives judgment there.
He leaves his towers and gorgeous palaces

To build the trimmest house in Stratford town;
Saves money, spends it, owns the worth of things,
Giulio Romano's pictures, Dowland's lute;
Enjoys a show, respects the puppets, too,
And none more, had he seen its entry once,
Than "Pandulph, of fair Milan cardinal."
Why then should I who play that personage,
The very Pandulph Shakespeare's fancy made,
Be told that had the poet chanced to start
From where I stand now (some degree like mine
Being just the goal he ran his race to reach)
He would have run the whole race back, forsooth,
And left being Pandulph, to begin write plays?
Ah, the earth's best can be but the earth's best!
Did Shakespeare live, he could but sit at home
And get himself in dreams the Vatican,
Greek busts, Venetian paintings, Roman walls,
And English books, none equal to his own,
Which I read, bound in gold, (he never did).
—Terni's fall Naples' bay and Gothard's top—
Eh, friend? I could not fancy one of these—
But, as I pour this claret, there they are—
I've gained them—crossed St. Gothards last July
With ten mules to the carriage and a bed
Slung inside; is my hap the worse for that?
We want the same things, Shakespeare and myself,
And what I want, I have: he, gifted more,
Could fancy he too had it when he liked,

But not so thoroughly that if fate allowed
He would not have it also in my sense.
We play one game. I send the ball aloft
No less adroitly that of fifty strokes
Scarce five go o'er the wall so wide and
　　high
Which sends them back to me: I wish and
　　get.
He struck balls higher and with better
　　skill,
But at a poor fence level with his head,
And hit—his Stratford house, a coat of
　　arms,
Successful dealings in his grain and
　　wool,—
While I receive heaven's incense in my
　　nose
And style myself the cousin of Queen
　　Bess.
Ask him, if this life's all, who wins the
　　game?

Believe—and our whole argument
　　breaks up.
Enthusiasm's the best thing, I repeat;
Only, we can't command it; fire and life
Are all, dead matter's nothing, we agree:
And be it a mad dream or God's very
　　breath,
The fact's the same,—belief's fire once
　　in us,
Makes of all else mere stuff to show
　　itself:
We penetrate our life with such a glow
As fire lends wood and iron—this turns
　　steel,
That burns to ash—all's one, fire proves
　　its power
For good or ill, since men call flare suc-
　　cess.
But paint a fire, it will not therefore burn.
Light one in me, I'll find it food enough!
Why, to be Luther—that's a life to lead,
Incomparably better than my own.
He comes, reclaims God's earth for God,
　　he says,
Sets up God's rule again by simple means,
Re-opens a shut book, and all is done.
He flared out in the flaring of mankind;

Such Luther's luck was—how shall such
　　be mine?
If he succeeded, nothing's left to do:
And if he did not altogether—well,
Strauss is the next advance. All Strauss
　　should be
I might be also. But to what result?
He looks upon no Future: Luther did.
What can I gain on the denying side?
Ice makes no conflagration. State the
　　facts,
Read the text right, emancipate the
　　world—
The emancipated world enjoys itself
With scarce a thank-you—Blougram told
　　it first
It could not owe a farthing,—not to him
More than Saint Paul! 'twould press its
　　pay, you think?
Then add there's still that plaguy hun-
　　dredth chance
Strauss may be wrong. And so a risk is
　　run—
For what gain? not for Luther's, who
　　secured
A real heaven in his heart throughout his
　　life,
Supposing death a little altered things.

"Ay, but since really you lack faith,"
　　you cry,
"You run the same risk really on all sides,
In cool indifference as bold unbelief.
As well be Strauss as swing 'twixt Paul
　　and him.
It's not worth having, such imperfect
　　faith,
Nor more available to do faith's work
Than unbelief like mine. Whole faith, or
　　none!"

Softly, my friend! I must dispute that
　　point.
Once own the use of faith, I'll find you
　　faith.
We're back on Christian ground. You
　　call for faith:
I show you doubt, to prove that faith
　　exists.

The more of doubt, the stronger faith, I
    say,
If faith o'ercomes doubt. How I know
    it does?
By life and man's free will, God gave for
    that!
To mould life as we choose it, shows our
    choice:
That's our one act, the previous work's
    His own.
You criticize the soil? it reared this
    tree—
This broad life and whatever fruit it
    bears!
What matter though I doubt at every
    pore,
Head-doubts, heart-doubts, doubts at my
    fingers' ends,
Doubts in the trivial work of every day,
Doubts at the very bases of my soul
In the grand moments when she probes
    herself—
If finally I have a life to show,
The thing I did, brought out in evidence
Against the thing done to me under-
    ground
By Hell and all its brood, for aught I
    know?
I say, whence sprang this? shows it faith
    or doubt?
All's doubt in me; where's break of faith
    in this?
It is the idea, the feeling and the love
God means mankind should strive for and
    show forth,
Whatever be the process to that end,—
And not historic knowledge, logic sound,
And metaphysical acumen, sure!
"What think ye of Christ," friend? when
    all's done and said,
Like you this Christianity or not?
It may be false, but will you wish it
    true?
Has it your vote to be so if it can?
Trust you an instinct silenced long ago
That will break silence and enjoin you
    love
What mortified philosophy is hoarse,
And all in vain, with bidding you despise?

If you desire faith—then you've faith
    enough:
What else seeks God—nay, what else seek
    ourselves?
You form a notion of me, we'll suppose,
On hearsay; it's a favourable one:
"But still," (you add) "there was no such
    good man,
Because of contradictions in the facts.
One proves, for instance, he was born in
    Rome,
This Blougram—yet throughout the tales
    of him
I see he figures as an Englishman."
Well, the two things are reconcilable.
But would I rather you discovered that,
Subjoining—"Still, what matter though
    they be?
Blougram concerns me nought, born here
    or there."

Pure faith indeed—you know not what
    you ask!
Naked belief in God the Omnipotent,
Omniscient, Omnipresent, sears too much
The sense of conscious creatures to be
    borne.
It were the seeing Him, no flesh shall
    dare.
Some think, Creation's meant to show
    Him forth:
I say, it's meant to hide Him all it can,
And that's what all the blessed evil's for.
Its use in Time is to environ us,
Our breath, our drop of dew, with shield
    enough
Against that sight till we can bear its
    stress.
Under a vertical sun, the exposed brain
And lidless eye and disemprisoned heart
Less certainly would wither up at once
Than mind, confronted with the truth of
    Him.
But time and earth case-harden us to live;
The feeblest sense is trusted most; the
    child
Feels God a moment, ichors o'er the place,
Plays on and grows to be a man like us.
With me, faith means perpetual unbelief

Kept quiet like the snake 'neath Michael's
     foot
Who stands calm just because he feels
     it writhe.
Or, if that's too ambitious,—here's my
     box—
I need the excitation of a pinch
Threatening the torpor of the inside-nose
Nigh on the imminent sneeze that never
     comes.
"Leave it in peace" advise the simple
     folk—
Make it aware of peace by itching-fits,
Say I—let doubt occasion still more faith!

     You'll say, once all believed, man,
          woman, child,
In that dear middle-age these noodles
     praise.
How you'd exult if I could put you back
Six hundred years, blot out cosmogony,
Geology, ethnology, what not,
(Greek endings with the little passing-bell
That signifies some faith's about to die)
And set you square with Genesis again,—
When such a traveller told you his last
     news,
He saw the ark a-top of Ararat
But did not climb there since 'twas get-
     ting dusk
And robber-bands infest the mountain's
     foot!
How should you feel, I ask, in such an
     age,
How act? As other people felt and did;
With soul more blank than this decanter's
     knob,
Believe—and yet lie, kill, rob, fornicate
Full in belief's face, like the beast you'd
     be!

     No, when the fight begins within him-
          self,
A man's worth something. God stoops
     o'er his head,
Satan looks up between his feet—both
     tug—
He's left, himself, in the middle: the soul
     wakes

And grows. Prolong that battle through
     his life!
Never leave growing till the life to come!
Here, we've got callous to the Virgin's
     winks
That used to puzzle people whole-
     somely—
Men have outgrown the shame of being
     fools.
What are the laws of nature, not to bend
If the Church bid them?—brother New-
     man asks.
Up with the Immaculate Conception,
     then—
On to the rack with faith!—is my advice.
Will not that hurry us upon our knees,
Knocking our breasts, "It can't be—yet
     it shall!
Who am I, the worm, to argue with my
     Pope?
Low things confound the high things!"
     and so forth.
That's better than acquitting God with
     grace
As some folks do. He's tried—no case is
     proved,
Philosophy is lenient—He may go!

     You'll say—the old system's not so
          obsolete
But men believe still: ay, but who and
     where?
King Bomba's lazzaroni foster yet
The sacred flame, so Antonelli writes;
But even of these, what ragamuffin-saint
Believes God watches him continually,
As he believes in fire that it will burn,
Or rain that it will drench him? Break
     fire's law,
Sin against rain, although the penalty
Be just a singe or soaking? "No," he
     smiles;
"Those laws are laws that can enforce
     themselves."

     The sum of all is—yes, my doubt is
          great,
My faith's still greater—then my faith's
     enough,

I have read much, thought much, experi-
enced much,
Yet would die rather than avow my fear
The Naples' liquefaction may be false,
When set to happen by the palace-clock
According to the clouds or dinner-time.
I hear you recommend, I might at least
Eliminate, decrassify my faith
Since I adopt it; keeping what I must
And leaving what I can—such points as
this!
I won't—that is, I can't throw one away.
Supposing there's no truth in what I said
About the need of trials to man's faith,
Still, when you bid me purify the same,
To such a process I discern no end,
Clearing off one excrescence to see two;
There's ever a next in size, now grown
as big,
That meets the knife—I cut and cut
again!
First cut the Liquefaction, what comes
last
But Fichte's clever cut at God Himself?
Experimentalize on sacred things!
I trust nor hand nor eye nor heart nor
brain
To stop betimes: they all get drunk alike.
The first step, I am master not to take.

You'd find the cutting-process to your
taste
As much as leaving growths of lies un-
pruned,
Nor see more danger in it, you retort.
Your taste's worth mine; but my taste
proves more wise
When we consider that the steadfast hold
On the extreme end of the chain of faith
Gives all the advantage, makes the differ-
ence,
With the rough purblind mass we seek
to rule.
We are their lords, or they are free of
us
Just as we tighten or relax that hold.
So, other matters equal, we'll revert
To the first problem—which, if solved my
way

And thrown into the balance, turns the
scale—
How we may lead a comfortable life,
How suit our luggage to the cabin's size.

Of course you are remarking all this
time
How narrowly and grossly I view life,
Respect the creature-comforts, care to
rule
The masses, and regard complacently
"The cabin," in our old phrase! Well,
I do.
I act for, talk for, live for this world now,
As this world calls for action, life and
talk—
No prejudice to what next world may
prove,
Whose new laws and requirements, my
best pledge
To observe then, is that I observe these
now,
Shall do hereafter what I do meanwhile.
Let us concede (gratuitously though)
Next life relieves the soul of body, yields
Pure spiritual enjoyments: well, my
friend,
Why lose this life in the meantime, since
its use
May be to make the next life more in-
tense?

Do you know, I have often had a dream
(Work it up in your next month's article)
Of man's poor spirit in its progress still
Losing true life for ever and a day
Through ever trying to be and ever being
In the evolution of successive spheres,
Before its actual sphere and place of life,
Halfway into the next, which having
reached,
It shoots with corresponding foolery
Halfway into the next still, on and off!
As when a traveller, bound from North
to South,
Scouts fur in Russia—what's its use in
France?
In France spurns flannel—where's its
need in Spain?

In Spain drops cloth—too cumbrous for
  Algiers!
Linen goes next, and last the skin itself,
A superfluity at Timbuctoo.
When, through his journey, was the fool
  at ease?
I'm at ease now, friend—worldly in this
  world
I take and like its way of life; I think
My brothers who administer the means
Live better for my comfort—that's good
  too;
And God, if He pronounce upon it all,
Approves my service, which is better still.
If He keep silence,—why, for you or me
Or that brute-beast pulled-up in to-day's
  "Times,"
What odds is't, save to ourselves, what
  life we lead?

You meet me at this issue—you declare,
All special-pleading done with, truth is
  truth,
And justifies itself by undreamed ways.
You don't fear but it's better, if we
  doubt,
To say so, acting up to our truth per-
  ceived
However feebly. Do then,—act away!
'Tis there I'm on the watch for you!
  How one acts
Is, both of us agree, our chief concern:
And how you'll act is what I fain would
  see
If, like the candid person you appear,
You dare to make the most of your life's
  scheme
As I of mine, live up to its full law
Since there's no higher law that counter-
  checks.
Put natural religion to the test
You've just demolished the revealed with
  —quick,
Down to the root of all that checks your
  will,
All prohibition to lie, kill and thieve
Or even to be an atheistic priest!
Suppose a pricking to incontinence—
Philosophers deduce your chastity

Or shame, from just the fact that at the
  first
Whoso embraced a woman in the plain,
Threw club down, and forewent his
  brains beside,
So stood a ready victim in the reach
Of any brother-savage club in hand—
Hence saw the use of going out of sight
In wood or cave to prosecute his loves—
I read this in a French book t' other day.
Does law so analysed coerce you much?
Oh, men spin clouds of fuzz where mat-
  ters end,
But you who reach where the first thread
  begins,
You'll soon cut that!—which means you
  can, but won't
Through certain instincts, blind, unrea-
  soned-out,
You dare not set aside, you can't tell
  why,
But there they are, and so you let them
  rule.
Then, friend, you seem as much a slave
  as I,
A liar, conscious coward and hypocrite,
Without the good the slave expects to get,
Suppose he has a master after all!
You own your instincts—why, what else
  do I,
Who want, am made for, and must have
  a God
Ere I can be aught, do aught?—no mere
  name
Want, but the true thing with what proves
  its truth,
To wit, a relation from that thing to me,
Touching from head to foot—which touch
  I feel,
And with it take the rest, this life of ours!
I live my life here; yours you dare not
  live.

—Not as I state it, who (you please
  subjoin)
Disfigure such a life and call it names,
While, in your mind, remains another way
For simple men: knowledge and power
  have rights,

But ignorance and weakness have rights
    too.
There needs no crucial effort to find truth
If here or there or anywhere about—
We ought to turn each side, try hard and
    see,
And if we can't, be glad we've earned at
    least
The right, by one laborious proof the
    more,
To graze in peace earth's pleasant pas-
    turage.
Men are not angels, neither are they
    brutes.
Something we may see, all we cannot
    see—
What need of lying? I say, I see all,
And swear to each detail the most minute
In what I think a Pan's face—you, mere
    cloud:
I swear I hear him speak and see him
    wink,
For fear, if once I drop the emphasis,
Mankind may doubt there's any cloud
    at all.
You take the simpler life—ready to see,
Willing to see—for no cloud's worth a
    face—
And leaving quiet what no strength can
    move,
And which, who bids you move? who has
    the right?
I bid you; but you are God's sheep, not
    mine—
"*Pastor est tui Dominus.*" You find
In these the pleasant pastures of this life
Much you may eat without the least
    offence,
Much you don't eat because your maw
    objects,
Much you would eat but that your fellow-
    flock
Open great eyes at you and even butt,
And thereupon you like your mates so
    well
You cannot please yourself, offending
    them—
Though when they seem exorbitantly
    sheep,

You weigh your pleasure with their butts
    and bleats
And strike the balance. Sometimes cer-
    tain fears
Restrain you—real checks since you find
    them so—
Sometimes you please yourself and noth-
    ing checks;
And thus you graze through life with not
    one lie,
And like it best.

        But do you, in truth's name?
If so, you beat—which means, you are
    not I—
Who needs must make earth mine and
    feed my fill
Not simply unbutted at, unbickered with,
But motioned to the velvet of the sward
By those obsequious wethers' very selves.
Look at me, sir; my age is double yours:
At yours, I knew beforehand, so enjoyed,
What now I should be—as, permit the
    word,
I pretty well imagine your whole range
And stretch of tether twenty years to
    come.
We both have minds and bodies much
    alike.
In truth's name, don't you want my
    bishopric,
My daily bread, my influence and my
    state?
You're young, I'm old, you must be old
    one day;
Will you find then, as I do hour by hour,
Women their lovers kneel to, that cut
    curls
From your fat lap-dog's ears to grace a
    brooch—
Dukes, that petition just to kiss your
    ring—
With much beside you know or may
    conceive?
Suppose we die to-night: well, here am I,
Such were my gains, life bore this fruit
    to me,
While writing all the same my articles
On music, poetry, the fictile vase

Found at Albano, chess, or Anacreon's
    Greek.
But you—the highest honour in your life,
The thing you'll crown yourself with, all
    your days,
Is—dining here and drinking this last
    glass
I pour you out in sign of amity
Before we part for ever. Of your power
And social influence, worldly worth in
    short,
Judge what's my estimation by the fact,
I do not condescend to enjoin, beseech,
Hint secrecy on one of all these words!
You're shrewd and know that should you
    publish one
The world would brand the lie—my
    enemies first,
Who'd sneer—"the bishop's an arch-
    hypocrite,
And knave perhaps, but not so frank a
    fool."
Whereas I should not dare for both my
    ears
Breathe one such syllable, smile one such
    smile,
Before my chaplain who reflects myself—
My shade's so much more potent than
    your flesh.
What's your reward, self-abnegating
    friend?
Stood you confessed of those exceptional
And privileged great natures that dwarf
    mine—
A zealot with a mad ideal in reach,
A poet just about to print his ode,
A statesman with a scheme to stop this
    war,
An artist whose religion is his art,
I should have nothing to object! such men
Carry the fire, all things grow warm to
    them,
Their drugget's worth my purple, they
    beat me.
But you,—you're just as little those as
    I—
You, Gigadibs, who, thirty years of age,
Write stately for Blackwood's Maga-
    zine,

Believe you see two points in Hamlet's
    soul
Unseized by the Germans yet—which
    view you'll print—
Meantime the best you have to show be-
    ing still
That lively lightsome article we took
Almost for the true Dickens,—what's its
    name?
"The Slum and Cellar—or Whitechapel
    life
Limned after dark!" it made me laugh, I
    know,
And pleased a month and brought you in
    ten pounds.
—Success I recognize and compliment,
And therefore give you, if you choose,
    three words
(The card and pencil-scratch is quite
    enough)
Which whether here, in Dublin or New
    York,
Will get you, prompt as at my eyebrow's
    wink,
Such terms as never you aspired to get
In all our own reviews and some not ours.
Go write your lively sketches—be the first
"Blougram, or The Eccentric Confi-
    dence"—
Or better simply say, "The Outward-
    bound."
Why, men as soon would throw it in my
    teeth
As copy and quote the infamy chalked
    broad
About me on the church-door opposite.
You will not wait for that experience
    though,
I fancy, howsoever you decide,
To discontinue—not detesting, not
Defaming, but at least—despising me!

Over his wine so smiled and talked his
    hour
Sylvester Blougram, styled *in partibus
Episcopus, nec non*—(the deuce knows
    what
It's changed to by our novel hierarchy)

With Gigadibs the literary man,
Who played with spoons, explored his
    plate's design,
And ranged the olive-stones about its
    edge,
While the great bishop rolled him out a
    mind
Long crumpled, till creased consciousness
    lay smooth.

For Blougram, he believed, say, half he
    spoke.
The other portion, as he shaped it thus
For argumentatory purposes,
He felt his foe was foolish to dispute.
Some arbitrary accidental thoughts
That crossed his mind, amusing because
    new,
He chose to represent as fixtures there,
Invariable convictions (such they seemed
Beside his interlocutor's loose cards
Flung daily down, and not the same way
    twice)
While certain hell-deep instincts, man's
    weak tongue
Is never bold to utter in their truth
Because styled hell-deep ('tis an old mis-
    take
To place hell at the bottom of the earth)
He ignored these,—not having in readi-
    ness
Their nomenclature and philosophy:
He said true things, but called them by
    wrong names.
"On the whole," he thought, "I justify
    myself
On every point where cavillers like this
Oppugn my life: he tries one kind of
    fence—
I close—he's worsted, that's enough for
    him;
He's on the ground! if the ground should
    break away
I take my stand on, there's a firmer yet
Beneath it, both of us may sink and reach.
His ground was over mine and broke the
    first:
So let him sit with me this many a year!"

He did not sit five minutes. Just a
    week
Sufficed his sudden healthy vehemence.
(Something had struck him in the "Out-
    ward-bound"
Another way than Blougram's purpose
    was)
And having bought, not cabin-furniture
But settler's-implements (enough **for**
    three)
And started for Australia—there, I hope,
By this time he has tested his first plough,
And studied his last chapter of St. John.

One Word More

TO E. B. B.

London, September, 1855

I

THERE they are, my fifty men and women
Naming me the fifty poems finished!
Take them, Love, the book and me to-
    gether:
Where the heart lies, let the brain lie also.

II

Rafael made a century of sonnets,
Made and wrote them in a certain volume
Dinted with the silver-pointed pencil
Else he only used to draw Madonnas:
These, the world might view—but one,
    the volume.
Who that one, you ask? Your heart in-
    structs you.
Did she live and love it all her lifetime?
Did she drop, his lady of the sonnets,
Die, and let it drop beside her pillow
Where it lay in place of Rafael's glory,
Rafael's cheek so duteous and so loving—
Cheek, the world was wont to hail a
    painter's,
Rafael's cheek, her love had turned **a**
    poet's?

III

You and I would rather read that volume,
(Taken to his beating bosom by it)
Lean and list the bosom-beats of Rafael,
Would we not? than wonder at Ma-
    donnas—
Her, San Sisto names, and Her, Foligno,
Her, that visits Florence in a vision,
Her, that's left with lilies in the Louvre—
Seen by us and all the world in circle.

IV

You and I will never read that volume.
Guido Reni, like his own eye's apple
Guarded long the treasure-book and loved
    it.
Guido Reni dying, all Bologna
Cried, and the world cried too, "Ours—
    the treasure!"
Suddenly, as rare things will, it vanished.

V

Dante once prepared to paint an angel:
Whom to please? You whisper "Beatrice."
While he mused and traced it and re-
    traced it,
(Peradventure with a pen corroded
Still by drops of that hot ink he dipped
    for,
When, his left-hand i' the hair o' the
    wicked,
Back he held the brow and pricked its
    stigma,
Bit into the live man's flesh for parch-
    ment,
Loosed him, laughed to see the writing
    rankle,
Let the wretch go festering through
    Florence)—
Dante, who loved well because he hated,
Hated wickedness that hinders loving,
Dante standing, studying his angel,—
In there broke the folk of his Inferno.
Says he—"Certain people of importance"
(Such he gave his daily, dreadful line to)

"Entered and would seize, forsooth, the
    poet."
Says the poet—"Then I stopped my paint-
    ing."

VI

You and I would rather see that angel,
Painted by the tenderness of Dante,
Would we not?—than read a fresh
    Inferno.

VII

You and I will never see that picture.
While he mused on love and Beatrice,
While he softened o'er his outlined angel,
In they broke, those "people of impor-
    tance:"
We and Bice bear the loss for ever.

VIII

What of Rafael's sonnets, Dante's pic-
    ture?
This: no artist lives and loves, that longs
    not
Once, and only once, and for one only,
(Ah, the prize!) to find his love a lan-
    guage
Fit and fair and simple and sufficient—
Using nature that's an art to others,
Not, this one time, art that's turned his
    nature.
Ay, of all the artists living, loving,
None but would forego his proper
    dowry,—
Does he paint? he fain would write a
    poem,—
Does he write? he fain would paint a
    picture,
Put to proof art alien to the artist's,
Once, and only once, and for one only,
So to be the man and leave the artist,
Gain the man's joy, miss the artist's sor-
    row.

IX

Wherefore? Heaven's gift takes earth's
    abatement!
He who smites the rock and spreads the
    water,

Bidding drink and live a crowd beneath
  him,
Even he, the minute makes immortal
Proves, perchance, his mortal in the
  minute,
Desecrates, belike, the deed in doing.
While he smites, how can he but re-
  member,
So he smote before, in such a peril,
When they stood and mocked—"Shall
  smiting help us?"
When they drank and sneered—"A stroke
  is easy!"
When they wiped their mouths and went
  their journey,
Throwing him for thanks—"But drought
  was pleasant."
Thus old memories mar the actual
  triumph;
Thus the doing savours of disrelish;
Thus achievement lacks a gracious some-
  what;
O'er-importuned brows becloud the man-
  date,
Carelessness or consciousness, the ges-
  ture.
For he bears an ancient wrong about
  him,
Sees and knows again those phalanxed
  faces,
Hears, yet one time more, the 'customed
  prelude—
"How shouldst thou, of all men, smite,
  and save us?"
Guesses what is like to prove the
  sequel—
"Egypt's flesh-pots—nay, the drought was
  better."

X

Oh, the crowd must have emphatic warrant!
Theirs, the Sinai-forehead's cloven brilliance,
Right-arm's rod-sweep, tongue's imperial
  fiat.
Never dares the man put off the
  prophet.

XI

Did he love one face from out the thou-
  sands,
(Were she Jethro's daughter, white and
  wifely,
Were she but the Æthiopian bond-slave,)
He would envy yon dumb patient camel,
Keeping a reserve of scanty water
Meant to save his own life in the desert;
Ready in the desert to deliver
(Kneeling down to let his breast be
  opened)
Hoard and life together for his mistress.

XII

I shall never, in the years remaining,
Paint you pictures, no, nor carve you
  statues,
Make you music that should all-express
  me;
So it seems: I stand on my attainment.
This of verse alone, one life allows me;
Verse and nothing else have I to give you.
Other heights in other lives, God will-
  ing—
All the gifts from all the heights, your
  own, Love!

XIII

Yet a semblance of resource avails us—
Shade so finely touched, love's sense must
  seize it.
Take these lines, look lovingly and nearly,
Lines I write the first time and the last
  time.
He who works in fresco, steals a hair-
  brush,
Curbs the liberal hand, subservient
  proudly,
Cramps his spirit, crowds its all in little,
Makes a strange art of an art familiar,
Fills his lady's missal-marge with
  flowerets.
He who blows through bronze, may
  breathe through silver,
Fitly serenade a slumbrous princess.
He who writes, may write for once, as I
  do.

XIV

Love, you saw me gather men and
women,
Live or dead or fashioned by my fancy,
Enter each and all, and use their service,
Speak from every mouth,—the speech,
a poem.
Hardly shall I tell my joys and sorrows,
Hopes and fears, belief and disbelieving:
I am mine and yours—the rest be all
men's,
Karshook, Cleon, Norbert and the fifty.
Let me speak this once in my true person,
Not as Lippo, Roland or Andrea,
Though the fruit of speech be just this
sentence—
Pray you, look on these my men and
women,
Take and keep my fifty poems finished;
Where my heart lies, let my brain lie also!
Poor the speech; be how I speak, for all
things.

XV

Not but that you know me! Lo, the
moon's self!
Here in London, yonder late in Florence,
Still we find her face, the thrice-trans-
figured.
Curving on a sky imbrued with colour,
Drifted over Fiesole by twilight,
Came she, our new crescent of a hair's-
breadth.
Full she flared it, lamping Samminiato,
Rounder 'twixt the cypresses and rounder,
Perfect till the nightingales applauded.
Now, a piece of her old self, impoverished,
Hard to greet, she traverses the house-
roofs,
Hurries with unhandsome thrift of silver,
Goes dispiritedly, glad to finish.

XVI

What, there's nothing in the moon note-
worthy?
Nay—for if that moon could love a
mortal,
Use, to charm him (so to fit a fancy)
All her magic ('tis the old sweet mythos)

She would turn a new side to her mortal,
Side unseen of herdsman, huntsman,
steersman—
Blank to Zoroaster on his terrace,
Blind to Galileo on his turret,
Dumb to Homer, dumb to Keats—him,
even!
Think, the wonder of the moonstruck
mortal—
When she turns round, comes again in
heaven,
Opens out anew for worse or better?
Proves she like some portent of an iceberg
Swimming full upon the ship it founders,
Hungry with huge teeth of splintered
crystals?
Proves she as the paved-work of a sap-
phire
Seen by Moses when he climbed the
mountain?
Moses, Aaron, Nadab and Abihu
Climbed and saw the very God, the
Highest,
Stand upon the paved-work of a sapphire.
Like the bodied heaven in his clearness
Shone the stone, the sapphire of that
paved-work,
When they ate and drank and saw God
also!

XVII

What were seen? None knows, none
ever shall know.
Only this is sure—the sight were other,
Not the moon's same side, born late in
Florence,
Dying now impoverished here in London.
God be thanked, the meanest of his
creatures
Boasts two soul-sides, one to face the
world with,
One to show a woman when he loves her.

XVIII

This I say of me, but think of you, Love!
This to you—yourself my moon of poets!
Ah, but that's the world's side, there's
the wonder,

Thus they see you, praise you, think they
    know you.
There, in turn I stand with them and
    praise you,
Out of my own self, I dare to phrase it.
But the best is when I glide from out
    them,
Cross a step or two of dubious twilight,
Come out on the other side, the novel
Silent silver lights and darks undreamed
    of,
Where I hush and bless myself with
    silence.

XIX

Oh, their Rafael of the dear Madonnas,
Oh, their Dante of the dread Inferno,
Wrote one song—and in my brain I
    sing it,
Drew one angel—borne, see, on my
    bosom!
                  R. B.

Confessions

WHAT is he buzzing in my ears?
    "Now that I come to die,
Do I view the world as a vale of tears?"
    Ah, reverend sir, not I!

What I viewed there once, what I view
    again
    Where the physic bottles stand
On the table's edge,—is a suburb lane,
    With a wall to my bedside hand.

That lane sloped, much as the bottles do,
    From a house you could descry
O'er the garden-wall: is the curtain blue
    Or green to a healthy eye?

To mine, it serves for the old June
    weather
    Blue above lane and wall;
And that farthest bottle labelled "Ether"
    Is the house o'er-topping all.

At a terrace, somewhat near its stopper,
    There watched for me, one June,
A girl: I know, sir, it's improper,
    My poor mind's out of tune.

Only, there was a way . . . you crept
    Close by the side, to dodge
Eyes in the house, two eyes except:
    They styled their house "The Lodge."

What right had a lounger up their lane?
    But, by creeping very close,
With the good wall's help,—their eyes
    might strain
    And stretch themselves to Oes,

Yet never catch her and me together,
    As she left the attic, there,
By the rim of the bottle labelled "Ether,"
    And stole from stair to stair,

And stood by the rose-wreathed gate.
    Alas,
    We loved, sir—used to meet:
How sad and bad and mad it was—
    But then, how it was sweet!

Prospice

FEAR death?—to feel the fog in my
    throat,
    The mist in my face,
When the snows begin, and the blasts
    denote
    I am nearing the place,
The power of the night, the press of the
    storm,
    The post of the foe;
Where he stands, the Arch Fear in a
    visible form,
    Yet the strong man must go:
For the journey is done and the summit
    attained,
    And the barriers fall,
Though a battle's to fight ere the guerdon
    be gained,
    The reward of it all.
I was ever a fighter, so—one fight more,
    The best and the last!
I would hate that death bandaged my
    eyes, and forbore,
    And bade me creep past.
No! let me taste the whole of it, fare like
    my peers
    The heroes of old,

Bear the brunt, in a minute pay glad life's
    arrears
Of pain, darkness and cold.
For sudden the worst turns the best to
    the brave,
    The black minute's at end,
And the elements' rage, the fiend-voices
    that rave,
    Shall dwindle, shall blend,
Shall change, shall become first a peace,
    then a joy,
    Then a light, then thy breast,
O thou soul of my soul! I shall clasp thee
    again,
    And with God be the rest!

The Householder

SHALL I sonnet-sing you about myself?
    Do I live in a house you would like to
    see?
Is it scant of gear, has it store of pelf?
    "Unlock my heart with a sonnet-key?"

Invite the world, as my betters have done?
    "Take notice: this building remains on
    view,
Its suites of reception every one,
    Its private apartment and bedroom too;

"For a ticket, apply to the Publisher."
    No: thanking the public, I must decline.
A peep through my window, if folk
    prefer;
    But, please you, no foot over threshold
    of mine!

I have mixed with a crowd and heard free
    talk
    In a foreign land where an earthquake
    chanced
And a house stood gaping, naught to balk
    Man's eye wherever he gazed or
    glanced.

The whole of the frontage shaven sheer,
    The inside gaped: exposed to day,
Right and wrong and common and queer,
    Bare, as the palm of your hand, it lay.

The owner? Oh, he had been crushed,
    no doubt!

"Odd tables and chairs for a man of
    wealth!
What a parcel of musty old books about!
    He smoked,—no wonder he lost his
    health!

"I doubt if he bathed before he dressed.
    A brasier?—the pagan, he burned per-
    fumes!
You see it is proved, what the neighbors
    guessed:
    His wife and himself had separate
    rooms."

Friends, the goodman of the house at
    least
    Kept house to himself till an earth-
    quake came:
'Tis the fall of its frontage permits you
    feast
    On the inside arrangement you praise
    or blame.

Outside should suffice for evidence:
    And whoso desires to penetrate
Deeper, must dive by the spirit-sense—
    No optics like yours, at any rate!

"Hoity-toity! A street to explore,
    Your house the exception! 'With this
    same key
Shakespeare unlocked his heart,' once
    more!"
    Did Shakespeare? If so, the less
    Shakespeare he!

Pheidippides

FIRST I salute this soil of the blessed,
    river and rock!
Gods of my birthplace, dæmons and
    heroes, honor to all!
Then I name thee, claim thee for our
    patron, co-equal in praise
—Ay, with Zeus the Defender, with Her
    of the ægis and spear!
Also, ye of the bow and the buskin,
    praised be your peer,
Now, henceforth and forever,—O latest
    to whom I upraise

Hand and heart and voice! For Athens,
leave pasture and flock!
Present to help, potent to save, Pan—
patron I call!

Archons of Athens, topped by the tettix,
see, I return!
See, 'tis myself here standing alive, no
spectre that speaks!
Crowned with the myrtle, did you com-
mand me, Athens and you,
"Run, Pheidippides, run and race, reach
Sparta for aid!
Persia has come, we are here, where is
She?" Your command I obeyed,
Ran and raced: like stubble, some field
which a fire runs through,
Was the space between city and city: two
days, two nights did I burn
Over the hills, under the dales, down pits
and up peaks.

Into their midst I broke: breath served
but for "Persia has come!
Persia bids Athens proffer slaves'-tribute,
water and earth;
Razed to the ground is Eretria—but
Athens, shall Athens sink,
Drop into dust and die—the flower of
Hellas utterly die,
Die, with the wide world spitting at
Sparta, the stupid, the stander-by?
Answer me quick, what help, what hand
do you stretch o'er destruction's
brink?
How,—when? No care for my limbs!—
there's lightning in all and some—
Fresh and fit your message to bear, once
lips give it birth!"

O my Athens—Sparta love thee? Did
Sparta respond?
Every face of her leered in a furrow of
envy, mistrust,
Malice,—each eye of her gave me its
glitter of gratified hate!
Gravely they turned to take counsel, to
cast for excuses. I stood

Quivering,—the limbs of me fretting as
fire frets, an inch from dry wood:
"Persia has come, Athens asks aid, and
still they debate?
Thunder, thou Zeus! Athene, are Spar-
tans a quarry beyond
Swing of thy spear? Phoibos and Arte-
mis, clang them 'Ye must'!"

No bolt launched from Olympus! Lo,
their answer at last!
"Has Persia come,—does Athens ask aid,
—may Sparta befriend?
Nowise precipitate judgment — too
weighty the issue at stake!
Count we no time lost time which lags
through respect to the gods!
Ponder that precept of old, 'No warfare,
whatever the odds
In your favor, so long as the moon, half-
orbed, is unable to take
Full-circle her state in the sky!' Already
she rounds to it fast:
Athens must wait, patient as we—who
judgment suspend."

Athens,—except for that sparkle,—thy
name, I had mouldered to ash!
That sent a blaze through my blood; off,
off and away was I back,
—Not one word to waste, one look to lose
on the false and the vile!
Yet "O gods of my land!" I cried, as each
hillock and plain,
Wood and stream, I knew, I named, rushing past them again,
"Have ye kept faith, proved mindful of
honors we paid you erewhile?
Vain was the filleted victim, the fulsome
libation! Too rash
Love in its choice, paid you so largely
service so slack!

"Oak and olive and bay,—I bid you cease
to enwreathe
Brows made bold by your leaf! Fade at
the Persian's foot,
You that, our patrons were pledged,
should never adorn a slave!

Rather I hail thee, Parnes,—trust to thy
wild waste tract!
Treeless, herbless, lifeless mountain!
What matter if slacked
My speed may hardly be, for homage to
crag and to cave
No deity deigns to drape with verdure?
at least I can breathe,
Fear in thee no fraud from the blind, no
lie from the mute!"

Such my cry as, rapid, I ran over Parnes'
ridge;
Gully and gap I clambered and cleared
till, sudden, a bar
Jutted, a stoppage of stone against me,
blocking the way.
Right! for I minded the hollow to tra-
verse, the fissure across:
"Where I could enter, there I depart by!
Night in the fosse?
Athens to aid? Though the dive were
through Erebos, thus I obey—
Out of the day dive, into the day as
bravely arise! No bridge
Better!"—when—ha! what was it I came
on, of wonders that are?

There, in the cool of a cleft, sat he—
majestical Pan!
Ivy drooped wanton, kissed his head,
moss cushioned his hoof:
All the great god was good in the eyes
grave-kindly—the curl
Carved on the bearded cheek, amused at
a mortal's awe,
As, under the human trunk, the goat-
thighs grand I saw.
"Halt, Pheidippides!"—halt I did, my
brain of a whirl:
"Hither to me! Why pale in my presence?" he gracious began:
"How is it,—Athens, only in Hellas, holds
me aloof?

"Athens, she only, rears me no fane,
makes me no feast!
Wherefore? Than I what godship to
Athens more helpful of old?

Go, bid Athens take heart, laugh Persia
to scorn, have faith
In the temples and tombs! Go, say to
Athens, 'The Goat-God saith:
When Persia—so much as strews not the
soil—is cast in the sea,
Then praise Pan who fought in the ranks
with your most and least,
Goat-thigh to greaved-thigh, made one
cause with the free and the bold!'

"Say Pan saith: 'Let this, foreshowing
the place, be the pledge!'"
(Gay, the liberal hand held out this
herbage I bear
—Fennel—I grasped it a-tremble with
dew—whatever it bode)
"While, as for thee" . . . But enough!
He was gone. If I ran hitherto—
Be sure that, the rest of my journey, I
ran no longer, but flew.
Parnes to Athens—earth no more, the air
was my road:
Here am I back. Praise Pan, we stand
no more on the razor's edge!
Pan for Athens, Pan for me! I too have
a guerdon rare!

Then spoke Miltiades. "And thee, best
runner of Greece,
Whose limbs did duty indeed,—what gift
is promised thyself?
Tell it us straightway,—Athens the
mother demands of her son!"
Rosily blushed the youth: he paused: but,
lifting at length
His eyes from the ground, it seemed as he
gathered the rest of his strength
Into the utterance—"Pan spoke thus:
'For what thou hast done
Count on a worthy reward! Henceforth
be allowed thee release
From the racer's toil, no vulgar reward
in praise or in pelf!'

"I am bold to believe, Pan means reward
the most to my mind!
Fight I shall, with our foremost, wherever this fennel may grow,—

Pound—Pan helping us—Persia to dust,
  and, under the deep,
Whelm her away forever; and then,—no
  Athens to save,—
Marry a certain maid, I know keeps faith
  to the brave,—
Hie to my house and home: and, when
  my children shall creep
Close to my knees,—recount how the God
  was awful yet kind,
Promised their sire reward to the full—
  rewarding him—so!"

———

Unforeseeing one! Yes, he fought on the
  Marathon day:
So, when Persia was dust, all cried "To
  Akropolis!
Run, Pheidippides, one race more! the
  meed is thy due!
'Athens is saved, thank Pan,' go shout!"
  He flung down his shield,
Ran like fire once more: and the space
  'twixt the Fennel-field
And Athens was stubble again, a field
  which a fire runs through,
Till in he broke: "Rejoice, we conquer!"
  Like wine through clay,
Joy in his blood bursting his heart, he
  died—the bliss!

So, to this day, when friend meets friend,
  the word of salute
Is still "Rejoice!"—his word which
  brought rejoicing indeed.
So is Pheidippides happy forever,—the
  noble strong man
Who could race like a god, bear the face
  of a god, whom a god loved so well;
He saw the land saved he had helped to
  save, and was suffered to tell
Such tidings, yet never decline, but, gloriously as he began,
So to end gloriously—once to shout, there-
  after be mute:
"Athens is saved!"—Pheidippides dies in
  the shout for his meed.

From ASOLANDO: FANCIES AND FACTS

Epilogue

AT the midnight in the silence of the
  sleep-time,
  When you set your fancies free,
Will they pass to where—by death, fools
  think, imprisoned—
Low he lies who once so loved you, whom
  you loved so,
      —Pity me?

Oh to love so, be so loved, yet so mistaken!
  What had I on earth to do
With the slothful, with the mawkish, the
  unmanly?
Like the aimless, helpless, hopeless did I
  drivel
      —Being—who?

One who never turned his back but
  marched breast forward,
  Never doubted clouds would break,
Never dreamed, though right were
  worsted, wrong would triumph,
Held we fall to rise, are baffled to fight
  better,
      Sleep to wake.

No, at noonday in the bustle of man's
  work-time
  Greet the unseen with a cheer!
Bid him forward, breast and back as
  either should be,
"Strive and thrive!" cry "Speed,—fight
  on, fare ever
      There as here!"

EDWARD LEAR (1812-1888)

The Jumblies

I

THEY went to sea in a Sieve, they did,
  In a Sieve they went to sea:
In spite of all their friends could say,
On a winter's morn, on a stormy day,
  In a Sieve they went to sea!

And when the Sieve turned round and round,
And every one cried, "You'll all be drowned!"
They called aloud, "Our Sieve ain't big,
But we don't care a button! we don't care a fig!
  In a Sieve we'll go to sea!"
    Far and few, far and few,
      Are the lands where the Jumblies live;
    Their heads are green, and their hands are blue,
      And they went to sea in a Sieve.

II

They sailed away in a Sieve, they did,
  In a Sieve they sailed so fast,
With only a beautiful pea-green veil
Tied with a riband by way of a sail,
  To a small tobacco-pipe mast;
And every one said, who saw them go,
"O won't they be soon upset, you know!
For the sky is dark, and the voyage is long,
And happen what may, it's extremely wrong
  In a Sieve to sail so fast!"
    Far and few, far and few,
      Are the lands where the Jumblies live;
    Their heads are green, and their hands are blue,
      And they went to sea in a Sieve.

III

The water it soon came in, it did,
  The water it soon came in;
So to keep them dry, they wrapped their feet
In a pinky paper all folded neat,
  And they fastened it down with a pin.
And they passed the night in a crockery-jar,
And each of them said, "How wise we are!
Though the sky be dark, and the voyage be long,

Yet we never can think we were rash or wrong,
While round in our Sieve we spin!"
  Far and few, far and few,
    Are the lands where the Jumblies live;
  Their heads are green, and their hands are blue,
    And they went to sea in a Sieve.

IV

And all night long they sailed away;
  And when the sun went down,
They whistled and warbled a moony song
To the echoing sound of a coppery gong,
  In the shade of the mountains brown.
"O Timballo! How happy we are,
When we live in a sieve and a crockery-jar,
And all night long in the moonlight pale,
We sail away with a pea-green sail,
  In the shade of the mountains brown!"
    Far and few, far and few,
      Are the lands where the Jumblies live;
    Their heads are green, and their hands are blue,
      And they went to sea in a Sieve.

V

They sailed to the Western Sea, they did,
  To a land all covered with trees,
And they bought an Owl, and a useful Cart,
And a pound of Rice, and a Cranberry Tart,
  And a hive of silvery Bees.
And they bought a Pig, and some green Jack-daws,
And a lovely Monkey with lollipop paws,
And forty bottles of Ring-Bo-Ree,
  And no end of Stilton Cheese.
    Far and few, far and few,
      Are the lands where the Jumblies live;
    Their heads are green, and their hands are blue,
      And they went to sea in a Sieve.

VI

And in twenty years they all came back,
  In twenty years or more,
And every one said, "How tall they've
    grown!
For they've been to the Lakes, and the
    Terrible Zone,
  And the hills of the Chankly Bore;"
And they drank their health, and gave
    them a feast
Of dumplings made of beautiful yeast;
And every one said, "If we only live,
We too will go to sea in a Sieve,—
  To the hills of the Chankly Bore!"
    Far and few, far and few,
      Are the lands where the Jumblies
        live;
      Their heads are green, and their
        hands are blue,
      And they went to sea in a Sieve.

The Pobble who has no Toes

I

THE Pobble who has no toes
  Had once as many as we;
When they said, "Some day you may lose
    them all;"—
He replied,—"Fish fiddle de-dee!"
And his Aunt Jobiska made him drink
Lavender water tinged with pink,
For she said, "The World in general
    knows
"There's nothing so good for a Pobble's
    toes!"

II

The Pobble who has no toes,
  Swam across the Bristol Channel;
But before he set out he wrapped his nose,
  In a piece of scarlet flannel.
For his Aunt Jobiska said, "No harm
"Can come to his toes if his nose is
    warm;
"And it's perfectly known that a Pobble's
    toes
"Are safe,—provided he minds his nose."

III

The Pobble swam fast and well,
  And when boats or ships came near him
He tinkledy-binkledy-winkled a bell,
  So that all the world could hear him.
And all the Sailors and Admirals cried,
When they saw him nearing the further
    side,—
"He has gone to fish, for his Aunt
    Jobiska's
"Runcible Cat with crimson whiskers!"

IV

But before he touched the shore,
  The shore of the Bristol Channel,
A sea-green Porpoise carried away
  His wrapper of scarlet flannel.
And when he came to observe his feet,
Formerly garnished with toes so neat,
His face at once became forlorn
On perceiving that all his toes were gone!

V

And nobody ever knew
  From that dark day to the present,
Whoso had taken the Pobble's toes,
  In a manner so far from pleasant.
Whether the shrimps or crawfish gray,
Or crafty Mermaids stole them away—
Nobody knew; and nobody knows
How the Pobble was robbed of his twice
    five toes!

VI

The Pobble who has no toes
  Was placed in a friendly Bark,
And they rowed him back, and carried
    him up,
  To his Aunt Jobiska's Park.
And she made him a feast at his earnest
    wish
Of eggs and buttercups fried with fish;—
And she said,—"It's a fact the whole
    world knows,
"That Pobbles are happier without their
    toes."

JAMES ANTHONY FROUDE (1818-1894)

From THE HISTORY OF ENGLAND FROM THE FALL OF WOLSEY TO
THE DEATH OF ELIZABETH

The Coronation of Anne Boleyn

IN anticipation of the timely close of the proceedings at Dunstable, notice had been given in the city early in May, that preparations should be made for the coronation on the first of the following month. Queen Anne was at Greenwich, but, according to custom, the few preceding days were to be spent at the Tower; and on the 19th of May she was conducted thither in state by the lord mayor and the city companies, with one of those splendid exhibitions upon the water which in the days when the silver Thames deserved its name, and the sun could shine down upon it out of the blue summer sky, were spectacles scarcely rivalled in gorgeousness by the world-famous wedding of the Adriatic. The river was crowded with boats; the banks and the ships in the pool swarmed with people; and fifty great barges formed the procession, all blazing with gold and banners. The queen herself was in her own barge, close to that of the lord mayor; and, in keeping with the fantastic genius of the time, she was preceded up the water by "a foyst or wafter full of ordnance, in which was a great dragon continually moving and casting wildfire, and round about the foyst stood terrible monsters and wild men, casting fire and making hideous noise." So, with trumpets blowing, cannon pealing, the Tower guns answering the guns of the ships, in a blaze of fireworks and splendour, Anne Boleyn was borne along to the great archway of the Tower, where the king was waiting on the stairs to receive her.

And now let us suppose eleven days to have elapsed, the welcome news to have arrived at length from Dunstable, and the fair summer morning of life dawning in treacherous beauty after the long night of expectation. No bridal ceremonial had been possible; the marriage had been huddled over like a stolen love-match, and the marriage feast had been eaten in vexation and disappointment. These past mortifications were to be atoned for by a coronation pageant which the art and the wealth of the richest city in Europe should be poured out in the most lavish profusion to adorn.

On the morning of the 31st of May, the families of the London citizens were stirring early in all houses. From Temple Bar to the Tower, the streets were fresh strewed with gravel, the footpaths were railed off along the whole distance, and occupied on one side by the guilds, their workmen, and apprentices, on the other by the city constables and officials in their gaudy uniforms, "with their staves in hand for to cause the people to keep good room and order." Cornhill and Gracechurch-street had dressed their fronts in scarlet and crimson, in arras and tapestry, and the rich carpet-work from Persia and the East. Cheapside, to outshine her rivals, was draped even more splendidly in cloth of gold, and tissue, and velvet. The sheriffs were pacing up and down on their great Flemish horses, hung with liveries, and all the windows were thronged with ladies crowding to see the procession pass. At length the Tower guns opened, the grim gates rolled back, and under the archway in the bright May sunshine, the long column began slowly to defile. Two states only permitted their representatives to grace the scene with their presence—Venice and France. It was, perhaps, to make the most of this isolated countenance, that the French ambassador's train formed the van of the cavalcade. Twelve French knights came riding foremost in surcoats of blue velvet with sleeves of yellow silk, their horses trapped in blue, with white crosses powdered on their hanging. After them followed a troop of English gentlemen, two and two, and then the Knights of the Bath, "in gowns of violet, with hoods purfled with miniver like doctors." Next, perhaps at a little interval, the abbots passed on, mitred in their robes; the barons followed in crimson velvet, the bishops then, and then the earls and marquises, the dresses of each order increasing in elaborate gorgeousness. All these rode on in pairs. Then came alone Audeley, lord-chancellor, and behind him the Venetian ambassador and the Archbishop of York; the Archbishop of Canterbury, and Du Bellay, Bishop of Bayonne and of Paris, not now with bugle and hunting-frock, but solemn with stole and crozier. Next, the lord mayor, with the city mace in hand, and Garter in his coat of arms; and then Lord William Howard—Belted Will Howard, of the Scottish Border, Marshal of England. The officers of the queen's household succeeded the marshal in scarlet and gold, and the van of the procession was closed by the Duke of Suffolk, as high constable, with his silver wand. It is no easy matter to picture to ourselves the blazing trail of splendour which in such a pageant must have drawn along the London streets,—those streets which now we know so black and smoke-grimed, themselves then radiant with masses of colour, gold, and crimson, and violet. Yet there it was, and there the sun could shine upon it, and tens of thousands of eyes were gazing on the scene out of the crowded lattices.

Glorious as the spectacle was, perhaps however, it passed unheeded.

Those eyes were watching all for another object, which now drew near. In an open space behind the constable there was seen approaching "a white chariot," drawn by two palfreys in white damask which swept the ground, a golden canopy borne above it making music with silver bells: and in the chariot sat the observed of all observers, the beautiful occasion of all this glittering homage; fortune's plaything of the hour, the Queen of England—queen at last—borne along upon the waves of this sea of glory, breathing the perfumed incense of greatness which she had risked her fair name, her delicacy, her honour, her self-respect, to win; and she had won it.

There she sate, dressed in white tissue robes, her fair hair flowing loose over her shoulders, and her temples circled with a light coronet of gold and diamonds—most beautiful—loveliest—most favoured perhaps, as she seemed at that hour, of all England's daughters. Alas! "within the hollow round" of that coronet—

> Kept death his court, and there the antick sate,
> Scoffing her state and grinning at her pomp.
> Allowing her a little breath, a little scene
> To monarchize, be feared, and kill with looks,
> Infusing her with self and vain conceit,
> As if the flesh which walled about her life
> Were brass impregnable; and humoured thus,
> Bored through her castle walls; and farewell, Queen.

Fatal gift of greatness! so dangerous ever! so more than dangerous in those tremendous times when the fountains are broken loose of the great deeps of thought; and nations are in the throes of revolution;—when ancient order and law and tradition are splitting in the social earthquake; and as the opposing forces wrestle to and fro, those unhappy ones who stand out above the crowd become the symbols of the struggle, and fall the victims of its alternating fortunes. And what if into an unsteady heart and brain, intoxicated with splendour, the outward chaos should find its way, converting the poor silly soul into an image of the same confusion,—if conscience should be deposed from her high place, and the Pandora box be broken loose of passions and sensualities and follies; and at length there be nothing left of all which man or woman ought to value, save hope of God's forgiveness.

Three short years have yet to pass, and again, on a summer morning, Queen Anne Boleyn will leave the Tower of London,—not radiant then with beauty on a gay errand of coronation, but a poor wandering ghost, on a sad tragic errand, from which she will never more return, passing away out of an earth where she may stay no longer, into a presence where, nevertheless, we know that all is well—for all of us—and therefore for her.

But let us not cloud her shortlived sunshine with the shadow of the future. She went on in her loveliness, the peeresses following in their carriages, with the royal guard in their rear. In Fenchurch-street she was met by the children of the city schools; and at the corner of Gracechurch-street a masterpiece had been prepared of the pseudo-classic art, then so fashionable, by the merchants of the Styllyard. A Mount Parnassus had been constructed, and a Helicon fountain upon it playing into a basin with four jets of Rhenish wine. On the top of the mountain sat Apollo with Calliope at his feet, and on either side the remaining Muses, holding lutes or harps, and singing each of them some "posy" or epigram in praise of the queen, which was presented, after it had been sung, written in letters of gold.

From Gracechurch-street the procession passed to Leadenhall, where there was a spectacle in better taste, of the old English Catholic kind, quaint perhaps and forced, but truly and even beautifully emblematic. There was again a "little mountain," which was hung with red and white roses; a gold ring was placed on the summit, on which, as the queen appeared, a white falcon was made to "descend as out of the sky,"—"and then incontinent came down an angel with great melody, and set a close crown of gold upon the falcon's head; and in the same pageant sat Saint Anne with all her issue beneath her; and Mary Cleophas with her four children, of the which children one made a goodly oration to the queen, of the fruitfulness of Saint Anne, trusting that like fruit should come of her."

With such "pretty conceits," at that time the honest tokens of an English welcome, the new queen was received by the citizens of London. These scenes must be multiplied by the number of the streets, where some fresh fancy met her at every turn. To preserve the festivities from flagging, every fountain and conduit within the walls ran all day with wine; the bells of every steeple were ringing; children lay in wait with songs, and ladies with posies, in which all the resources of fantastic extravagance were exhausted; and thus in an unbroken triumph—and to outward appearance received with the warmest affection—she passed under Temple Bar, down the Strand by Charing Cross to Westminster Hall. The king was not with her throughout the day; nor did he intend to be with her in any part of the ceremony. She was to reign without a rival, the undisputed sovereign of the hour.

Saturday being passed in showing herself to the people, she retired for the night to "the king's manour house at Westminster," where she slept. On the following morning, between eight and nine o'clock, she returned to the hall, where the lord mayor, the city council, and the peers were again assembled, and took her place on the high dais at the top of the stairs under the cloth of state; while the bishops, the abbots, and the monks of the abbey formed in the area. A railed way had been laid with carpets across Palace Yard and the Sanctuary to the abbey gates, and when all was ready, preceded by the peers in their robes of parliament, the Knights of the Garter in the dress of the order, she swept out under her canopy, the bishops and the monks "solemnly singing." The train was borne by the old Duchess of Norfolk her aunt, the Bishops of London and Winchester on either side "bearing up the lappets of her robe." The Earl of Oxford carried the crown on its cushion immediately before her. She was dressed in purple velvet furred with ermine, her hair escaping loose, as she usually wore it, under a wreath of diamonds.

On entering the abbey, she was led to the coronation chair, where she sat while the train fell into their places, and the preliminaries of the ceremonial were despatched. Then she was conducted up to the high altar, and anointed Queen of England, and she received from the hands of Cranmer, fresh come in haste from Dunstable, with the last words of his sentence upon Catherine scarcely silent upon his lips, the golden sceptre, and St. Edward's crown.

Did any twinge of remorse, any pang of painful recollection, pierce at that moment the incense of glory which she was inhaling? Did any vision flit across her of a sad mourning figure which once had stood where she was standing, now desolate, neglected, sinking into the darkening twilight of a life cut short by sorrow? Who can tell? At such a time, that figure would have weighed heavily upon a noble mind, and a wise mind would have been taught by the thought of it, that, although life be fleeting as a dream, it is long enough to experience strange vicissitudes of fortune. But Anne Boleyn was not noble and was not wise, —too probably she felt nothing but the delicious, all-absorbing, all-intoxicating present; and if that plain, suffering face presented itself to her memory at all, we may fear that it was rather as a foil to her own surpassing loveliness. Two years later she was able to exult over Catherine's death; she is not likely to have thought of her with gentler feelings in the first glow and flush of triumph.

The Execution of Mary, Queen of Scots

HER last night was a busy one. As she said herself there was much to be done and the time was short. A few lines to the King of France were dated two hours after midnight. They were to insist for the last time that she was innocent of the conspiracy, that she was dying for religion, and for having asserted her right to the crown; and to beg that out of the sum which he owed her, her servants' wages might be paid, and masses provided for her soul. After this she slept for three or four hours, and then rose and with the most elaborate care prepared to encounter the end.

At eight in the morning the Provost-marshal knocked at the outer door which communicated with her suite of apartments. It was locked and no one answered, and he went back in some trepidation lest the fears prove true which had been entertained the preceding evening. On his returning with the Sheriff, however, a few minutes later, the door was open, and they were confronted with the tall majestic figure of Mary Stuart standing before them in splendour. The plain grey dress had been exchanged for a robe of black satin; her jacket was of black satin also, looped and slashed and trimmed with velvet. Her false hair was arranged studiously with a coif, and over her head and falling down over her back was a white veil of delicate lawn. A crucifix of gold hung from her neck. In her hand she held a crucifix of ivory, and a number of jewelled Paternosters was attached to her girdle. Led by two of Paulet's gentlemen, the Sheriff walking before her, she passed to the chamber of presence in which she had been tried, where Shrewsbury, Kent, Paulet, Drury and others were waiting to receive her. Andrew Melville, Sir Robert's brother, who had been master of her household, was kneeling in tears. "Melville," she said, "you should rather rejoice than weep that the end of my troubles is come. Tell my friends I die a true Catholic. Commend me to my son. Tell him I have done nothing to prejudice his kingdom of Scotland, and so good Melville, farewell." She kissed him, and turning asked for her chaplain Du Preau. He was not present. There had been a fear of some religious melodrama which it was thought well to avoid. Her ladies, who had attempted to follow her, had been kept back also. She could not afford to leave the account of her death to be reported by enemies and Puritans, and she required assistance for the scene which she meditated. Missing them she asked the reason of their absence, and said she wished them to see her die. Kent said he feared they might scream or faint, or attempt perhaps to dip their handkerchiefs in her blood. She undertook that they should be quiet and obedient. "The Queen," she said, "would never deny her so slight a request;" and when Kent still hesitated, she added with tears, "You know I am cousin to your Queen, of the blood of Henry the Seventh, a married Queen of France, and anointed Queen of Scotland."

It was impossible to refuse. She was allowed to take six of her own people with her, and select them herself. She chose her physician Burgoyne, Andrew Melville, the apothecary Gorion, and her surgeon, with two ladies, Elizabeth Kennedy and Curle's young wife Barbara Mowbray, whose child she had baptised.

"Allons donc," she then said—"Let us go," and passing out attended by the Earls, and leaning on the arm of an officer of the guard, she descended the great staircase to the hall. The news had spread far through the country. Thousands of people were collected outside the walls. About three hundred knights and gentlemen of the country had been admitted to witness the execution. The tables and forms had been removed, and a great wood fire was blazing in the chimney. At the upper end of the hall, above the fire-place, but near it, stood the scaffold, twelve feet square and two feet and a half high. It was covered with black cloth; a low rail ran round it covered with black cloth also, and the Sheriff's guard of halberdiers were ranged on the floor below on the four sides to keep off the crowd. On the scaffold was the block, black like the rest; a square black cushion was placed behind it, and behind the cushion a black chair; on the right were two other chairs for the Earls. The axe leant against the rail, and two masked figures stood like mutes on either side at the back. The Queen of Scots as she swept in seemed as if coming to take a part in some solemn pageant. Not a muscle of her face could be seen to quiver; she ascended the scaffold with absolute composure, looked round her smiling, and sate down. Shrewsbury and Kent followed and took their places, the Sheriff stood at her left hand, and Beale then mounted a platform and read the warrant aloud.

In all the assembly Mary Stuart appeared the person least interested in the words which were consigning her to death.

"Madam," said Lord Shrewsbury to her, when the reading was ended, "you hear what we are commanded to do."

"You will do your duty," she answered, and rose as if to kneel and pray.

The Dean of Peterborough, Dr. Fletcher, approached the rail. "Madam," he began, with a low obeisance, "the Queen's most excellent Majesty;" "Madam, the Queen's most excellent Majesty"—thrice he

MARY STUART RECEIVING HER DEATH SENTENCE

commenced his sentence, wanting words to pursue it. When he repeated the words a fourth time, she cut him short.

"Mr. Dean," she said, "I am a Catholic, and must die a Catholic. It is useless to attempt to move me, and your prayers will avail me but little."

"Change your opinion, Madam," he cried, his tongue being loosed at last: "repent of your sins, settle your faith in Christ, by him to be saved."

"Trouble not yourself further, Mr. Dean," she answered; "I am settled in my own faith, for which I mean to shed my blood."

"I am sorry, Madam," said Shrewsbury, "to see you so addicted to Popery."

"That image of Christ you hold there," said Kent, "will not profit you if he be not engraved in your heart."

She did not reply, and turning her back on Fletcher knelt for her own devotions.

He had been evidently instructed to impair the Catholic complexion of the scene, and the Queen of Scots was determined that he should not succeed. When she knelt he commenced an extempore prayer in which the assembly joined. As his voice sounded out in the hall she raised her own, reciting with powerful deep-chested tones the penitential Psalms in Latin, introducing English sentences at intervals, that the audience might know what she was saying, and praying with especial distinctness for her holy father the Pope.

From time to time, with conspicuous vehemence, she struck the crucifix against her bosom, and then, as the Dean gave up the struggle, leaving her Latin, she prayed in English wholly, still clear and loud. She prayed for the Church which she had been ready to betray, for her son, whom she had disinherited, for the Queen whom she had endeavoured to murder. She prayed God to avert his wrath from England, that England which she had sent a last message to Philip to beseech him to invade. She forgave her enemies, whom she had invited Philip not to forget, and then, praying to the saints to intercede for her with Christ, and kissing the crucifix and crossing her own breast, "Even as thy arms, O Jesus," she cried, "were spread upon the cross, so receive me into thy mercy and forgive my sins."

With these words she rose; the black mutes stepped forward, and in the usual form begged her forgiveness.

"I forgive you," she said, "for now I hope you shall end all my troubles." They offered their help in arranging her dress. "Truly, my lords," she said with a smile to the Earls, "I never had such grooms waiting on me before." Her ladies were allowed to come up upon the scaffold to assist her; for the work to be done was considerable, and had been prepared with no common thought.

She laid her crucifix on her chair. The chief executioner took it as a perquisite, but was ordered instantly to lay it down. The lawn veil was lifted carefully off, not to disturb the hair, and was hung upon the rail. The black robe was next removed. Below it was a petticoat of crimson velvet. The black jacket followed, and under the jacket was a body of crimson satin. One of her ladies handed her a pair of crimson sleeves, with which she hastily covered her arms; and thus she stood on the black scaffold with the black figures all around her, blood-red from head to foot.

Her reasons for adopting so extraordinary a costume must be left to conjecture. It is only certain that it must have been carefully studied, and that the pictorial effect must have been appalling.

The women, whose firmness had hitherto borne the trial, began now to give way, spasmodic sobs bursting from them which they could not check. "Ne criez vous," she said, "j'ay promis pour vous." Struggling bravely, they crossed their breasts again and again, she crossing them in turn and bidding them pray for her. Then she knelt on the cushion. Barbara Mowbray bound her eyes with a handkerchief. "Adieu," she said, smiling for the last time and waving her hand to them, "Adieu, au revoir." They stepped back from off the scaffold and left her alone. On her knees she repeated the Psalm, In te, Domine, confido, "In thee, O Lord, have I put my trust." Her shoulders being exposed, two scars became visible, one on either side, and the Earls being now a little behind her, Kent pointed to them with his white wand and looked enquiringly at his companion. Shrewsbury whispered that they were the remains of two abscesses from which she had suffered while living with him at Sheffield.

When the psalm was finished she felt for the block, and laying down her head muttered: "In manus, Domine tuas, commendo animam meam." The hard wood seemed to hurt her, for she placed her hands under her neck. The executioners gently removed them, lest they should deaden the blow, and then one of them holding her slightly, the other raised the axe and struck. The scene had been too trying even for the practised headsman of the Tower. His arm wandered. The blow fell on the knot of the handkerchief, and scarcely broke the skin. She neither spoke nor moved. He struck again, this time effectively. The head hung by a shred of skin, which he divided without withdrawing the axe; and at once a metamorphosis was witnessed, strange as was ever wrought by wand of fabled enchanter. The coif fell off and the false plaits. The laboured illusion vanished. The lady who had knelt before the block was in the maturity of grace and loveliness. The executioner, when he raised the head, as usual, to shew it to the crowd, exposed the withered features of a grizzled, wrinkled old woman.

"So perish all enemies of the Queen," said the Dean of Peterborough. A loud Amen rose over the hall. "Such end," said the Earl of Kent, rising and standing over the body, "to the Queen's and the Gospel's enemies."

EMILY JANE BRONTË (1818-1848)

Stanzas: A little while, a little while

A LITTLE while, a little while,
    The weary task is put away,
And I can sing and I can smile,
    Alike, while I have holiday.

Where wilt thou go, my harassed heart—
    What thought, what scene invites thee
        now?
What spot, or near or far apart,
    Has rest for thee, my weary brow?

There is a spot, 'mid barren hills,
    Where winter howls, and driving rain;
But, if the dreary tempest chills,
    There is a light that warms again.

The house is old, the trees are bare,
    Moonless above bends twilight's dome;
But what on earth is half so dear,
    So longed for, as the hearth of home?

The mute bird sitting on the stone,
    The dank moss dripping from the wall,
The thorn-trees gaunt, the walks o'er-
        grown,
    I love them, how I love them all!

Still, as I mused, the naked room,
    The alien firelight died away;
And from the midst of cheerless gloom,
    I passed to bright, unclouded day.

A little and a lone green lane
    That opened on a common wide;

A distant, dreamy, dim blue chain
    Of mountains circling every side:

A heaven so clear, an earth so calm,
    So sweet, so soft, so hushed an air;
And, deepening still the dream-like charm,
    Wild moor-sheep feeding everywhere.

That was the scene, I knew it well;
    I knew the turfy pathway's sweep,
That, winding o'er each billowy swell,
    Marked out the tracks of wandering
        sheep.

Even as I stood with raptured eye,
    Absorbed in bliss so deep and dear,
My hour of rest had fleeted by,
    And back came labour, bondage, care.

Last Lines: No coward soul is mine

No coward soul is mine,
No trembler in the world's storm-troubled
        sphere.
    I see Heaven's glories shine,
And faith shines equal, arming me from
        fear.

O God within my breast,
Almighty, ever-present Deity!
    Life—that in me has rest,
As I—undying Life—have power in
        Thee!

Vain are the thousand creeds
That move men's hearts: unutterably
        vain;

Worthless as withered weeds,
Or idlest froth amid the boundless main,

To waken doubt in one
Holding so fast by Thine infinity;
So surely anchored on
The steadfast rock of immortality.

With wide embracing love
Thy Spirit animates eternal years,
Pervades and broods above,
Changes, sustains, dissolves, creates, and
rears.

Though earth and man were gone
And suns and universes ceased to be,
And Thou were left alone,
Every existence would exist in Thee.

There is not room for Death,
Nor atom that his might could render
void:
Thou—THOU art Being and Breath,
And what THOU art may never be de-
stroyed.

ARTHUR HUGH CLOUGH
(1819-1861)

Say not the struggle nought availeth

SAY not the struggle nought availeth,
The labour and the wounds are vain,
The enemy faints not, nor faileth,
And as things have been they remain.

If hopes were dupes, fears may be liars;
It may be, in yon smoke concealed,
Your comrades chase e'en now the fliers,
And, but for you, possess the field.

For while the tired waves, vainly break-
ing,
Seem here no painful inch to gain,
Far back, through creeks and inlets mak-
ing,
Comes silent, flooding in, the main.

And not by eastern windows only,
When daylight comes, comes in the
light,
In front, the sun climbs slow, how slowly,
But westward, look, the land is bright.

MATTHEW ARNOLD (1822-1888)

The Forsaken Merman

COME, dear children, let us away;
Down and away below.
Now my brothers call from the bay;
Now the great winds shoreward blow;
Now the salt tides seaward flow;
Now the wild white horses play,
Champ and chafe and toss in the spray.
    Children dear, let us away.
    This way, this way!

Call her once before you go.
    Call once yet.
In a voice that she will know:
    "Margaret! Margaret!"
Children's voices should be dear
(Call once more) to a mother's ear;
Children's voices, wild with pain.
Surely she will come again.
Call her once and come away.
    This way, this way!
"Mother dear, we cannot stay."
The wild white horses foam and fret.
    Margaret! Margaret!

Come, dear children, come away down.
    Call no more.
One last look at the white-wall'd town,
And the little grey church on the windy
        shore.
    Then come down.
She will not come though you call all
        day.
    Come away, come away.

Children dear, was it yesterday
We heard the sweet bells over the bay?
In the caverns where we lay,
Through the surf and through the
        swell,

The far-off sound of a silver bell?
Sand-strewn caverns, cool and deep,
Where the winds are all asleep;
Where the spent lights quiver and
    gleam;
Where the salt weed sways in the
    stream;
Where the sea-beasts, ranged all round,
Feed in the ooze of their pasture-
    ground;
Where the sea-snakes coil and twine,
Dry their mail, and bask in the brine;
Where great whales come sailing by,
Sail and sail, with unshut eye,
Round the world for ever and aye?
When did music come this way?
Children dear, was it yesterday?

Children dear, was it yesterday
(Call yet once) that she went away?
Once she sate with you and me,
On a red gold throne in the heart of the
    sea,
  And the youngest sate on her knee.
She comb'd its bright hair, and she tended
    it well,
When down swung the sound of the far-
    off bell.
She sigh'd, she look'd up through the clear
    green sea.
She said, "I must go, for my kinsfolk pray
In the little grey church on the shore
    to-day.
'Twill be Easter-time in the world—ah
    me!
And I lose my poor soul, Merman, here
    with thee."
I said, "Go up, dear heart, through the
    waves.
Say thy prayer, and come back to the kind
    sea-caves."
She smiled, she went up through the
    surf in the bay.
  Children dear, was it yesterday?

Children dear, were we long alone?
"The sea grows stormy, the little ones
    moan.

Long prayers," I said, "in the world they
    say.
Come," I said, and we rose through the
    surf in the bay.
We went up the beach, by the sandy down
Where the sea-stocks bloom, to the white-
    wall'd town.
Through the narrow paved streets, where
    all was still,
To the little grey church on the windy
    hill.
From the church came a murmur of folk
    at their prayers,
But we stood without in the cold-blowing
    airs.
We climb'd on the graves, on the stones
    worn with rains,
And we gazed up the aisle through the
    small leaded panes.
  She sate by the pillar; we saw her
    clear:
  "Margaret, hist! come quick, we are
    here.
Dear heart," I said, "we are long alone.
The sea grows stormy, the little ones
    moan."
But, ah! she gave me never a look,
For her eyes were seal'd to the holy book.
Loud prays the priest; shut stands the
    door.
  Come away, children, call no more.
  Come away, come down, call no
    more.

    Down, down, down;
  Down to the depths of the sea.
She sits at her wheel in the humming
    town,
  Singing most joyfully.
Hark what she sings: "O joy, O joy,
For the humming street, and the child
    with its toy.
For the priest, and the bell, and the holy
    well.
  For the wheel where I spun,
  And the blessèd light of the sun."

    And so she sings her fill,
    Singing most joyfully,

Till the shuttle falls from her hand,
And the whizzing wheel stands still.
She steals to the window, and looks at
    the sand;
And over the sand at the sea;
And her eyes are set in a stare;
And anon there breaks a sigh,
And anon there drops a tear,
From a sorrow-clouded eye,
And a heart sorrow-laden,
    A long, long sigh
For the cold strange eyes of a little
    Mermaiden,
And the gleam of her golden hair.

Come away, away, children.
Come children, come down.
The hoarse wind blows colder;
Lights shine in the town.
She will start from her slumber
When gusts shake the door;
She will hear the winds howling,
Will hear the waves roar.
We shall see, while above us
The waves roar and whirl,
A ceiling of amber,
A pavement of pearl.
Singing, "Here came a mortal,
But faithless was she:
And alone dwell for ever
The kings of the sea."

But, children, at midnight,
When soft the winds blow;
When clear falls the moonlight;
When spring-tides are low:
When sweet airs come seaward
From heaths starr'd with broom;
And high rocks throw mildly
On the blanch'd sands a gloom:
Up the still, glistening beaches,
Up the creeks we will hie;
Over banks of bright seaweed
The ebb-tide leaves dry.
We will gaze, from the sand-hills,
At the white, sleeping town;
At the church on the hill-side—
    And then come back down.

Singing, "There dwells a loved one,
    But cruel is she.
She left lonely for ever
    The kings of the sea."

Memorial Verses. April, 1850

(William Wordsworth, 1770-1850)

GOETHE in Weimar sleeps, and Greece,
Long since, saw Byron's struggle cease.
But one such death remained to come;
The last poetic voice is dumb—
We stand to-day by Wordsworth's tomb.

When Byron's eyes were shut in death,
We bowed our head and held our breath.
He taught us little; but our soul
Had *felt* him like the thunder's roll.
With shivering heart the strife we saw
Of passion with eternal law;
And yet with reverential awe
We watched the fount of fiery life
Which served for that Titanic strife.

When Goethe's death was told, we said
Sunk, then, is Europe's sagest head.
Physician of the iron age,
Goethe has done his pilgrimage.
He took the suffering human race,
He read each wound, each weakness
    clear:
And struck his finger on the place,
And said: *Thou ailest here, and here!*
He looked on Europe's dying hour
Of fitful dream and feverish power;
His eye plunged down the weltering strife,
The turmoil of expiring life—
He said: *The end is everywhere,*
Art still has truth, take refuge there!
And he was happy, if to know
Causes of things, and far below
His feet to see the lurid flow
Of terror, and insane distress,
And headlong fate, be happiness.

And Wordsworth!—Ah, pale ghosts, re-
    joice!
For never has such soothing voice

Been to your shadowy world conveyed,
Since erst, at morn, some wandering shade
Heard the clear song of Orpheus come
Through Hades, and the mournful gloom.
Wordsworth has gone from us—and ye,
Ah, may ye feel his voice as we!
He too upon a wintery clime
Had fallen—on this iron time
Of doubts, disputes, distractions, fears.
He found us when the age had bound
Our souls in its benumbing round;
He spoke, and loosed our hearts in tears.
He laid us as we lay at birth
On the cool flowery lap of earth,
Smiles broke from us, and we had ease;
The hills were round us, and the breeze
Went o'er the sun-lit fields again;
Our foreheads felt the wind and rain.
Our youth returned; for there was shed
On spirits that had long been dead,
Spirits dried up and closely furled,
The freshness of the early world.

Ah! since dark days still bring to light
Man's prudence and man's fiery might,
Time may restore us in his course
Goethe's sage mind and Byron's force;
But where will Europe's latter hour
Again find Wordsworth's healing power?
Others will teach us how to dare,
And against fear our breast to steel;
Others will strengthen us to bear—
But who, ah! who, will make us feel?
The cloud of mortal destiny,
Others will front it fearlessly—
But who, like him, will put it by?

Keep fresh the grass upon his grave,
O Rotha, with thy living wave!
Sing him thy best! for few or none
Hears thy voice right, now he is gone.

Requiescat

STREW on her roses, roses,
    And never a spray of yew!
In quiet she reposes;
    Ah, would that I did too!

Her mirth the world required;
    She bathed it in smiles of glee,
But her heart was tired, tired,
    And now they let her be.

Her life was turning, turning,
    In mazes of heat and sound.
But for peace her soul was yearning,
    And now peace laps her round.

Her cabin'd, ample spirit,
    It flutter'd and fail'd for breath.
To-night it doth inherit
    The vasty hall of death.

The Scholar Gipsy

Go, for they call you, Shepherd, from the
        hill;
    Go, Shepherd, and untie the wattled
        cotes:
        No longer leave thy wistful flock
            unfed,
    Nor let thy bawling fellows rack their
        throats,
        Nor the cropp'd grasses shoot an-
        other head.
        But when the fields are still,
And the tired men and dogs all gone to
        rest,
    And only the white sheep are some-
        times seen
    Cross and recross the strips of moon-
        blanch'd green;
    Come, Shepherd, and again begin the
        quest.

Here, where the reaper was at work of
        late,
    In this high field's dark corner, where
        he leaves
        His coat, his basket, and his earthen
            cruse,
    And in the sun all morning binds
        the sheaves,
        Then here, at noon, comes back his
            stores to use;
        Here will I sit and wait,
    While to my ear from uplands far away

The bleating of the folded flocks is borne,
With distant cries of reapers in the corn—
All the live murmur of a summer's day.

Screen'd is this nook o'er the high, half-reap'd field,
And here till sundown, Shepherd, will I be.
Through the thick corn the scarlet poppies peep,
And round green roots and yellowing stalks I see
Pale blue convolvulus in tendrils creep:
And air-swept lindens yield
Their scent, and rustle down their perfumed showers
Of bloom on the bent grass where I am laid,
And bower me from the August sun with shade;
And the eye travels down to Oxford's towers:

And near me on the grass lies Glanvil's book—
Come, let me read the oft-read tale again:
The story of that Oxford scholar poor,
Of pregnant parts and quick inventive brain,
Who, tired of knocking at Preferment's door,
One summer morn forsook
His friends, and went to learn the Gipsy lore,
And roam'd the world with that wild brotherhood,
And came, as most men deem'd, to little good,
But came to Oxford and his friends no more.

But once, years after, in the country lanes,
Two scholars, whom at college erst he knew,

Met him, and of his way of life inquired.
Whereat he answer'd that the Gipsy crew,
His mates, had arts to rule as they desired
The workings of men's brains;
And they can bind them to what thoughts they will:
"And I," he said, "the secret of their art,
When fully learn'd, will to the world impart:
But it needs Heaven-sent moments for this skill!"

This said, he left them, and return'd no more,
But rumours hung about the country-side,
That the lost Scholar long was seen to stray,
Seen by rare glimpses, pensive and tongue-tied,
In hat of antique shape, and cloak of grey,
The same the Gipsies wore.
Shepherds had met him on the Hurst in spring;
At some lone alehouse in the Berkshire moors,
On the warm ingle-bench, the smock-frock'd boors
Had found him seated at their entering,

But, 'mid their drink and clatter, he would fly:
And I myself seem half to know thy looks,
And put the shepherds, Wanderer, on thy trace;
And boys who in lone wheatfields scare the rooks
I ask if thou hast pass'd their quiet place;
Or in my boat I lie
Moor'd to the cool bank in the summer heats,

'Mid wide grass meadows which the
  sunshine fills,
  And watch the warm green-muffled
    Cumnor hills,
  And wonder if thou haunt'st their shy
    retreats.

For most, I know, thou lov'st retirèd
  ground.
  Thee, at the ferry, Oxford riders blithe,
    Returning home on summer nights,
    have met
  Crossing the stripling Thames at Bab-
    lock-hithe,
    Trailing in the cool stream thy
      fingers wet,
  As the slow punt swings round:
  And leaning backwards in a pensive
    dream,
    And fostering in thy lap a heap of
      flowers
  Pluck'd in shy fields and distant
    Wychwood bowers,
  And thine eyes resting on the moonlit
    stream:

And then they land, and thou art seen no
  more.
  Maidens who from the distant hamlets
    come
    To dance around the Fyfield elm in
      May,
  Oft through the darkening fields have
    seen thee roam,
    Or cross a stile into the public way.
  Oft thou hast given them store
  Of flowers—the frail-leaf'd, white ane-
    mone—
    Dark bluebells drench'd with dews
      of summer eves,
    And purple orchises with spotted
      leaves—
  But none has words she can report of
    thee.

And, above Godstow Bridge, when hay-
  time's here
  In June, and many a scythe in sunshine
    flames,

Men who through those wide fields
  of breezy grass
  Where black-wing'd swallows haunt
    the glittering Thames,
    To bathe in the abandon'd lasher
      pass,
  Have often pass'd thee near
  Sitting upon the river bank o'ergrown:
    Mark'd thine outlandish garb, thy
      figure spare,
    Thy dark vague eyes, and soft ab-
      stracted air;
  But, when they came from bathing,
    thou wert gone.

At some lone homestead in the Cumnor
  hills,
  Where at her open door the housewife
    darns,
    Thou hast been seen, or hanging on
      a gate
  To watch the threshers in the mossy
    barns.
    Children, who early range these
      slopes and late
    For cresses from the rills,
  Have known thee watching, all an
    April day,
    The springing pastures and the feed-
      ing kine;
    And mark'd thee, when the stars
      come out and shine,
  Through the long dewy grass move
    slow away.

In autumn, on the skirts of Bagley Wood,
  Where most the Gipsies by the turf-
    edged way
    Pitch their smoked tents, and every
      bush you see
  With scarlet patches tagg'd and shreds
    of gray,
    Above the forest-ground call'd Thes-
      saly—
    The blackbird picking food
  Sees thee, nor stops his meal, nor fears
    at all;
    So often has he known thee past him
      stray

Rapt, twirling in thy hand a wither'd
    spray,
And waiting for the spark from Heaven
    to fall.

And once, in winter, on the causeway chill
  Where home through flooded fields
    foot-travellers go,
    Have I not pass'd thee on the wooden
      bridge
  Wrapt in thy cloak and battling with
    the snow,
    Thy face towards Hinksey and its
      wintry ridge?
    And thou hast climb'd the hill
And gain'd the white brow of the Cum-
  nor range;
    Turn'd once to watch, while thick
    the snowflakes fall,
    The line of festal light in Christ
    Church hall—
Then sought thy straw in some se-
  quester'd grange.

But what—I dream! Two hundred years
  are flown
  Since first thy story ran through Oxford halls,
    And the grave Glanvil did the tale
    inscribe
That thou wert wander'd from the
  studious walls
    To learn strange arts, and join a
    Gipsy tribe:
    And thou from earth art gone
Long since, and in some quiet churchyard laid;
    Some country nook, where o'er thy
    unknown grave
    Tall grasses and white flowering
    nettles wave—
Under a dark red-fruited yew-tree's
  shade.

—No, no, thou hast not felt the lapse of
  hours.
  For what wears out the life of mortal
  men?

'Tis that from change to change their
    being rolls:
'Tis that repeated shocks, again, again,
    Exhaust the energy of strongest souls,
    And numb the elastic powers.
Till having used our nerves with bliss
  and teen,
    And tired upon a thousand schemes
    our wit,
    To the just-pausing Genius we remit
Our worn-out life, and are—what we
  have been.

Thou hast not lived, why shouldst thou
  perish, so?
  Thou hadst *one* aim, *one* business, *one*
  desire:
    Else wert thou long since number'd
    with the dead—
  Else hadst thou spent, like other men,
    thy fire.
    The generations of thy peers are fled,
    And we ourselves shall go;
  But thou possessest an immortal lot,
    And we imagine thee exempt from
    age
    And living as thou liv'st on Glanvil's
    page,
  Because thou hadst—what we, alas,
    have not!

For early didst thou leave the world, with
  powers
  Fresh, undiverted to the world without,
    Firm to their mark, not spent on
    other things;
  Free from the sick fatigue, the languid
    doubt,
    Which much to have tried, in much
    been baffled, brings.
    O Life unlike to ours!
Who fluctuate idly without term or
  scope,
    Of whom each strives, nor knows for
    what he strives,
    And each half-lives a hundred dif-
    ferent lives;
Who wait like thee, but not, like thee,
  in hope.

Thou waitest for the spark from Heaven:
 and we,
 Vague half-believers of our casual
  creeds,
 Who never deeply felt, nor clearly
  will'd,
Whose insight never has borne fruit
 in deeds,
Whose weak resolves never have been
 fulfill'd;
 For whom each year we see
Breeds new beginnings, disappointments
 new;
 Who hesitate and falter life away,
 And lose to-morrow the ground won
  to-day—
Ah, do not we, Wanderer, await it too?

Yes, we await it, but it still delays,
 And then we suffer; and amongst us
  One,
 Who most has suffer'd, takes de-
  jectedly
His seat upon the intellectual throne;
 And all his store of sad experience he
 Lays bare of wretched days;
Tells us his misery's birth and growth
 and signs,
 And how the dying spark of hope was
  fed,
 And how the breast was soothed, and
  how the head,
And all his hourly varied anodynes.

This for our wisest: and we others pine,
 And wish the long unhappy dream
  would end,
 And waive all claim to bliss, and try
  to bear,
With close-lipp'd Patience for our only
 friend,
 Sad Patience, too near neighbour to
  Despair:
 But none has hope like thine.
Thou through the fields and through
 the woods dost stray,
 Roaming the country-side, a truant
  boy,

 Nursing thy project in unclouded
  joy,
And every doubt long blown by time
 away.

O born in days when wits were fresh and
 clear,
 And life ran gaily as the sparkling
  Thames;
 Before this strange disease of modern
  life,
With its sick hurry, its divided aims,
 Its heads o'ertax'd, its palsied hearts,
  was rife—
  Fly hence, our contact fear!
Still fly, plunge deeper in the bowering
 wood!
 Averse, as Dido did with gesture
  stern
 From her false friend's approach in
  Hades turn,
Wave us away, and keep thy solitude.

Still nursing the unconquerable hope,
 Still clutching the inviolable shade,
 With a free onward impulse brushing
  through,
 By night, the silver'd branches of the
  glade—
 Far on the forest-skirts, where none
  pursue,
 On some mild pastoral slope
Emerge, and resting on the moonlit
 pales,
 Freshen thy flowers, as in former
  years,
 With dew, or listen with enchanted
  ears,
From the dark dingles, to the nightin-
 gales.

But fly our paths, our feverish contact fly!
 For strong the infection of our mental
  strife,
 Which, though it gives no bliss, yet
  spoils for rest;
 And we should win thee from thy own
  fair life,

Like us distracted, and like us un-
blest.
    Soon, soon thy cheer would die,
Thy hopes grow timorous, and un-
fix'd thy powers,
And thy clear aims be cross and shift-
ing made:
And then thy glad perennial youth
would fade,
Fade, and grow old at last, and die like
ours.

Then fly our greetings, fly our speech and
    smiles!
—As some grave Tyrian trader, from
    the sea,
Descried at sunrise an emerging prow
Lifting   the   cool-hair'd   creepers
    stealthily,
    The fringes of a southward-facing
    brow
        Among the Ægean isles;
And saw the merry Grecian coaster
    come,
    Freighted with amber grapes, and
    Chian wine,
    Green bursting figs, and tunnies
    steep'd in brine;
And knew the intruders on his ancient
home,

The young light-hearted Masters of the
    waves;
And snatch'd his rudder, and shook out
    more sail,
And day and night held on indignantly
O'er the blue Midland waters with the
    gale,
    Betwixt the Syrtes and soft Sicily,
    To where the Atlantic raves
Outside the Western Straits, and un-
    bent sails
    There, where down cloudy cliffs,
    through sheets of foam,
    Shy traffickers, the dark Iberians
    come;
And on the beach undid his corded
bales.

Rugby Chapel—November, 1857

COLDLY, sadly descends
The autumn evening. The field
Strewn with its dank yellow drifts
Of withered leaves, and the elms,
Fade into dimness apace,
Silent;—hardly a shout
From a few boys late at their play!
The lights come out in the street,
In the schoolroom windows;—but cold
Solemn, unlighted, austere,
Through the gathering darkness, arise
The chapel-walls, in whose bound
Thou, my father! art laid.

There thou dost lie, in the gloom
Of the autumn evening. But ah!
That word *gloom* to my mind
Brings thee back in the light
Of thy radiant vigor again.
In the gloom of November we passed
Days not dark at thy side;
Seasons impaired not the ray
Of thy buoyant cheerfulness clear.
Such thou wast! and I stand
In the autumn evening, and think
Of bygone autumns with thee.

Fifteen years have gone round
Since thou arosest to tread,
In the summer-morning, the road
Of death, at a call unforeseen,
Sudden. For fifteen years,
We who till then in thy shade
Rested as under the boughs
Of a mighty oak, have endured
Sunshine and rain as we might,
Bare, unshaded, alone,
Lacking the shelter of thee.

O strong soul, by what shore
Tarriest thou now? For that force,
Surely, has not been left vain!
Somewhere, surely, afar,
In the sounding labor-house vast
Of being, is practised that strength,
Zealous, beneficent, firm!

Yes, in some far-shining sphere,
Conscious or not of the past,
Still thou performest the word
Of the Spirit in whom thou dost live,
Prompt, unwearied, as here!
Still thou upraisest with zeal
The humble good from the ground,
Sternly repressest the bad;
Still, like a trumpet, dost rouse
Those who with half-open eyes
Tread the border-land dim
'Twixt vice and virtue; reviv'st,
Succorest. This was thy work,
This was thy life upon earth.

What is the course of the life
Of mortal men on the earth?
Most men eddy about
Here and there—eat and drink,
Chatter and love and hate,
Gather and squander, are raised
Aloft, are hurled in the dust,
Striving blindly, achieving
Nothing; and then they die,—
Perish; and no one asks
Who or what they have been,
More than he asks what waves,
In the moonlit solitudes mild
Of the midmost Ocean, have swelled,
Foamed for a moment, and gone.
And there are some whom a thirst
Ardent, unquenchable, fires,
Not with the crowd to be spent,
Not without aim to go round
In an eddy of purposeless dust,
Effort unmeaning and vain.
Ah yes! some of us strive
Not without action to die
Fruitless, but something to snatch
From dull oblivion, nor all
Glut the devouring grave.
We, we have chosen our path,—
Path to a clear-purposed goal,
Path of advance; but it leads
A long, steep journey, through sunk
Gorges, o'er mountains in snow.
Cheerful, with friends, we set forth:
Then, on the height, comes the storm.

Thunder crashes from rock
To rock; the cataracts reply;
Lightnings dazzle our eyes;
Roaring torrents have breached
The track; the stream-bed descends
In the place where the wayfarer once
Planted his footstep—the spray
Boils o'er its borders! aloft,
The unseen snow-beds dislodge
Their hanging ruin. Alas,
Havoc is made in our train!
Friends who set forth at our side
Falter, are lost in the storm.
We, we only are left!
With frowning foreheads, with lips
Sternly compressed, we strain on,
On—and at nightfall at last
Come to the end of our way,
To the lonely inn 'mid the rocks;
Where the gaunt and taciturn host
Stands on the threshold, the wind
Shaking his thin white hairs,
Holds his lantern to scan
Our storm-beat figures, and asks,—
Whom in our party we bring?
Whom we have left in the snow?

Sadly we answer, We bring
Only ourselves! we lost
Sight of the rest in the storm.
Hardly ourselves we fought through,
Stripped, without friends, as we are.
Friends, companions, and train,
The avalanche swept from our side.

But thou wouldst not *alone*
Be saved, my father! *alone*
Conquer and come to thy goal,
Leaving the rest in the wild.
We were weary, and we
Fearful, and we in our march
Fain to drop down and to die.
Still thou turnedst, and still
Beckonedst the trembler, and still
Gavest the weary thy hand.
If, in the paths of the world,
Stones might have wounded thy feet,
Toil or dejection have tried

Thy spirit, of that we saw
Nothing: to us thou wast still
Cheerful, and helpful, and firm!
Therefore to thee it was given
Many to save with thyself,
And, at the end of thy day,
O faithful shepherd, to come,
Bringing thy sheep in thy hand.

And through thee I believe
In the noble and great who are gone;
Pure souls honored and blest
By former ages, who else—
Such, so soulless, so poor,
Is the race of men whom I see—
Seemed but a dream of the heart,
Seemed but a cry of desire.
Yes! I believe that there lived
Others like thee in the past,
Not like the men of the crowd
Who all around me to-day
Bluster or cringe, and make life
Hideous and arid and vile;
But souls tempered with fire,
Fervent, heroic, and good,
Helpers and friends of mankind.

Servants of God!—or sons
Shall I not call you? because
Not as servants ye knew
Your Father's innermost mind,
His who unwillingly sees
One of his little ones lost,—
Yours is the praise, if mankind
Hath not as yet in its march
Fainted and fallen and died.

See! In the rocks of the world
Marches the host of mankind,
A feeble, wavering line.
Where are they tending? A God
Marshalled them, gave them their goal.
Ah, but the way is so long!
Years have they been in the wild:
Sore thirst plagues them; the rocks,
Rising all round, overawe;
Factions divide them; their host
Threatens to break, to dissolve.
—Ah! keep, keep them combined!

Else, of the myriads who fill
That army, not one shall arrive;
Sole they shall stray; in the rocks
Stagger forever in vain,
Die one by one in the waste.

Then, in such hour of need
Of your fainting, dispirited race,
Ye like angels appear,
Radiant with ardor divine.
Beacons of hope, ye appear!
Languor is not in your heart,
Weakness is not in your word,
Weariness not on your brow.
Ye alight in our van! at your voice,
Panic, despair, flee away.
Ye move through the ranks, recall
The stragglers, refresh the outworn,
Praise, re-inspire the brave.
Order, courage, return;
Eyes rekindling, and prayers,
Follow your steps as ye go.
Ye fill up the gaps in our files,
Strengthen the wavering line,
Stablish, continue our march,
On, to the bound of the waste,
On to the City of God.

Thyrsis

A MONODY, *to commemorate the author's
friend,* ARTHUR HUGH CLOUGH, *who
died at Florence,* 1861.

How changed is here each spot man
            makes or fills!
In the two Hinkseys nothing keeps the
            same;
      The village street its haunted man-
            sion lacks,
And from the sign is gone Sibylla's
            name,
      And from the roofs the twisted chim-
            ney-stacks—
            Are ye too changed, ye hills?
See, 'tis no foot of unfamiliar men
      To-night from Oxford up your path-
            way strays!

Here came I often, often, in old
    days—
Thyrsis and I; we still had Thyrsis
    then.

Runs it not here, the track by Childs-
    worth Farm,
    Past the high wood, to where the elm-
        tree crowns
    The hill behind whose ridge the sun-
        set flames?
The signal-elm, that looks on Ilsley
    Downs,
    The Vale, the three lone weirs, the
        youthful Thames?—
      This winter-eve is warm,
Humid the air! leafless, yet soft as
    spring,
    The tender purple spray on copse and
        briers!
And that sweet city with her dream-
    ing spires,
She needs not June for beauty's height-
    ening,

Lovely all times she lies, lovely to-
    night!—
Only, methinks, some loss of habit's
    power
    Befalls me wandering through this
        upland dim.
Once pass'd I blindfold here, at any
    hour;
    Now seldom come I, since I came
        with him.
      That single elm-tree bright
Against the west—I miss it! is it gone?
    We prized it dearly; while it stood,
      we said,
    Our friend, the Gipsy Scholar, was
        not dead;
While the tree lived, he in these fields
    lived on.

Too rare, too rare, grow now my visits
    here,
    But once I knew each field, each flower,
      each stick;
    And with the country-folk acquaint-
        ance made

By barn in threshing-time, by new-
    built rick.
Here, too, our shepherd-pipes we
    first assay'd.
    Ah me! this many a year
My pipe is lost, my shepherd's holiday!
    Needs must I lose them, needs with
      heavy heart
    Into the world and wave of men de-
      part;
But Thyrsis of his own will went away.

It irk'd him to be here, he could not rest.
    He loved each simple joy the country
      yields,
    He loved his mates; but yet he could
      not keep,
For that a shadow lour'd on the fields,
    Here with the shepherds and the
      silly sheep.
    Some life of men unblest
He knew, which made him droop, and
    fill'd his head.
    He went; his piping took a troubled
      sound
    Of storms that rage outside our
      happy ground;
He could not wait their passing, he is
    dead.

So, some tempestuous morn in early June,
    When the year's primal burst of bloom
      is o'er,
    Before the roses and the longest
      day—
    When garden-walks and all the grassy
      floor
    With blossoms red and white of
      fallen May
      And chestnut-flowers are strewn—
So have I heard the cuckoo's parting
    cry,
    From the wet field, through the vext
      garden-trees,
    Come with the volleying rain and
      tossing breeze:
The bloom is gone, and with the bloom
    go I!

Too quick despairer, wherefore wilt thou
    go?
  Soon will the high Midsummer pomps
    come on.
    Soon will the musk carnations break
      and swell,
  Soon shall we have gold-dusted snap-
    dragon,
    Sweet-William with his homely cot-
      tage-smell,
      And stocks in fragrant blow;
  Roses that down the alleys shine afar,
  And open, jasmine-muffled lattices,
  And groups under the dreaming gar-
    den-trees,
  And the full moon, and the white eve-
    ning-star.

He hearkens not! light comer, he is flown!
  What matters it? next year he will re-
    turn,
    And we shall have him in the sweet
      spring-days,
  With whitening hedges, and uncrump-
    ling fern,
    And blue-bells trembling by the
      forest-ways,
    And scent of hay new-mown.
  But Thyrsis never more we swains
    shall see;
    See him come back, and cut a
      smoother reed,
    And blow a strain the world at last
      shall heed—
  For Time, not Corydon, hath con-
    quer'd thee!

Alack, for Corydon no rival now!—
  But when Sicilian shepherds lost a mate,
    Some good survivor with his flute
      would go,
  Piping a ditty sad for Bion's fate;
    And cross the unpermitted ferry's
      flow,
    And relax Pluto's brow,
  And make leap up with joy the beau-
    teous head
    Of Proserpine, among whose
    crownèd hair

  Are flowers first open'd on Sicilian
    air,
  And flute his friend, like Orpheus, from
    the dead.

O easy access to the hearer's grace
  When Dorian shepherds sang to Pros-
    erpine!
    For she herself had trod Sicilian
      fields,
  She knew the Dorian water's gush
    divine,
    She knew each lily white which Enna
      yields,
      Each rose with blushing face;
  She loved the Dorian pipe, the Dorian
    strain.
    But ah, of our poor Thames she
      never heard!
    Her foot the Cumner cowslips never
      stirr'd;
  And we should tease her with our plaint
    in vain!

Well! wind-dispersed and vain the words
    will be,
  Yet, Thyrsis, let me give my grief its
    hour
    In the old haunt, and find our tree-
    topp'd hill!
  Who, if not I, for questing here hath
    power?
    I know the wood which hides the
      daffodil,
      I know the Fyfield tree,
  I know what white, what purple fritil-
    laries
    The grassy harvest of the river-fields,
    Above by Ensham, down by Sandford,
      yields,
  And what sedged brooks are Thames's
    tributaries;

I know these slopes; who knows them if
    not I?—
  But many a dingle on the loved hill-
    side,
    With thorns once studded, old, white-
      blossom'd trees,

Where thick the cowslips grew, and far
    descried
  High tower'd the spikes of purple
    orchises,
    Hath since our day put by
The coronals of that forgotten time;
  Down each green bank hath gone the
    ploughboy's team,
  And only in the hidden brookside
    gleam
Primroses, orphans of the flowery
    prime.

Where is the girl, who by the boatman's
    door,
  Above the locks, above the boating
    throng,
    Unmoor'd our skiff when through
    the Wytham flats,
Red loosestrife and blond meadow-
    sweet among
  And darting swallows and light
    water-gnats,
    We track'd the shy Thames shore?
Where are the mowers, who, as the tiny
    swell
  Of our boat passing heaved the
    river-grass,
  Stood with suspended scythe to see
    us pass?—
They all are gone, and thou art gone
    as well!

Yes, thou art gone! and round me too the
    night
  In ever-nearing circle weaves her
    shade.
  I see her veil draw soft across the
    day,
I feel her slowly chilling breath
    invade
  The cheek grown thin, the brown
    hair sprent with grey;
    I feel her finger light
Laid pausefully upon life's headlong
    train;—
  The foot less prompt to meet the
    morning dew,

The heart less bounding at emotion
    new,
And hope, once crush'd, less quick to
    spring again.

And long the way appears, which seem'd
    so short
  To the less practised eye of sanguine
    youth;
  And high the mountain-tops, in
    cloudy air,
  The mountain-tops where is the throne
    of Truth,
  Tops in life's morning-sun so bright
    and bare!
    Unbreachable the fort
Of the long-batter'd world uplifts its
    wall;
  And strange and vain the earthly tur-
    moil grows,
  And near and real the charm of thy
    repose,
And night as welcome as a friend would
    fall.

But hush! the upland hath a sudden loss
  Of quiet!—Look, adown the dusk hill-
    side,
  A troop of Oxford hunters going
    home,
  As in old days, jovial and talking, ride!
    From hunting with the Berkshire
    hounds they come.
    Quick! let me fly, and cross
Into yon farther field!—'Tis done; and
    see,
  Back'd by the sunset, which doth
    glorify
  The orange and pale violet evening-
    sky,
Bare on its lonely ridge, the Tree! the
    Tree!

I take the omen! Eve lets down her veil,
  The white fog creeps from bush to bush
    about,
  The west unflushes, the high stars
    grow bright,

And in the scatter'd farms the lights
    come out.
  I cannot reach the signal-tree to-
    night,
    Yet, happy omen, hail!
Hear it from thy broad lucent Arno-
    vale
  (For there thine earth-forgetting
    eyelids keep
  The morningless and unawakening
    sleep
Under the flowery oleanders pale),

Hear it, O Thyrsis, still our tree is
  there!—
Ah, vain! These English fields, this
  upland dim,
  These brambles pale with mist en-
    garlanded,
That lone, sky-pointing tree, are not
  for him;
  To a boon southern country he is fled,
    And now in happier air,
Wandering with the great Mother's
  train divine
  (And purer or more subtle soul than
    thee,
  I trow, the mighty Mother doth not
    see)
Within a folding of the Apennine,

Thou hearest the immortal chants of
  old!—
  Putting his sickle to the perilous grain
    In the hot cornfield of the Phrygian
    king,
  For thee the Lityerses-song again
    Young Daphnis with his silver voice
    doth sing;
    Sings his Sicilian fold,
His sheep, his hapless love, his blinded
  eyes—
  And how a call celestial round him
    rang,
  And heavenward from the fountain-
    brink he sprang,
And all the marvel of the golden skies.

There thou art gone, and me thou leavest
  here
  Sole in these fields! yet will I not
    despair.
    Despair I will not, while I yet descry
'Neath the mild canopy of English air
    That lonely tree against the western
    sky.
    Still, still these slopes, 'tis clear,
Our Gipsy Scholar haunts, outliving
  thee!
  Fields where soft sheep from cages
    pull the hay,
  Woods with anemones in flower till
    May,
Know him a wanderer still; then why
    not me?

A fugitive and gracious light he seeks,
  Shy to illumine; and I seek it too.
    This does not come with houses or
    with gold,
  With place, with honour, and a flat-
    tering crew;
    'Tis not in the world's market bought
    and sold—
    But the smooth-slipping weeks
  Drop by, and leave its seeker still un-
    tired;
    Out of the heed of mortals he is gone,
    He wends unfollow'd, he must house
    alone;
  Yet on he fares, by his own heart in-
    spired.

Thou too, O Thyrsis, on like quest wast
  bound;
  Thou wanderedst with me for a little
    hour!
    Men gave thee nothing; but this
    happy quest,
  If men esteem'd thee feeble, gave thee
    power,
    If men procured thee trouble, gave
    thee rest.
    And this rude Cumner ground,
  Its fir-topped Hurst, its farms, its quiet
    fields,

Here cam'st thou in thy jocund
    youthful time,
Here was thine height of strength,
    thy golden prime!
And still the haunt beloved a virtue
    yields.

What though the music of thy rustic flute
    Kept not for long its happy, country
        tone;
      Lost it too soon, and learnt a stormy
        note
Of men contention-tost, of men who
      groan,
    Which task'd thy pipe too sore, and
        tired thy throat—
      It fail'd, and thou wast mute!
Yet hadst thou alway visions of our
    light,
    And long with men of care thou
      couldst not stay,
    And soon thy foot resumed its wan-
      dering way,
Left human haunt, and on alone till
    night.

Too rare, too rare, grow now my visits
    here!
    'Mid city-noise, not, as with thee of
      yore,
      Thyrsis! in reach of sheep-bells is my
        home.
—Then through the great town's harsh,
      heart-wearying roar,
    Let in thy voice a whisper often come,
      To chase fatigue and fear:
Why faintest thou? I wander'd till I
    died.
    Roam on! The light we sought is
    shining still.
    Dost thou ask proof? Our tree yet
    crowns the hill,
Our Scholar travels yet the loved hill-
    side.

Dover Beach

THE sea is calm to-night,
The tide is full, the moon lies fair

Upon the straits;—on the French coast
    the light
Gleams and is gone; the cliffs of England
    stand,
Glimmering and vast, out in the tranquil
    bay.
Come to the window, sweet is the night-
    air!
Only, from the long line of spray
Where the sea meets the moon-blanch'd
    land,
Listen! you hear the grating roar
Of pebbles which the waves draw back,
    and fling,
At their return, up the high strand,
Begin, and cease, and then again begin,
With tremulous cadence slow, and bring
The eternal note of sadness in.

Sophocles long ago
Heard it on the Ægean, and it brought
Into his mind the turbid ebb and flow
Of human misery; we
Find also in the sound a thought,
Hearing it by this distant northern sea.

The Sea of Faith
Was once, too, at the full, and round
    earth's shore
Lay like the folds of a bright girdle furl'd.
But now I only hear
Its melancholy, long, withdrawing roar,
Retreating, to the breath
Of the night-wind, down the vast edges
    drear
And naked shingles of the world.

Ah, love, let us be true
To one another! for the world, which
    seems
To lie before us like a land of dreams,
So various, so beautiful, so new,
Hath really neither joy, nor love, nor
    light,
Nor certitude, nor peace, nor help for
    pain;
And we are here as on a darkling plain
Swept with confused alarms of struggle
    and flight,
Where ignorant armies clash by night.

DANTE GABRIEL ROSSETTI
(1828-1882)

The Blessed Damozel

THE blessed damozel leaned out
  From the gold bar of Heaven;
Her eyes were deeper than the depth
  Of waters stilled at even;
She had three lilies in her hand,
  And the stars in her hair were seven.

Her robe, ungirt from clasp to hem,
  No wrought flowers did adorn,
But a white rose of Mary's gift,
  For service meetly worn;
Her hair that lay along her back
  Was yellow like ripe corn.

Her seemed she scarce had been a day
  One of God's choristers;
The wonder was not yet quite gone
  From that still look of hers;
Albeit, to them she left, her day
  Had counted as ten years.

(To one, it is ten years of years.
  . . . Yet now, and in this place,
Surely she leaned o'er me—her hair
  Fell all about my face. . . .
Nothing: the autumn fall of leaves.
  The whole year sets apace.)

It was the rampart of God's house
  That she was standing on;
By God built over the sheer depth
  The which is Space begun;
So high, that looking downward thence
  She scarce could see the sun.

It lies in Heaven, across the flood
  Of ether, as a bridge.
Beneath, the tides of day and night
  With flame and darkness ridge
The void, as low as where this earth
  Spins like a fretful midge.

Around her, lovers, newly met
  'Mid deathless love's acclaims,
Spoke evermore among themselves
  Their heart-remembered names;

And the souls mounting up to God
  Went by her like thin flames.

And still she bowed herself and stooped
  Out of the circling charm;
Until her bosom must have made
  The bar she leaned on warm,
And the lilies lay as if asleep
  Along her bended arm.

From the fixed place of Heaven she saw
  Time like a pulse shake fierce
Through all the world. Her gaze still
    strove
  Within the gulf to pierce
Its path; and now she spoke as when
  The stars sang in their spheres.

The sun was gone now; the curled
    moon
  Was like a little feather
Fluttering far down the gulf; and now
  She spoke through the still weather.
Her voice was like the voice the stars
  Had when they sang together.

(Ah sweet! Even now, in that bird's
    song,
  Strove not her accents there,
Fain to be hearkened? When those bells
  Possessed the mid-day air,
Strove not her steps to reach my side
  Down all the echoing stair?)

"I wish that he were come to me,
  For he will come," she said.
"Have I not prayed in Heaven?—on
    earth,
  Lord, Lord, has he not pray'd?
Are not two prayers a perfect strength?
  And shall I feel afraid?

"When round his head the aureole clings,
  And he is clothed in white,
I'll take his hand and go with him
  To the deep wells of light;
As unto a stream we will step down,
  And bathe there in God's sight.

"We two will stand beside that shrine,
  Occult, withheld, untrod,

Whose lamps are stirred continually
  With prayer sent up to God;
And see our old prayers, granted, melt
  Each like a little cloud.

"We two will lie i' the shadow of
  That living mystic tree
Within whose secret growth the Dove
  Is sometimes felt to be,
While every leaf that His plumes touch
  Saith His Name audibly.

"And I myself will teach to him,
  I myself, lying so,
The songs I sing here; which his voice
  Shall pause in, hushed and slow,
And find some knowledge at each pause,
  Or some new thing to know."

(Alas! We two, we two, thou say'st!
  Yea, one wast thou with me
That once of old. But shall God lift
  To endless unity
The soul whose likeness with thy soul
  Was but its love for thee?)

"We two," she said, "will seek the groves
  Where the lady Mary is,
With her five handmaidens, whose names
  Are five sweet symphonies,
Cecily, Gertrude, Magdalen,
  Margaret and Rosalys.

"Circlewise sit they, with bound locks
  And foreheads garlanded;
Into the fine cloth white like flame
  Weaving the golden thread,
To fashion the birth-robes for them
  Who are just born, being dead.

"He shall fear, haply, and be dumb:
  Then will I lay my cheek
To his, and tell about our love,
  Not once abashed or weak:
And the dear Mother will approve
  My pride, and let me speak.

"Herself shall bring us, hand in hand,
  To Him round whom all souls

Kneel, the clear-ranged unnumbered
    heads
  Bowed with their aureoles:
And angels meeting us shall sing
  To their citherns and citoles.

"There will I ask of Christ the Lord
  Thus much for him and me:—
Only to live as once on earth
  With Love, only to be,
As then awhile, forever now
  Together, I and he."

She gazed and listened and then said,
  Less sad of speech than mild,—
"All this is when he comes." She ceased.
  The light thrilled towards her, fill'd
With angels in strong level flight.
  Her eyes prayed, and she smil'd.

(I saw her smile.) But soon their path
  Was vague in distant spheres:
And then she cast her arms along
  The golden barriers,
And laid her face between her hands,
  And wept. (I heard her tears.)

Sister Helen

"Why did you melt your waxed man,
          Sister Helen?
To-day is the third since you began."
"The time was long, yet the time ran,
          Little brother."
    (O Mother, Mary Mother,
Three days to-day, between Hell and
  Heaven!)

"But if you have done your work aright,
          Sister Helen,
You'll let me play, for you said I might."
"Be very still in your play to-night,
          Little brother."
    (O Mother, Mary Mother,
Third night, to-night, between Hell and
  Heaven!)

"You said it must melt ere vesper-bell,
          Sister Helen;
If now it be molten, all is well."

"Even so,—nay, peace! you cannot tell,
Little brother."
(*O Mother, Mary Mother,*
O what is this, between Hell and
Heaven?)

"Oh the waxen knave was plump to-day,
Sister Helen;
How like dead folk he has dropped
away!"
"Nay now, of the dead what can you say,
Little brother?"
(*O Mother, Mary Mother,*
What of the dead, between Hell and
Heaven?)

"See, see, the sunken pile of wood,
Sister Helen,
Shines through the thinned wax red as
blood!"
"Nay now, when looked you yet on blood,
Little brother?"
(*O Mother, Mary Mother,*
How pale she is, between Hell and
Heaven!)

"Now close your eyes, for they're sick and
sore,
Sister Helen,
And I'll play without the gallery door."
"Aye, let me rest,—I'll lie on the floor,
Little brother."
(*O Mother, Mary Mother,*
What rest to-night, between Hell and
Heaven?)

"Here high up in the balcony,
Sister Helen,
The moon flies face to face with me."
"Aye, look and say whatever you see,
Little brother."
(*O Mother, Mary Mother,*
What sight to-night, between Hell and
Heaven?)

"Outside it's merry in the wind's wake,
Sister Helen;
In the shaken trees the chill stars shake."
"Hush, heard you a horse-tread as you
spake,
Little brother?"

(*O Mother, Mary Mother,*
What sound to-night, between Hell and
Heaven?)

"I hear a horse-tread, and I see,
Sister Helen,
Three horsemen that ride terribly."
"Little brother, whence come the three,
Little brother?"
(*O Mother, Mary Mother,*
Whence should they come, between Hell
and Heaven?)

"They come by the hill-verge from Boyne
Bar,
Sister Helen,
And one draws nigh, but two are afar."
"Look, look, do you know them who they
are,
Little brother?"
(*O Mother, Mary Mother,*
Who should they be, between Hell and
Heaven?)

"Oh, it's Keith of Eastholm rides so fast,
Sister Helen,
For I know the white mane on the blast."
"The hour has come, has come at last,
Little brother!"
(*O Mother, Mary Mother,*
Her hour at last, between Hell and
Heaven!)

"He has made a sign and called Halloo!
Sister Helen,
And he says that he would speak with
you."
"Oh tell him I fear the frozen dew,
Little brother."
(*O Mother, Mary Mother,*
Why laughs she thus, between Hell and
Heaven?)

"The wind is loud, but I hear him cry,
Sister Helen,
That Keith of Ewern's like to die."
"And he and thou, and thou and I,
Little brother."
(*O Mother, Mary Mother,*
And they and we, between Hell and
Heaven!)

"For three days now he has lain abed,
          Sister Helen,
And he prays in torment to be dead."
"The thing may chance, if he have prayed,
          Little brother!"
          (*O Mother, Mary Mother,
If he have prayed, between Hell and
Heaven!*)

"But he has not ceased to cry to-day,
          Sister Helen,
That you should take your curse away."
"*My* prayer was heard,—he need but
pray,
          Little brother!"

          (*O Mother, Mary Mother,
Shall God not hear, between Hell and
Heaven?*)

"But he says, till you take back your ban,
          Sister Helen,
His soul would pass, yet never can."
"Nay then, shall I slay a living man,
          Little brother?"
          (*O Mother, Mary Mother,
A living soul, between Hell and Heaven!*)

"But he calls for ever on your name,
          Sister Helen,
And says that he melts before a flame."
"My heart for his pleasure fared the
same,
          Little brother."
          (*O Mother, Mary Mother,
Fire at the heart, between Hell and
Heaven!*)

"Here's Keith of Westholm riding fast,
          Sister Helen,
For I know the white plume on the blast."
"The hour, the sweet hour I forecast,
          Little brother!"
          (*O Mother, Mary Mother,
Is the hour sweet, between Hell and
Heaven?*)

"He stops to speak, and he stills his horse,
          Sister Helen;
But his words are drowned in the wind's
course."

"Nay hear, nay hear, you must hear per-
force,
          Little brother!"
          (*O Mother, Mary Mother,
A word ill heard, between Hell and
Heaven!*)

"Oh he says that Keith of Ewern's cry,
          Sister Helen,
Is ever to see you ere he die."
"He sees me in earth, in moon and sky,
          Little brother!"
          (*O Mother, Mary Mother,
Earth, moon and sky, between Hell and
Heaven!*)

"He sends a ring and a broken coin,
          Sister Helen,
And bids you mind the banks of Boyne."
"What else he broke will he ever join,
          Little brother?"
          (*O Mother, Mary Mother,
Oh, never more, between Hell and
Heaven!*)

"He yields you these and craves full fain,
          Sister Helen,
You pardon him in his mortal pain."
"What else he took will he give again,
          Little brother?"
          (*O Mother, Mary Mother,
No more, no more, between Hell and
Heaven!*)

"He calls your name in an agony,
          Sister Helen,
That even dead Love must weep to see."
"Hate, born of Love, is blind as he,
          Little brother!"
          (*O Mother, Mary Mother,
Love turned to hate, between Hell and
Heaven!*)

"Oh it's Keith of Keith now that rides
fast,
          Sister Helen,

For I know the white hair on the blast."
"The short short hour will soon be past,
          Little brother!"

(O Mother, Mary Mother,
Will soon be past, between Hell and
Heaven!)

"He looks at me and he tries to speak,
          Sister Helen,
But oh! his voice is sad and weak!"
"What here should the mighty Baron
   seek,
          Little brother?"
    (O Mother, Mary Mother,
Is this the end, between Hell and
Heaven?)

"Oh his son still cries, if you forgive,
          Sister Helen,
The body dies but the soul shall live."
"Fire shall forgive me as I forgive,
          Little brother!"
    (O Mother, Mary Mother,
As she forgives, between Hell and
Heaven!)

"Oh he prays you, as his heart would
   rive,
          Sister Helen,
To save his dear son's soul alive."
"Nay, flame cannot slay it, it shall thrive,
          Little brother!"
    (O Mother, Mary Mother,
Alas, alas, between Hell and Heaven!)

"He cries to you, kneeling in the road,
          Sister Helen,
To go with him for the love of God!"
"The way is long to his son's abode,
          Little brother."
    (O Mother, Mary Mother,
The way is long, between Hell and
Heaven!)

"O Sister Helen, you heard the bell,
          Sister Helen!
More loud than the vesper-chime it fell."
"No vesper-chime, but a dying knell,
          Little brother!"
    (O Mother, Mary Mother,
His dying knell, between Hell and
Heaven!)

"Alas! but I fear the heavy sound,
          Sister Helen;
Is it in the sky or in the ground?"
"Say, have they turned their horses round,
          Little brother?"
    (O Mother, Mary Mother,
What would she more, between Hell and
Heaven?)

"They have raised the old man from his
   knee,
          Sister Helen,
And they ride in silence hastily."
"More fast the naked soul doth flee,
          Little brother!"
    (O Mother, Mary Mother,
The naked soul, between Hell and
Heaven!)

"Oh the wind is sad in the iron chill,
          Sister Helen,
And weary sad they look by the hill."
"But Keith of Ewern's sadder still,
          Little brother!"
    (O Mother, Mary Mother,
Most sad of all, between Hell and
Heaven!)

"See, see, the wax has dropped from its
   place,
          Sister Helen,
And the flames are winning up apace!"
"Yet here they burn but for a space,
          Little brother!"
    (O Mother, Mary Mother,
Here for a space, between Hell and
Heaven!)

"Ah! what white thing at the door has
   cross'd,
          Sister Helen?
Ah! what is this that sighs in the frost?"
"A soul that's lost as mine is lost,
          Little brother!"
    (O Mother, Mary Mother,
Lost, lost, all lost, between Hell and
Heaven!)

GEORGE MEREDITH (1829-1882)

France. December, 1870

I

WE look for her that sunlike stood
Upon the forehead of our day,
An orb of nations, radiating food
For body and for mind alway.
Where is the Shape of glad array;
The nervous hands, the front of steel,
The clarion tongue? Where is the bold
    proud face?
We see a vacant place;
We hear an iron heel.

II

O she that made the brave appeal
For manhood when our time was dark,
And from our fetters drove the spark
Which was as lightning to reveal
New seasons, with the swifter play
Of pulses, and benigner day;
She that divinely shook the dead
From living man; that stretched ahead
Her resolute forefinger straight,
And marched toward the gloomy gate
Of earth's Untried, gave note, and in
The good name of Humanity
Called forth the daring vision! she,
She likewise half corrupt of sin,
Angel and Wanton! can it be?
Her star has foundered in eclipse,
The shriek of madness on her lips;
Shreds of her, and no more, we see.
There is horrible convulsion, smothered
    din,
As of one that in a grave-cloth struggles
    to be free.

III

Look not for spreading boughs
On the riven forest tree.
Look down where deep in blood and mire
Black thunder plants his feet and ploughs
The soil for ruin: that is France:
Still thrilling like a lyre,
Amazed to shivering discord from a fall

Sudden as that the lurid hosts recall
Who met in heaven the irreparable mis-
    chance.
O that is France!
The brilliant eyes to kindle bliss,
The shrewd quick lips to laugh and kiss,
Breasts that a sighing world inspire,
And laughter-dimpled countenance
Where soul and senses caught desire!

IV

Ever invoking fire from heaven, the fire
Has grasped her, unconsumable, but
    framed
For all the ecstasies of suffering dire.
Mother of Pride, her sanctuary shamed:
Mother of Delicacy, and made a mark
For outrage: Mother of Luxury, stripped
    stark:
Mother of Heroes, bondsmen: through
    the rains,
Across her boundaries, lo the league-long
    chains!
Fond Mother of her martial youth; they
    pass,
Are spectres in her sight, are mown as
    grass!
Mother of Honour, and dishonoured:
    Mother
Of Glory, she condemned to crown with
    bays
Her victor, and be fountain of his praise.
Is there another curse? There is another:
Compassionate her madness: is she not
Mother of Reason? she that sees them
    mown
Like grass, her young ones! Yea, in the
    low groan
And under the fixed thunder of this hour
Which holds the animate world in one
    foul blot
Tranced circumambient while relentless
    Power
Breaks at her heart and claws her limbs
    down-thrown,
She, with the plunging lightnings overshot,
With madness for an armour against
    pain,

With milkless breasts for little ones
   athirst,
And round her all her noblest dying in
   vain,
Mother of Reason is she, trebly cursed,
To feel, to see, to justify the blow;
Chamber to chamber of her sequent brain
Gives answer of the cause of her great
   woe,
Inexorably echoing through the vaults,
"'Tis thus they reap in blood, in blood
   who sow:
This is the sum of self-absolvèd faults."
Doubt not that through her grief, with
   sight supreme,
Through her delirium and despair's last
   dream,
Through pride, through bright illusion
   and the brood
Bewildering of her various Motherhood,
The high strong light within her, though
   she bleeds,
Traces the letters of returned misdeeds.
She sees what seed long sown, ripened of
   late,
Bears this fierce crop; and she discerns
   her fate
From origin to agony, and on
As far as the wave washes long and was
Off one disastrous impulse: for of waves
Our life is, and our deeds are pregnant
   graves
Blown rolling to the sunset from the
   dawn.

V

Ah, what a dawn of splendour, when her
   sowers
Went forth and bent the necks of popu-
   lations,
And of their terrors and humiliations
Wove her the starry wreath that earth-
   ward lowers
Now in the figure of a burning yoke!
Her legions traversed North and South
   and East,
Of triumph they enjoyed the glutton's
   feast:

They grafted the green sprig, they lopped
   the oak.
They caught by the beard the tempests,
   by the scalp
The icy precipices, and clove sheer
   through
The heart of horror of the pinnacled Alp,
Emerging not as men whom mortals
   knew.
They were the earthquake and the hurri-
   cane,
The lightnings and the locusts, plagues
   of blight,
Plagues of the revel: they were Deluge
   rain,
And dreaded Conflagration; lawless
   Might.
Death writes a reeling line along the
   snows,
Where under frozen mists they may be
   tracked,
Who men and elements provoked to foes,
And Gods: they were of god and beast
   compact:
Abhorred of all. Yet, how they sucked
   the teats
Of Carnage, thirsty issue of their dam,
Whose eagles, angrier than their ori-
   flamme,
Flushed the vext earth with blood, green
   earth forgets.
The gay young generations mask her
   grief;
Where bled her children hangs the loaded
   sheaf.
Forgetful is green earth; the Gods alone
Remember everlastingly: they strike
Remorselessly, and ever like for like.
By their great memories the Gods are
   known.

VI

They are with her now, and in her ears,
   and known.
'Tis they that cast her to the dust for
   Strength,
Their slave, to feed on her fair body's
   length,

That once the sweetest and the proudest
    shone;
Scoring for hideous dismemberment
Her limbs, as were the anguish-taking
    breath
Gone out of her in the insufferable
    descent
From her high chieftainship; as were she
    death,
Who hears a voice of justice, feels the
    knife
Of torture, drinks all ignominy of life.
They are with her, and the painful Gods
    might weep,
If ever rain of tears came out of heaven
To flatter Weakness and bid Conscience
    sleep,
Viewing the woe of this Immortal, driven
For the soul's life to drain the madden-
    ing cup
Of her own children's blood implacably:
Unsparing even as they to furrow up
The yellow land to likeness of a sea:
The bountiful fair land of vine and
    grain,
Of wit and grace and ardour, and strong
    roots,
Fruits perishable, imperishable fruits;
Furrowed to likeness of the dim grey
    main
Behind the black obliterating cyclone.

VII

Behold, the Gods are with her, and are
    known.
Whom they abandon misery persecutes
No more: them half-eyed apathy may
    loan
The happiness of pitiable brutes.
Whom the just Gods abandon have no
    light,
No ruthless light of introspective eyes
That in the midst of misery scrutinize
The heart and its iniquities outright.
They rest, they smile and rest; have
    earned perchance
Of ancient service quiet for a term;
Quiet of old men dropping to the worm;

And so goes out the soul. But not of
    France.
She cries for grief, and to the Gods she
    cries,
For fearfully their loosened hands chas-
    tize,
And icily they watch the rod's caress
Ravage her flesh from scourges merciless,
But she, inveterate of brain, discerns
That Pity has as little place as Joy
Among their roll of gifts; for Strength
    she yearns,
For Strength, her idol once, too long her
    toy.
Lo, Strength is of the plain root-Virtues
    born:
Strength shall ye gain by service, prove
    in scorn,
Train by endurance, by devotion shape.
Strength is not won by miracle or rape.
It is the offspring of the modest years,
The gift of sire to son, through those
    firm laws
Which we name Gods; which are the
    righteous cause,
The cause of man, and manhood's min-
    isters.
Could France accept the fables of her
    priests,
Who blest her banners in this game of
    beasts,
And now bid hope that heaven will in-
    tercede
To violate its laws in her sore need,
She would find comfort in their opiates:
Mother of Reason! can she cheat the
    Fates?
Would she, the champion of the open
    mind,
The Omnipotent's prime gift—the gift of
    growth—
Consent even for a night-time to be
    blind,
And sink her soul on the delusive sloth,
For fruits ethereal and material, both,
In peril of her place among mankind?
The Mother of the many Laughters
    might

Call one poor shade of laughter in the
  light
Of her unwavering lamp to mark what
  things
The world puts faith in, careless of the
  truth:
What silly puppet-bodies danced on
  strings,
Attached by credence, we appear in sooth,
Demanding intercession, direct aid,
When the whole tragic tale hangs on a
  broken blade!

She swung the sword for centuries; in a
  day
It slipped her, like a stream cut off from
  source.
She struck a feeble hand, and tried to
  pray,
Clamoured of treachery, and had re-
  course
To drunken outcries in her dream that
  Force
Needed but hear her shouting to obey.
Was she not formed to conquer?   The
  bright plumes
Of crested vanity shed graceful nods:
Transcendent in her foundries, Arts and
  looms,
Had France to fear the vengeance of the
  Gods?
Her faith was on her battle-roll of names
Sheathed in the records of old war; with
  dance
And song she thrilled her warriors and
  her dames,
Embracing her Dishonour: gave him
  France
From head to foot, France present and
  to come,
So she might hear the trumpet and the
  drum—
Bellona and Bacchante! rushing forth
On yon stout marching Schoolmen of the
  North.

Inveterate of brain, well knows she why
Strength failed her, faithful to himself
  the first:

Her dream is done, and she can read the
  sky,
And she can take into her heart the worst
Calamity to drug the shameful thought
Of days that made her as the man she
  served,
A name of terror, but a thing unnerved:
Buying the trickster, by the trickster
  bought,
She for dominion, he to patch a throne.

VIII

Henceforth of her the Gods are known,
Open to them her breast is laid.
Inveterate of brain, heart-valiant,
Never did fairer creature pant
Before the altar and the blade!

IX

Swift fall the blows, and men upbraid,
And friends give echo blunt and cold,
The echo of the forest to the axe.
Within her are the fires that wax
For resurrection from the mould.

X

She snatched at heaven's flame of old,
And kindled nations: she was weak:
Frail sister of her heroic prototype,
The Man; for sacrifice unripe,
She too must fill a Vulture's beak.
Deride the vanquished, and acclaim
The conqueror, who stains her fame,
Still the Gods love her, for that of high
  aim
Is this good France, the bleeding thing
  they stripe.

XI

She shall rise worthier of her prototype
Through her abasement deep; the pain
  that runs
From nerve to nerve some victory
  achieves.
They lie like circle-strewn soaked
  Autumn-leaves
Which stain the forest scarlet, her fair
  sons!

And of their death her life is: of their
blood
From many streams now urging to a
flood,
No more divided, France shall rise afresh.
Of them she learns the lesson of the
flesh:—
The lesson writ in red since first Time
ran
A hunter hunting down the beast in man:
That till the chasing out of its last vice,
The flesh was fashioned but for sacrifice.

Immortal Mother of a mortal host!
Thou suffering of the wounds that will
not slay,
Wounds that bring death but take not
life away!—
Stand fast and hearken while thy victors
boast:
Hearken, and loathe that music evermore.
Slip loose thy garments woven of pride
and shame:
The torture lurks in them, with them the
blame
Shall pass to leave thee purer than before.
Undo thy jewels, thinking whence they
came,
For what, and of the abominable name
Of her who in imperial beauty wore.

O Mother of a fated fleeting host
Conceived in the past days of sin, and
born
Heirs of disease and arrogance and scorn,
Surrender, yield the weight of thy great
ghost,
Like wings on air, to what the heavens
proclaim
With trumpets from the multitudinous
mounds
Where peace has filled the hearing of thy
sons:
Albeit a pang of dissolution rounds
Each new discernment of the undying
ones,
Do thou stoop to these graves here scat-
tered wide
Along thy fields, as sunless billows roll;

These ashes have the lesson for the soul.
"Die to thy Vanity, and strain thy Pride,
Strip off thy Luxury: that thou may'st
live,
Die to thyself," they say, "as we have died
From dear existence and the foe forgive,
Nor pray for aught save in our little space
To warn good seed to greet the fair
earth's face."
O Mother! take their counsel, and so
shall
The broader world breathe in on this thy
home,
Light clear for thee the counter-changing
dome,
Strength give thee, like an ocean's vast
expanse
Off mountain cliffs, the generations all,
Not whirling in their narrow rings of
foam,
But as a river forward. Soaring France!
Now is Humanity on trial in thee:
Now may'st thou gather humankind in
fee:
Now prove that Reason is a quenchless
scroll;
Make of calamity thine aureole,
And bleeding head us through the
troubles of the sea.

CHRISTINA ROSSETTI (1830-1894)

Uphill

Does the road wind uphill all the way?
  Yes, to the very end.
Will the day's journey take the whole
    long day?
  From morn to night, my friend.

But is there for the night a resting-place?
  A roof for when the slow, dark hours
    begin.
May not the darkness hide it from my
    face?
  You cannot miss that inn.

Shall I meet other wayfarers at night?
  Those who have gone before.

Then must I knock, or call when just in
  sight?
  They will not keep you waiting at that
    door.

Shall I find comfort, travel-sore and
  weak?
  Of labour you shall find the sum.
Will there be beds for me and all who
  seek?
  Yea, beds for all who come.

A Christmas Carol

THANK God, thank God, we do believe;
Thank God that this is Christmas Eve.
Even as we kneel upon this day,
Even so, the ancient legends say,
Nearly two thousand years ago
The stalled ox knelt, and even so
The ass knelt full of praise, which they
Could not express, while we can pray.
Thank God, thank God, for Christ was
  born
Ages ago, as on this morn.
In the snow-season undefiled
God came to earth a little child:
He put His ancient glory by
To live for us and then to die.

How shall we thank God? How shall
  we
Thank Him and praise Him worthily?
What will He have who loved us thus?
What presents will He take from us?
Will He take gold, or precious heap
Of gems? or shall we rather steep
The air with incense, or bring myrrh?
What man will be our messenger
To go to Him and ask His will?
Which having learned, we will fulfil
Though He choose all we most prefer:—
What man will be our messenger?

Thank God, thank God, the Man is
  found,
Sure-footed, knowing well the ground.
He knows the road, for this the way
He travelled once, as on this day.
He is our Messenger beside,
He is our door and path and Guide:
He also is our Offering:
He is the gift that we must bring.
Let us kneel down with one accord
And render thanks unto the Lord:
For unto us a Child is born
Upon this happy Christmas morn;
For unto us a Son is given,
Firstborn of God and Heir of Heaven.

LEWIS CARROLL (1832-1892)

From ALICE IN WONDERLAND

Down the Rabbit Hole

ALICE was beginning to get very tired of sitting by her sister on
the bank, and of having nothing to do: once or twice she had peeped
into the book her sister was reading, but it had no pictures or conversations in it, "and what is the use of a book," thought Alice, "without
pictures or conversations?"

So she was considering, in her own mind (as well as she could, for
the hot day made her feel very sleepy and stupid), whether the pleasure
of making a daisy-chain would be worth the trouble of getting up and
picking the daisies, when suddenly a White Rabbit with pink eyes ran
close by her.

There was nothing so *very* remarkable in that; nor did Alice think it so *very* much out of the way to hear the Rabbit say to itself "Oh dear! Oh dear! I shall be too late!" (when she thought it over afterwards, it occurred to her that she ought to have wondered at this, but at the time it all seemed quite natural); but, when the Rabbit actually *took a watch out of its waistcoat-pocket*, and looked at it, and then hurried on, Alice started to her feet, for it flashed across her mind that she had never before seen a rabbit with either a waistcoat-pocket, or a watch to take out of it, and burning with curiosity, she ran across the field after it, and was just in time to see it pop down a large rabbit-hole under the hedge.

In another moment down went Alice after it, never once considering how in the world she was to get out again.

The rabbit-hole went straight on like a tunnel for some way, and then dipped suddenly down, so suddenly that Alice had not a moment to think about stopping herself before she found herself falling down what seemed to be a very deep well.

Either the well was very deep, or she fell very slowly, for she had plenty of time as she went down to look about her, and to wonder what was going to happen next. First, she tried to look down and make out what she was coming to, but it was too dark to see anything: then she looked at the sides of the well, and noticed that they were filled with cupboards and book-shelves: here and there she saw maps and pictures hung upon pegs. She took down a jar from one of the shelves as she passed: it was labeled "ORANGE MARMALADE," but to her great disappointment it was empty: she did not like to drop the jar, for fear of killing somebody underneath, so managed to put it into one of the cupboards as she fell past it.

"Well!" thought Alice to herself. "After such a fall as this, I shall think nothing of tumbling down-stairs! How brave they'll think me at home! Why, I wouldn't say anything about it, even if I fell off the top of the house!" (Which was very likely true.)

Down, down, down. Would the fall *never* come to an end? "I wonder how many miles I've fallen by this time?" she said aloud. "I must be getting somewhere near the centre of the earth. Let me see: that would be four thousand miles down, I think—" (for, you see, Alice had learnt several things of this sort in her lessons in the school-room, and though this was not a *very* good opportunity for showing off her knowledge, as there was no one to listen to her, still it was good practice to say it over)"—yes, that's about the right distance—but then I wonder what Latitude or Longitude I've got to?" (Alice had not the slightest idea what Latitude was, or Longitude either, but she thought they were nice grand words to say.)

Presently she began again. "I wonder if I shall fall right *through* the earth! How funny it'll seem to come out among the people that walk with their heads downwards! The antipathies, I think—" (she was rather glad there *was* no one listening, this time, as it didn't sound at all the right word) "—but I shall have to ask them what the name of the country is, you know. Please, Ma'am, is this New Zealand? Or Australia?" (and she tried to curtsey as she spoke—fancy, *curtseying* as you're falling through the air! Do you think you could manage it?) "And what an ignorant little girl she'll think me for asking! No, it'll never do to ask: perhaps I shall see it written up somewhere."

Down, down, down. There was nothing else to do, so Alice soon began talking again. "Dinah'll miss me very much to-night, I should think!" (Dinah was the cat.) "I hope they'll remember her saucer of milk at tea-time. Dinah, my dear! I wish you were down here with me! There are no mice in the air, I'm afraid, but you might catch a bat, and that's very like a mouse, you know. But do cats eat bats, I wonder?" And here Alice began to get rather sleepy, and went on saying to herself, in a dreamy sort of way, "Do cats eat bats? Do cats eat bats?" and sometimes "Do bats eat cats?", for, you see, as she couldn't answer either question, it didn't much matter which way she put it. She felt that she was dozing off, and had just begun to dream that she was walking hand in hand with Dinah, and was saying to her, very earnestly, "Now, Dinah, tell me the truth: did you ever eat a bat?", when suddenly, thump! thump! down she came upon a heap of sticks and dry leaves, and the fall was over.

Alice was not a bit hurt, and she jumped up on to her feet in a moment: she looked up, but it was all dark overhead: before her was another long passage, and the White Rabbit was still in sight, hurrying down it. There was not a moment to be lost: away went Alice like the wind, and was just in time to hear it say, as it turned a corner, "Oh my ears and whiskers, how late it's getting!" She was close behind it when she turned the corner, but the Rabbit was no longer to be seen: she found herself in a long, low hall, which was lit up by a row of lamps hanging from the roof.

There were doors all round the hall, but they were all locked; and when Alice had been all the way down one side and up the other, trying every door, she walked sadly down the middle, wondering how she was ever to get out again.

Suddenly she came upon a little three-legged table, all made of solid glass: there was nothing on it but a tiny golden key, and Alice's first idea was that this might belong to one of the doors of the hall; but, alas! either the locks were too large, or the key was too small, but at any rate it would not open any of them. However, on the second time round, she came upon a low curtain she had not noticed before, and behind it was a little door about fifteen inches high: she tried the little golden key in the lock, and to her great delight it fitted!

Alice opened the door and found that it led into a small passage, not much larger than a rat-hole: she knelt down and looked along the passage into the loveliest garden you ever saw. How she longed to get out of that dark hall, and wander about among those beds of bright flowers and those cool fountains, but she could not even get her head through the doorway; "and even if my head *would* go through," thought poor Alice, "it would be of very little use without my shoulders. Oh, how I wish I could shut up like a telescope! I think I could, if I only knew how to begin." For, you see, so many out-of-the-way things had happened lately, that Alice had begun to think that very few things indeed were really impossible.

There seemed to be no use in waiting by the little door, so she went back to the table, half hoping she might find another key on it, or at any rate a book of rules for shutting people up like telescopes: this time she found a little bottle on it ("which certainly was not here before," said Alice), and tied round the neck of the bottle was a paper label, with the words "DRINK ME" beautifully printed on it in large letters.

It was all very well to say "Drink me," but the wise little Alice was not going to do *that* in a hurry. "No, I'll look first," she said, "and see whether it's marked '*poison*' or not"; for she had read several nice little stories about children who had got burnt, and eaten up by wild beasts, and other unpleasant things, all because they *would* not remember the simple rules their friends had taught them: such as, that a red-hot poker will burn you if you hold it too long; and that, if you cut your finger *very* deeply with a knife, it usually bleeds; and she had never forgotten that, if you drink much from a bottle marked "poison," it is almost certain to disagree with you, sooner or later.

However, this bottle was *not* marked "poison," so Alice ventured to taste it, and, finding it very nice (it had, in fact, a sort of mixed flavour of cherry-tart, custard, pine-apple, roast turkey, toffy, and hot buttered toast), she very soon finished it off.

        *   *   *   *   *   *   *

          *   *   *   *   *

       *   *   *   *   *   *

"What a curious feeling!" said Alice. "I must be shutting up like a telescope!"

And so it was indeed: she was now only ten inches high, and her face brightened up at the thought that she was now the right size for going through the little door into that lovely garden. First, however, she waited for a few minutes to see if she was going to shrink any further: she felt a little nervous about this; "for it might end, you know," said Alice to herself, "in my going out altogether, like a candle. I wonder what I should be like then?" And she tried to fancy what the flame of a candle looks like after the candle is blown out, for she could not remember ever having seen such a thing.

After a while, finding that nothing more happened, she decided on going into the garden at once; but, alas for poor Alice! when she got to the door, she found she had forgotten the little golden key, and when she went back to the table for it, she found she could not possibly reach it: she could see it quite plainly through the glass, and she tried her best to climb up one of the legs of the table, but it was too slippery; and when she had tired herself out with trying, the poor little thing sat down and cried.

"Come, there's no use in crying like that!" said Alice to herself rather sharply. "I advise you to leave off this minute!" She generally gave herself very good advice (though she very seldom followed it), and sometimes she scolded herself so severely as to bring tears into her eyes; and once she remembered trying to box her own ears for having cheated herself in a game of croquet she was playing against herself, for this curious child was very fond of pretending to be two people. "But it's no use now," thought poor Alice, "to pretend to be two people! Why, there's hardly enough of me left to make *one* respectable person!"

Soon her eye fell on a little glass box that was lying under the table: she opened it, and found in it a very small cake, on which the words "EAT ME" were beautifully marked in currants. "Well, I'll eat it," said Alice, "and if it makes me grow longer, I can reach the key; and if it makes me grow smaller, I can creep under the door: so either way I'll get into the garden, and I don't care which happens!"

She ate a little bit, and said anxiously to herself "Which way? Which way?", holding her hand on the top of her head to feel which way it was growing; and she was quite surprised to find that she remained the same size. To be sure, this is what generally happens when one eats cake; but Alice had got so much into the way of expecting nothing but out-of-the-way things to happen, that it seemed quite dull and stupid for life to go on in the common way.

So she set to work, and very soon finished off the cake.

The Pool of Tears

"CURIOUSER and curiouser!" cried Alice (she was so much surprised, that for the moment she quite forgot how to speak good English). "Now I'm opening out like the largest telescope that ever was! Good-bye, feet!" (for when she looked down at her feet, they seemed to be almost out of sight, they were getting so far off). "Oh, my poor little feet, I wonder who will put on your shoes and stockings for you now, dears? I'm sure *I* sha'n't be able! I shall be a great deal too far off to trouble myself about you: you must manage the best way you can—but I must be kind to them," thought Alice, "or perhaps they won't walk the way I want to go! Let me see. I'll give them a new pair of boots every Christmas."

And she went on planning to herself how she would manage it. "They must go by the carrier," she thought; "and how funny it'll seem, sending presents to one's own feet! And how odd the directions will look!

> *Alice's Right Foot, Esq.*
> *Hearthrug,*
> *near the Fender,*
> *(with Alice's love).*

Oh dear, what nonsense I'm talking!

Just at this moment her head struck against the roof of the hall: in fact she was now rather more than nine feet high, and she at once took up the little golden key and hurried off to the garden door.

Poor Alice! It was as much as she could do, lying down on one side, to look through into the garden with one eye; but to get through was more hopeless than ever: she sat down and began to cry again.

"You ought to be ashamed of yourself," said Alice, "a great girl like you," (she might well say this), "to go on crying in this way! Stop this moment, I tell you!" But she went on all the same, shedding gallons of tears, until there was a large pool all round her, about four inches deep, and reaching half down the hall.

After a time she heard a little pattering of feet in the distance, and she hastily dried her eyes to see what was coming. It was the White Rabbit returning, splendidly dressed, with a pair of white kid-gloves in one hand and a large fan in the other: he came trotting along in a great hurry, muttering to himself, as he came, "Oh! The Duchess, the Duchess! Oh! *Won't* she be savage if I've kept her waiting!" Alice felt so desperate that she was ready to ask help of any one: so, when the Rabbit came near her, she began, in a low, timid voice, "If you please, Sir——" The Rabbit started violently, dropped the white kid-gloves and the fan, and skurried away into the darkness as hard as he could go.

Alice took up the fan and gloves, and, as the hall was very hot, she kept fanning herself all the time she went on talking. "Dear, dear! How queer everything is to-day! And yesterday things went on just as usual. I wonder if I've been changed in the night? Let me think: *was* I the same when I got up this morning? I almost think I can remember feeling a little different. But if I'm not the same, the next question is 'Who in the world am I?' Ah, *that's* the great puzzle!" And she began thinking over all the children she knew that were of the same age as herself, to see if she could have been changed for any of them.

"I'm sure I'm not Ada," she said, "for her hair goes in such long ringlets, and mine doesn't go in ringlets at all; and I'm sure I can't be Mabel, for I know all sorts of things, and she, oh, she knows such a very little! Besides, *she's* she, and *I'm* I, and—oh dear, how puzzling it all is! I'll try if I know all the things I used to know. Let me see: four times five is twelve, and four times six is thirteen, and four times seven is—oh dear! I shall never get to twenty at that rate! However, the Multiplication-Table doesn't signify: let's try Geography. London is the capital of Paris, and Paris is the capital of Rome, and Rome— no, *that's* all wrong, I'm certain! I must have been changed for Mabel! I'll try and say '*How doth the little—*'," and she crossed her hands on her lap, as if she were saying lessons, and began to repeat it, but her voice sounded hoarse and strange, and the words did not come the same as they used to do:—

> "*How doth the little crocodile*
> *Improve his shining tail,*
> *And pour the waters of the Nile*
> *On every golden scale!*
>
> "*How cheerfully he seems to grin,*
> *How neatly spreads his claws,*
> *And welcomes little fishes in,*
> *With gently smiling jaws!*"

"I'm sure those are not the right words," said poor Alice, and her eyes filled with tears again as she went on, "I must be Mabel after all, and I shall have to go and live in that poky little house, and have next to no toys to play with, and oh, ever so many lessons to learn! No, I've made up my mind about it: if I'm Mabel, I'll stay down here! It'll be no use their putting their heads down and saying 'Come up again, dear!' I shall only look up and say 'Who am I, then? Tell me that first, and then, if I like being that person, I'll come up: if not, I'll stay down here till I'm somebody else'—but, oh dear!" cried Alice, with a sudden burst of tears, "I do wish they *would* put their heads down! I am so *very* tired of being all alone here!"

As she said this she looked down at her hands, and was surprised to see that she had put on one of the Rabbit's little white kid-gloves while she was talking. "How *can* I have done that?" she thought. "I must be growing small again." She got up and went to the table to measure herself by it, and found that, as nearly as she could guess, she was now about two feet high, and was going on shrinking rapidly: she soon found out that the cause of this was the fan she was holding, and she dropped it hastily, just in time to save herself from shrinking away altogether.

"That *was* a narrow escape!" said Alice, a good deal frightened at the sudden change, but very glad to find herself still in existence! "And now for the garden!" And she ran with all speed back to the little door; but, alas! the little door was shut again, and the little golden key was lying on the glass table as before, "and things are worse than ever," thought the poor child, "for I never was so small as this before, never! And I declare it's too bad, that it is!"

As she said these words, her foot slipped, and in another moment, splash! she was up to her chin in salt-water. Her first idea was that she had somehow fallen into the sea, "and in that case I can go back by railway," she said to herself. (Alice had been to the seaside once in her life, and had come to the general conclusion that, wherever you go to on the English coast, you find a number of bathing-machines in the sea, some children digging in the sand with wooden spades, then a row of lodging-houses, and behind them a railway-station.) However, she soon made out that she was in the pool of tears which she had wept when she was nine feet high.

"I wish I hadn't cried so much!" said Alice, as she swam about, trying to find her way out. "I shall be punished for it now, I suppose, by being drowned in my own tears! That *will* be a queer thing, to be sure! However, everything is queer to-day."

Just then she heard something splashing about in the pool a little way off, and she swam nearer to make out what it was: at first she thought it must be a walrus or hippopotamus, but then she remembered how small she was now, and she soon made out that it was only a mouse, that had slipped in like herself.

"Would it be of any use, now," thought Alice, "to speak to this mouse? Everything is so out-of-the-way down here, that I should think very likely it can talk: at any rate, there's no harm in trying." So she began: "O Mouse, do you know the way out of this pool? I am very tired of swimming about here, O Mouse!" (Alice thought this must be the right way of speaking to a mouse: she had never done such a thing before, but she remembered having seen, in her brother's Latin Grammar, "A mouse—of a mouse—to a mouse—a mouse—O mouse!" The mouse looked at her rather inquisitively, and seem to her to wink with one of its little eyes, but it said nothing.

"Perhaps it doesn't understand English," thought Alice. "I daresay it's a French mouse, come over with William the Conqueror." (For, with all her knowledge of history, Alice had no very clear notion how long ago anything had happened.) So she began again: "Où est ma chatte?" which was the first sentence in her French lesson-book. The Mouse gave a sudden leap out of the water, and seemed to quiver all over with fright. "Oh, I beg your pardon!" cried Alice hastily, afraid that she had hurt the poor animal's feelings. "I quite forgot you didn't like cats."

"Not like cats!" cried the Mouse in a shrill, passionate voice. "Would *you* like cats, if you were me?"

"Well, perhaps not," said Alice in a soothing tone: "don't be angry about it. And yet I wish I could show you our cat Dinah. I think you'd take a fancy to cats, if you could only see her. She is such a dear quiet thing," Alice went on, half to herself, as she swam lazily about in the pool, "and she sits purring so nicely by the fire, licking her paws and washing her face—and she is such a nice soft thing to nurse—and she's such a capital one for catching mice—oh, I beg your pardon!" cried Alice again, for this time the Mouse was bristling all over, and she felt certain it must be really offended. "We won't talk about her any more, if you'd rather not."

"We, indeed!" cried the Mouse, who was trembling down to the end of its tail. "As if *I* would talk on such a subject! Our family always *hated* cats: nasty, low, vulgar things! Don't let me hear the name again!"

"I won't indeed!" said Alice, in a great hurry to change the subject of conversation. "Are you—are you fond—of—of dogs?" The Mouse did not answer, so Alice went on eagerly: "There is such a nice little dog, near the house, I should like to show you! A little bright-eyed terrier, you know, with oh, such long curly brown hair! And it'll fetch things when you throw them, and it'll sit up and beg for its dinner, and all sorts of things—I can't remember half of them—and it belongs to a farmer, you know, and he says it's so useful, it's worth a hundred pounds! He says it kills all the rats and—oh dear!" cried Alice in a sorrowful tone. "I'm afraid I've offended it again!" For the Mouse was swimming away from her as hard as it could go, and making quite a commotion in the pool as it went.

So she called softly after it, "Mouse dear! Do come back, and we won't talk about cats, or dogs either, if you don't like them!" When the Mouse heard this, it turned round and swam slowly back to her: its face was quite pale (with passion, Alice thought), and it said, in a low trembling voice, "Let us get to the shore, and then I'll tell you my history, and you'll understand why it is I hate cats and dogs."

It was high time to go, for the pool was getting quite crowded with the birds and animals that had fallen into it: there was a Duck and a Dodo, a Lory and an Eaglet, and several other curious creatures. Alice led the way, and the whole party swam to the shore.

Father William

"You are old, Father William," the
    young man said,
  "And your hair has become very
    white;
And yet you incessantly stand on your
    head—
  Do you think, at your age, it is right?"

"In my youth," Father William replied
    to his son,
  "I feared it might injure the brain;
But, now that I'm perfectly sure I have
    none,
  Why, I do it again and again."

"You are old," said the youth, "as I
    mentioned before,
  And have grown most uncommonly
    fat;
Yet you turned a back-somersault in at
    the door—
  Pray, what is the reason of that?"

"In my youth," said the sage, as he shook
    his grey locks,
  "I kept all my limbs very supple
By the use of this ointment—one shilling
    the box—
  Allow me to sell you a couple?"

"You are old," said the youth, "and your
    jaws are too weak
  For anything tougher than suet;
Yet you finished the goose, with the bones
    and the beak—
  Pray, how did you manage to do it?"

"In my youth," said his father, "I took
    to the law,
  And argued each case with my wife;
And the muscular strength which it gave
    to my jaw
  Has lasted the rest of my life."

"You are old," said the youth, "one would
    hardly suppose
  That your eye was as steady as ever;

Yet you balanced an eel on the end of
   your nose—
What made you so awfully clever?"

"I have answered three questions, and
   that is enough,"
   Said his father. "Don't give yourself
   airs!
Do you think I can listen all day to such
   stuff?
   Be off, or I'll kick you down-stairs!"

The Whiting and the Snail

"WILL you walk a little faster?" said a
   whiting to a snail,
"There's a porpoise close behind us, and
   he's treading on my tail.
See how eagerly the lobsters and the
   turtles all advance!
They are waiting on the shingle—will you
   come and join the dance?
   Will you, won't you, will you, won't
   you, will you join the dance?
   Will you, won't you, will you, won't
   you, won't you join the dance?

"You can really have no notion how delightful it will be
When they take us up and throw us, with
   the lobsters, out to sea!"
But the snail replied "Too far, too far!",
   and gave a look askance—
Said he thanked the whiting kindly, but he
   would not join the dance.
   Would not, could not, would not, could
   not, would not join the dance.
   Would not, could not, would not, could
   not, could not join the dance.

"What matters it how far we go?" his
   scaly friend replied.
"There is another shore, you know, upon
   the other side.
The further off from England the nearer
   is to France—
Then turn not pale, beloved snail, but
   come and join the dance.

Will you, won't you, will you, won't
   you, will you join the dance?
Will you, won't you, will you, won't
   you, won't you join the dance?"

From THROUGH THE LOOKING-GLASS

Jabberwocky

'TWAS brillig, and the slithy toves
   Did gyre and gimble in the wabe:
All mimsy were the borogoves,
   And the mome raths outgrabe.

"Beware the Jabberwock, my son!
   The jaws that bite, the claws that
   catch!
Beware the Jubjub bird, and shun
   The frumious Bandersnatch!"

He took his vorpal sword in hand:
   Long time the manxome foe he
   sought—
So rested he by the Tumtum tree,
   And stood awhile in thought.

And, as in uffish thought he stood,
   The Jabberwock, with eyes of flame,
Came whiffling through the tulgey
   wood,
   And burbled as it came!

One, two! One, two! And through and
   through
   The vorpal blade went snicker-
   snack!
He left it dead, and with its head
   He went galumphing back.

"And hast thou slain the Jabberwock?
   Come to my arms, my beamish boy!
O frabjous day! Callooh! Callay!"
   He chortled in his joy.

'Twas brillig, and the slithy toves
   Did gyre and gimble in the wabe:
All mimsy were the borogoves,
   And the mome raths outgrabe.

The Walrus and the Carpenter

THE sun was shining on the sea,
  Shining with all his might:
He did his very best to make
  The billows smooth and bright—
And this was odd, because it was
  The middle of the night.

The moon was shining sulkily,
  Because she thought the sun
Had got no business to be there
  After the day was done—
'It's very rude of him," she said,
  To come and spoil the fun!"

The sea was wet as wet could be,
  The sands were dry as dry.
You could not see a cloud, because
  No cloud was in the sky:
No birds were flying overhead—
  There were no birds to fly.

The Walrus and the Carpenter
  Were walking close at hand:
They wept like anything to see
  Such quantities of sand:
'If this were only cleared away,"
  They said, it *would* be grand!"

'If seven maids with seven mops
  Swept it for half a year,
Do you suppose," the Walrus said,
  "That they could get it clear?"
'I doubt it," said the Carpenter,
  And shed a bitter tear.

'O Oysters, come and walk with us!"
  The Walrus did beseech.
"A pleasant walk, a pleasant talk,
  Along the briny beach:
We cannot do with more than four,
  To give a hand to each."

The eldest Oyster looked at him,
  But never a word he said:
The eldest Oyster winked his eye,
  And shook his heavy head—
Meaning to say he did not choose
  To leave the oyster-bed.

But four young Oysters hurried up,
  All eager for the treat:
Their coats were brushed, their faces
    washed,
  Their shoes were clean and neat—
And this was odd, because, you know,
  They hadn't any feet.

Four other Oysters followed them,
  And yet another four;
And thick and fast they came at last,
  And more, and more, and more—
All hopping through the frothy waves,
  And scrambling to the shore.

The Walrus and the Carpenter
  Walked on a mile or so,
And then they rested on a rock
  Conveniently low:
And all the little Oysters stood
  And waited in a row.

"The time has come," the Walrus said
  "To talk of many things:
Of shoes—and ships—and sealing-wax—
  Of cabbages—and kings—
And why the sea is boiling hot—
  And whether pigs have wings."

"But wait a bit," the Oysters cried,
  Before we have our chat;
For some of us are out of breath,
  And all of us are fat!"
"No hurry!" said the Carpenter.
  They thanked him much for that.

"A loaf of bread," the Walrus said,
  "Is what we chiefly need:
Pepper and vinegar besides
  Are very good indeed—
Now, if you're ready, Oysters dear,
  We can begin to feed."

"But not on us!" the Oysters cried,
  Turning a little blue.
"After such kindness, that would be
  A dismal thing to do!"
"The night is fine," the Walrus said.
  "Do you admire the view?

"It was so kind of you to come!
  And you are very nice!"
The Carpenter said nothing but
  "Cut us another slice.
I wish you were not quite so deaf—
  I've had to ask you twice!"

"It seems a shame," the Walrus said,
  "To play them such a trick.
After we've brought them out so far,
  And made them trot so quick!"
The Carpenter said nothing but
  "The butter's spread too thick!"

"I weep for you," the Walrus said:
  "I deeply sympathize."
With sobs and tears he sorted out
  Those of the largest size,
Holding his pocket-handkerchief
  Before his streaming eyes.

"O Oysters," said the Carpenter,
  "You've had a pleasant run!
Shall we be trotting home again?"
  But answer came there none—
And this was scarcely odd, because
  They'd eaten every one.

RICHARD WATSON DIXON
(1833-1900)

Ode on Advancing Age

THOU goest more and more
To the silent things; thy hair is hoar,
Emptier thy weary face; like to the shore
Far-ruined, and the desolate billow white,
That recedes and leaves it waif-wrinkled,
  gap-rocked, weak.

The shore and the billow white
Groan, they cry and rest not; they would
  speak,
And call the eternal Night
To cease them for ever; bidding new
  things issue
From her cold tissue:
Night that is ever young, nor knows
  decay,
Though older by eternity than they.

Go down upon the shore.
The breakers dash, the smitten spray
  drops to the roar;
The spit upsprings, and drops again,
Where'er the white waves clash in the
  main.
Their sound is but one: 'tis the cry
That has risen from of old to the sky,
'Tis their silence!
          Go now from the shore
Far-ruined: the grey shingly floor
To thy crashing step answers; the doteril
  cries,
And on dipping wings flies:
'Tis their silence!
          And thou, oh thou
To that wild silence sinkest now.
No more remains to thee than the cry of
  silence, the cry
Of the waves, of the shore, of the bird to
  the sky.
The bald eyes 'neath as bald a brow
Ask but what nature gives
To the inarticulate cries
Of the waves, of the shore, of the bird.
Earth in earth thou art being interred:
No longer in thee lives
The lordly essence which was unlike all,
That was thy flower of soul, the imperial
Glory that separated thee
From all others that might be.

Thy dog hath died before.
Didst thou not mark him? did he not neg-
  lect
What roused his rapture once, but still
  loved thee?
Till, weaker grown, was he not fain reject
Thy pitying hand, thy meat and drink,
For all thou could'st implore?
Then, at the last, how mournfully
Did not his eyelids sink
With wearied sighs?
He sought at last that never-moving night
Which is the same in darkness, as in light,
The closing of the eyes.

So, Age, thou dealest us
To the elements: but no! Resume thy
  pride.

O man, that musest thus.
Be to the end what thou hast been before:
The ancient joy shall wrap thee still—
 the tide
Return upon the shore.

WILLIAM MORRIS (1834-1896)

Mother and Son

Now sleeps the land of houses,
 and dead night holds the street,
And there thou liest, my baby,
 and sleepest soft and sweet;
My man is away for awhile,
 but safe and alone we lie,
And none heareth thy breath but thy
 mother,
 and the moon looking down from the
 sky
On the weary waste of the town,
 as it looked on the grass-edged road
Still warm with yesterday's sun,
 when I left my old abode;
Hand in hand with my love,
 that night of all nights in the year;
When the river of love o'erflowed
 and drowned all doubt and fear,
And we two were alone in the world,
 and once if never again,
We knew of the secret of earth
 and the tale of its labour and pain.

Lo amidst London I lift thee,
 and how little and light thou art,
And thou without hope or fear
 thou fear and hope of my heart!
Lo here thy body beginning,
 O son, and thy soul and thy life;
But how will it be if thou livest,
 and enterest into the strife,
And in love we dwell together
 when the man is grown in thee,
When thy sweet speech I shall hearken,
 and yet 'twixt thee and me
Shall rise that wall of distance,
 that round each one doth grow,
And maketh it hard and bitter
 each other's thought to know?

Now, therefore, while yet thou art little
 and hast no thought of thine own,
I will tell thee a word of the world,
 of the hope whence thou hast grown;
Of the love that once begat thee,
 of the sorrow that hath made
Thy little heart of hunger,
 and thy hands on my bosom laid.
Then mayst thou remember hereafter
 as whiles when people say
All this hath happened before
 in the life of another day;
So mayst thou dimly remember
 this tale of thy mother's voice,
As oft in the calm of dawning
 I have heard the birds rejoice,
As oft I have heard the storm-wind
 go moaning through the wood;
And I knew that earth was speaking,
 and the mother's voice was good.

Now, to thee alone will I tell it
 that thy mother's body is fair,
In the guise of the country maidens
 who play with the sun and the air;
Who have stood in the row of the reapers
 in the August afternoon,
Who have sat by the frozen water
 in the high day of the moon,
When the lights of the Christmas feasting
 were dead in the house on the hill,
And the wild geese gone to the salt-
 marsh
 had left the winter still.
Yea, I am fair, my firstling;
 if thou couldst but remember me!
The hair that thy small hand clutcheth
 is a goodly sight to see;
I am true, but my face is a snare;
 soft and deep are my eyes,
And they seem for men's beguiling
 fulfilled with the dreams of the wise.
Kind are my lips, and they look
 as though my soul had learned
Deep things I have never heard of,
 my face and my hands are burned
By the lovely sun of the acres;
 three months of London town

And thy birth-bed have bleached them indeed,
 "But lo, where the edge of the gown"
(So said thy father) "is parting
 the wrist that is white as the curd
From the brown of the hand that I love
 bright as the wing of a bird."

Such is thy mother, O firstling,
 yet strong as the maidens of old,
Whose spears and whose swords were the
 warders
 of homestead, of field and of fold.
Oft were my feet on the highway,
 often they wearied the grass;
From dusk unto dusk of the summer
 three times in a week would I pass
To the downs from the house on the river
 through the waves of the blossoming
 corn.
Fair then I lay down in the even,
 and fresh I arose on the morn,
And scarce in the noon was I weary.
 Ah, son, in the days of thy strife,
If thy soul could but harbour a dream
 of the blossom of my life!
It would be as the sunlit meadows
 beheld from a tossing sea,
And the soul should look on a vision
 of the peace that is to be.

Yet, yet the tears on my cheek!
 and what is this doth move
My heart to thy heart, beloved,
 save the flood of yearning love?
For fair and fierce is thy father,
 and soft and strange are his eyes
That look on the day that shall be
 with the hope of the brave and the
 wise.
It was many a day that we laughed,
 as over the meadows we walked,
And many a day I hearkened
 and the pictures came as he talked;
It was many a day that we longed,
 and we lingered late at eve
Ere speech from speech was sundered,
 and my hand his hand could leave.

Then I wept when I was alone,
 and I longed till the daylight came;
And down the stairs I stole,
 and there was our housekeeping dame
(No mother of me, the foundling)
 kindling the fire betimes
Ere the haymaking folk went forth
 to the meadows down by the limes;
All things I saw at a glance;
 the quickening fire-tongues leapt
Through the crackling heap of sticks,
 and the sweet smoke up from it
 crept.
And close to the very hearth
 the low sun flooded the floor,
And the cat and her kittens played
 in the sun by the open door.
The garden was fair in the morning,
 and there in the road he stood
Beyond the crimson daisies
 and the bush of southernwood.
Then side by side together
 through the grey-walled place we
 went,
And O the fear departed,
 and the rest and sweet content!

Son, sorrow and wisdom he taught me,
 and sore I grieved and learned
As we twain grew into one;
 and the heart within me burned
With the very hopes of his heart.
 Ah, son, it is piteous,
But never again in my life
 shall I dare to speak to thee thus;
So may these lonely words
 about thee creep and cling,
These words of the lonely night
 in the days of our wayfaring.
Many a child of woman
 to-night is born in the town,
The desert of folly and wrong;
 and of what and whence are they
 grown?
Many and many an one
 of wont and use is born;
For a husband is taken to bed
 as a hat or a ribbon is worn.

Prudence begets her thousands;
  "good is a housekeeper's life,
So shall I sell my body
  that I may be matron and wife."
"And I shall endure foul wedlock
  and bear the children of need."
Some are there born of hate,
  many the children of greed.
"I, I too can be wedded,
  though thou my love hast got."
"I am fair and hard of heart,
  and riches shall be my lot."
And all these are the good and the
  happy,
  on whom the world dawns fair.
O son, when wilt thou learn
  of those that are born of despair,
As the fabled mud of the Nile
  that quickens under the sun
With a growth of creeping things,
  half dead when just begun?
E'en such is the care of Nature
  that man should never die,
Though she breed of the fools of the
  earth,
  and the dregs of the city sty.
But thou, O son, O son,
  of very love wert born,
When our hope fulfilled bred hope,
  and fear was a folly outworn.
On the eve of the toil and the battle
  all sorrow and grief we weighed,
We hoped and we were not ashamed,
  we knew and we were not afraid.

Now waneth the night and the moon;
  ah, son, it is piteous
That never again in my life
  shall I dare to speak to thee thus.
But sure from the wise and the simple
  shall the mighty come to birth;
And fair were my fate, beloved,
  if I be yet on the earth
When the world is awakened at last,
  and from mouth to mouth they tell
Of thy love and thy deeds and thy
  valour,
  and thy hope that nought can quell.

ALGERNON CHARLES SWINBURNE (1837-1909)

From ATALANTA IN CALYDON

The Youth of the Year

WHEN the hounds of spring are on win-
  ter's traces,
  The mother of months in meadow or
    plain
Fills the shadows and windy places
  With lisp of leaves and ripple of rain;
And the brown bright nightingale amour-
  ous
Is half assuaged for Itylus,
For the Thracian ships and the foreign
  faces,
The tongueless vigil, and all the pain.

Come with bows bent and with emptying
  of quivers,
  Maiden most perfect, lady of light,
With a noise of winds and many rivers,
  With a clamour of waters, and with
    might;
Bind on thy sandals, O thou most fleet,
Over the splendour and speed of thy feet,
For the faint east quickens, the wan west
  shivers,
  Round the feet of the day and the feet
    of the night.

Where shall we find her, how shall we
  sing to her,
  Fold our hands round her knees, and
    cling?
O that man's heart were as fire and could
  spring to her,
  Fire, or the strength of the streams
    that spring!
For the stars and the winds are unto her
As raiment, as songs of the harp-player;
For the risen stars and the fallen cling to
  her,
  And the southwest-wind and the west-
    wind sing.

For winter's rains and ruins are over,
  And all the season of snows and sins;

The days dividing lover and lover,
  The light that loses, the night that
    wins;
And time remembered is grief forgotten,
And frosts are slain and flowers begotten,
And in green underwood and cover
  Blossom by blossom the spring begins.

The full streams feed on flower of
    rushes,
  Ripe grasses trammel a travelling foot,
The faint fresh flame of the young year
    flushes
  From leaf to flower and flower to fruit;
And fruit and leaf are as gold and fire,
And the oat is heard above the lyre,
And the hoofed heel of a satyr crushes
  The chestnut-husk at the chestnut root.

And Pan by noon and Bacchus by night,
  Fleeter of foot than the fleet-foot kid,
Follows with dancing and fills with de-
    light
  The Mænad and the Bassarid;
And soft as lips that laugh and hide,
The laughing leaves of the trees divide,
And screen from seeing and leave in sight
  The god pursuing, the maiden hid.

The ivy falls with the Bacchanal's hair
  Over her eyebrows hiding her eyes;
The wild vine slipping down leaves bare
  Her bright breast shortening into sighs;
The wild vine slips with the weight of its
    leaves,
But the berried ivy catches and cleaves
To the limbs that glitter, the feet that
    scare
  The wolf that follows, the fawn that
    flies.

A Forsaken Garden

In a coign of the cliff between lowland
    and highland,
  At the sea-down's edge between wind-
    ward and lee,
Walled round with rocks as an inland
    island,

The ghost of a garden fronts the sea.
A girdle of brushwood and thorn
    encloses
The steep square slope of the blossom-
    less bed
Where the weeds that grew green from
    the graves of its roses
  Now lie dead.

The fields fall southward, abrupt and
    broken,
  To the low last edge of the long lone
    land.
If a step should sound or a word be
    spoken,
  Would a ghost not rise at the strange
    guest's hand?
So long have the gray bare walks lain
    guestless,
  Through branches and briars if a man
    make way,
He shall find no life but the sea-wind's,
    restless
  Night and day.

The dense hard passage is blind and
    stifled
  That crawls by a track none turn to
    climb
To the strait waste place that the years
    have rifled
  Of all but the thorns that are touched
    not of time.
The thorns he spares when the rose is
    taken;
  The rocks are left when he wastes the
    plain;
The wind that wanders, the weeds wind-
    shaken,
  These remain.

Not a flower to be pressed of the foot
    that falls not;
  As the heart of a dead man the seed-
    plots are dry;
From the thicket of thorns whence the
    nightingale calls not,
  Could she call, there were never a rose
    to reply.

Over the meadows that blossom and
    wither,
  Rings but the note of a sea-bird's song.
Only the sun and the rain come hither
  All year long.

The sun burns sear, and the rain dis-
    hevels
  One gaunt bleak blossom of scentless
    breath.
Only the wind here hovers and revels
  In a round where life seems barren as
    death.
Here there was laughing of old, there was
    weeping,
  Haply, of lovers none ever will know,
Whose eyes went seaward a hundred
    sleeping
  Years ago.

Heart handfast in heart as they stood,
    "Look thither,"
  Did he whisper? "Look forth from
    the flowers to the sea;
For the foam-flowers endure when the
    rose-blossoms wither,
  And men that love lightly may die—
    But we?"
And the same wind sang, and the same
    waves whitened,
  And or ever the garden's last petals
    were shed,
In the lips that had whispered, the eyes
    that had lightened,
  Love was dead.

Or they loved their life through, and then
    went whither?
  And were one to the end—but what
    end who knows?
Love deep as the sea as a rose must
    wither,
  As the rose-red seaweed that mocks the
    rose.
Shall the dead take thought for the dead
    to love them?
  What love was ever as deep as a
    grave?

They are loveless now as the grass above
    them
  Or the wave.

All are at one now, roses and lovers,
  Not known of the cliffs and the fields
    and the sea.
Not a breath of the time that has been
    hovers
  In the air now soft with a summer to
    be.
Not a breath shall there sweeten the sea-
    sons hereafter
  Of the flowers or the lovers that laugh
    now or weep,
When, as they that are free now of weep-
    ing and laughter,
  We shall sleep.

Here death may deal not again forever;
  Here change may come not till all
    change end.
From the graves they have made they
    shall rise up never,
  Who have left naught living to ravage
    and rend.
Earth, stones, and thorns of the wild
    ground growing,
  When the sun and the rain live, these
    shall be;
Till a last wind's breath upon all these
    blowing
  Roll the sea.

Till the slow sea rise and the sheer cliff
    crumble,
  Till terrace and meadow the deep gulfs
    drink,
Till the strength of the waves of the high
    tides humble
  The fields that lessen, the rocks that
    shrink,
Here now in his triumph where all things
    falter,
  Stretched out on the spoils that his own
    hand spread,
As a god self-slain on his own strange
    altar,
  Death lies dead.

A Jacobite's Farewell
1716

THERE'S nae mair lands to tyne, my dear,
  And nae mair lives to gie:
Though a man think sair to live nae mair,
  There's but one day to die.

For a' things come and a' days gane,
  What needs ye rend your hair?
But kiss me till the morn's morrow,
  Then I'll kiss ye nae mair.

O lands are lost and life's losing,
  And what were they to gie?
Fu' mony a man gives all he can,
  But nae man else gives ye.

Our king wons ower the sea's water,
  And I in prison sair:
But I'll win out the morn's morrow,
  And ye'll see me nae mair.

A Jacobite's Exile
1746

THE weary day rins down and dies,
  The weary night wears through:
And never an hour is fair wi' flower,
  And never a flower wi' dew.

I would the day were night for me,
  I would the night were day:
For then would I stand in my ain fair
    land,
  As now in dreams I may.

O lordly flow the Loire and Seine,
  And loud the dark Durance:
But bonnier shine the braes of Tyne
  Than a' the fields of France;
And the waves of Till that speak sae still
  Gleam goodlier where they glance.

O weel were they that fell fighting
  On dark Drumossie's day:
They keep their hame ayont the faem,
  And we die far away.

O sound they sleep, and saft, and deep,
  But night and day wake we;

And ever between the sea-banks green
  Sounds loud the sundering sea.

And ill we sleep, sae sair we weep,
  But sweet and fast sleep they;
And the mool that haps them roun' and
    laps them
  Is e'en their country's clay;
But the land we tread that are not dead
  Is strange as night by day.

Strange as night in a strange man's sight,
  Though fair as dawn it be:
For what is here that a stranger's cheer
  Should yet wax blithe to see?

The hills stand steep, the dells lie deep,
  The fields are green and gold:
The hill-streams sing, and the hill-sides
    ring,
  As ours at home of old.

But hills and flowers are nane of ours,
  And ours are oversea:
And the kind strange land whereon we
    stand,
  It wotsna what were we
Or ever we came, wi' scathe and shame,
  To try what end might be.

Scathe, and shame, and a waefu' name,
  And a weary time and strange,
Have they that seeing a weird for dreeing
  Can die, and cannot change.

Shame and scorn may we thole that
    mourn,
  Though sair be they to dree:
But ill may we bide the thoughts we hide,
  Mair keen than wind and sea.

Ill may we thole the night's watches,
  And ill the weary day:
And the dreams that keep the gates of
    sleep,
  A waefu' gift gie they;
For the sangs they sing us, the sights they
    bring us,
  The morn blaws all away.

On Aikenshaw the sun blinks braw,
  The burn rins blithe and fain:

There's nought wi' me I wadna gie
  To look thereon again.

On Keilder-side the wind blaws wide;
  There sounds nae hunting-horn
That rings sae sweet as the winds that
    beat
  Round banks where Tyne is born.

The Wansbeck sings with all her springs,
  The bents and braes give ear;
But the wood that rings wi' the sang she
    sings
  I may not see nor hear;
For far and far thae blithe burns are,
  And strange is a' thing near.

The light there lightens, the day there
    brightens,
  The loud wind there lives free:
Nae light comes nigh me or wind blaws
    by me
  That I wad hear or see.

But O gin I were there again,
  Afar ayont the faem,
Cauld and dead in the sweet saft bed
  That haps my sires at hame!

We'll see nae mair the sea-banks fair,
  And the sweet grey gleaming sky,
And the lordly strand of Northumber-
    land,
  And the goodly towers thereby:
And none shall know but the winds that
    blow
  The graves wherein we lie.

AUSTIN DOBSON (1840-1921)

A Gentleman of the Old School

HE lived in that past Georgian day,
When men were less inclined to say
That "Time is Gold," and overlay
          With toil their pleasure;
He held some land, and dwelt thereon,—
Where, I forget,—the house is gone;
His Christian name, I think, was John,—
          His surname, Leisure.

Reynolds has painted him,—a face
Filled with a fine, old-fashioned grace,
Fresh-coloured, frank, with ne'er a trace
          Of trouble shaded;
The eyes are blue, the hair is drest
In plainest way,—one hand is prest
Deep in a flapped canary vest,
          With buds brocaded.

He wears a brown old Brunswick coat,
With silver buttons,—round his throat,
A soft cravat;—in all you note
          An elder fashion,—
A strangeness, which, to us who shine
In shapely hats,—whose coats combine
All harmonies of hue and line,—
          Inspires compassion.

He lived so long ago, you see!
Men were untravelled then, but we,
Like Ariel, post o'er land and sea
          With careless parting;
He found it quite enough for him
To smoke his pipe in "garden trim,"
And watch, about the fish-tank's brim,
          The swallows darting.

He liked the well-wheel's creaking
    tongue,—
He liked the thrush that fed her young,—
He liked the drone of flies among
          His netted peaches;
He liked to watch the sunlight fall
Athwart his ivied orchard wall;
Or pause to catch the cuckoo's call
          Beyond the beeches.

His were the times of Paint and Patch,
And yet no Ranelagh could match
The sober doves that round his thatch
          Spread tails and sidled;
He liked their ruffling, puffed content,—
For him their drowsy wheelings meant
More than a Mall of Beaux that bent,
          Or Belles that bridled.

Not that, in truth, when life began,
He shunned the flutter of the fan;
He too had maybe "pinked his man"
          In Beauty's quarrel;

But now his "fervent youth" had flown
Where lost things go; and he was grown
As staid and slow-paced as his own
   Old hunter, Sorrel.

Yet still he loved the chase, and held
That no composer's score excelled
The merry horn, when Sweetlip swelled
   Its jovial riot;
But most his measured words of praise
Caressed the angler's easy ways,—
His idly meditative days,—
   His rustic diet.

Not that his "meditating" rose
Beyond a sunny summer doze;
He never troubled his repose
   With fruitless prying;
But held, as law for high and low,
What God withholds no man can know,
And smiled away inquiry so,
   Without replying.

We read—alas, how much we read!
The jumbled strifes of creed and creed
With endless controversies feed
   Our groaning tables;
His books—and they sufficed him—were
Cotton's "Montaigne," "The Grave" of
  Blair,
A "Walton"—much the worse for wear—
   And "Æsop's Fables."

One more,—"The Bible." Not that he
Had searched its page as deep as we;
No sophistries could make him see
   Its slender credit;
It may be that he could not count
The sires and sons to Jesse's fount,—
He liked the "Sermon on the Mount,"—
   And more, he read it.

Once he had loved, but failed to wed,
A red-cheeked lass who long was dead;
His ways were far too slow, he said,
   To quite forget her;
And still when time had turned him gray
The earliest hawthorn buds in May
Would find his lingering feet astray,
   Where first he met her.

"*In Cælo Quies*" heads the stone
On Leisure's grave,—now little known,
A tangle of wild-rose has grown
   So thick across it;
The "Benefactions" still declare
He left the clerk an elbow-chair,
And "12 Pence Yearly to Prepare
   A Christmas Posset."

Lie softly, Leisure! Doubtless you
With too serene a conscience drew
Your easy breath, and slumbered through
   The gravest issue;
But we, to whom our age allows
Scarce space to wipe our weary brows,
Look down upon your narrow house,
   Old friend, and miss you!

The Curé's Progress

Monsieur the Curé down the street
 Comes with his kind old face,—
With his coat worn bare, and his strag-
  gling hair,
 And his green umbrella-case.

You may see him pass by the little
 "*Grande Place*,"
 And the tiny "*Hôtel-de-Ville*";
He smiles, as he goes, to the *fleuriste*
  Rose,
 And the *pompier* Théophile.

He turns, as a rule, through the
 "*Marché*" cool,
 Where the noisy fish-wives call;
And his compliment pays to the "*Belle
  Thérèse*,"
 As she knits in her dusky stall.

There's a letter to drop at the locksmith's
 shop,
 And Toto, the locksmith's niece,
Has jubilant hopes, for the Curé gropes
 In his tails for a *pain d'épice*.

There's a little dispute with a merchant
 of fruit,
 Who is said to be heterodox,
That will ended be with a "*Ma foi, oui!*"
 And a pinch from the Curé's box.

There is also a word that no one heard
  To the furrier's daughter Lou;
And a pale cheek fed with a flickering
    red,
  And a *"Bon Dieu garde M'sieu!"*

But a grander way for the *Sous-Préfet,*
  And a bow for Ma'am'selle Anne;
And a mock "off-hat" to the Notary's cat,
  And a nod to the Sacristan:—

For ever through life the Curé goes
  With a smile on his kind old face—
With his coat worn bare, and his strag-
    gling hair,
  And his green umbrella-case.

A Ballad of Heroes

BECAUSE you passed, and now are not,—
  Because, in some remoter day,
Your sacred dust from doubtful spot
  Was blown of ancient airs away,—
  Because you perished,—must men say
Your deeds were naught, and so profane
  Your lives with that cold burden? Nay
The deeds you wrought are not in vain!

Though, it may be, above the plot
  That hid your once imperial clay,
No greener than o'er men forgot
  The unregarding grasses sway;—
  Though there no sweeter is the lay
From careless bird,—though you remain
  Without distinction of decay,—
The deeds you wrought are not in vain!

No. For while yet in tower or cot
  Your story stirs the pulses' play;
And men forget the sordid lot—
  The sordid care, of cities gray;—
  While yet, beset in homelier fray,
They learn from you the lesson plain
  That Life may go, so Honour stay,—
The deeds you wrought are not in vain!

ENVOY

Heroes of old! I humbly lay
  The laurel on your graves again;

Whatever men have done, men may,—
  The deeds you wrought are not in vain.

The Ballad of Imitation

"C'est imiter quelqu'un que de planter des choux."—Alfred de Musset.

IF they hint, O Musician, the piece that
    you played
Is naught but a copy of Chopin or
    Spohr;
That the ballad you sing is but merely
    "conveyed"
  From the stock of the Arnes and the
    Purcells of yore;
  That there's nothing, in short, in the
    words or the score
That is not as out-worn as the "Wan-
    dering Jew,"
  Make answer—Beethoven could scarce-
    ly do more—
That the man who plants cabbages imi-
    tates, too!

If they tell you, Sir Artist, your light and
    your shade
  Are simply "adapted" from other men's
    lore;
That—plainly to speak of a "spade" as a
    "spade"—
  You've "stolen" your grouping from
    three or from four;
  That (however the writer the truth
    may deplore),
'Twas Gainsborough painted *your* "Little
    Boy Blue";
  Smile only serenely—though cut to the
    core—
For the man who plants cabbages imi-
    tates, too!

And you too, my Poet, be never dis-
    mayed
  If they whisper your Epic—"Sir Éperon
    d'Or"—
Is nothing but Tennyson thinly arrayed
  In a tissue that's taken from Morris's
    store;

That no one, in fact, but a child could ignore
That you "lift" or "accommodate" all that you do;
Take heart—though your Pegasus' withers be sore—
For the man who plants cabbages imitates, too!

Postscriptum—And you, whom we all so adore,
Dear Critics, whose verdicts are always so new!—
One word in your ear. There were Critics before . . .
And the man who plants cabbages imitates, too!

THOMAS HARDY

From THE MAYOR OF CASTERBRIDGE

Chapter I

ONE evening of late summer, before the present century had reached its thirtieth year, a young man and woman, the latter carrying a child, were approaching the large village of Weydon-Priors, in Upper Wessex, on foot. They were plainly but not ill clad, though the thick hoar of dust which had accumulated on their shoes and garments from an obviously long journey lent a disadvantageous shabbiness to their appearance just now.

The man was of fine figure, swarthy, and stern in aspect; and he showed in profile a facial angle so slightly inclined as to be almost perpendicular. He wore a short jacket of brown corduroy, newer than the remainder of his suit, which was a fustian waistcoat with white horn buttons, breeches of the same, tanned leggings, and a straw hat overlaid with black glazed canvas. At his back he carried by a looped strap a rush basket, from which protruded at one end the crutch of a hay-knife, a wimble for hay-bonds being also visible in the aperture. His measured, springless walk was the walk of the skilled countryman as distinct from the desultory shamble of the general labourer; while in the turn and plant of each foot there was, further, a dogged and cynical indifference, personal to himself, showing its presence even in the regularly interchanging fustian folds, now in the left leg, now in the right, as he paced along.

What was really peculiar, however, in this couple's progress, and would have attracted the attention of any casual observer otherwise disposed to overlook them, was the perfect silence they preserved. They walked side by side in such a way as to suggest afar off the low, easy, confidential chat of people full of reciprocity; but on closer view it could be discerned that the man was reading, or pretending to read, a ballad sheet which he kept before his eyes with some difficulty by the hand that was passed through the basket strap. Whether this apparent cause were the real cause, or whether it were an assumed one to escape an intercourse that would have been irksome to him, nobody but himself could have said precisely; but his taciturnity was unbroken, and the woman enjoyed no society whatever from his presence. Virtually she walked the highway alone, save for the child she bore. Sometimes the man's bent elbow almost touched her shoulder, for she kept as close to his side as was possible without actual contact; but she seemed to have no idea of taking his arm, nor he of offering it; and far from exhibiting surprise at his ignoring silence, she appeared to receive it as a natural thing. If any word at all were uttered by the little group, it was an occasional whisper of the woman to the child—a tiny girl in short clothes and blue boots of knitted yarn—and the murmured babble of the child in reply.

The chief—almost the only—attraction of the young woman's face was its mobility. When she looked down sideways to the girl she became pretty, and even handsome, particularly that in the action her features caught slantwise the rays of the strongly coloured sun, which made transparencies of her eyelids and nostrils, and set fire on her lips. When she plodded on in the shade of the hedge, silently thinking, she had the hard, half-apathetic expression of one who deems anything possible at the hands of Time and Chance, except, perhaps, fair play. The first phase was the work of Nature, the second probably of civilization.

That the man and woman were husband and wife, and the parents of the girl in arms, there could be little doubt. No other than such relationship would have accounted for the atmosphere of stale familiarity which the trio carried along with them like a nimbus as they moved down the road.

The wife mostly kept her eyes fixed ahead, though with little interest —the scene for that matter being one that might have been matched at almost any spot in any county in England at this time of the year; a road neither straight nor crooked, neither level nor hilly, bordered by hedges, trees, and other vegetation, which had entered the blackened-green stage of colour that the doomed leaves pass through on their way to dingy and yellow, and red. The grassy margin of the bank, and the nearest hedgerow boughs, were powdered by the dust that had been stirred over them by hasty vehicles, the same dust as it lay on the road deadening their footfalls like a carpet; and this, with the aforesaid total absence of conversation, allowed every extraneous sound to be heard.

For a long time there was none, beyond the voice of a weak bird singing a trite old evening song that might doubtless have been heard on the hill at the same hour, and with the self-same trills, quavers, and breves, at any sunset of that season for centuries untold. But as they approached the village sundry distant shouts and rattles reached their ears from some elevated spot in that direction, as yet screened from view by foliage. When the outlying houses of Weydon-Priors could just be descried, the family group was met by a turnip-hoer with his hoe on his shoulder, and his dinner-bag suspended from it. The reader promptly glanced up.

"Any trade doing here?" he asked phlegmatically, designating the village in his van by a wave of the broadsheet. And thinking the labourer did not understand him, he added, "Anything in the hay-trussing line?"

The turnip-hoer had already begun shaking his head. "Why, save the man, what wisdom's in him that 'a should come to Weydon for a job of that sort this time o' year?"

"Then is there any house to let—a little small new cottage just a builded, or such like?" asked the other.

The pessimist still maintained a negative. "Pulling down is more the nater of Weydon. There were five houses cleared away last year, and three this; and the volk nowhere to go—no, not so much as a thatched hurdle; that's the way o' Weydon-Priors."

The hay-trusser, which he obviously was, nodded with some superciliousness. Looking towards the village, he continued, "There is something going on here, however, is there not?"

"Ay. 'Tis Fair Day. Though what you hear now is little more than the clatter and scurry of getting away the money o' children and fools, for the real business is done earlier than this. I've been working within sound o't all day, but I didn't go up—not I. 'Twas no business of mine"

The trusser and his family proceeded on their way, and soon entered the Fair-field, which showed standing-places and pens where many hundreds of horses and sheep had been exhibited and sold in the forenoon, but were now in great part taken away. At present, as their informant had observed, but little real business remained on hand, the chief being the sale by auction of a few inferior animals, that could not otherwise be disposed of, and had been absolutely refused by the better class of traders, who came and went early. Yet the crowd was denser now than during the morning hours, the frivolous contingent of visitors, including journeymen out for a holiday, a stray soldier or two home on furlough, village shopkeepers, and the like, having latterly flocked in; persons whose activities found a congenial field among the peep-shows, toy-stands, waxworks, inspired monsters, disinterested medical men who travelled for the public good, thimble-riggers, nick-nack vendors, and readers of Fate.

Neither of our pedestrians had much heart for these things, and they looked around for a refreshment tent among the many which dotted the down. Two, which stood nearest to them in the ochreous haze of expiring sunlight, seemed almost equally inviting. One was formed of new, milk-hued canvas, and bore red flags on its summit; it announced "Good Home-brewed Beer, Ale, and Cyder." The other was less new; a little iron stove-pipe came out of it at the back, and in front appeared the placard, "Good Furmity Sold Hear." The man mentally weighed the two inscriptions, and inclined to the former tent.

"No—no—the other one," said the woman. "I always like furmity; and so does Elizabeth-Jane; and so will you. It is nourishing after a long hard day."

"I've never tasted it," said the man. However, he gave way to her representations, and they entered the furmity booth forthwith.

A rather numerous company appeared within, seated at the long narrow tables that ran down the tent on each side. At the upper end stood a stove, containing a charcoal fire, over which hung a large three-legged crock, sufficiently polished round the rim to show that it was made of bell-metal. A haggish creature of about fifty presided, in a white apron, which, as it threw an air of respectability over her as far as it extended, was made so wide as to reach nearly round her waist. She slowly stirred the contents of the pot. The dull scrape of her large spoon was audible throughout the tent as she thus kept from burning the mixture of corn in the grain, milk, raisins, currants, and what not, that composed the antiquated slop in which she dealt. Vessels holding the separate ingredients stood on a white-clothed table of boards and trestles close by.

The young man and woman ordered a basin each of the mixture, steaming hot, and sat down to consume it at leisure. This was very well so far, for furmity, as the woman had said, was nourishing, and as proper a food as could be obtained within the four seas; though, to those not accustomed to it, the grains of wheat, swollen as large as lemon-pips, which floated on its surface, might have a deterrent effect at first.

But there was more in that tent than met the cursory glance; and the man, with the instinct of a perverse character, scented it quickly. After a mincing attack on his bowl, he watched the hag's proceedings from the corner of his eye, and saw the game she played. He winked to her, and passed up his basin in reply to her nod; when she took a bottle from under the table, slily measured out a quantity of its contents, and tipped the same into the man's furmity. The liquor poured in was rum. The man as slily sent back money in payment.

He found the concoction, thus strongly laced, much more to his satisfaction than it had been in its natural state. His wife had observed the proceeding with much uneasiness; but he persuaded her to have hers laced also, and she agreed to a milder allowance after some misgiving.

The man finished his basin, and called for another, the rum being signalled for in yet stronger proportion. The effect of it was soon apparent in his manner, and his wife but too sadly perceived that in strenuously steering off the rocks of the licensed liquor-tent she had only got into maelstrom depths here amongst the smugglers.

The child began to prattle impatiently, and the wife more than once said to her husband, "Michael, how about our lodging? You know we may have trouble in getting it if we don't go soon."

But he turned a deaf ear to those bird-like chirpings. He talked loud to the company. The child's black eyes, after slow, round, ruminating gazes at the candles when they were lighted, fell together; then they opened, then shut again, and she slept.

At the end of the first basin the man had risen to serenity; at the second he was jovial; at the third, argumentative; at the fourth, the qualities signified by the shape of his face, the occasional clench of his mouth, and the fiery spark of his dark eye, began to tell in his conduct; he was overbearing—even brilliantly quarrelsome.

The conversation took a high turn, as it often does on such occasions. The ruin of good men by bad wives, and more particularly, the frustration of many a promising youth's high aims and hopes, and the extinction of his energies, by an early imprudent marriage, was the theme.

"I did for myself that way thoroughly," said the trusser, with a contemplative bitterness that was well-nigh resentful. "I married at eighteen, like the fool that I was; and this is the consequence o't." He pointed at himself and family with a wave of the hand intended to bring out the penuriousness of the exhibition.

The young woman his wife, who seemed accustomed to such remarks, acted as if she did not hear them, and continued her intermittent private words on tender trifles to the sleeping and waking child, who was just big enough to be placed for a moment on the bench beside her when she wished to ease her arms. The man continued—

"I haven't more than fifteen shillings in the world, and yet I am a good experienced hand in my line. I'd challenge England to beat me in the fodder business; and if I were a free man again, I'd be worth a thousand pound before I'd done o't. But a fellow never knows these little things till all chance of acting upon 'em is past."

The auctioneer selling the old horses in the field outside could be heard saying, "Now this is the last lot—now who'll take the last lot for a song? Shall I say forty shillings? 'Tis a very promising brood-mare, a trifle over five years old, and nothing the matter with the hoss at all, except that she's a little holler in the back and had her left eye knocked out by the kick of another, her own sister, coming along the road."

"For my part I don't see why men who have got wives, and don't want 'em, shouldn't get rid of 'em as these gipsy fellows do their old horses," said the man in the tent. "Why shouldn't they put 'em up and sell 'em by auction to men who are in want of such articles? Hey? Why, begad, I'd sell mine this minute if anybody would buy her!"

"There's them that would do that," some of the guests replied, looking at the woman, who was by no means ill-favoured.

"True," said a smoking gentleman, whose coat had the fine polish about the collar, elbows, seams, and shoulder-blades that long-continued friction with grimy surfaces will produce, and which is usually more desired on furniture than on clothes. From his appearance he had possibly been in former time groom or coachman to some neighbouring county family. "I've had my breedings in as good circles, I may say, as any man," he added, "and I know true cultivation, or nobody do; and I can declare she's got it—in the bone, mind ye, I say—as much as any female in the fair—though it may want a little bringing out." Then, crossing his legs, he resumed his pipe with a nicely-adjusted gaze at a point in the air.

The fuddled young husband stared for a few seconds at this unexpected praise of his wife, half in doubt of the wisdom of his own attitude towards the possessor of such qualities. But he speedily lapsed into his former conviction, and said harshly—

"Well, then, now is your chance; I am open to an offer for this gem o' creation."

She turned to her husband and murmured, "Michael, you have talked this nonsense in public places before. A joke is a joke, but you may make it once too often, mind!"

"I know I've said it before; I meant it. All I want is a buyer."

At the moment a swallow, one among the last of the season, which had by chance found its way through an opening into the upper part of the tent, flew to and fro in quick curves above their heads, causing all eyes to follow it absently. In watching the bird till it made its escape the assembled company neglected to respond to the workman's offer, and the subject dropped.

But a quarter of an hour later the man, who had gone on lacing his furmity more and more heavily, though he was either so strong-minded or such an intrepid toper that he still appeared fairly sober, recurred to the old strain, as in a musical fantasy the instrument fetches up the original theme. "Here—I am waiting to know about this offer of mine. The woman is no good to me. Who'll have her?"

The company had by this time decidedly degenerated, and the renewed inquiry was received with a laugh of appreciation. The woman whispered; she was imploring and anxious: "Come, come, it is getting dark, and this nonsense won't do. If you don't come along, I shall go without you. Come!"

She waited and waited; yet he did not move. In ten minutes the man broke in upon the desultory conversation of the furmity drinkers with, "I asked this question, and nobody answered to 't. Will any Jack Rag or Tom Straw among ye buy my goods?"

The woman's manner changed, and her face assumed the grim shape and colour of which mention has been made.

"Mike, Mike," said she; "this is getting serious. Oh!—too serious!"

"Will anybody buy her?" said the man.

"I wish somebody would," said she firmly. "Her present owner is not at all to her liking!"

"Nor you to mine," said he. "So we are agreed about that. Gentlemen, you hear? It's an agreement to part. She shall take the girl if she wants to, and go her ways. I'll take my tools, and go my ways. 'Tis simple as Scripture history. Now then, stand up, Susan, and show yourself."

"Don't, my chiel," whispered a buxom staylace dealer in voluminous petticoats, who sat near the woman; "yer good man don't know what he's saying."

The woman, however, did stand up. "Now, who's auctioneer?" cried the hay-trusser.

"I be," promptly answered a short man, with a nose resembling a copper knob, a damp voice, and eyes like button-holes. "Who'll make an offer for this lady?"

The woman looked on the ground, as if she maintained her position by a supreme effort of will.

"Five shillings," said some one, at which there was a laugh.

"No insults," said the husband. "Who'll say a guinea?"

Nobody answered; and the female dealer in staylaces interposed.

"Behave yerself moral, good man, for Heaven's love! Ah, what a cruelty is the poor soul married to! Bed and board is dear at some figures, 'pon my 'vation 'tis!"

"Set it higher, auctioneer," said the trusser.

"Two guineas!" said the auctioneer; and no one replied.

"If they don't take her for that, in ten seconds they'll have to give more," said the husband. "Very well. Now, auctioneer, add another."

"Three guineas—going for three guineas!" said the rheumy man.

"No bid?" said the husband. "Good Lord, why she's cost me fifty times the money, if a penny. Go on."

"Four guineas!" cried the auctioneer.

"I'll tell ye what—I won't sell her for less than five," said the husband, bringing down his fist so that the basins danced. "I'll sell her for five guineas to any man that will pay me the money, and treat her well; and he shall have her for ever, and never hear aught o' me. But she shan't go for less. Now then—five guineas—and she's yours. Susan, you agree?"

She bowed her head with absolute indifference.

"Five guineas," said the auctioneer, "or she'll be withdrawn. Do anybody give it? The last time. Yes or no?"

"Yes," said a loud voice from the doorway.

All eyes were turned. Standing in the triangular opening which formed the door of the tent was a sailor, who, unobserved by the rest, had arrived there within the last two or three minutes. A dead silence followed his affirmation.

"You say you do?" asked the husband, staring at him.

"I say so," replied the sailor.

"Saying is one thing, and paying is another. Where's the money?"

The sailor hesitated a moment, looked anew at the woman, came in, unfolded five crisp pieces of paper, and threw them down upon the table-cloth. They were Bank-of-England notes for five pounds. Upon the face of this he chinked down the shillings severally—one, two, three, four, five.

The sight of real money in full amount, in answer to a challenge for the same till then deemed slightly hypothetical, had a great effect upon the spectators. Their eyes became riveted upon the faces of the chief actors, and then upon the notes as they lay, weighted by the shillings, on the table.

Up to this moment it could not positively have been asserted that the man, in spite of his tantalizing declaration, was really in earnest.

The spectators had indeed taken the proceedings throughout as a piece of mirthful irony carried to extremes; and had assumed that, being out of work, he was, as a consequence, out of temper with the world, and society, and his nearest kin. But with the demand and response of real cash the jovial frivolity of the scene departed. A lurid colour seemed to fill the tent, and change the aspect of all therein. The mirth-wrinkles left the listeners' faces, and they waited with parting lips.

"Now," said the woman, breaking the silence, so that her low dry voice sounded quite loud, "before you go further, Michael, listen to me. If you touch that money, I and this girl go with the man. Mind, it is a joke no longer."

"A joke? Of course it is not a joke!" shouted her husband, his resentment rising at her suggestion. "I take the money: the sailor takes you. That's plain enough. It has been done elsewhere—and why not here?"

"'Tis quite on the understanding that the young woman is willing," said the sailor blandly. "I wouldn't hurt her feelings for the world."

"Faith, nor I," said her husband. "But she is willing, provided she can have the child. She said so only the other day when I talked o't!"

"That you swear?" said the sailor to her

"I do," said she, after glancing at her husband's face and seeing no repentance there.

"Very well, she shall have the child, and the bargain's complete," said the trusser. He took the sailor's notes and deliberately folded them, and put them with the shillings in a high remote pocket, with an air of finality.

The sailor looked at the woman and smiled. "Come along!" he said kindly. "The little one too—the more the merrier!" She paused for an instant, with a close glance at him. Then dropping her eyes again, and saying nothing, she took up the child and followed him as he made towards the door. On reaching it, she turned, and pulling off her wedding-ring, flung it across the booth in the hay-trusser's face.

"Mike," she said, "I've lived with thee a couple of years, and had nothing but temper! Now I'm no more to 'ee; I'll try my luck elsewhere. 'Twill be better for me and the child, both. So good-bye!"

Seizing the sailor's arm with her right hand, and mounting the little girl on her left, she went out of the tent sobbing bitterly.

A stolid look of concern filled the husband's face, as if, after all, he had not quite anticipated this ending; and some of the guests laughed.

"Is she gone?" he said.

"Faith, ay; she gone clane enough," said some rustics near the door.

He rose and walked to the entrance with the careful tread of one conscious of his alcoholic load. Some others followed, and they stood looking into the twilight. The difference between the peacefulness of inferior nature and the wilful hostilities of mankind was very apparent at this place. In contrast with the harshness of the act just ended within the tent was the sight of several horses crossing their necks and rubbing each other lovingly as they waited in patience to be harnessed for the homeward journey. Outside the fair, in the valleys and woods, all was quiet. The sun had recently set, and the west heaven was hung with rosy cloud, which seemed permanent, yet slowly changed. To watch it was like looking at some grand feat of stagery from a darkened auditorium. In presence of this scene, after the other, there was a natural instinct to abjure man as the blot on an otherwise kindly universe; till it was remembered that all terrestrial conditions were intermittent, and that mankind might some night be innocently sleeping when these quiet objects were raging loud.

"Where do the sailor live?" asked a spectator, when they had vainly gazed around.

"God knows that," replied the man who had seen high life. "He's without doubt a stranger here."

"He came in about five minutes ago," said the furmity woman, joining the rest with her hands on her hips. "And then 'a stepped back, and then 'a looked in again. I'm not a penny the better for him."

"Serves the husband well be-right," said the staylace vendor. "A comely respectable body like her—what can a man want more? I glory in the woman's sperrit. I'd ha' done it myself—od send if I wouldn't, if a husband had behaved so to me! I'd go, and 'a might call, and call, till his keacorn was raw; but I'd never come back—no, not till the great trumpet, would I!"

"Well, the woman will be better off," said another of a more deliberative turn. "For seafaring naters be very good shelter for shorn lambs, and the man do seem to have plenty of money, which is what she's not been used to lately, by all showings."

"Mark me—I'll not go after her!" said the trusser, returning doggedly to his seat. "Let her go! If she's up to such vagaries she must suffer for 'em. She'd no business to take the maid—'tis my maid; and if it were the doing again she shouldn't have her!"

Perhaps from some little sense of having countenanced an indefensible proceeding, perhaps because it was late, the customers thinned away from the tent shortly after this episode. The man stretched his elbows forward on the table, leant his face upon his arms, and soon began to snore. The furmity seller decided to close for the night, and after seeing the rum-bottles, milk, corn, raisins, &c., that remained on hand, loaded into the cart, came to where the man reclined. She shook him, but could not wake him. As the tent was not to be struck that night, the fair continuing for two or three days, she decided to let the sleeper, who was obviously no tramp, stay where he was, and his basket with him. Extinguishing the last candle, and lowering the flap of the tent, she left it, and drove away.

The Darkling Thrush

I LEANT upon a coppice gate
　　When Frost was spectre-gray,
And Winter's dregs made desolate
　　The weakening eye of day.
The tangled bine-stems scored the sky
　　Like strings of broken lyres,
And all mankind that haunted nigh
　　Had sought their household fires.

The land's sharp features seemed to be
　　The Century's corpse outleant,
His crypt the cloudy canopy,
　　The wind his death-lament.
The ancient pulse of germ and birth
　　Was shrunken hard and dry,
And every spirit upon earth
　　Seemed fervourless as I.

At once a voice arose among
　　The bleak twigs overhead
In a full-hearted evensong
　　Of joy illimited;
An aged thrush, frail, gaunt, and small,
　　In blast-beruffled plume,
Had chosen thus to fling his soul
　　Upon the growing gloom.

So little cause for carollings
　　Of such ecstatic sound
Was written on terrestrial things
　　Afar or nigh around,
That I could think there trembled through
　　His happy good-night air
Some blessed Hope, whereof he knew
　　And I was unaware.

ANDREW LANG (1844-1912)

From LETTERS TO DEAD AUTHORS

To Jane Austen

MADAM,—

If to the enjoyments of your present state be lacking a view of the minor infirmities or foibles of men, I cannot but think (were the thought permitted) that your pleasures are yet incomplete. Moreover, it is certain that a woman of parts who has once meddled with literature will never wholly lose her love for the discussion of that delicious topic, nor cease to relish what (in the cant of our new age) is styled "literary shop." For these reasons I attempt to convey to you some inkling of the present state of that agreeable art which you, madam, raised to its highest pitch of perfection.

As to your own works (immortal, as I believe), I have but little that is wholly cheering to tell one who, among women of letters, was almost alone in her freedom from a lettered vanity. You are not a very popular author: your volumes are not found in gaudy colors on every bookstall; or, if found, are not perused with avidity by the Emmas and Catherines of our generation. 'Tis not long since a blow was dealt (in the estimation of the unreasoning) at your character as an author by the publication of your familiar letters. The editor of these epistles, unfortunately, did not always take your witticisms, and he added others which were too unmistakably his own. While the injudicious were disappointed by the absence of your exquisite style and humor, the wiser sort were the more convinced of your wisdom. In your letters (knowing your correspondents) you gave but the small personal talk of the hour, for them sufficient; for your books you reserved matter and expression which are imperishable. Your admirers, if not very numerous, include all persons of taste, who, in your favor, are apt somewhat to abate the rule, or shake off the habit, which commonly confines them to but temperate laudation.

'Tis the fault of all art to seem antiquated and faded in the eyes of the succeeding generation. The manners of your age were not the manners of to-day, and young gentlemen and ladies who think Scott "slow," think Miss Austen "prim" and "dreary." Yet, even could you return among us, I scarcely believe that, speaking the language of the hour, as you might, and versed in its habits, you would win the general admiration. For how tame, madam, are your characters, especially your favorite heroines! how limited the life which you knew and described! how narrow the range of your incidents! how correct your grammar!

As heroines, for example, you chose ladies like Emma, and Elizabeth, and Catherine: women remarkable neither for the brilliance nor for the degradation of their birth; women wrapped up in their own and the parish's concerns, ignorant of evil, as it seems, and unacquainted with vain yearnings and interesting doubts. Who can engage his fancy with their match-makings and the conduct of their affections, when so many daring and dazzling heroines approach and solicit his regard?

Here are princesses dressed in white velvet stamped with golden fleurs-de-lys—ladies with hearts of ice and lips of fire, who count their rubles by the million, their lovers by the score, and even their husbands, very often, in figures of some arithmetical importance. With these are the immaculate daughters of itinerant Italian musicians, maids whose souls are unsoiled amidst the contaminations of our streets, and whose acquaintance with the art of Phidias and Praxiteles, of Dædalus and

Scopas, is the more admirable because entirely derived from loving study of the inexpensive collections vended by the plaster-of-Paris man round the corner. When such heroines are wooed by the nephews of dukes, where are your Emmas and Elizabeths? Your volumes neither excite nor satisfy the curiosities provoked by that modern and scientific fiction, which is greatly admired, I learn, in the United States as well as in France and at home.

You erred, it cannot be denied, with your eyes open. Knowing Lydia and Kitty so intimately as you did, why did you make of them almost insignificant characters? With Lydia for a heroine you might have gone far; and, had you devoted three volumes, and the chief of your time, to the passions of Kitty, you might have held your own, even now, in the circulating library. How Lyddy, perched on a corner of the roof, first beheld her Wickham; how, on her challenge, he climbed up by a ladder to her side; how they kissed, caressed, swung on gates together, met at odd seasons, in strange places, and finally eloped: all this might have been put in the mouth of a jealous elder sister, say Elizabeth, and you would not have been less popular than several favorites of our time. Had you cast the whole narrative into the present tense, and lingered lovingly over the thickness of Mary's legs, and the softness of Kitty's cheeks, and the blond fluffiness of Wickham's whiskers, you would have left a romance still dear to young ladies.

Or again, you might entrance your students still, had you concentrated your attention on Mrs. Rushworth, who eloped with Henry Crawford. These should have been the chief figures of "Mansfield Park." But you timidly decline to tackle Passion. "Let other pens," you write, "dwell on guilt and misery. I quit such odious subjects as soon as I can." Ah, *there* is the secret of your failure! Need I add that the vulgarity and narrowness of the social circles you describe impair your popularity? I scarce remember more than one lady of title, and but very few lords (and these unessential), in all your tales. Now, when we all wish to be in society, we demand plenty of titles in our novels, at any rate, and we get lords (and very queer lords) even from Republican authors, born in a country which in your time was not renowned for its literature. I have heard a critic remark, with a decided air of fashion, on the brevity of the notice which your characters give each other when they offer invitations to dinner. "An invitation to dinner next day was despatched," and this demonstrates that your acquaintance "went out" very little, and had but few engagements. How vulgar, too, is one of your heroines, who bids Mr. Darcy "keep his breath to cool his porridge." I blush for Elizabeth! It was superfluous to add that your characters are debased by being invariably mere members of the Church of England as by law established. The dissenting enthusiast, the open soul that glides from Esoteric Buddhism to the Salvation Army, and from the Higher Pantheism to the Higher Paganism, we look for in vain among your studies of character. Nay, the very words I employ are of unknown sound to you; so how can you help us in the stress of the soul's travailings?

You may say that the soul's travailings are no affair of yours; proving thereby that you have indeed but a lowly conception of the duty of the novelist. I only remember one reference, in all your works, to that controversy which occupies the chief of our attention—the great controversy on Creation or Evolution. Your Jane Bennet cries: "I have no idea of there being so much Design in the world as some persons imagine." Nor do you touch on our mighty social question, the Land Laws, save when Mrs. Bennet appears as a Land Reformer, and rails bitterly against the cruelty "of settling an estate away from a family of five daughters, in favor of a man whom nobody cared anything about." There, madam, in that cruelly unjust performance, what a text you had for a *Tendenz-Roman*. Nay, you can allow Kitty to report that a Private had been flogged, without introducing a chapter on Flogging in the Army. But you formally declined to stretch your matter out, here and there, "with solemn specious nonsense about something unconnected with the story." No "padding" for Miss Austen! In fact, madam, as you were born before Analysis came in, or Passion, or Realism, or Naturalism, or Irreverence, or Religious Open-mindedness, you really cannot hope to rival your literary sisters in the minds of a perplexed generation. Your heroines are not passionate, we do not see their red wet cheeks, and tresses dishevelled in the manner of our frank young Mænads. What says your best successor, a lady who adds fresh lustre to a name that in fiction equals yours? She says of Miss Austen: "Her heroines have a stamp of their own. They have *a certain gentle self-respect and humor and hardness of heart.* . . . Love with them does not mean a passion as much as an interest, deep and silent." I think one prefers them so, and that English-women should be more like Anne Elliot than Maggie Tulliver. "All the privilege I claim for my own sex is that of loving longest when existence or when hope is gone," said Anne; perhaps she insisted on a monopoly that neither sex has all to itself. Ah, madam, what a relief it is to come back to your witty volumes, and forget the follies of to-day in those of Mr. Collins and of Mrs. Bennet! How fine, nay, how noble is your art in its delicate reserve, never insisting, never forcing the note, never pushing the sketch into the caricature!

You worked without thinking of it, in the spirit of Greece, on a labor happily limited, and exquisitely organized. "Dear books," we say, with Miss Thackeray—"dear books, bright, sparkling with wit and animation, in which the homely heroines charm, the dull hours fly, and the very bores are enchanting."

To Sir Walter Scott, Bart.

Rodono, St. Mary's Loch:
Sept. 8, 1885.

SIR,—In your biography it is recorded that you not only won the favor of all men and women; but that a domestic fowl conceived an affection for you, and that a pig, by his will, had never been severed from your company. If some Circe had repeated in my case her favorite miracle of turning mortals into swine, and had given me a choice, into that fortunate pig, blessed among his race, would I have been converted! You, almost alone among men of letters, still, like a living friend, win and charm us out of the past; and if one might call up a poet, as the scholiast tried to call Homer, from the shades, who would not, out of all the rest, demand some hours of your society? Who that ever meddled with letters, what child of the irritable race, possessed even a tithe of your simple manliness, of the heart that never knew a touch of jealousy, that envied no man his laurels, that took honor and wealth as they came, but never would have deplored them had you missed both and remained but the Border sportsman and the Border antiquary?

Were the word "genial" not so much profaned, were it not misused, in easy good-nature, to extenuate lettered and sensual indolence, that worn old term might be applied, above all men, to "the Shirra." But perhaps we scarcely need a word (it would be seldom in use) for a character so rare, or rather so lonely, in its nobility and charm as that of Walter Scott. Here, in the heart of your own country, among your own gray round-shouldered hills (each so like the other that the shadow of one falling on its neighbor exactly outlines that neighbor's shape), it is of you and of your works that a native of the Forest is most frequently brought in mind. All the spirits of the river and the hill, all the dying refrains of ballad and the fading echoes of story, all the memory of the wild past, each legend of burn and loch, seem to have combined to inform your spirit, and to secure themselves an immortal life in your song. It is through you that we remember them; and in recalling them, as in treading each hillside in this land, we again remember you and bless you.

It is not "Sixty Years Since" the echo of the Tweed among his pebbles fell for the last time on your ear; not sixty years since, and how much is altered! But two generations have passed; the lad who used to ride from Edinburgh to Abbotsford, carrying new books for you, and old, is still vending, in George Street, old books and new. Of politics I have not the heart to speak. Little joy would you have had in most that has befallen since the Reform Bill was passed, to the chivalrous cry of "burke Sir Walter." We are still very Radical in the Forest, and you were taken away from many evils to come. How would the cheek of Walter Scott, or of Leyden, have blushed at the names of Majuba, The Soudan, Maiwand, and many others that recall political cowardice or military incapacity! On the other hand, who but you could have sung the dirge of Gordon, or wedded with immortal verse the names of Hamilton (who fell with Cavagnari), of the two Stewarts, of many another clansman, brave among the bravest! Only he who told how

> The stubborn spearmen still made good
> Their dark impenetrable wood

could have fitly rhymed a score of feats of arms in which, as at M'Neill's Zareeba and at Abu Klea,

> Groom fought like noble, squire like knight,
> As fearlessly and well.

Ah, Sir, the hearts of the rulers may wax faint, and the voting classes may forget that they are Britons; but when it comes to blows our fighting men might cry, with Leyden,

> My name is little Jock Elliot,
> And wha daur meddle wi' me!

Much is changed, in the country-side as well as in the country; but much remains. The little towns of your time are populous and excessively black with the smoke of factories—not, I fear, at present very flourishing. In Galashiels you still see the little change-house and the cluster of cottages round the Laird's lodge, like the clachan of Tully Veolan. But these plain remnants of the old Scotch towns are almost buried in a multitude of "smoky dwarf houses"—a living poet, Mr. Matthew Arnold, has found the fitting phrase for these dwellings, once for all. All over the Forest the waters are dirty and poisoned: I think they are filthiest below Hawick; but this may be mere local prejudice in a Selkirk man. To keep them clean costs money; and, though improvements are often promised, I cannot see much change for the better. Abbotsford, luckily, is above Galashiels, and only receives the dirt and dyes of Selkirk, Peebles,

Walkerburn, and Innerlethen. On the other hand, your ill-omened later dwelling, "the unhappy palace of your race," is overlooked by villas that prick a cockney ear among their larches, hotels of the future. Ah, Sir, Scotland is a strange place. Whiskey is exiled from some of our caravansaries, and they have banished Sir John Barleycorn. It seems as if the views of the excellent critic (who wrote your life lately, and said you had left no descendants, *le pauvre homme!*) were beginning to prevail. This pious biographer was greatly shocked by that capital story about the keg of whiskey that arrived at the Liddesdale farmer's during family prayers. Your Toryism also was an offence to him.

Among these vicissitudes of things and the overthrow of customs, let us be thankful that, beyond the reach of the manufacturers, the Border country remains as kind and homely as ever. I looked at Ashiestiel some days ago: the house seemed just as it may have been when you left it for Abbotsford, only there was a lawn-tennis net on the lawn, the hill on the opposite bank of the Tweed was covered to the crest with turnips, and the burn did not sing below the little bridge, for in this arid summer the burn was dry. But there was still a grilse that rose to a big March brown in the shrunken stream below Elibank. This may not interest you, who styled yourself

> No fisher,
> But a well-wisher
> To the game!

Still, as when you were thinking over Marmion, a man might have "grand gallops among the hills"—those grave wastes of heather and bent that sever all the watercourses and roll their sheep-covered pastures from Dollar Law to White Combe, and from White Combe to the Three Brethren Cairn and the Windburg and Skelf-hill Pen. Yes, Teviotdale is pleasant still, and there is not a drop of dye in the water, *purior electro,* of Yarrow. St. Mary's Loch lies beneath me, smitten with wind and rain—the St. Mary's of North and of the Shepherd. Only the trout, that see a myriad of artificial flies, are shyer than of yore. The Shepherd could no longer fill a cart up Meggat with trout so much of a size that the country people took them for herrings.

The grave of Piers Cockburn is still not desecrated: hard by it lies, within a little wood; and beneath that slab of old sandstone, and the graven letters, and the sword and shield, sleep "Piers Cockburn and Marjory his wife." Not a hundred yards off was the castle-door where they hanged him; this is the tomb of the ballad, and the lady that buried him rests now with her wild lord.

Oh, wat ye no my heart was sair,
When I happit the mouls on his yellow hair;
Oh, wat ye no my heart was wae,
When I turned about and went my way!

Here too hearts have broken, and there is a sacredness in the shadow and beneath these clustering berries of the rowan-tree. That sacredness, that reverent memory of our old land, it is always and inextricably blended with our memories, with our thoughts, with our love of you. Scotchmen, methinks, who owe so much to you, owe you most for the example you gave of the beauty of a life of honor, showing them what, by Heaven's blessing, a Scotchman still might be.

Words, empty and unavailing—for what words of ours can speak our thoughts or interpret our affections! From you first, as we followed the deer with King James, or rode with William of Deloraine on his midnight errand, did we learn what Poetry means, and all the happiness that is in the gift of song. This, and more than may be told, you gave us, that are not forgetful, not ungrateful, though our praise be unequal to our gratitude. *Fungor inani munere!*

ROBERT LOUIS STEVENSON
(1845-1894)

From A CHILD'S GARDEN OF VERSES

Whole Duty of Children

A CHILD should always say what's true
And speak when he is spoken to,
And behave mannerly at table;
At least as far as he is able.

Foreign Lands

UP into the cherry tree
Who should climb but little me?
I held the trunk with both my hands
And looked abroad on foreign lands.

I saw the next door garden lie,
Adorned with flowers, before my eye,
And many pleasant places more
That I had never seen before.

I saw the dimpling river pass
And be the sky's blue looking-glass;
The dusty roads go up and down
With people tramping into town.

If I could find a higher tree
Farther and farther I should see,
To where the grown-up river slips
Into the sea among the ships,

To where the roads on either hand
Lead onward into fairy land,
Where all the children dine at five,
And all the playthings come alive.

The Land of Counterpane

WHEN I was sick and lay a-bed,
I had two pillows at my head,
And all my toys beside me lay
To keep me happy all the day.

And sometimes for an hour or so
I watched my leaden soldiers go,
With different uniforms and drills,
Among the bed-clothes, through the hills;

And sometimes sent my ships in fleets
All up and down among the sheets;
Or brought my trees and houses out,
And planted cities all about.

I was the giant great and still
That sits upon the pillow-hill,
And sees before him, dale and plain,
The pleasant land of counterpane.

System

EVERY night my prayers I say,
And get my dinner every day;
And every day that I've been good,
I get an orange after food.

The child that is not clean and neat,
With lots of toys and things to eat,
He is a naughty child, I'm sure—
Or else his dear papa is poor.

Good and Bad Children

CHILDREN, you are very little,
And your bones are very brittle;
If you would grow great and stately,
You must try to walk sedately.

You must still be bright and quiet,
And content with simple diet;
And remain, through all bewild'ring,
Innocent and honest children.

Happy hearts and happy faces,
Happy play in grassy places—
That was how, in ancient ages,
Children grew to kings and sages.

But the unkind and the unruly,
And the sort who eat unduly,
They must never hope for glory—
Theirs is quite a different story!

Cruel children, crying babies,
All grow up as geese and gabies,
Hated, as their age increases,
By their nephews and their nieces.

The Unseen Playmate

WHEN children are playing alone on the
green
In comes the playmate that never was
seen.

When children are happy and lonely and
good,
The Friend of the Children comes out of
the wood.

Nobody heard him and nobody saw,
His is a picture you never could draw,
But he's sure to be present, abroad or at
home,
When children are happy and playing
alone.

He lies in the laurels, he runs on the
grass,
He sings when you tinkle the musical
glass;
Whene'er you are happy and cannot tell
why,
The Friend of the Children is sure to be
by!

He loves to be little, he hates to be big,
'Tis he that inhabits the caves that you
dig;
'Tis he when you play with your soldiers
of tin
That sides with the Frenchmen and never
can win.

'Tis he, when at night you go off to your
bed,
Bids you go to your sleep and not trouble
your head;
For wherever they're lying, in cupboard
or shelf,
'Tis he will take care of your playthings
himself!

From UNDERWOODS

Requiem

UNDER the wide and starry sky,
Dig the grave and let me lie.
Glad did I live and gladly die,
And I laid me down with a will.

This be the verse you grave for me:
Here he lies where he longed to be;
Home is the sailor, home from sea,
And the hunter home from the hill.

The Celestial Surgeon

IF I have faltered more or less
In my great task of happiness;
If I have moved among my race
And shown no glorious morning face;
If beams from happy human eyes
Have moved me not; if morning
  skies,
Books, and my food, and summer rain
Knocked on my sullen heart in vain:—
Lord, thy most pointed pleasure take
And stab my spirit broad awake;
Or, Lord, if too obdurate I,
Choose thou, before that spirit die,
A piercing pain, a killing sin,
And to my dead heart run them in!

Say not of me that weakly I declined

SAY not of me that weakly I declined
The labours of my sires, and fled the sea,
The towers we founded and the lamps we
  lit,
To play at home with paper like a child.
But rather say: *In the afternoon of time*
A strenuous family dusted from its hands
The sand of granite, and beholding far
Along the sounding coast its pyramids
And tall memorials catch the dying sun,
Smiled well content, and to this childish
  task
Around the fire addressed its evening
  hours.

From THE MANSE

Probably Arboreal

Now I often wonder what I have inherited from this old minister.
I must suppose, indeed, that he was fond of preaching sermons, and so
am I, though I never heard it maintained that either of us loved to hear
them. He sought health in his youth in the Isle of Wight, and I have
sought it in both hemispheres; but whereas he found and kept it, I am still
on the quest. He was a great lover of Shakespeare, whom he read aloud,
I have been told, with taste; well, I love my Shakespeare also, and am
persuaded I can read him well, though I own I never have been told so.
He made embroidery, designing his own patterns; and in that kind of
work I never made anything but a kettle-holder in Berlin wool, and an
odd garter of knitting, which was as black as the chimney before I had
done with it. He loved port, and nuts, and porter; and so do I, but they
agreed better with my grandfather, which seems to me a breach of
contract. He had chalk-stones in his fingers; and these, in good time,
I may possibly inherit, but I would much rather have inherited his noble
presence. Try as I please, I cannot join myself on with the reverend
doctor; and all the while, no doubt, and even as I write the phrase,
he moves in my blood, and whispers words to me, and sits efficient in
the very knot and centre of my being. In his garden, as I played there, I
learned the love of mills—or had I an ancestor a miller?—and a kindness
for the neighborhood of graves, as homely things not without their
poetry—or had I an ancestor a sexton? But what of the garden where

he played himself?—for that, too, was a scene of my education. Some part of me played there in the eighteenth century, and ran races under the green avenue at Pilrig; some part of me trudged up Leith Walk, which was still a country place, and sat on the High School benches, and was thrashed, perhaps, by Dr. Adam. The house where I spent my youth was not yet thought upon; but we made holiday parties among the corn-fields on its site, and ate strawberries and cream near by at a gardener's. All this I had forgotten; only my grandfather remembered and once reminded me. I have forgotten, too, how we grew up, and took orders, and went to our first Ayrshire parish, and fell in love with and married a daughter of Burns's Dr. Smith—"Smith opens out his cauld harangues." I have forgotten, but I was there all the same, and heard stories of Burns at first hand.

And there is a thing stranger than all that; for this *homunculus* or part-man of mine that walked about the eighteenth century with Dr. Balfour in his youth, was in the way of meeting other *homunculos* or part-men, in the persons of my other ancestors. These were of a lower order, and doubtless we looked down upon them duly. But as I went to college with Dr. Balfour, I may have seen the lamp and oil man taking down the shutters from his shop beside the Tron;—we may have had a rabbit-hutch or a bookshelf made for us by a certain carpenter in I know not what wynd of the old, smoky city; or, upon some holiday excursion, we may have looked into the windows of a cottage in a flower-garden and seen a certain weaver plying his shuttle. And these were all kinsmen of mine upon the other side; and from the eyes of the lamp and oil man one-half of my unborn father, and one-quarter of my-self, looked out upon us as we went by to college. Nothing of all this would cross the mind of the young student, as he posted up the Bridges with trim, stockinged legs, in that city of cocked hats and good Scotch still unadulterated. It would not cross his mind that he should have a daughter; and the lamp and oil man, just then beginning, by a not unnatural metastasis, to bloom into a lighthouse-engineer, should have a grandson; and that these two, in the fulness of time, should wed; and some portion of that student himself should survive yet a year or two longer in the person of their child.

But our ancestral adventures are beyond even the arithmetic of fancy; and it is the chief recommendation of long pedigrees, that we can follow backward the careers of our *homunculi* and be reminded of our antenatal lives. Our conscious years are but a moment in the history of the elements that build us. Are you a bank-clerk, and do you live at Peck-ham? It was not always so. And though to-day I am only a man of

letters, either tradition errs or I was present when there landed at St.
Andrews a French barber-surgeon, to tend the health and the beard of
the great Cardinal Beaton; I have shaken a spear in the Debatable Land
and shouted the slogan of the Elliots; I was present when a skipper,
plying from Dundee, smuggled Jacobites to France after the '15; I was
in a West India merchant's office, perhaps next door to Bailie
Nichol Jarvie's, and managed the business of a plantation in St. Kitt's;
I was with my engineer-grandfather (the son-in-law of the lamp
and oil man) when he sailed north about Scotland on the famous
cruise that gave us the *Pirate* and the *Lord of the Isles;* I was with him,
too, on the Bell Rock, in the fog, when the *Smeaton* had drifted from
her moorings, and the Aberdeen men, pick in hand, had seized upon the
only boats, and he must stoop and lap sea-water before his tongue could
utter audible words; and once more with him when the Bell Rock
beacon took a "thrawe," and his workmen fled into the tower, then nearly
finished, and he sat unmoved reading in his Bible—or affecting to read—
till one after another slunk back with confusion of countenance to their
engineer.   Yes, parts of me have seen life, and met adventures, and sometimes met them well.   And away in the still cloudier past, the threads
that make me up can be traced by fancy into the bosoms of thousands
and millions of ascendants: Picts who rallied round Macbeth and the
old (and highly preferable) system of descent by females, fleërs from
before the legions of Agricola, marchers in Pannonian morasses, star-
gazers on Chaldæan plateaus; and, furthest of all, what face is this that
fancy can see peering through the disparted branches?   What sleeper in
green tree-tops, what muncher of nuts, concludes my pedigree?   Probably
arboreal in his habits. . . .

   And I know not which is the more strange, that I should carry about
with me some fibres of my minister-grandfather; or that in him, as he
sat in his cool study, grave, reverend, contented gentleman, there was an
aboriginal frisking of the blood that was not his; tree-top memories,
like undeveloped negatives, lay dormant in his mind; tree-top instincts
awoke and were trod down; and Probably Arboreal (scarce to be distinguished from a monkey) gambolled and chattered in the brain of the
old divine.

A Lodging for the Night

IT was late in November, 1456.   The snow fell over Paris with
rigorous, relentless persistence; sometimes the wind made a sally and
scattered it in flying vortices; sometimes there was a lull, and flake after

flake descended out of the black night air, silent, circuitous, interminable. To poor people, looking up under moist eyebrows, it seemed a wonder where it all came from. Master Francis Villon had propounded an alternative that afternoon, at a tavern window: was it only Pagan Jupiter plucking geese upon Olympus? or were the holy angels moulting? He was only a poor Master of Arts, he went on; and as the question somewhat touched upon divinity, he durst not venture to conclude. A silly old priest from Montargis, who was among the company, treated the young rascal to a bottle of wine in honor of the jest and grimaces with which it was accompanied, and swore on his own white beard that he had been just such another irreverent dog when he was Villon's age.

The air was raw and pointed, but not far below freezing; and the flakes were large, damp, and adhesive. The whole city was sheeted up. An army might have marched from end to end and not a footfall given the alarm. If there were any belated birds in heaven, they saw the island like a large white patch, and the bridges like slim white spars, on the black ground of the river. High up overhead the snow settled among the tracery of the cathedral towers. Many a niche was drifted full; many a statue wore a long white bonnet on its grotesque or sainted head. The gargoyles had been transformed into great false noses, drooping towards the point. The crockets were like upright pillows swollen on one side. In the intervals of the wind, there was a dull sound of dripping about the precincts of the church.

The cemetery of St. John had taken its own share of the snow. All the graves were decently covered; tall white housetops stood around in grave array; worthy burghers were long ago in bed, benightcapped like their domiciles; there was no light in all the neighborhood but a little peep from a lamp that hung swinging in the church choir, and tossed the shadows to and fro in time to its oscillations. The clock was hard on ten when the patrol went by with halberds and a lantern, beating their hands; and they saw nothing suspicious about the cemetery of St. John.

Yet there was a small house, backed up against the cemetery wall, which was still awake, and awake to evil purpose, in that snoring district. There was not much to betray it from without; only a stream of warm vapor from the chimney-top, a patch where the snow melted on the roof, and a few half-obliterated footprints at the door. But within, behind the shuttered windows, Master Francis Villon the poet, and some of the thievish crew with whom he consorted, were keeping the night alive and passing round the bottle.

A great pile of living embers diffused a strong and ruddy glow from the arched chimney. Before this straddled Dom Nicolas, the Picardy monk, with his skirts picked up and his fat legs bared to the comfortable warmth. His dilated shadow cut the room in half; and the firelight only escaped on either side of his broad person, and in a little pool between his outspread feet. His face had the beery, bruised appearance of the continual drinker's; it was covered with a network of congested veins, purple in ordinary circumstances, but now pale violet, for even with his back to the fire the cold pinched him on the other side. His cowl had half fallen back, and made a strange excrescence on either side of his bull neck. So he straddled, grumbling, and cut the room in half with the shadow of his portly frame.

On the right, Villon and Guy Tabary were huddled together over a scrap of parchment; Villon making a ballade which he was to call the "Ballade of Roast Fish," and Tabary spluttering admiration at his shoulder. The poet was a rag of a man, dark, little, and lean, with hollow cheeks and thin black locks. He carried his four-and-twenty years with feverish animation. Greed had made folds about his eyes, evil smiles had puckered his mouth. The wolf and pig struggled together in his face. It was an eloquent, sharp, ugly, earthly countenance. His hands were small and prehensile, with fingers knotted like a cord; and they were continually flickering in front of him in violent and expressive pantomime. As for Tabary, a broad, complacent, admiring imbecility breathed from his squash nose and slobbering lips: he had become a thief, just as he might have become the most decent of burgesses, by the imperious chance that rules the lives of human geese and human donkeys.

At the monk's other hand, Montigny and Thevenin Pensete played a game of chance. About the first there clung some flavor of good birth and training, as about a fallen angel; something long, lithe, and courtly in the person; something aquiline and darkling in the face. Thevenin, poor soul, was in great feather: he had done a good stroke of knavery that afternoon in the Faubourg St. Jacques, and all night he had been gaining from Montigny. A flat smile illuminated his face; his bald head shone rosily in a garland of red curls; his little protuberant stomach shook with silent chucklings as he swept in his gains.

"Doubles or quits?" said Thevenin.

Montigny nodded grimly.

"*Some men prefer to dine in state,*" wrote Villon, "*On bread and cheese on silver plate.* Or, or—help me out, Guido!"

Tabary giggled.

"*Or parsley on a golden dish,*" scribbled the poet.

The wind was freshening without; it drove the snow before it, and sometimes raised its voice in a victorious whoop, and made sepulchral grumblings in the chimney. The cold was growing sharper as the night went on. Villon, protruding his lips, imitated the gust with something between a whistle and a groan. It was an eerie, uncomfortable talent of the poet's, much detested by the Picardy monk.

"Can't you hear it rattle in the gibbet?" said Villon. "They are all dancing the devil's jig on nothing, up there. You may dance, my gallants, you'll be none the warmer! Whew! what a gust! Down went somebody just now! A medlar the fewer on the three-legged medlar-tree!—I say, Dom Nicolas, it'll be cold to-night on the St. Denis Road?" he asked.

Dom Nicolas winked both his big eyes, and seemed to choke upon his Adam's apple. Montfaucon, the great grisly Paris gibbet, stood hard by the St. Denis Road, and the pleasantry touched him on the raw. As for Tabary, he laughed immoderately over the medlars; he had never heard anything more light-hearted; and he held his sides and crowed. Villon fetched him a fillip on the nose, which turned his mirth into an attack of coughing.

"Oh, stop that row," said Villon, "and think of rhymes to 'fish.' "

"Doubles or quits," said Montigny doggedly.

"With all my heart," quoth Thevenin.

"Is there any more in that bottle?" asked the monk.

"Open another," said Villon. "How do you ever hope to fill that big hogshead, your body, with little things like bottles? And how do you expect to get to heaven? How many angels, do you fancy, can be spared to carry up a single monk from Picardy? Or do you think yourself another Elias—and they'll send the coach for you?"

"*Hominibus impossibile,*" replied the monk as he filled his glass.

Tabary was in ecstasies.

Villon filliped his nose again.

"Laugh at my jokes, if you like," he said.

"It was very good," objected Tabary.

Villon made a face at him. "Think of rhymes to 'fish,' " he said. "What have you to do with Latin? You'll wish you knew none of it at the great assizes, when the devil calls for Guido Tabary, clericus—the devil with the hump-back and red-hot finger-nails. Talking of the devil," he added in a whisper, "look at Montigny!"

All three peered covertly at the gamester. He did not seem to be enjoying his luck. His mouth was a little to a side; one nostril nearly shut, and the other much inflated. The black dog was on his back, as people say, in terrifying nursery metaphor; and he breathed hard under the gruesome burthen.

"He looks as if he could knife him," whispered Tabary, with round eyes.

The monk shuddered, and turned his face and spread his open hands to the red embers. It was the cold that thus affected Dom Nicolas, and not any excess of moral sensibility.

"Come now," said Villon—"about this ballade. How does it run so far?" And beating time with his hand, he read it aloud to Tabary.

They were interrupted at the fourth rhyme by a brief and fatal movement among the gamesters. The round was completed, and Thevenin was just opening his mouth to claim another victory, when Montigny leaped up, swift as an adder, and stabbed him to the heart. The blow took effect before he had time to utter a cry, before he had time to move. A tremor or two convulsed his frame; his hands opened and shut, his heels rattled on the floor; then his head rolled backward over one shoulder with the eyes wide open; and Thevenin Pensete's spirit had returned to Him who made it.

Every one sprang to his feet; but the business was over in two twos. The four living fellows looked at each other in rather a ghastly fashion; the dead man contemplating a corner of the roof with a singular and ugly leer.

"My God!" said Tabary; and he began to pray in Latin.

Villon broke out into hysterical laughter. He came a step forward and ducked a ridiculous bow at Thevenin, and laughed still louder. Then he sat down suddenly, all of a heap, upon a stool, and continued laughing bitterly, as though he would shake himself to pieces.

Montigny recovered his composure first.

"Let's see what he has about him," he remarked, and he picked the dead man's pockets with a practised hand, and divided the money into four equal portions on the table. "There's for you," he said.

The monk received his share with a deep sigh, and a single stealthy glance at the dead Thevenin, who was beginning to sink into himself and topple sideways off the chair.

"We're all in for it," cried Villon, swallowing his mirth. "It's a hanging job for every man jack of us that's here—not to speak of those who aren't." He made a shocking gesture in the air with his raised right hand, and put out his tongue and threw his head on one side, so as to counterfeit the appearance of one who has been hanged. Then he pocketed his share of the spoil, and executed a shuffle with his feet as if to restore the circulation.

Tabary was the last to help himself; he made a dash at the money, and retired to the other end of the apartment.

Montigny stuck Thevenin upright in the chair, and drew out the dagger, which was followed by a jet of blood.

"You fellows had better be moving," he said, as he wiped the blade on his victim's doublet.

"I think we had," returned Villon, with a gulp. "Damn his fat head!" he broke out. "It sticks in my throat like phlegm. What right has a man to have red hair when he is dead?" And he fell all of a heap again upon the stool, and fairly covered his face with his hands.

Montigny and Dom Nicolas laughed aloud, even Tabary feebly chiming in.

"Cry baby," said the monk.

"I always said he was a woman," added Montigny, with a sneer. "Sit up, can't you?" he went on, giving another shake to the murdered body. "Tread out that fire, Nick!"

But Nick was better employed; he was quietly taking Villon's purse, as the poet sat, limp and trembling, on the stool where he had been making a ballade not three minutes before. Montigny and Tabary dumbly demanded a share of the booty, which the monk silently promised as he passed the little bag into the bosom of his gown. In many ways an artistic nature unfits a man for practical existence.

No sooner had the theft been accomplished than Villon shook himself, jumped to his feet, and began helping to scatter and extinguish the embers. Meanwhile Montigny opened the door and cautiously peered into the street. The coast was clear; there was no meddlesome patrol in sight. Still it was judged wiser to slip out severally; and as Villon was himself in a hurry to escape from the neighborhood of the dead Thevenin, and the rest were in a still greater hurry to get rid of him before he should discover the loss of his money, he was the first by general consent to issue forth into the street.

The wind had triumphed and swept all the clouds from heaven. Only a few vapors, as thin as moonlight, fleeted rapidly across the stars. It was bitter cold; and by a common optical effect, things seemed almost more definite than in the broadest daylight. The sleeping city was absolutely still; a company of white hoods, a field full of little alps, below the twinkling stars. Villon cursed his fortune. Would it were still snowing! Now, wherever he went, he left an indelible trail behind him on the glittering streets; wherever he went he was still tethered to the house by the cemetery of St. John; wherever he went he must weave, with his own plodding feet, the rope that bound him to the crime and would bind him to the gallows. The leer of the dead man came back to him with a new significance. He snapped his fingers as if to pluck up his own spirits, and choosing a street at random, stepped boldly forward in the snow.

Two things preoccupied him as he went: the aspect of the gallows at Montfaucon in this bright, windy phase of the night's existence, for one; and for another, the look of the dead man with his bald head and garland of red curls. Both struck cold upon his heart, and he kept quickening his pace as if he could escape from unpleasant thoughts by mere fleetness of foot. Sometimes he looked back over his shoulder with a sudden nervous jerk; but he was the only moving thing in the white streets, except when the wind swooped round a corner and threw up the snow, which was beginning to freeze, in spouts of glittering dust.

Suddenly he saw, a long way before him, a black clump and a couple of lanterns. The clump was in motion, and the lanterns swung as though carried by men walking. It was a patrol. And though it was merely crossing his line of march he judged it wiser to get out of eyeshot as speedily as he could. He was not in the humor to be challenged, and he was conscious of making a very conspicuous mark upon the snow. Just on his left hand there stood a great hotel, with some turrets and a large porch before the door; it was half ruinous, he remembered, and had long stood empty; and so he made three steps of it, and jumped into the shelter of the porch. It was pretty dark inside, after the glimmer of the snowy streets, and he was groping forward with outspread hands, when he stumbled over some substance which offered an indescribable mixture of resistances, hard and soft, firm and loose. His heart gave a leap, and he sprang two steps back and stared dreadfully at the obstacle. Then he gave a little laugh of relief. It was only a woman, and she dead. He knelt beside her to make sure upon this latter point. She was freezing cold, and rigid like a stick. A little ragged finery fluttered in the wind about her hair, and her cheeks had been heavily rouged that same afternoon. Her pockets were quite empty; but in her stocking, underneath the garter, Villon found two of the small coins that went by the name of whites. It was little enough; but it was always something; and the poet was moved with a deep sense of pathos that she should have died before she had spent her money. That seemed to him a dark and pitiable mystery; and he looked from the coins in his hands to the dead woman, and back again to the coins, shaking his head over the riddle of man's life. Henry V. of England, dying at Vincennes just after he had conquered France, and this poor jade cut off by a cold draught in a great man's doorway, before she had time to spend her couple of whites—it seemed a cruel way to carry on the world. Two whites would have taken such a little while to squander; and yet it would have been one more good taste in the mouth, one more smack of the lips, before the devil got the soul, and the body was left to birds and vermin. He would like to use all his tallow before the light was blown out and the lantern broken.

While these thoughts were passing through his mind, he was feeling, half mechanically, for his purse. Suddenly his heart stopped beating; a feeling of cold scales passed up the back of his legs, and a cold blow seemed to fall upon his scalp. He stood petrified for a moment; then he felt again with one feverish movement; and then his loss burst upon him, and he was covered at once with perspiration. To spendthrifts money is so living and actual—it is such a thin veil between them and their pleasures! There is only one limit to their fortune—that of time; and a spendthrift with only a few crowns is the Emperor of Rome until they are spent. For such a person to lose his money is to suffer the most shocking reverse, and fall from heaven to hell, from all to nothing, in a breath. And all the more if he has put his head in the halter for it; if he may be hanged to-morrow for that same purse, so dearly earned, so foolishly departed! Villon stood and cursed; he threw the two whites into the street; he shook his fist at heaven; he stamped, and was not horrified to find himself trampling the poor corpse. Then he began rapidly to retrace his steps towards the house beside the cemetery. He had forgotten all fear of the patrol, which was long gone by at any rate, and had no idea but that of his lost purse. It was in vain that he looked right and left upon the snow: nothing was to be seen. He had not dropped it in the streets. Had it fallen in the house? He would have liked dearly to go in and see; but the idea of the grisly occupant un-manned him. And he saw besides, as he drew near, that their efforts to put out the fire had been unsuccessful; on the contrary, it had broken into a blaze, and a changeful light played in the chinks of door and window, and revived his terror for the authorities and Paris gibbet.

He returned to the hotel with the porch, and groped about upon the snow for the money he had thrown away in his childish passion. But he could only find one white; the other had probably struck sideways and sunk deeply in. With a single white in his pocket, all his projects for a rousing night in some wild tavern vanished utterly away. And it was not only pleasure that fled laughing from his grasp; positive dis-comfort, positive pain, attacked him as he stood ruefully before the porch. His perspiration had dried upon him; and although the wind had now fallen, a binding frost was setting in stronger with every hour, and he felt benumbed and sick at heart. What was to be done? Late as was the hour, improbable as was success, he would try the house of his adopted father, the chaplain of St. Benoît.

He ran there all the way, and knocked timidly. There was no answer.
He knocked again and again, taking heart with every stroke; and at last
steps were heard approaching from within. A barred wicket fell open
in the iron-studded door, and emitted a gush of yellow light.

"Hold up your face to the wicket," said the chaplain from within.

"It's only me," whimpered Villon.

"Oh, it's only you, is it?" returned the chaplain; and he cursed him
with foul unpriestly oaths for disturbing him at such an hour, and bade
him be off to hell, where he came from.

"My hands are blue to the wrist," pleaded Villon; "my feet are dead
and full of twinges; my nose aches with the sharp air; the cold lies at my
heart. I may be dead before morning. Only this once, father, and before
God, I will never ask again!"

"You should have come earlier," said the ecclesiastic coolly. "Young
men require a lesson now and then." He shut the wicket and retired
deliberately into the interior of the house.

Villon was beside himself; he beat upon the door with his hands and
feet, and shouted hoarsely after the chaplain.

"Wormy old fox!" he cried. "If I had my hand under your twist,
I would send you flying headlong into the bottomless pit."

A door shut in the interior, faintly audible to the poet down long
passages. He passed his hand over his mouth with an oath. And then
the humor of the situation struck him, and he laughed and looked lightly
up to heaven, where the stars seemed to be winking over his discomfiture.

What was to be done? It looked very like a night in the frosty
streets. The idea of the dead woman popped into his imagination, and
gave him a hearty fright; what had happened to her in the early night
might very well happen to him before morning. And he so young! and
with such immense possibilities of disorderly amusement before him! He
felt quite pathetic over the notion of his own fate, as if it had been some
one else's, and made a little imaginative vignette of the scene in the morning when they should find his body.

He passed all his chances under review, turning the white between
his thumb and forefinger. Unfortunately he was on bad terms with
some old friends who would once have taken pity on him in such a plight.
He had lampooned them in verses; he had beaten and cheated them; and
yet now, when he was in so close a pinch, he thought there was at least one
who might perhaps relent. It was a chance. It was worth trying at
least, and he would go and see.

On the way, two little accidents happened to him which colored his
musings in a very different manner. For, first he fell in with the track

of a patrol, and walked in it for some hundred yards, although it lay out of his direction. And this spirited him up; at least he had confused his trail; for he was still possessed with the idea of people tracking him all about Paris over the snow, and collaring him next morning before he was awake. The other matter affected him quite differently. He passed a street corner, where, not so long before, a woman and her child had been devoured by wolves. This was just the kind of weather, he reflected, when wolves might take it into their heads to enter Paris again; and a lone man in these deserted streets would run the chance of something worse than a mere scare. He stopped and looked upon the place with an unpleasant interest—it was a centre where several lanes intersected each other; and he looked down them all, one after another, and held his breath to listen, lest he should detect some galloping black things on the snow or hear the sound of howling between him and the river. He remembered his mother telling him the story and pointing out the spot, while he was yet a child. His mother! If he only knew where she lived, he might make sure at least of shelter. He determined he would inquire upon the morrow; nay, he would go and see her too, poor old girl! So thinking, he arrived at his destination—his last hope for the night.

The house was quite dark, like its neighbors; and yet after a few taps, he heard a movement overhead, a door opening, and a cautious voice asking who was there. The poet named himself in a loud whisper, and waited, not without some trepidation, the result. Nor had he to wait long. A window was suddenly opened, and a pailful of slops splashed down upon the doorstep. Villon had not been unprepared for something of the sort, and had put himself as much in shelter as the nature of the porch admitted; but for all that, he was deplorably drenched below the waist. His hose began to freeze almost at once. Death from cold and exposure stared him in the face; he remembered he was of phthisical tendency, and began coughing tentatively. But the gravity of the danger steadied his nerves. He stopped a few hundred yards from the door where he had been so rudely used, and reflected with his finger to his nose. He could only see one way of getting a lodging, and that was to take it. He had noticed a house not far away, which looked as if it might be easily broken into, and thither he betook himself promptly, entertaining himself on the way with the idea of a room still hot, with a table still loaded with the remains of supper, where he might pass the rest of the black hours and whence he should issue, on the morrow, with an armful of valuable plate. He even considered on what viands and what wines he should prefer; and as he was calling the roll of his favorite dainties, roast fish presented itself to his mind with an odd mixture of amusement and horror.

"I shall never finish that ballade," he thought to himself; and then, with another shudder at the recollection, "Oh, damn his fat head!" he repeated fervently, and spat upon the snow.

The house in question looked dark at first sight; but as Villon made a preliminary inspection in search of the handiest point of attack, a little twinkle of light caught his eye from behind a curtained window.

"The devil!" he thought. "People awake! Some student or some saint, confound the crew! Can't they get drunk and lie in bed snoring like their neighbors? What's the good of curfew, and poor devils of bell-ringers jumping at a rope's end in bell-towers? What's the use of day, if people sit up all night? The gripes to them!" He grinned as he saw where his logic was leading him. "Every man to his business, after all," added he, "and if they're awake, by the Lord, I may come by a supper honestly for once, and cheat the devil."

He went boldly to the door and knocked with an assured hand. On both previous occasions, he had knocked timidly and with some dread of attracting notice; but now when he had just discarded the thought of a burglarious entry, knocking at a door seemed a mighty simple and innocent proceeding. The sound of his blows echoed through the house with thin, phantasmal reverberations, as though it were quite empty; but these had scarcely died away before a measured tread drew near, a couple of bolts were withdrawn, and one wing was opened broadly, as though no guile or fear of guile were known to those within. A tall figure of a man, muscular and spare, but a little bent, confronted Villon. The head was massive in bulk, but finely sculptured; the nose blunt at the bottom, but refining upward to where it joined a pair of strong and honest eyebrows; the mouth and eyes surrounded with delicate markings, and the whole face based upon a thick white beard, boldly and squarely trimmed. Seen as it was by the light of a flickering hand-lamp, it looked perhaps nobler than it had a right to do; but it was a fine face, honorable rather than intelligent, strong, simple, and righteous.

"You knock late, sir," said the old man in resonant, courteous tones.

Villon cringed and brought up many servile words of apology; at a crisis of this sort the beggar was uppermost in him, and the man of genius hid his head with confusion.

"You are cold," repeated the old man, "and hungry? Well, step in." And he ordered him into the house with a noble enough gesture.

"Some great seigneur," thought Villon, as his host, setting down the lamp on the flagged pavement of the entry, shot the bolts once more into their places.

"You will pardon me if I go in front," he said, when this was done; and he preceded the poet up-stairs into a large apartment, warmed with a pan of charcoal and lit by a great lamp hanging from the roof. It was very bare of furniture: only some gold plate on a sideboard; some folios; and a stand of armor between the windows. Some smart tapestry hung upon the walls, representing the crucifixion of our Lord in one piece, and in another a scene of shepherds and shepherdesses by a running stream. Over the chimney was a shield of arms.

"Will you seat yourself," said the old man, "and forgive me if I leave you? I am alone in my house to-night, and if you are to eat I must forage for you myself."

No sooner was his host gone than Villon leaped from the chair on which he had just seated himself, and began examining the room, with the stealth and passion of a cat. He weighed the gold flagons in his hand, opened all the folios, and investigated the arms upon the shield, and the stuff with which the seats were lined. He raised the window curtains, and saw that the windows were set with rich stained glass in figures, so far as he could see, of martial import. Then he stood in the middle of the room, drew a long breath, and retaining it with puffed cheeks, looked round and round him, turning on his heels, as if to impress every feature of the apartment on his memory.

"Seven pieces of plate," he said. "If there had been ten, I would have risked it. A fine house, and a fine old master, so help me all the saints!"

And just then, hearing the old man's tread returning along the corridor, he stole back to his chair, and began humbly toasting his wet legs before the charcoal pan.

His entertainer had a plate of meat in one hand and a jug of wine in the other. He set down the plate upon the table, motioning Villon to draw in his chair, and going to the sideboard, brought back two goblets which he filled.

"I drink your better fortune," he said, gravely touching Villon's cup with his own.

"To our better acquaintance," said the poet, growing bold. A mere man of the people would have been awed by the courtesy of the old seigneur, but Villon was hardened in that matter; he had made mirth for great lords before now, and found them as black rascals as himself. And so he devoted himself to the viands with a ravenous gusto, while the old man, leaning backward, watched him with steady, curious eyes.

"You have blood on your shoulder, my man," he said.

Montigny must have laid his wet right hand upon him as he left the house. He cursed Montigny in his heart.

"It was none of my shedding," he stammered.

"I had not supposed so," returned his host quietly. "A brawl?"

"Well, something of that sort," Villon admitted with a quaver.

"Perhaps a fellow murdered?"

"Oh, no, not murdered," said the poet, more and more confused. "It was all fair play—murdered by accident. I had no hand in it, God strike me dead!" he added fervently.

"One rogue the fewer, I dare say," observed the master of the house.

"You may dare to say that," agreed Villon, infinitely relieved. "As big a rogue as there is between here and Jerusalem. He turned up his toes like a lamb. But it was a nasty thing to look at. I dare say you've seen dead men in your time, my lord?" he added, glancing at the armor.

"Many," said the old man. "I have followed the wars, as you imagine."

Villon laid down his knife and fork, which he had just taken up again.

"Were any of them bald?" he asked.

"Oh, yes, and with hair as white as mine."

"I don't think I should mind the white so much," said Villon. "His was red." And he had a return of his shuddering and tendency to laughter, which he drowned with a great draught of wine. "I'm a little put out when I think of it," he went on. "I knew him—damn him! And then the cold gives a man fancies—or the fancies give a man cold, I don't know which."

"Have you any money?" asked the old man.

"I have one white," returned the poet, laughing. "I got it out of a dead jade's stocking in a porch. She was as dead as Cæsar, poor wench, and as cold as a church, with bits of ribbon sticking in her hair. This is a hard world in winter for wolves and wenches and poor rogues like me."

"I," said the old man, "am Enguerrand de la Feuillée, seigneur de Brisetout, bailly du Patatrac. Who and what may you be?"

Villon rose and made a suitable reverence. "I am called Francis Villon," he said, "a poor Master of Arts of this university. I know some Latin, and a deal of vice. I can make chansons, ballades, lais, virelais, and roundels, and I am very fond of wine. I was born in a garret, and I shall not improbably die upon the gallows. I may add, my lord, that from this night forward I am your lordship's very obsequious servant to command."

"No servant of mine," said the knight; "my guest for this evening, and no more."

"A very grateful guest," said Villon politely, and he drank in dumb show to his entertainer.

"You are shrewd," began the old man, tapping his forehead, "very shrewd; you have learning; you are a clerk; and yet you take a small piece of money off a dead woman in the street. Is it not a kind of theft?"

"It is a kind of theft much practised in the wars, my lord."

"The wars are the field of honor," returned the old man proudly. "There a man plays his life upon the cast; he fights in the name of his lord the king, his Lord God, and all their lordships the holy saints and angels."

"Put it," said Villon, "that I were really a thief, should I not play my life also, and against heavier odds?"

"For gain but not for honor."

"Gain?" repeated Villon with a shrug. "Gain! The poor fellow wants supper, and takes it. So does the soldier in a campaign. Why, what are all these requisitions we hear so much about? If they are not gain to those who take them, they are loss enough to the others. The men-at-arms drink by a good fire, while the burgher bites his nails to buy them wine and wood. I have seen a good many ploughmen swinging on trees about the country; ay, I have seen thirty on one elm, and a very poor figure they made; and when I asked some one how all these came to be hanged, I was told it was because they could not scrape together enough crowns to satisfy the men-at-arms."

"These things are a necessity of war, which the low-born must endure with constancy. It is true that some captains drive overhard; there are spirits in every rank not easily moved by pity; and indeed many follow arms who are no better than brigands."

"You see," said the poet, "you cannot separate the soldier from the brigand; and what is a thief but an isolated brigand with circumspect manners? I steal a couple of mutton chops, without so much as disturbing people's sleep; the farmer grumbles a bit, but sups none the less wholesomely on what remains. You come up blowing gloriously on a trumpet, take away the whole sheep, and beat the farmer pitifully into the bargain. I have no trumpet; I am only Tom, Dick, or Harry; I am a rogue and a dog, and hanging's too good for me—with all my heart; but just ask the farmer which of us he prefers, just find out which of us he lies awake to curse on cold nights."

"Look at us two," said his lordship. "I am old, strong, and honored. If I were turned from my house to-morrow, hundreds would be proud to shelter me. Poor people would go out and pass the night in the streets with their children, if I merely hinted that I wished to be alone. And I find you up, wandering homeless, and picking farthings off dead women by the wayside! I fear no man and nothing; I have seen you tremble and lose countenance at a word. I wait God's summons contentedly in my own house, or, if it please the king to call me out again, upon the field of battle. You look for the gallows; a rough, swift death, without hope or honor. Is there no difference between these two?"

"As far as to the moon," Villon acquiesced. "But if I had been born lord of Brisetout, and you had been the poor scholar Francis, would the difference have been any the less? Should not I have been warming my knees at this charcoal pan, and would not you have been groping for farthings in the snow? Should not I have been the soldier, and you the thief?"

"A thief?" cried the old man. "I a thief! If you understood your words, you would repent them."

Villon turned out his hands with a gesture of inimitable impudence. "If your lordship had done me the honor to follow my argument!" he said.

"I do you too much honor in submitting to your presence," said the knight. "Learn to curb your tongue when you speak with old and honorable men, or some one hastier than I may reprove you in a sharper fashion." And he rose and paced the lower end of the apartment, struggling with anger and antipathy. Villon surreptitiously refilled his cup, and settled himself more comfortably in the chair, crossing his knees and leaning his head upon one hand and the elbow against the back of the chair. He was now replete and warm; and he was in nowise frightened for his host, having gauged him as justly as was possible between two such different characters. The night was far spent, and in a very comfortable fashion after all; and he felt morally certain of a safe departure on the morrow.

"Tell me one thing," said the old man, pausing in his walk. "Are you really a thief?"

"I claim the sacred rights of hospitality," returned the poet. "My lord, I am."

"You are very young," the knight continued.

"I should never have been so old," replied Villon, showing his fingers, "if I had not helped myself with these ten talents. They have been my nursing mothers and my nursing fathers."

"You may still repent and change."

"I repent daily," said the poet. "There are few people more given to repentance than poor Francis. As for change, let somebody change my circumstances. A man must continue to eat, if it were only that he may continue to repent."

"The change must begin in the heart," returned the old man solemnly.

"My dear lord," answered Villon, "do you really fancy that I steal for pleasure? I hate stealing, like any other piece of work or of danger. My teeth chatter when I see a gallows. But I must eat, I must drink, I must mix in society of some sort. What the devil! Man is not a solitary animal—*Cui Deus fœminam tradit*. Make me king's pantler—make me abbot of St. Denis; make me bailly of the Patatrac; and then I shall be changed indeed. But as long as you leave me the poor scholar Francis Villon, without a farthing, why, of course, I remain the same."

"The grace of God is all-powerful."

"I should be a heretic to question it," said Francis. "It has made you lord of Brisetout and bailly of the Patatrac; it has given me nothing but the quick wits under my hat and these ten toes upon my hands. May I help myself to wine? I thank you respectfully. By God's grace, you have a very superior vintage."

The lord of Brisetout walked to and fro with his hands behind his back. Perhaps he was not yet quite settled in his mind about the parallel between thieves and soldiers; perhaps Villon had interested him by some cross-thread of sympathy; perhaps his wits were simply muddled by so much unfamiliar reasoning; but whatever the cause, he somehow yearned to convert the young man to a better way of thinking, and could not make up his mind to drive him forth again into the street.

"There is something more than I can understand in this," he said at length. "Your mouth is full of subtleties, and the devil has led you very far astray; but the devil is only a very weak spirit before God's truth, and all his subtleties vanish at a word of true honor, like darkness at morning. Listen to me once more. I learned long ago that a gentleman should live chivalrously and lovingly to God, and the king, and his lady; and though I have seen many strange things done, I have still striven to command my ways upon that rule. It is not only written in all noble histories, but in every man's heart, if he will take care to read. You speak of food and wine, and I know very well that hunger is a difficult trial to endure; but you do not speak of other wants; you say nothing of honor, of faith to God and other men, of courtesy, of love without reproach. It may be that I am not very wise—and yet I think I am—but you seem to me like one who has lost his way and made a great error in life. You are attending to the little wants, and you have totally forgotten the great and only real ones, like a man who should be doctoring toothache on the Judgment Day. For such things as honor and love and faith are not only nobler than food and drink, but indeed I think we desire them more, and suffer more sharply for their absence. I speak to you as I think you will most easily understand me. Are you not, while careful to fill your belly, disregarding another appetite in your heart, which spoils the pleasure of your life and keeps you continually wretched?"

Villon was sensibly nettled under all this sermonising. "You think I have no sense of honor!" he cried. "I'm poor enough, God knows! It's hard to see rich people with their gloves, and you blowing in your hands. An empty belly is a bitter thing, although you speak so lightly of it. If you had had as many as I, perhaps you would change your tune. Anyway I'm a thief—make the most of that—but I'm not a devil from hell, God strike me dead. I would have you know I've an honor of my own, as good as yours, though I don't prate about it all day long, as if it was a God's miracle to have any. It seems quite natural to me; I keep it in its box till it's wanted. Why now, look you here, how long have I been in this room with you? Did you not tell me you were alone in the house? Look at your gold plate! You're strong, if you like, but you're old and unarmed, and I have my knife. What did I want but a jerk of the elbow and here would have been you with the cold steel in your bowels, and there would have been me, linking in the streets, with an armful of golden cups! Did you suppose I hadn't wit enough to see that? And I scorned the action. There are your damned goblets, as safe as in a church; there are you, with your heart ticking as good as new; and here am I, ready to go out again as poor as I came in, with my one white that you threw in my teeth! And you think I have no sense of honor—God strike me dead!"

The old man stretched out his right arm. "I will tell you what you are," he said. "You are a rogue, my man, an impudent and black-hearted rogue and vagabond. I have passed an hour with you. Oh! believe me, I feel myself disgraced! And you have eaten and drunk at my table. But now I am sick at your presence; the day has come, and the night-bird should be off to his roost. Will you go before, or after?"

"Which you please," returned the poet, rising. "I believe you to be strictly honorable." He thoughtfully emptied his cup. "I wish I could add you were intelligent," he went on, knocking on his head with his knuckles. "Age! age! the brains stiff and rheumatic."

The old man preceded him from a point of self-respect. Villon followed, whistling, with his thumbs in his girdle.

"God pity you," said the lord of Brisetout at the door.

"Good-bye, papa," returned Villon with a yawn. "Many thanks for the cold mutton."

The door closed behind him. The dawn was breaking over the white roofs. A chill, uncomfortable morning ushered in the day. Villon stood and heartily stretched himself in the middle of the road.

"A very dull old gentleman," he thought. "I wonder what his goblets may be worth."

Will o' the Mill

THE PLAIN AND THE STARS

THE Mill where Will lived with his adopted parents stood in a falling valley between pine-woods and great mountains. Above, hill after hill soared upwards until they soared out of the depth of the hardiest timber, and stood naked against the sky. Some way up, a long grey village lay like a seam or a rag of vapor on a wooded hillside; and when the wind was favorable, the sound of the church bells would drop down, thin and silvery, to Will. Below, the valley grew ever steeper and steeper, and at the same time widened out on either hand; and from an eminence beside the mill it was possible to see its whole length and away beyond it over a wide plain, where the river turned and shone, and moved on from city to city on its voyage towards the sea. It chanced that over this valley there lay a pass into a neighboring kingdom, so that, quiet and rural as it was, the road that ran along beside the river was a high thoroughfare between two splendid and powerful societies. All through the summer, travelling-carriages came crawling up, or went plunging briskly downwards past the mill; and as it happened that the other side was very much easier of ascent, the path was not much frequented, except by people going in one direction; and of all the carriages that Will saw go by, five-sixths were plunging briskly downwards and only one-sixth crawling up. Much more was this the case with foot-passengers. All the light-footed tourists, all the pedlers laden with strange wares, were tending downward like the river that accompanied their path. Nor was this all; for when Will was yet a child a disastrous war arose over a great part of the world. The newspapers were full of defeats and victories, the earth rang with cavalry hoofs, and often for days together and for miles around the coil of battle terrified good people from their labors in the field. Of all this, nothing was heard for a long time in the valley; but at last one of the commanders pushed an army over the pass by forced marches, and for three days horse and foot, cannon and tumbril, drum and standard, kept pouring downward past the mill. All day the child stood and watched them on their passage—the rhythmical stride, the pale, unshaven faces tanned about the eyes, the discolored regimentals and the tattered flags, filled him with a sense of weariness, pity, and wonder; and all night long, after he was in bed, he could hear the cannon pounding and the feet trampling, and the great armament sweeping onward and downward past the mill. No one in the valley ever heard the fate of the expedition, for they lay out of the way of gossip in those troublous times; but Will saw one thing plainly, that not a man returned. Whither had they all gone? Whither went all the tourists and pedlers with strange wares? whither all the brisk barouches with servants in the dicky? whither the water of the stream, ever coursing downward and ever renewed from above? Even the wind blew oftener down the valley, and carried the dead leaves along with it in the fall. It seemed like a great conspiracy of things animate and inanimate; they all went downward, fleetly and gaily downward, and only he, it seemed, remained behind, like a stock upon the wayside. It sometimes made him glad when he noticed how the fishes kept their heads up stream. They, at least, stood faithfully by him, while all else were posting downward to the unknown world.

One evening he asked the miller where the river went.

"It goes down the valley," answered he, "and turns a power of mills— six-score mills, they say, from here to Unterdeck—and it none the wearier after all. And then it goes out into the lowlands, and waters the great corn country, and runs through a sight of fine cities (so they say) where kings live all alone in great palaces, with a sentry walking up and down before the door. And it goes under bridges with stone men upon them, looking down and smiling so curious at the water, and living folks leaning their elbows on the wall and looking over too. And then it goes on and on, and down through marshes and sands, until at last it falls into the sea, where the ships are that bring parrots and tobacco from the Indies. Ay, it has a long trot before it as it goes singing over our weir, bless its heart!"

"And what is the sea?" asked Will.

"The sea!" cried the miller. "Lord help us all, it is the greatest thing God made! That is where all the water in the world runs down into a great salt lake. There it lies, as flat as my hand and as innocent-like as a child; but they do say when the wind blows it gets up into water-mountains bigger than any of ours, and swallows down great ships bigger than our mill, and makes such a roaring that you can hear it miles away upon the land. There are great fish in it five times bigger than a bull, and one old serpent as long as our river and as old as all the world, with whiskers like a man, and a crown of silver on her head."

Will thought he had never heard anything like this, and he kept on asking question after question about the world that lay away down the river, with all its perils and marvels, until the old miller became quite interested himself, and at last took him by the hand and led him to the hill-top that overlooks the valley and the plain. The sun was near setting, and hung low down in a cloudless sky. Everything was defined and glorified in golden light. Will had never seen so great an expanse of country in his life; he stood and gazed with all his eyes. He could see the cities, and the woods and fields, and the bright curves of the river, and far away to where the rim of the plain trenched along the shining heavens. An overmastering emotion seized upon the boy, soul and body; his heart beat so thickly that he could not breathe; the scene swam before his eyes; the sun seemed to wheel round and round, and throw off, as it turned, strange shapes which disappeared with the rapidity of thought, and were succeeded by others. Will covered his face with his hands, and burst into a violent fit of tears; and the poor miller, sadly disappointed and perplexed, saw nothing better for it than to take him up in his arms and carry him home in silence.

From that day forward Will was full of new hopes and longings. Something kept tugging at his heartstrings; the running water carried his desires along with it as he dreamed over its fleeting surface; the wind, as it ran over innumerable tree-tops, hailed him with encouraging words; branches beckoned downward; the open road, as it shouldered round the angles and went turning and vanishing faster and faster down the valley, tortured him with its solicitations. He spent long whiles on the eminence, looking down the river-shed and abroad on the flat lowlands, and watched the clouds that travelled forth upon the sluggish wind and trailed their purple shadows on the plain; or he would linger by the wayside, and follow the carriages with his eyes as they rattled downward by the river. It did not matter what it was; everything that went that way, were it cloud or carriage, bird or brown water in the stream, he felt his heart flow out after it in an ecstasy of longing.

We are told by men of science that all the ventures of mariners on the sea, all that countermarching of tribes and races that confounds old history with its dust and rumor, sprang from nothing more abstruse than the laws of supply and demand, and a certain natural instinct for cheap rations. To any one thinking deeply, this will seem a dull and pitiful explanation. The tribes that came swarming out of the North and East, if they were indeed pressed onward from behind by others, were drawn at the same time by the magnetic influence of the South and West. The fame of other lands had reached them; the name of the eternal city rang in their ears; they were not colonists, but pilgrims; they travelled towards wine and gold and sunshine, but their hearts were set on something higher. That divine unrest, that old stinging trouble of humanity that makes all high achievements and all miserable failure, the same that spread wings with Icarus, the same that sent Columbus into the desolate Atlantic, inspired and supported these barbarians on their perilous march. There is one legend which profoundly represents their spirit, of how a flying party of these wanderers encountered a very old man shod with iron. The old man asked them whither they were going; and they answered with one voice: "To the Eternal City!" He looked upon them gravely, "I have sought it," he said, "over the most part of the world. Three such pairs as I now carry on my feet have I worn out upon this pilgrimage, and now the fourth is growing slender underneath my steps. And all this while I have not found the city." And he turned and went his own way alone, leaving them astonished.

And yet this would scarcely parallel the intensity of Will's feeling for the plain. If he could only go far enough out there, he felt as if his eyesight would be purged and clarified, as if his hearing would grow more delicate, and his very breath would come and go with luxury. He was transplanted and withering where he was; he lay in a strange country and was sick for home. Bit by bit, he pieced together broken notions of the world below: of the river, ever moving and growing until it sailed forth into the majestic ocean; of the cities, full of brisk and beautiful people, playing fountains, bands of music and marble palaces, and lighted up at night from end to end with artificial stars of gold; of the great churches, wise universities, brave armies, and untold money lying stored in vaults; of the high-flying vice that moved in the sunshine, and the stealth and swiftness of midnight murder. I have said he was sick as if for home: the figure halts. He was like some one lying in twilit, formless pre-existence, and stretching out his hands lovingly towards many-colored, many-sounding life. It was no wonder he was unhappy, he would go and tell the fish: they were made for their life, wished for no more than worms and running water, and a hole below a falling bank; but he was differently designed, full of desires and aspirations, itching at the fingers, lusting with the eyes, whom the whole variegated world could not satisfy with aspects. The true life, the true bright sunshine, lay far out upon the plain. And O! to see this sunlight once before he died! to move with a jocund spirit in a golden land! to hear the trained singers and sweet church bells, and see the holiday gardens; "And O fish!" he would cry, "if you would only turn your noses down stream, you could swim so easily into the fabled waters and see the vast ships passing over your head like clouds, and hear the great water-hills making music over you all day long!" But the fish kept looking patiently in their own direction, until Will hardly knew whether to laugh or cry.

Hitherto the traffic on the road had passed by Will, like something seen in a picture: he had perhaps exchanged salutations with a tourist, or caught sight of an old gentleman in a travelling-cap at a carriage window; but for the most part it had been a mere symbol, which he contemplated from apart and with something of a superstitious feeling. A time came at last when this was to be changed. The miller, who was a greedy man in his way, and never forewent an opportunity of honest profit, turned the mill-house into a little wayside inn, and, several pieces of good fortune falling in opportunely, built stables and got the position of post master on the road. It now became Will's duty to wait upon people, as they sat to break their fasts in the little arbor at the top of the mill garden; and you may be sure that he kept his ears open, and learned many new things about the outside world as he brought the omelette or the wine. Nay, he would often get into conversation with single guests, and by adroit questions and polite attention, not only gratify his own curiosity, but win the good-will of the travellers. Many complimented the old couple on their serving-boy; and a professor was eager to take him away with him, and have him properly educated in the plain. The miller and his wife were mightily astonished and even more pleased. They thought it a very good thing that they should have opened their inn. "You see," the old man would remark, "he has a kind of talent for a publican; he never would have made anything else!" And so life wagged on in the valley, with high satisfaction to all concerned but Will. Every carriage that left the inn-door seemed to take a part of him away with it; and when people jestingly offered him a lift, he could with difficulty command his emotion. Night after night he would dream that he was awakened by flustered servants, and that a splendid equipage waited at the door to carry him down into the plain; night after night; until the dream, which had seemed all jollity to him at first, began to take on a color of gravity, and the nocturnal summons and waiting equipage occupied a place in his mind as something to be both feared and hoped for.

One day, when Will was about sixteen, a fat young man arrived at sunset to pass the night. He was a contented-looking fellow, with a jolly eye, and carried a knapsack. While dinner was preparing, he sat in the arbor to read a book; but as soon as he had begun to observe Will, the book was laid aside; he was plainly one of those who prefer living people to people made of ink and paper. Will, on his part, although he had not been much interested in the stranger at first sight, soon began to take a great deal of pleasure in his talk, which was full of good-nature and good-sense, and at last conceived a great respect for his character and wisdom. They sat far into the night; and about two in the morning Will opened his heart to the young man, and told him how he longed to leave the valley and what bright hopes he had connected with the cities of the plain. The young man whistled, and then broke into a smile.

"My young friend," he remarked, "you are a very curious little fellow, to be sure, and wish a great many things which you will never get. Why, you would feel quite ashamed if you knew how the little fellows in these fairy cities of yours are all after the same sort of nonsense, and keep breaking their hearts to get up into the mountains. And let me tell you, those who go down into the plains are a very short while there before they wish themselves heartily back again. The air is not so light nor so pure; nor is the sun any brighter. As for the beautiful men and women, you would see many of them in rags and many of them deformed with horrible disorders; and a city is so hard a place for people who are poor and sensitive that many choose to die by their own hand."

"You must think me very simple," answered Will. "Although I have never been out of this valley, believe me, I have used my eyes. I know how one thing lives on another; for instance, how the fish hangs in the eddy to catch his fellows; and the shepherd, who makes so pretty a picture carrying home the lamb, is only carrying it home for dinner. I do not expect to find all things right in your cities. That is not what troubles me; it might have been that once upon a time; but although I live here always, I have asked many questions and learned a great deal in these last years, and certainly enough to cure me of my old fancies. But you would not have me die like a dog and not see all that is to be seen, and do all that a man can do, let it be good or evil? you would not have me spend all my days between this road here and the river, and not so much as make a motion to be up and live my life?—I would rather die out of hand," he cried, "than linger on as I am doing."

"Thousands of people," said the young man, "live and die like you, and are none the less happy."

"Ah!" said Will, "if there are thousands who would like, why should not one of them have my place?"

It was quite dark; there was a hanging lamp in the arbor which lit up the table and the faces of the speakers; and along the arch, the leaves upon the trellis stood out illuminated against the night sky, a pattern of transparent green upon a dusky purple. The fat young man rose, and, taking Will by the arm, led him out under the open heavens.

"Did you ever look at the stars?" he asked, pointing upwards.

"Often and often," answered Will.

"And do you know what they are?"

"I have fancied many things."

"They are worlds like ours," said the young man. "Some of them less; many of them a million times greater; and some of the least sparkles that you see are not only worlds, but whole clusters of worlds turning about each other in the midst of space. We do not know what there may be in any of them; perhaps the answer to all our difficulties or the cure of all our sufferings: and yet we can never reach them; not all the skill of the craftiest of men can fit out a ship for the nearest of these our neighbors, nor would the life of the most aged suffice for such a journey. When a great battle has been lost or a dear friend is dead, when we are hipped or in high spirits, there they are unweariedly shining overhead. We may stand down here, a whole army of us together, and shout until we break our hearts, and not a whisper reaches them. We may climb the highest mountain, and we are no nearer them. All we can do is to stand down here in the garden and take off our hats; the starshine lights upon our heads, and where mine is a little bald, I dare say you can see it glisten in the darkness. The mountain and the mouse. That is like to be all we shall ever have to do with Arcturus or Aldebaran. Can you apply a parable?" he added, laying his hand upon Will's shoulder. "It is not the same thing as a reason, but usually vastly more convincing."

Will hung his head a little, and then raised it once more to heaven. The stars seemed to expand and emit a sharper brilliancy; and as he kept turning his eyes higher and higher, they seemed to increase in multitude under his gaze.

"I see," he said, turning to the young man. "We are in a rat-trap."

"Something of that size. Did you ever see a squirrel turning in a cage? and another squirrel sitting philosophically over his nuts? I needn't ask you which of them looked more of a fool."

THE PARSON'S MARJORY

After some years the old people died, both in one winter, very carefully tended by their adopted son, and very quietly mourned when they were gone. People who had heard of his roving fancies supposed he would hasten to sell the property, and go down the river to push his fortunes. But there was never any sign of such an intention on the part of Will. On the contrary, he had the inn set on a better footing, and hired a couple of servants to assist him in carrying it on; and there he settled down, a kind, talkative, inscrutable young man, six feet three in his stockings, with an iron constitution and a friendly voice. He soon began to take rank in the district as a bit of an oddity: it was not much to be wondered at from the first, for he was always full of notions, and kept calling the plainest common-sense in question; but what most raised the report upon him was the odd circumstance of his courtship with the parson's Marjory.

The parson's Marjory was a lass about nineteen, when Will would be about thirty; well enough looking, and much better educated than any other girl in that part of the country, as became her parentage. She held her head very high, and had already refused several offers of marriage with a grand air, which had got her hard names among the neighbors. For all that she was a good girl, and one that would have made any man well contented.

Will had never seen much of her; for although the church and parsonage were only two miles from his own door, he was never known to go there but on Sundays. It chanced, however, that the parsonage fell into disrepair, and had to be dismantled; and the parson and his daughter took lodgings for a month or so, on very much reduced terms, at Will's inn. Now, what with the inn, and the mill, and the old miller's savings, our friend was a man of substance; and besides that, he had a name for good temper and shrewdness, which make a capital portion in marriage; and so it was currently gossiped, among their ill-wishers, that the parson and his daughter had not chosen their temporary lodging with their eyes shut. Will was about the last man in the world to be cajoled or frightened into marriage. You had only to look into his eyes, limpid and still like pools of water, and yet with a sort of clear light that seemed to come from within, and you would understand at once that here was one who knew his own mind, and would stand to it immovably. Marjory herself was no weakling by her looks, with strong, steady eyes and a resolute and quiet bearing. It might be a question whether she was not Will's match in steadfastness, after all, or which of them would rule the roast in marriage. But Marjory had never given it a thought, and accompanied her father with the most unshaken innocence and unconcern.

The season was still so early that Will's customers were few and far between; but the lilacs were already flowering, and the weather was so mild that the party took dinner under the trellis, with the noise of the river in their ears and the woods ringing about them with the songs of birds. Will soon began to take a particular pleasure in these dinners. The parson was rather a dull companion, with a habit of dozing at table; but nothing rude or cruel ever fell from his lips. And as for the parson's daughter, she suited her surroundings with the best grace imaginable; and whatever she said seemed so pat and pretty that Will conceived a great idea of her talents. He could see her face, as she leaned forward, against a background of rising pine-woods; her eyes shone peaceably; the light lay around her hair like a kerchief; something that was hardly a smile rippled her pale cheeks, and Will could not contain himself from gazing on her in an agreeable dismay. She looked, even in her quietest moments, so complete in herself, and so quick with life down to her finger tips and the very skirts of her dress, that the remainder of created things became no more than a blot by comparison; and if Will glanced away from her to her surroundings, the trees looked inanimate and senseless, the clouds hung in heaven like dead things, and even the mountain tops were disenchanted. The whole valley could not compare in looks with this one girl.

Will was always observant in the society of his fellow-creatures; but his observation became almost painfully eager in the case of Marjory. He listened to all she uttered, and read her eyes, at the same time, for the unspoken commentary. Many kind, simple, and sincere speeches found an echo in his heart. He became conscious of a soul beautifully poised upon itself, nothing doubting, nothing desiring, clothed in peace. It was not possible to separate her thoughts from her appearance. The turn of her wrist, the still sound of her voice, the light in her eyes, the lines of her body, fell in tune with her grave and gentle words, like the accompaniment that sustains and harmonizes the voice of the singer. Her influence was one thing, not to be divided or discussed, only to be felt with gratitude and joy. To Will, her presence recalled something of his childhood, and the thought of her took its place in his mind beside that of dawn, of running water, and of the earliest violets and lilacs. It is the property of things seen for the first time, or for the first time after long, like the flowers in spring, to reawaken in us the sharp edge of sense and that impression of mystic strangeness which otherwise passes out of life with the coming of years; but the sight of a loved face is what renews a man's character from the fountain upwards.

One day after dinner Will took a stroll among the firs, a grave beatitude possessed him from top to toe, and he kept smiling to himself and the landscape as he went. The river ran between the stepping-stones with a pretty wimple; a bird sang loudly in the wood; the hill-tops looked immeasurably high, and as he glanced at them from time to time seemed to contemplate his movements with a beneficent but awful curiosity. His way took him to the eminence which overlooked the plain; and there he sat down upon a stone, and fell into deep and pleasant thought. The plain lay abroad with its cities and silver river; everything was asleep, except a great eddy of birds which kept rising and falling and going round and round in the blue air. He repeated Marjory's name aloud, and the sound of it gratified his ear. He shut his eyes, and her image sprang up before him, quietly luminous and attended with good thoughts. The river might run for ever; the birds fly higher and higher till they touched the stars. He saw it was empty bustle after all; for here, without stirring a foot, waiting patiently in his own narrow valley, he also had attained the better sunlight.

The next day Will made a sort of declaration across the dinner-table, while the parson was filling his pipe.

"Miss Marjory," he said, "I never knew any one I liked so well as you. I am mostly a cold, unkindly sort of man; not from want of heart, but out of strangeness in my way of thinking; and people seem far away from me. 'Tis as if there were a circle round me, which kept every one out but you; I can hear the others talking and laughing; but you come quite close. Maybe, this is disagreeable to you?" he asked.

Marjory made no answer.

"Speak up, girl," said the parson.

"Nay, now," returned Will, "I wouldn't press her, parson. I feel tongue-tied myself, who am not used to it; and she's a woman, and little more than a child, when all is said. But for my part, as far as I can understand what people mean by it, I fancy I must be what they call in love. I do not wish to be held as committing myself; for I may be wrong; but that is how I believe things are with me. And if Miss Marjory should feel any otherwise on her part, mayhap she would be so kind as shake her head."

Marjory was silent, and gave no sign that she had heard.

"How is that, parson?" asked Will.

"The girl must speak," replied the parson, laying down his pipe. "Here's our neighbor who says he loves you, Madge. Do you love him, ay or no?"

"I think I do," said Marjory, faintly.

"Well then, that's all that could be wished!" cried Will, heartily. And he took her hand across the table, and held it a moment in both of his with great satisfaction.

"You must marry," observed the parson, replacing his pipe in his mouth.

"Is that the right thing to do, think you?" demanded Will.

"It is indispensable," said the parson.

"Very well," replied the wooer.

Two or three days passed away with great delight to Will, although a bystander might scarce have found it out. He continued to take his meals opposite Marjory, and to talk with her and gaze upon her in her father's presence; but he made no attempt to see her alone, nor in any other way changed his conduct towards her from what it had been since the beginning. Perhaps the girl was a little disappointed, and perhaps not unjustly; and yet if it had been enough to be always in the thoughts of another person, and so pervade and alter his whole life, she might have been thoroughly contented. For she was never out of Will's mind for an instant. He sat over the stream, and watched the dust of the eddy, and the poised fish, and straining weeds; he wandered out alone into the purple even, with all the blackbirds piping round him in the wood; he rose early in the morning, and saw the sky turn from grey to gold, and the light leap upon the hill-tops; and all the while he kept wondering if he had never seen such things before, or how it was that they should look so different now. The sound of his own mill-wheel, or of the wind among the trees, confounded and charmed his heart. The most enchanting thoughts presented themselves unbidden in his mind. He was so happy that he could not sleep at night, and so restless that he could hardly sit still out of her company. And yet it seemed as if he avoided her rather than sought her out.

One day, as he was coming home from a ramble, Will found Marjory in the garden picking flowers, and as he came up with her, slackened his pace and continued walking by her side.

"You like flowers?" he said.

"Indeed I love them dearly," she replied. "Do you?"

"Why, no," said he, "not so much. They are a very small affair, when all is done. I can fancy people caring for them greatly, but not doing as you are just now."

"How?" she asked, pausing and looking up at him.

"Plucking them," said he. "They are a deal better off where they are, and look a deal prettier, if you go to that."

"I wish to have them for my own," she answered, "to carry them near my heart, and keep them in my room. They tempt me when they grow here; they seem to say, 'Come and do something with us;' but once I have cut them and put them by, the charm is laid, and I can look at them with quite an easy heart."

"You wish to possess them," replied Will, "in order to think no more about them. It's a bit like killing the goose with the golden eggs. It's a bit like what I wished to do when I was a boy. Because I had a fancy for looking out over the plain, I wished to go down there—where I couldn't look out over it any longer. Was not that fine reasoning? Dear, dear, if they only thought of it, all the world would do like me; and you would let your flowers alone, just as I stay up here in the mountains." Suddenly he broke off sharp. "By the Lord!" he cried. And when she asked him what was wrong, he turned the question off, and walked away into the house with rather a humorous expression of face.

He was silent at table; and after the night had fallen and the stars had come out overhead, he walked up and down for hours in the court-yard and garden with an uneven pace. There was still a light in the window of Marjory's room: one little oblong patch of orange in a world of dark blue hills and silver starlight. Will's mind ran a great deal on the window; but his thoughts were not very lover-like. "There she is in her room," he thought, "and there are the stars overhead:—a blessing upon both!" Both were good influences in his life; both soothed and braced him in his profound contentment with the world. And what more should he desire with either? The fat young man and his councils were so present to his mind, that he threw back his head, and, putting his hands before his mouth, shouted aloud to the populous heavens. Whether from the position of his head or the sudden strain of the exertion, he seemed to see a momentary shock among the stars, and a diffusion of frosty light pass from one to another along the sky. At the same instant, a corner of the blind was lifted up and lowered again at once. He laughed a loud ho-ho! "One and another!" thought Will, "The stars tremble, and the blind goes up. Why, before Heaven, what a great magician I must be! Now if I were only a fool, should not I be in a pretty way?" And he went off to bed, chuckling to himself: "If I were only a fool!"

The next morning, pretty early, he saw her once more in the garden, and sought her out.

"I have been thinking about getting married," he began abruptly; "and after having turned it all over, I have made up my mind it's not worth while."

She turned upon him for a single moment; but his radiant, kindly appearance would, under the circumstances, have disconcerted an angel, and she looked down again upon the ground in silence. He could see her tremble.

"I hope you don't mind," he went on, a little taken aback. "You ought not. I have turned it all over, and upon my soul there's nothing in it. We should never be one whit nearer than we are just now, and, if I am a wise man, nothing like so happy."

"It is unnecessary to go round about with me," she said. "I very well remember that you refused to commit yourself; and now that I see you were mistaken, and in reality have never cared for me, I can only feel sad that I have been so far misled."

"I ask your pardon," said Will stoutly; "you do not understand my meaning. As to whether I have ever loved you or not, I must leave that to others. But for one thing, my feeling is not changed; and for another, you may make it your boast that you have made my whole life and character something different from what they were. I mean what I say; no less. I do not think getting married is worth while. I would rather you went on living with your father, so that I could walk over and see you once, or maybe twice a week, as people go to church, and then we should both be all the happier between whiles. That's my notion. But I'll marry you if you will," he added.

"Do you know that you are insulting me?" she broke out.

"Not I, Marjory," said he; "if there is anything in a clear conscience, not I. I offer all my heart's best affections; you can take it or want it, though I suspect it's beyond either your power or mine to change what has once been done, and set me fancy-free. I'll marry you, if you like; but I tell you again and again, it's not worth while, and we had best stay friends. Though I am a quiet man I have noticed a heap of things in my life. Trust in me, and take things as I propose; or, if you don't like that, say the word, and I'll marry you out of hand."

There was a considerable pause, and Will, who began to feel uneasy, began to grow angry in consequence.

"It seems you are too proud to say your mind," he said. "Believe me that's a pity. A clean shrift makes simple living. Can a man be more downright or honorable to a woman than I have been? I have said my say, and given you your choice. Do you want me to marry you? or will you take my friendship, as I think best? or have you had enough of me for good? Speak out for the dear God's sake! You know your father told you a girl should speak her mind in these affairs."

She seemed to recover herself at that, turned without a word, walked rapidly through the garden, and disappeared into the house, leaving Will in some confusion as to the result. He walked up and down the garden, whistling softly to himself. Sometimes he stopped and contemplated the sky and hill-tops; sometimes he went down to the tail of the weir and sat there, looking foolishly in the water. All this dubiety and perturbation was so foreign to his nature and the life which he had resolutely chosen for himself, that he began to regret Marjory's arrival. "After all," he thought, "I was as happy as a man need be. I could come down here and watch my fishes all day long if I wanted: I was as settled and contented as my old mill."

Marjory came down to dinner, looking very trim and quiet; and no sooner were all three at table than she made her father a speech, with her eyes fixed upon her plate, but showing no other sign of embarrassment or distress.

"Father," she began, "Mr. Will and I have been talking things over. We see that we have each made a mistake about our feelings, and he has agreed, at my request, to give up all idea of marriage, and be no more than my very good friend, as in the past. You see, there is no shadow of a quarrel, and indeed I hope we shall see a great deal of him in the future, for his visits will always be welcome in our house. Of course, father, you will know best, but perhaps we should do better to leave Mr. Will's house for the present. I believe, after what has passed, we should hardly be agreeable inmates for some days."

Will, who had commanded himself with difficulty from the first, broke out upon this into an inarticulate noise, and raised one hand with an appearance of real dismay, as if he were about to interfere and contradict. But she checked him at once, looking up at him with a swift glance and an angry flush upon her cheek.

"You will perhaps have the good grace," she said, "to let me explain these matters for myself."

Will was put entirely out of countenance by her expression and the ring of her voice. He held his peace, concluding that there were some things about this girl beyond his comprehension, in which he was exactly right.

The poor parson was quite crestfallen. He tried to prove that this was no more than a true lovers' tiff, which would pass off before night; and when he was dislodged from that position, he went on to argue that where there was no quarrel there could be no call for a separation; for the good man liked both his entertainment and his host. It was curious to see how the girl managed them, saying little all the time, and that very quietly, and yet twisting them round her finger and insensibly leading them wherever she would by feminine tact and generalship. It scarcely seemed to have been her doing—it seemed as if things had merely so fallen out—that she and her father took their departure that same afternoon in a farm-cart, and went farther down the valley, to wait, until their own house was ready for them, in another hamlet.

But Will had been observing closely, and was well aware of her dexterity and resolution. When he found himself alone he had a great many curious matters to turn over in his mind. He was very sad and solitary, to begin with. All the interest had gone out of his life, and he might look up at the stars as long as he pleased, he somehow failed to find support or consolation. And then he was in such a turmoil of spirit about Marjory. He had been puzzled and irritated at her behavior, and yet he could not keep himself from admiring it. He thought he recognized a fine, perverse angel in that still soul which he had never hitherto suspected; and though he saw it was an influence that would fit but ill with his own life of artificial calm, he could not keep himself from ardently desiring to possess it. Like a man who has lived among shadows and now meets the sun, he was both pained and delighted.

As the days went forward he passed from one extreme to another; now pluming himself on the strength of his determination, now despising his timid and silly caution. The former was, perhaps, the true thought of his heart, and represented the regular tenor of the man's reflections; but the latter burst forth from time to time with an unruly violence, and then he would forget all consideration, and go up and down his house and garden or walk among the fir-woods like one who is beside himself with remorse. To equable, steady-minded Will this state of matters was intolerable; and he determined, at whatever cost, to bring it to an end. So, one warm summer afternoon he put on his best clothes, took a thorn switch in his hand, and set out down the valley by the river. As soon as he had taken his determination, he had regained at a bound his customary peace of heart, and he enjoyed the bright weather and the variety of the scene without any admixture of alarm or unpleasant eagerness. It was nearly the same to him how the matter turned out. If she accepted him he would have to marry her this time, which perhaps was all for the best. If she refused him, he would have done his utmost, and might follow his own way in the future with an untroubled conscience. He hoped, on the whole, she would refuse him; and then, again, as he saw the brown roof which sheltered her, peeping through some willows at an angle of the stream, he was half inclined to reverse the wish, and more than half ashamed of himself for this infirmity of purpose.

Marjory seemed glad to see him, and gave him her hand without affectation or delay.

"I have been thinking about this marriage," he began.

"So have I," she answered. "And I respect you more and more for a very wise man. You understood me better than I understood myself; and I am now quite certain that things are all for the best as they are."

"At the same time—" ventured Will.

"You must be tired," she interrupted. "Take a seat and let me fetch you a glass of wine. The afternoon is so warm; and I wish you not to be displeased with your visit. You must come quite often; once a week, if you can spare the time; I am always so glad to see my friends."

"O, very well," thought Will to himself. "It appears I was right after all." And he paid a very agreeable visit, walked home again in capital spirits, and gave himself no further concern about the matter.

For nearly three years Will and Marjory continued on these terms, seeing each other once or twice a week without any word of love between them; and for all that time I believe Will was nearly as happy as a man can be. He rather stinted himself the pleasure of seeing her; and he would often walk half-way over to the parsonage, and then back again, as if to whet his appetite. Indeed there was one corner of the road, whence he could see the church-spire wedged into a crevice of the valley between sloping fir-woods, with a triangular snatch of plain by way of background, which he greatly affected as a place to sit and moralize in before returning homewards; and the peasants got so much into the habit of finding him there in the twilight that they gave it the name of "Will o' the Mill's Corner."

At the end of three years Marjory played him a sad trick by suddenly marrying somebody else. Will kept his countenance bravely, and merely remarked that, for as little as he knew of women, he had acted very prudently in not marrying her himself three years before. She plainly knew very little of her own mind, and, in spite of a deceptive manner, was as fickle and flighty as the rest of them. He had to congratulate himself on an escape, he said, and would take a higher opinion of his own wisdom in consequence. But at heart, he was reasonably displeased, moped a good deal for a month or two, and fell away in flesh, to the astonishment of his serving-lads.

It was perhaps a year after this marriage that Will was awakened late one night by the sound of a horse galloping on the road, followed by precipitate knocking at the inn-door. He opened his window and saw a farm servant, mounted and holding a led horse by the bridle, who told him to make what haste he could and go along with him; for Marjory was dying, and had sent urgently to fetch him to her bedside. Will was no horseman, and made so little speed upon the way that the poor young wife was very near her end before he arrived. But they

had some minutes' talk in private, and he was present and wept very
bitterly while she breathed her last.

DEATH

Year after year went away into nothing, with great explosions and
outcries in the cities on the plain: red revolt springing up and being
suppressed in blood, battle swaying hither and thither, patient astron-
omers in observatory towers picking out and christening new stars, plays
being performed in lighted theatres, people being carried into hospitals
on stretchers, and all the usual turmoil and agitation of men's lives in
crowded centres. Up in Will's valley only the winds and seasons made
an epoch; the fish hung in the swift stream, the birds circled overhead,
the pine-tops rustled underneath the stars, the tall hills stood over all;
and Will went to and fro, minding his wayside inn, until the snow began
to thicken on his head. His heart was young and vigorous; and if his
pulses kept a sober time, they still beat strong and steady in his wrists.
He carried a ruddy stain on either cheek, like a ripe apple; he stooped
a little, but his step was still firm; and his sinewy hands were reached
out to all men with a friendly pressure. His face was covered with
those wrinkles which are got in open air, and which, rightly looked at,
are no more than a sort of permanent sunburning; such wrinkles heighten
the stupidity of stupid faces; but to a person like Will, with his clear
eyes and smiling mouth, only give another charm by testifying to a
simple and easy life. His talk was full of wise sayings. He had a taste
for other people; and other people had a taste for him. When the
valley was full of tourists in the season, there were merry nights in
Will's arbor; and his views, which seemed whimsical to his neighbors,
were often enough admired by learned people out of towns and col-
leges. Indeed, he had a very noble old age, and grew daily better
known; so that his fame was heard of in the cities of the plain; and
young men who had been summer travellers spoke together in *cafés* of
Will o' the Mill and his rough philosophy. Many and many an invitation, you may be sure, he had; but nothing could tempt him from his
upland valley. He would shake his head and smile over his tobacco-
pipe with a deal of meaning. "You come too late," he would answer.
"I am a dead man now: I have lived and died already. Fifty years ago
you would have brought my heart into my mouth; and now you do not
even tempt me. But that is the object of long living, that man should
cease to care about life." And again: "There is only one difference
between a long life and a good dinner: that, in the dinner, the sweets

come last." Or once more: "When I was a boy, I was a bit puzzled, and hardly knew whether it was myself or the world that was curious and worth looking into. Now, I know it is myself, and stick to that."

He never showed any symptoms of frailty, but kept stalwart and firm to the last; but they say he grew less talkative towards the end, and would listen to other people by the hour in an amused and sympathetic silence. Only, when he did speak, it was more to the point and more charged with old experience. He drank a bottle of wine gladly; above all, at sunset on the hill-top or quite late at night under the stars in the arbor. The sight of something attractive and unattainable seasoned his enjoyment, he would say; and he professed he had lived long enough to admire a candle all the more when he could compare it with a planet.

One night, in his seventy-second year, he awoke in bed, in such uneasiness of body and mind that he arose and dressed himself and went out to meditate in the arbor. It was pitch dark, without a star; the river was swollen, and the wet woods and meadows loaded the air with perfume. It had thundered during the day, and it promised more thunder for the morrow. A murky, stifling night for a man of seventy-two! Whether it was the weather or the wakefulness, or some little touch of fever in his old limbs, Will's mind was besieged by tumultuous and crying memories. His boyhood, the night with the fat young man, the death of his adopted parents, the summer days with Marjory, and many of those small circumstances, which seem nothing to another, and are yet the very gist of a man's own life to himself—things seen, words heard, looks misconstrued—arose from their forgotten corners and usurped his attention. The dead themselves were with him, not merely taking part in this thin show of memory that defiled before his brain, but revisiting his bodily senses as they do in profound and vivid dreams. The fat young man leaned his elbows on the table opposite; Marjory came and went with an apronful of flowers between the garden and the arbor; he could hear the old parson knocking out his pipe or blowing his resonant nose. The tide of his consciousness ebbed and flowed: he was sometimes half asleep and drowned in his recollections of the past; and sometimes he was broad awake, wondering at himself. But about the middle of the night he was startled by the voice of the dead miller calling to him out of the house as he used to do on the arrival of custom. The hallucination was so perfect that Will sprang from his seat and stood listening for the summons to be repeated; and as he listened he became conscious of another noise besides the brawling of the river and the ringing in his feverish ears. It was like the stir of the horses and the creaking of harness, as though a carriage with an impatient team had been brought up upon the road before the courtyard gate. At such an hour, upon this rough and dangerous pass, the supposition was no better than absurd; and Will dismissed it from his mind, and resumed his seat upon the arbor chair; and sleep closed over him again like running water. He was once again awakened by the dead miller's call, thinner and more spectral than before; and once again he heard the noise of an equipage upon the road. And so thrice and four times, the same dream, or the same fancy, presented itself to his senses: until at length, smiling to himself as when one humors a nervous child, he proceeded towards the gate to set his uncertainty at rest.

From the arbor to the gate was no great distance, and yet it took Will some time; it seemed as if the dead thickened around him in the court, and crossed his path at every step. For, first, he was suddenly surprised by an overpowering sweetness of heliotropes; it was as if his garden had been planted with this flower from end to end, and the hot, damp night had drawn forth all their perfumes in a breath. Now the heliotrope had been Marjory's favorite flower, and since her death not one of them had ever been planted in Will's ground.

"I must be going crazy," he thought. "Poor Marjory and her heliotropes!"

And with that he raised his eyes towards the window that had once been hers. If he had been bewildered before, he was now almost terrified; for there was a light in the room; the window was an orange oblong as of yore; and the corner of the blind was lifted and let fall as on the night when he stood and shouted to the stars in his perplexity. The illusion only endured an instant; but it left him somewhat unmanned, rubbing his eyes and staring at the outline of the house and the black night behind it. While he thus stood, and it seemed as if he must have stood there quite a long time, there came a renewal of the noises on the road: and he turned in time to meet a stranger, who was advancing to meet him across the court. There was something like the outline of a great carriage discernible on the road behind the stranger, and, above that, a few black pine-tops, like so many plumes.

"Master Will?" asked the new-comer, in brief military fashion.

"That same, sir," answered Will. "Can I do anything to serve you?"

"I have heard you much spoken of, Master Will," returned the other; "much spoken of, and well. And though I have both hands full of business, I wish to drink a bottle of wine with you in your arbor. Before I go, I shall introduce myself."

Will led the way to the trellis, and got a lamp lighted and a bottle

uncorked. He was not altogether unused to such complimentary inter-
views, and hoped little enough from this one, being schooled by many
disappointments. A sort of cloud had settled on his wits and prevented
him from remembering the strangeness of the hour. He moved like a
person in his sleep; and it seemed as if the lamp caught fire and the
bottle came uncorked with the facility of thought. Still, he had some
curiosity about the appearance of his visitor, and tried in vain to turn
the light into his face; either he handled the lamp clumsily, or there
was a dimness over his eyes; but he could make out little more than a
shadow at table with him. He stared and stared at this shadow, as he
wiped out the glasses, and began to feel cold and strange about the heart.
The silence weighed upon him, for he could hear nothing now, not even
the river, but the drumming of his own arteries in his ears.

"Here's to you," said the stranger, roughly.

"Here is my service, sir," replied Will, sipping his wine, which somehow tasted oddly.

"I understand you are a very positive fellow," pursued the stranger.

Will made answer with a smile of some satisfaction and a little nod.

"So am I," continued the other; "and it is the delight of my heart
to tramp on people's corns. I will have nobody positive but myself; not
one. I have crossed the whims, in my time, of kings and generals and
great artists. And what would you say," he went on, "if I had come
up here on purpose to cross yours?"

Will had it on his tongue to make a sharp rejoinder; but the politeness of an old innkeeper prevailed; and he held his peace and made answer
with a civil gesture of the hand.

"I have," said the stranger. "And if I did not hold you in a particular esteem, I should make no words about the matter. It appears
you pride yourself on staying where you are. You mean to stick by
your inn. Now I mean you shall come for a turn with me in my
barouche; and before this bottle's empty, so you shall."

"That would be an odd thing, to be sure," replied Will, with a
chuckle. "Why, sir, I have grown here like an old oak-tree; the Devil
himself could hardly root me up: and for all I perceive you are a very
entertaining old gentleman, I would wager you another bottle you lose
your pains with me."

The dimness of Will's eyesight had been increasing all this while;
but he was somehow conscious of a sharp and chilling scrutiny which
irritated and yet overmastered him.

"You need not think," he broke out suddenly, in an explosive, febrile
manner that startled and alarmed himself, "that I am a stay-at-home,

because I fear anything under God. God knows I am tired enough of it all; and when the time comes for a longer journey than ever you dream of, I reckon I shall find myself prepared."

The stranger emptied his glass and pushed it away from him. He looked down for a little, and then, leaning over the table, tapped Will three times upon the forearm with a single finger. "The time has come!" he said solemnly.

An ugly thrill spread from the spot he touched. The tones of his voice were dull and startling, and echoed strangely in Will's heart.

"I beg your pardon," he said, with some discomposure. "What do you mean?"

"Look at me, and you will find your eyesight swim. Raise your hand; it is dead-heavy. This is your last bottle of wine, Master Will, and your last night upon the earth."

"You are a doctor?" quavered Will.

"The best that ever was," replied the other; "for I cure both mind and body with the same prescription. I take away all pain and I forgive all sins; and where my patients have gone wrong in life, I smooth out all complications and set them free again upon their feet."

"I have no need of you," said Will.

"A times comes for all men, Master Will," replied the doctor, "when the helm is taken out of their hands. For you, because you were prudent and quiet, it has been long of coming, and you have had long to discipline yourself for its reception. You have seen what is to be seen about your mill; you have sat close all your days like a hare in its form; but now that is at an end; and," added the doctor, getting on his feet, "you must arise and come with me."

"You are a strange physician," said Will, looking steadfastly upon his guest.

"I am a natural law," he replied, "and people call me Death."

"Why did you not tell me so at first?" cried Will. "I have been waiting for you these many years. Give me your hand, and welcome."

"Lean upon my arm," said the stranger, "for already your strength abates. Lean on me heavily as you need; for though I am old, I am very strong. It is but three steps to my carriage, and there all your trouble ends. Why, Will," he added, "I have been yearning for you as if you were my own son; and of all the men that ever I came for in my long days, I have come for you most gladly. I am caustic, and sometimes offend people at first sight; but I am a good friend at heart to such as you."

"Since Marjory was taken," returned Will, "I declare before God you were the only friend I had to look for."

So the pair went arm-in-arm across the courtyard.

One of the servants awoke about this time and heard the noise of horses pawing before he dropped asleep again; all down the valley that night there was a rushing as of a smooth and steady wind descending towards the plain; and when the world rose next morning, sure enough Will o' the Mill had gone at last upon his travels.

Markheim

"Yes," said the dealer, "our windfalls are of various kinds. Some customers are ignorant, and then I touch a dividend of my superior knowledge. Some are dishonest," and here he held up the candle, so that the light fell strongly on his visitor, "and in that case," he continued, "I profit by my virtue."

Markheim had but just entered from the daylight streets, and his eyes had not yet grown familiar with the mingled shine and darkness in the shop. At these pointed words, and before the near presence of the flame, he blinked painfully and looked aside.

The dealer chuckled. "You come to me on Christmas Day," he resumed, "when you know that I am alone in my house, put up my shutters, and make a point of refusing business. Well, you will have to pay for that; you will have to pay for my loss of time, when I should be balancing my books; you will have to pay, besides, for a kind of manner that I remark in you to-day very strongly. I am the essence of discretion, and ask no awkward questions; but when a customer cannot look me in the eyes, he has to pay for it." The dealer once more chuckled; and then, changing to his usual business voice, though still with a note of irony, "You can give, as usual, a clear account of how you came into the possession of the object?" he continued. "Still your uncle's cabinet? A remarkable collector, sir!"

And the little pale, round-shouldered dealer stood almost on tiptoe, looking over the top of his gold spectacles, and nodding his head with every mark of disbelief. Markheim returned his gaze with one of infinite pity, and a touch of horror.

"This time," said he, "you are in error. I have not come to sell, but to buy. I have no curios to dispose of; my uncle's cabinet is bare to the wainscot; even were it still intact, I have done well on the Stock Exchange, and should more likely add to it than otherwise, and my errand to-day is simplicity itself. I seek a Christmas present for a lady," he continued, waxing more fluent as he struck into the speech he had prepared; "and certainly I owe you every excuse for thus disturbing you upon so small a matter. But the thing was neglected yesterday; I must produce my little compliment at dinner; and, as you very well know, a rich marriage is not a thing to be neglected."

There followed a pause, during which the dealer seemed to weigh this statement incredulously. The ticking of many clocks among the curious lumber of the shop, and the faint rushing of the cabs in a near thoroughfare, filled up the interval of silence.

"Well, sir," said the dealer, "be it so. You are an old customer after all; and if, as you say, you have the chance of a good marriage, far be it from me to be an obstacle. Here is a nice thing for a lady now," he went on, "this hand glass—fifteenth century, warranted; comes from a good collection, too; but I reserve the name, in the interests of my customer, who was just like yourself, my dear sir, the nephew and sole heir of a remarkable collector."

The dealer, while he thus ran on in his dry and biting voice, had stooped to take the object from its place; and, as he had done so, a shock had passed through Markheim, a start both of hand and foot, a sudden leap of many tumultuous passions to the face. It passed as swiftly as it came, and left no trace beyond a certain trembling of the hand that now received the glass.

"A glass," he said hoarsely, and then paused, and repeated it more clearly. "A glass? For Christmas? Surely not?"

"And why not?" cried the dealer. "Why not a glass?"

Markheim was looking upon him with an indefinable expression. "You ask me why not?" he said. "Why, look here—look in it—look at yourself! Do you like to see it? No! nor I—nor any man."

The little man had jumped back when Markheim had so suddenly confronted him with the mirror; but now, perceiving there was nothing worse on hand, he chuckled. "Your future lady, sir, must be pretty hard favored," said he.

"I ask you," said Markheim, "for a Christmas present, and you give me this—this damned reminder of years, and sins and follies—this hand-conscience! Did you mean it? Had you a thought in your mind? Tell me. It will be better for you if you do. Come, tell me about yourself. I hazard a guess now, that you are in secret a very charitable man?"

The dealer looked closely at his companion. It was very odd, Markheim did not appear to be laughing; there was something in his face like an eager sparkle of hope, but nothing of mirth.

"What are you driving at?" the dealer asked.

"Not charitable?" returned the other, gloomily. "Not charitable; not pious; not scrupulous; unloving, unbeloved; a hand to get money, a safe to keep it. Is that all? Dear God, man, is that all?"

"I will tell you what it is," began the dealer, with some sharpness, and then broke off again into a chuckle. "But I see this is a love match of yours, and you have been drinking the lady's health."

"Ah!" cried Markheim, with a strange curiosity. "Ah, have you been in love? Tell me about that."

"I," cried the dealer. "I in love! I never had the time, nor have I the time to-day for all this nonsense. Will you take the glass?"

"Where is the hurry?" returned Markheim. "It is very pleasant to stand here talking; and life is so short and insecure that I would not hurry away from any pleasure—no, not even from so mild a one as this. We should rather cling, cling to what little we can get, like a man at a cliff's edge. Every second is a cliff, if you think upon it—a cliff a mile high—high enough, if we fall, to dash us out of every feature of humanity. Hence it is best to talk pleasantly. Let us talk of each other; why should we wear this mask? Let us be confidential. Who knows, we might become friends?"

"I have just one word to say to you," said the dealer. "Either make your purchase, or walk out of my shop."

"True, true," said Markheim. "Enough fooling. To business. Show me something else."

The dealer stooped once more, this time to replace the glass upon the shelf, his thin blond hair falling over his eyes as he did so. Markheim moved a little nearer, with one hand in the pocket of his great-coat; he drew himself up and filled his lungs; at the same time many different emotions were depicted together on his face—terror, horror, and resolve, fascination and a physical repulsion; and through a haggard lift of his upper lip, his teeth looked out.

"This, perhaps, may suit," observed the dealer; and then, as he began to re-arise, Markheim bounded from behind upon his victim. The long, skewer-like dagger flashed and fell. The dealer struggled like a hen, striking his temple on the shelf, and then tumbled on the floor in a heap.

Time had some score of small voices in that shop, some stately and slow as was becoming to their great age; others garrulous and hurried. All these told out the seconds in an intricate chorus of tickings. Then the passage of a lad's feet, heavily running on the pavement, broke in upon these smaller voices and startled Markheim into the consciousness of his surroundings. He looked about him awfully. The candle stood on the counter, its flame solemnly wagging in a draught; and by that inconsiderable movement, the whole room was filled with noiseless bustle and kept heaving like a sea: the tall shadows nodding, the gross blots of darkness swelling and dwindling as with respiration, the faces of the portraits and the china gods changing and wavering like images in water. The inner door stood ajar, and peered into that leaguer of shadows with a long slit of daylight like a pointing finger.

From these fear-stricken rovings, Markheim's eyes returned to the body of his victim, where it lay both humped and sprawling, incredibly small and strangely meaner than in life. In these poor, miserly clothes, in that ungainly attitude, the dealer lay like so much sawdust. Markheim had feared to see it, and, lo! it was nothing. And yet, as he gazed, this bundle of old clothes and pool of blood began to find eloquent voices. There it must lie; there was none to work the cunning hinges or direct the miracle of locomotion—there it must lie till it was found. Found! ay, and then? Then would this dead flesh lift up a cry that would ring over England, and fill the world with the echoes of pursuit. Ay, dead or not, this was still the enemy. "Time was, that when the brains were out," he thought; and the first word struck into his mind. Time, now that the deed was accomplished—time, which had closed for the victim, had become instant and momentous for the slayer.

The thought was yet in his mind, when, first one and then another, with every variety of pace and voice—one deep as the bell from a cathedral turret, another ringing on its treble notes the prelude of a waltz—the clocks began to strike the hour of three in the afternoon.

The sudden outbreak of so many tongues in that dumb chamber staggered him. He began to bestir himself, going to and fro with the candle, beleaguered by moving shadows, and startled to the soul by chance reflections. In many rich mirrors, some of home designs, some from Venice or Amsterdam, he saw his face repeated and repeated, as it were an army of spies; his own eyes met and detected him; and the sound of his own steps, lightly as they fell, vexed the surrounding quiet. And still as he continued to fill his pockets, his mind accused him, with a sickening iteration, of the thousand faults of his design. He should have chosen a more quiet hour; he should have prepared an alibi; he should not have used a knife; he should have been more cautious, and only bound and gagged the dealer, and not killed him; he should have been more bold, and killed the servant also; he should have done all things otherwise; poignant regrets, weary, incessant toiling of the mind to change what was unchangeable, to plan what was now useless, to be the architect of the irrevocable past. Meanwhile, and behind all this activity, brute terrors, like the scurrying of rats in a deserted attic, filled the more remote chambers of his brain with riot; the hand of the constable would fall heavy on his shoulder, and his nerves would jerk like a hooked fish; or he beheld, in galloping defile, the dock, the prison, the gallows, and the black coffin.

Terror of the people in the street sat down before his mind like a besieging army. It was impossible, he thought, but that some rumor of the struggle must have reached their ears and set on edge their curiosity; and now, in all the neighboring houses, he divined them sitting motionless and with uplifted ear—solitary people, condemned to spend Christmas dwelling alone on memories of the past, and now startlingly recalled from that tender exercise; happy family parties, struck into silence round the table, the mother still with raised finger: every degree and age and humor, but all, by their own hearts, prying and hearkening and weaving the rope that was to hang him. Sometimes it seemed to him he could not move too swiftly; the clink of the tall Bohemian goblets rang out loudly like a bell; and alarmed by the bigness of the ticking, he was tempted to stop the clocks. And then, again, with a swift transition of his terrors, the very silence of the place appeared a source of peril, and a thing to strike and freeze the passer-by; and he would step more boldly, and bustle aloud among the contents of the shop, and imitate, with elaborate bravado, the movements of a busy man at ease in his own house.

But he was now so pulled about by different alarms that, while one portion of his mind was still alert and cunning, another trembled on the brink of lunacy. One hallucination in particular took a strong hold on his credulity. The neighbor hearkening with white face beside his window, the passer-by arrested by a horrible surmise on the pavement—these could at worst suspect, they could not know; through the brick walls and shuttered windows only sounds could penetrate. But here, within the house, was he alone? He knew he was; he had watched the servant set forth sweet-hearting, in her poor best, "out for the day" written in every ribbon and smile. Yes, he was alone, of course; and yet, in the bulk of empty house above him, he could surely hear a stir of delicate footing—he was surely conscious, inexplicably conscious of some presence. Ay, surely; to every room and corner of the house his imagination followed it; and now it was a faceless thing, and yet had eyes to see with; and again it was a shadow of himself; and yet again behold the image of the dead dealer, reinspired with cunning and hatred.

At times, with a strong effort, he would glance at the open door which still seemed to repel his eyes. The house was tall, the skylight small and dirty, the day blind with fog; and the light that filtered down to the ground storey was exceedingly faint, and showed dimly on the threshold of the shop. And yet, in that strip of doubtful brightness, did there not hang wavering a shadow?

Suddenly, from the street outside, a very jovial gentleman began to beat with a staff on the shop-door, accompanying his blows with shouts and railleries in which the dealer was continually called upon by name. Markheim, smitten into ice, glanced at the dead man. But no! he lay quite still; he was fled away far beyond ear-shot of these blows and shoutings; he was sunk beneath seas of silence; and his name, which would once have caught his notice above the howling of a storm, had become an empty sound. And presently the jovial gentleman desisted from his knocking and departed.

Here was a broad hint to hurry what remained to be done, to get forth from this accusing neighborhood, to plunge into a bath of London multitudes, and to reach, on the other side of day, that haven of safety and apparent innocence—his bed. One visitor had come: at any moment another might follow and be more obstinate. To have done the deed, and yet not to reap the profit, would be too abhorrent a failure. The money, that was now Markheim's concern; and as a means to that, the keys.

He glanced over his shoulder at the open door, where the shadow was still lingering and shivering; and with no conscious repugnance of the mind, yet with a tremor of the belly, he drew near the body of his victim. The human character had quite departed. Like a suit half stuffed with bran, the limbs lay scattered, the trunk doubled, on the floor; and yet the thing repelled him. Although so dingy and inconsiderable to the eye, he feared it might have more significance to the touch. He took the body by the shoulders, and turned it on its back. It was strangely light and supple, and the limbs, as if they had been broken, fell into the oddest postures. The face was robbed of all expression; but it was pale as wax, and shockingly smeared with blood about one temple. That was, for Markheim, the one displeasing circumstance. It carried him back, upon the instant, to a certain fair day in a fishers' village: a grey day, a piping wind, a crowd upon the street, the blare of brasses, the booming of drums, the nasal voice of a ballad singer; and a boy going to and fro, buried over head in the crowd and divided between interest and fear, until, coming out upon the chief place of concourse, he beheld a booth and a great screen with pictures, dismally designed, garishly colored: Brownrigg with her apprentice; the Mannings with their murdered guest; We are in the death-grip of Thurtell; and a score besides of famous crimes. The thing was as clear as an illusion; he was once again that little boy; he was looking once again, and with the same sense of physical revolt, at these vile pictures; he was still stunned by the thumping of the drums. A bar of that day's music returned upon his memory; and at that, for the first time, a qualm came over him, a breath of nausea, a sudden weakness of the joints, which he must instantly resist and conquer.

He judged it more prudent to confront than to flee from these considerations; looking the more hardily in the dead face, bending his mind to realize the nature and greatness of his crime. So little a while ago that face had moved with every change of sentiment, that pale mouth had spoken, that body had been all on fire with governable energies; and now, and by his act, that piece of life had been arrested, as the horologist, with interjected finger, arrests the beating of the clock. So he reasoned in vain; he could rise to no more remorseful consciousness; the same heart which had shuddered before the painted effigies of crime, looked on its reality unmoved. At best, he felt a gleam of pity for one who had been endowed in vain with all those faculties that can make the world a garden of enchantment, one who had never lived and who was now dead. But of penitence, no, not a tremor.

With that, shaking himself clear of these considerations, he found the keys and advanced towards the open door of the shop. Outside, it had begun to rain smartly; and the sound of the shower upon the roof had banished silence. Like some dripping cavern, the chambers of the house were haunted by an incessant echoing, which filled the ear and mingled with the ticking of the clocks. And, as Markheim approached the door, he seemed to hear, in answer to his own cautious tread, the steps of another foot withdrawing up the stair. The shadow still palpitated loosely on the threshold. He threw a ton's weight of resolve upon his muscles, and drew back the door.

The faint, foggy daylight glimmered dimly on the bare floor and stairs; on the bright suit of armor posted, halbert in hand, upon the landing; and on the dark wood-carvings, and framed pictures that hung against the yellow panels of the wainscot. So loud was the beating of the rain through all the house that, in Markheim's ears, it began to be distinguished into many different sounds. Footsteps and sighs, the tread of regiments marching in the distance, the chink of money in the counting, and the creaking of doors held stealthily ajar, appeared to mingle with the patter of the drops upon the cupola and the gushing of the water in the pipes. The sense that he was not alone grew upon

him to the verge of madness. On every side he was haunted and begirt
by presences. He heard them moving in the upper chambers; from the
shop, he heard the dead man getting to his legs; and as he began with
a great effort to mount the stairs, feet fled quietly before him and followed stealthily behind. If he were but deaf, he thought, how tran-
quilly he would possess his soul! And then again, and hearkening with
ever fresh attention, he blessed himself for that unresting sense which
held the outposts and stood a trusty sentinel upon his life. His head
turned continually on his neck; his eyes, which seemed starting from
their orbits, scouted on every side, and on every side were half re-
warded as with the tail of something nameless vanishing. The four-
and-twenty steps to the first floor were four-and-twenty agonies.

On that first storey, the doors stood ajar, three of them like three
ambushes, shaking his nerves like the throats of cannon. He could
never again, he felt, be sufficiently immured and fortified from men's
observing eyes; he longed to be home, girt in by walls, buried among
bedclothes, and invisible to all but God. And at that thought he wondered a little, recollecting tales of other murderers and the fear they
were said to entertain of heavenly avengers. It was not so, at least,
with him. He feared the laws of nature, lest, in their callous and immu-
table procedure, they should preserve some damning evidence of his
crime. He feared tenfold more, with a slavish, superstitious terror, some
scission in the continuity of man's experience, some wilful illegality of
nature. He played a game of skill, depending on the rules, calculating
consequence from cause; and what if nature, as the defeated tyrant over-
threw the chess-board, should break the mold of their succession? The
like had befallen Napoleon (so writers said) when the winter changed
the time of its appearance. The like might befall Markheim: the solid
walls might become transparent and reveal his doings like those of bees
in a glass hive; the stout planks might yield under his foot like quick-
sands and detain him in their clutch; ay, and there were soberer accidents that might destroy him: if, for instance, the house should fall and
imprison him beside the body of his victim; or the house next door should
fly on fire, and the firemen invade him from all sides. These things
he feared; and, in a sense, these things might be called the hands of
God reached forth against sin. But about God himself he was at ease;
his act was doubtless exceptional, but so were his excuses, which God
knew; it was there, and not among men, that he felt sure of justice.

When he had got safe into the drawing-room, and shut the door
behind him, he was aware of a respite from alarms. The room was
quite dismantled, uncarpeted besides, and strewn with packing-cases and

incongruous furniture; several great pier-glasses, in which he beheld himself at various angles, like an actor on a stage; many pictures, framed and unframed, standing, with their faces to the wall; a fine Sheraton sideboard, a cabinet of marquetry, and a great old bed, with tapestry hangings. The windows opened to the floor; but by great good-fortune the lower part of the shutters had been closed, and this concealed him from the neighbors. Here, then, Markheim drew in a packing-case before the cabinet and began to search among the keys. It was a long business, for there were many; and it was irksome, besides; for after all, there might be nothing in the cabinet, and time was on the wing. But the closeness of the occupation sobered him. With the tail of his eye he saw the door—even glanced at it from time to time directly, like a besieged commander pleased to verify the good estate of his defences. But in truth he was at peace. The rain falling in the street sounded natural and pleasant. Presently, on the other side, the notes of a piano were wakened to the music of a hymn, and the voices of many children took up the air and words. How stately, how comfortable was the melody! How fresh the youthful voices! Markheim gave ear to it smilingly, as he sorted out the keys; and his mind was thronged with answerable ideas and images; church-going children and the pealing of the high organ; children afield, bathers by the brookside, ramblers on the brambly common, kite-fliers in the windy and cloud-navigated sky; and then, at another cadence of the hymn, back again to church, and the somnolence of summer Sundays, and the high genteel voice of the parson (which he smiled a little to recall) and the painted Jacobean tombs, and the dim lettering of the Ten Commandments in the chancel.

And as he sat thus, at once busy and absent, he was startled to his feet. A flash of ice, a flash of fire, a bursting gush of blood, went over him, and then he stood transfixed and thrilling. A step mounted the stair slowly and steadily, and presently a hand was laid upon the knob, and the lock clicked, and the door opened.

Fear held Markheim in a vice. What to expect he knew not, whether the dead man walking, or the official ministers of human justice, or some chance witness blindly stumbling in to consign him to the gallows. But when a face was thrust into the aperture, glanced round the room, looked at him, nodded and smiled as if in friendly recognition, and then withdrew again, and the door closed behind it, his fear broke loose from his control in a hoarse cry. At the sound of this the visitant returned.

"Did you call me?" he asked, pleasantly, and with that he entered the room and closed the door behind him.

Markheim stood and gazed at him with all his eyes. Perhaps there was a film upon his sight, but the outlines of the new-comer seemed to change and waver like those of the idols in the wavering candle-light of the shop; and at times he thought he knew him; and at times he thought he bore a likeness to himself; and always, like a lump of living terror, there lay in his bosom the conviction that this thing was not of the earth and not of God.

And yet the creature had a strange air of the commonplace, as he stood looking on Markheim with a smile; and when he added: "You are looking for the money, I believe?" it was in the tones of every-day politeness.

Markheim made no answer.

"I should warn you," resumed the other, "that the maid has left her sweetheart earlier than usual and will soon be here. If Mr. Markheim be found in this house, I need not describe to him the consequences."

"You know me?" cried the murderer.

The visitor smiled. "You have long been a favorite of mine," he said; "and I have long observed and often sought to help you."

"What are you?" cried Markheim: "the devil?"

"What I may be," returned the other, "cannot affect the service I propose to render you."

"It can," cried Markheim; "it does! Be helped by you? No, never; not by you! You do not know me yet; thank God, you do not know me!"

"I know you," replied the visitant, with a sort of kind severity or rather firmness. "I know you to the soul."

"Know me!" cried Markheim. "Who can do so? My life is but a travesty and slander on myself. I have lived to belie my nature. All men do; all men are better than this disguise that grows about and stifles them. You see each dragged away by life, like one whom bravos have seized and muffled in a cloak. If they had their own control— if you could see their faces, they would be altogether different, they would shine out for heroes and saints! I am worse than most; my self is more overlaid; my excuse is known to me and God. But, had I the time, I could disclose myself."

"To me?" inquired the visitant.

"To you before all," returned the murderer. "I supposed you were intelligent. I thought—since you exist—you would prove a reader of the heart. And yet you would propose to judge me by my acts! Think of it; my acts! I was born and I have lived in a land of giants; giants have dragged me by the wrists since I was born out of my mother— the giants of circumstance. And you would judge me by my acts! But can you not look within? Can you not understand that evil is hateful to me? Can you not see within me the clear writing of conscience, never blurred by any wilful sophistry, although too often disregarded? Can you not read me for a thing that surely must be common as humanity—the unwilling sinner?"

"All this is very feelingly expressed," was the reply, "but it regards me not. These points of consistency are beyond my province, and I care not in the least by what compulsion you may have been dragged away, so as you are but carried in the right direction. But time flies; the servant delays, looking in the faces of the crowd and at the pictures on the hoardings, but still she keeps moving nearer; and remember, it is as if the gallows itself was striding towards you through the Christmas streets! Shall I help you; I, who know all? Shall I tell you where to find the money?"

"For what price?" asked Markheim.

"I offer you the service for a Christmas gift," returned the other.

Markheim could not refrain from smiling with a kind of bitter triumph. "No," said he, "I will take nothing at your hands; if I were dying of thirst, and it was your hand that put the pitcher to my lips, I should find the courage to refuse. It may be credulous, but I will do nothing to commit myself to evil."

"I have no objection to a death-bed repentance," observed the visitant.

"Because you disbelieve their efficacy!" Markheim cried.

"I do not say so," returned the other; "but I look on these things from a different side, and when the life is done my interest falls. The man has lived to serve me, to spread black looks under color of religion, or to sow tares in the wheat-field, as you do, in a course of weak compliance with desire. Now that he draws so near to his deliverance, he can add but one act of service—to repent, to die smiling, and thus to build up in confidence and hope the more timorous of my surviving followers. I am not so hard a master. Try me. Accept my help. Please yourself in life as you have done hitherto; please yourself more amply, spread your elbows at the board; and when the night begins to fall and the curtains to be drawn, I tell you, for your greater comfort, that you will find it even easy to compound your quarrel with your conscience, and to make a truckling peace with God. I came but now from such a death-bed, and the room was full of sincere mourners, listening to the man's last words: and when I looked into that face, which had been set as a flint against mercy, I found it smiling with hope."

"And do you, then, suppose me such a creature?" asked Markheim. "Do you think I have no more generous aspirations than to sin, and sin, and sin, and, at last, sneak into heaven? My heart rises at the thought. Is this, then, your experience of mankind? or is it because you find me with red hands that you presume such baseness? and is this crime of murder indeed so impious as to dry up the very springs of good?"

"Murder is to me no special category," replied the other. "All sins are murder, even as all life is war. I behold your race, like starving mariners on a raft, plucking crusts out of the hands of famine and feeding on each other's lives. I follow sins beyond the moment of their acting; I find in all that the last consequence is death; and to my eyes, the pretty maid who thwarts her mother with such taking graces on a question of a ball, drips no less visibly with human gore than such a murderer as yourself. Do I say that I follow sins? I follow virtues also; they differ not by the thickness of a nail, they are both scythes for the reaping angel of Death. Evil, for which I live, consists not in action but in character. The bad man is dear to me; not the bad act, whose fruits, if we could follow them far enough down the hurtling cataract of the ages, might yet be found more blessed than those of the rarest virtues. And it is not because you have killed a dealer, but because you are Markheim, that I offered to forward your escape."

"I will lay my heart open to you," answered Markheim. "This crime on which you find me is my last. On my way to it I have learned many lessons; itself is a lesson, a momentous lesson. Hitherto I have been driven with revolt to what I would not; I was a bond-slave to poverty, driven and scourged. There are robust virtues that can stand in these temptations; mine was not so: I had a thirst of pleasure. But to-day, and out of this deed, I pluck both warning and riches—both the power and a fresh resolve to be myself. I become in all things a free actor in the world; I begin to see myself all changed, these hands the agents of good, this heart at peace. Something comes over me out of the past; something of what I have dreamed on Sabbath evenings to the sound of the church organ, of what I forecast when I shed tears over noble books, or talked, an innocent child, with my mother. There lies my life; I have wandered a few years, but now I see once more my city of destination."

"You are to use this money on the Stock Exchange, I think?" remarked the visitor; "and there, if I mistake not, you have already lost some thousands?"

"Ah," said Markheim, "but this time I have a sure thing."

"This time, again, you will lose," replied the visitor quietly.

"Ah, but I keep back the half!" cried Markheim.

"That also you will lose," said the other.

The sweat started upon Markheim's brow. "Well, then, what matter?" he exclaimed. "Say it be lost, say I am plunged again in poverty, shall one part of me, and that the worst, continue until the end to override the better? Evil and good run strong in me, haling me both ways. I do not love the one thing, I love all. I can conceive great deeds, renunciations, martyrdoms; and though I be fallen to such a crime as murder, pity is no stranger to my thoughts. I pity the poor; who knows their trials better than myself? I pity and help them; I prize love, I love honest laughter; there is no good thing nor true thing on earth but I love it from my heart. And are my vices only to direct my life, and my virtues to lie without effect, like some passive lumber of the mind? Not so; good, also, is a spring of acts."

But the visitant raised his finger. "For six-and-thirty years that you have been in this world," said he, "through many changes of fortune and varieties of humor, I have watched you steadily fall. Fifteen years ago you would have started at a theft. Three years back you would have blenched at the name of murder. Is there any crime, is there any cruelty or meanness, from which you still recoil?—five years from now I shall detect you in the fact! Downward, downward, lies your way; nor can anything but death avail to stop you."

"It is true," Markheim said huskily, "I have in some degree complied with evil. But it is so with all: the very saints, in the mere exercise of living, grow less dainty, and take on the tone of their surroundings."

"I will propound to you one simple question," said the other; "and as you answer, I shall read to you your moral horoscope. You have grown in many things more lax; possibly you do right to be so; and at any account, it is the same with all men. But granting that, are you in any one particular, however trifling, more difficult to please with your own conduct, or do you go in all things with a looser rein?"

"In any one?" repeated Markheim, with an anguish of consideration. "No," he added, with despair, "in none! I have gone down in all."

"Then," said the visitor, "content yourself with what you are, for you will never change; and the words of your part on this stage are irrevocably written down."

Markheim stood for a long while silent, and indeed it was the visitor who first broke the silence. "That being so," he said, "shall I show you the money?"

"And grace?" cried Markheim.

"Have you not tried it?" returned the other. "Two or three years ago, did I not see you on the platform of revival meetings, and was not your voice the loudest in the hymn?"

"It is true," said Markheim; "and I see clearly what remains for me by way of duty. I thank you for these lessons from my soul; my eyes are opened, and I behold myself at last for what I am."

At this moment, the sharp note of the door-bell rang through the house; and the visitant, as though this were some concerted signal for which he had been waiting, changed at once in his demeanor.

"The maid!" he cried. "She has returned, as I forewarned you, and there is now before you one more difficult passage. Her master, you must say, is ill; you must let her in, with an assured but rather serious countenance—no smiles, no overacting, and I promise you success! Once the girl within, and the door closed, the same dexterity that has already rid you of the dealer will relieve you of this last danger in your path. Thenceforward you have the whole evening—the whole night, if needful —to ransack the treasures of the house and to make good your safety. This is help that comes to you with the mask of danger. Up!" he cried: "up, friend; your life hangs trembling in the scales: up, and act!"

Markheim steadily regarded his counsellor. "If I be condemned to evil acts," he said, "there is still one door of freedom open—I can cease from action. If my life be an ill thing, I can lay it down. Though I be, as you say truly, at the beck of every small temptation, I can yet, by one decisive gesture, place myself beyond the reach of all. My love of good is damned to barrenness; it may, and let it be! But I have still my hatred of evil; and from that, to your galling disappointment, you shall see that I can draw both energy and courage."

The features of the visitor began to undergo a wonderful and lovely change: they brightened and softened with a tender triumph; and, even as they brightened, faded and dislimned. But Markheim did not pause to watch or understand the transformation. He opened the door and went down-stairs very slowly, thinking to himself. His past went soberly before him; he beheld it as it was, ugly and strenuous like a dream, random as chance-medley—a scene of defeat. Life, as he thus reviewed it, tempted him no longer; but on the further side he perceived a quiet haven for his bark. He paused in the passage, and looked into the shop, where the candle still burned by the dead body. It was strangely silent. Thoughts of the dealer swarmed into his mind, as he stood gazing. And then the bell once more broke out into impatient clamor.

He confronted the maid upon the threshold with something like a smile.

"You had better go for the police," said he: "I have killed your master."

WILLIAM ERNEST HENLEY
(1849-1903)

From HOSPITAL SKETCHES

Before

BEHOLD me waiting—waiting for the knife.
A little while, and at a leap I storm
The thick, sweet mystery of chloroform,
The drunken dark, the little death-in-life.
The gods are good to me: I have no wife,
No innocent child, to think of as I near
The fateful minute; nothing all too dear
Unmans me for my bout of passive strife.
Yet I am tremulous and a trifle sick,
And, face to face with chance, I shrink a little:
My hopes are strong, my will is something weak.
Here comes the basket? Thank you. I am ready.
But, gentlemen my porters, life is brittle:
You carry Cæsar and his fortunes—steady!

Operation

YOU are carried in a basket,
  Like a carcase from the shambles,
  To the theatre, a cockpit
  Where they stretch you on a table.

Then they bid you close your eyelids,
  And they mask you with a napkin,
  And the anæsthetic reaches
  Hot and subtle through your being.

And you gasp and reel and shudder
  In a rushing, swaying rapture,
While the voices at your elbow
  Fade—receding—fainter—farther.

Lights about you shower and tumble,
  And your blood seems crystallizing—
  Edged and vibrant, yet within you
  Racked and hurried back and forward.

Then the lights grow fast and furious,
  And you hear a noise of waters,
  And you wrestle, blind and dizzy,
  In an agony of effort,

Till a sudden lull accepts you,
  And you sound an utter darkness . . .
  And awaken . . . with a struggle . . .
  On a hushed, attentive audience.

Apparition

THIN-LEGGED, thin-chested, slight unspeakably,
Neat-footed and weak-fingered: in his face—
Lean, large-boned, curved of beak, and touched with race,
Bold-lipped, rich-tinted, mutable as the sea,
The brown eyes radiant with vivacity—
There shines a brilliant and romantic grace,
A spirit intense and rare, with trace on trace
Of passion and impudence and energy.
Valiant in velvet, light in ragged luck,
Most vain, most generous, sternly critical,
Buffoon and poet, lover and sensualist:
A deal of Ariel, just a streak of Puck,
Much Antony, of Hamlet most of all,
And something of the Shorter-Catechist.

JOSEPH CONRAD (1857-1924)

Youth

THIS could have occurred nowhere but in England, where men and sea interpenetrate, so to speak—the sea entering into the life of most men, and the men knowing something or everything about the sea, in the way of amusement, of travel, or of bread-winning.

We were sitting round a mahogany table that reflected the bottle, the claret-glasses, and our faces as we leaned on our elbows. There was a director of companies, an accountant, a lawyer, Marlow, and myself. The director had been a *Conway* boy, the accountant had served four years at sea, the lawyer—a fine crusted Tory, High Churchman, the best of old fellows, the soul of honour—had been chief officer in the P. & O. service in the good old days when mail-boats were square-rigged at least on two masts, and used to come down the China Sea before a fair monsoon with stun'-sails set alow and aloft. We all began life in the merchant service. Between the five of us there was the strong bond of the sea, and also the fellowship of the craft, which no amount of enthusiasm for yachting, cruising, and so on can give, since one is only the amusement of life and the other is life itself.

Marlow (at least I think that is how he spelt his name) told the story, or rather the chronicle, of a voyage:—

"Yes, I have seen a little of the Eastern seas; but what I remember best is my first voyage there. You fellows know there are those voyages that seem ordered for the illustration of life, that might stand for a symbol of existence. You fight, work, sweat, nearly kill yourself, some-times do kill yourself, trying to accomplish something—and you can't. Not from any fault of yours. You simply can do nothing, neither great nor little—not a thing in the world—not even marry an old maid, or get a wretched 600-ton cargo of coal to its port of destination.

"It was altogether a memorable affair. It was my first voyage to the East, and my first voyage as second mate; it was also my skipper's first command. You'll admit it was time. He was sixty if a day; a little man, with a broad, not very straight back, with bowed shoulders and one leg more bandy than the other, he had that queer twisted-about appearance you see so often in men who work in the fields. He had a nut-cracker face—chin and nose trying to come together over a sunken mouth—and it was framed in iron-gray fluffy hair, that looked like a chin-strap of cotton-wool sprinkled with coal-dust. And he had blue eyes in that old face of his, which were amazingly like a boy's, with that candid expression some quite common men preserve to the end of their days by a rare internal gift of simplicity of heart and rectitude of soul. What induced him to accept me was a wonder. I had come out of a crack Australian clipper, where I had been third officer, and he seemed to have a prejudice against crack clippers as aristocratic and high-toned. He said to me, 'You know, in this ship you will have to work.' I said I had to work in every ship I had ever been in. 'Ah, but this is different, and you gentlemen out of them big ships; . . . but there! I dare say you will do. Join to-morrow.'

"I joined to-morrow. It was twenty-two years ago; and I was just twenty. How time passes! It was one of the happiest days of my life. Fancy! Second mate for the first time—a really responsible officer! I wouldn't have thrown up my new billet for a fortune. The mate looked me over carefully. He was also an old chap, but of another stamp. He had a Roman nose, a snow-white, long beard, and his name was Mahon, but he insisted that it should be pronounced Mann. He was well connected; yet there was something wrong with his luck, and he had never got on.

"As to the captain, he had been for years in coasters, then in the Mediterranean, and last in the West Indian trade. He had never been round the Capes. He could just write a kind of sketchy hand, and didn't care for writing at all. Both were thorough good seamen of course, and between those two old chaps I felt like a small boy between two grandfathers.

"The ship also was old. Her name was the *Judea*. Queer name, isn't it? She belonged to a man Wilmer, Wilcox—some name like that; but he has been bankrupt and dead these twenty years or more, and his name don't matter. She had been laid up in Shadwell basin for ever so long. You may imagine her state. She was all rust, dust, grime—soot aloft, dirt on deck. To me it was like coming out of a palace into a ruined cottage. She was about 400 tons, had a primitive windlass, wooden latches to the doors, not a bit of brass about her, and a big square stern. There was on it, below her name in big letters, a lot of scrollwork, with the gilt off, and some sort of a coat of arms, with the motto 'Do or Die' underneath. I remember it took my fancy immensely. There was a touch of romance in it, something that made me love the old thing—something that appealed to my youth!

"We left London in ballast—sand ballast—to load a cargo of coal in a northern port for Bankok. Bankok! I thrilled. I had been six years at sea, but had only seen Melbourne and Sydney, very good places, charming places in their way—but Bankok!

"We worked out of the Thames under canvas, with a North Sea pilot on board. His name was Jermyn, and he dodged all day long about the galley drying his handkerchief before the stove. Apparently he never slept. He was a dismal man, with a perpetual tear sparkling at the end of his nose, who either had been in trouble, or was in trouble, or expected to be in trouble—couldn't be happy unless something went wrong. He mistrusted my youth, my common-sense, and my seamanship, and made a point of showing it in a hundred little ways. I dare say he was right. It seems to me I knew very little then, and I know not much more now; but I cherish a hate for that Jermyn to this day.

"We were a week working up as far as Yarmouth Roads, and then we got into a gale—the famous October gale of twenty-two years ago. It was wind, lightning, sleet, snow, and a terrific sea. We were flying light, and you may imagine how bad it was when I tell you we had smashed bulwarks and a flooded deck. On the second night she shifted her ballast into the lee bow, and by that time we had been blown off somewhere on the Dogger Bank. There was nothing for it but go below with shovels and try to right her, and there we were in that vast hold, gloomy like a cavern, the tallow dips stuck and flickering on the beams, the gale howling above, the ship tossing about like mad on her side; there we all were, Jermyn, the captain, every one, hardly able to keep our feet, engaged on that gravedigger's work, and trying to toss shovelfuls of wet sand up to windward. At every tumble of the ship you could see vaguely in the dim light men falling down with a great flourish of shovels. One of the ship's boys (we had two), impressed by the weirdness of the scene, wept as if his heart would break. We could hear him blubbering somewhere in the shadows.

"On the third day the gale died out, and by and by a north-country tug picked us up. We took sixteen days in all to get from London to the Tyne! When we got into dock we had lost our turn for loading, and they hauled us off to a tier where we remained for a month. Mrs. Beard (the captain's name was Beard) came from Colchester to see the old man. She lived on board. The crew of runners had left, and there remained only the officers, one boy and the steward, a mulatto who answered to the name of Abraham. Mrs. Beard was an old woman, with a face all wrinkled and ruddy like a winter apple, and the figure of a young girl. She caught sight of me once, sewing a button, and insisted on having my shirts to repair. This was something different from the captains' wives I had known on board crack clippers. When I brought her the shirts, she said: 'And the socks? They want mending, I am sure, and John's—Captain Beard's—things are all in order now. I would

be glad of something to do.' Bless the old woman. She overhauled my
outfit for me, and meantime I read for the first time *Sartor Resartus* and
Burnaby's *Ride to Khiva.* I didn't understand much of the first then;
but I remember I preferred the soldier to the philosopher at the time;
a preference which life has only confirmed. One was a man, and the
other was either more—or less. However, they are both dead and Mrs.
Beard is dead, and youth, strength, genius, thoughts, achievements, simple
hearts—all die. . . . No matter.

"They loaded us at last. We shipped a crew. Eight able seamen
and two boys. We hauled off one evening to the buoys at the dock-gates,
ready to go out, and with a fair prospect of beginning the voyage next
day. Mrs. Beard was to start for home by a late train. When the ship
was fast we went to tea. We sat rather silent through the meal—Mahon,
the old couple, and I. I finished first, and slipped away for a smoke,
my cabin being in a deck-house just against the poop. It was high water,
blowing fresh with a drizzle; the double dock-gates were opened, and
the steam-colliers were going in and out in the darkness with their
lights burning bright, a great plashing of propellers, rattling of winches,
and a lot of hailing on the pier-heads. I watched the procession of head-
lights gliding high and of green lights gliding low in the night, when
suddenly a red gleam flashed at me, vanished, came into view again, and
remained. The fore-end of a steamer loomed up close. I shouted down
the cabin, 'Come up, quick!' and then heard a startled voice saying afar in
the dark, 'Stop her, sir.' A bell jingled. Another voice cried warningly,
'We are going right into that barque, sir.' The answer to this was a
gruff 'All right' and the next thing was a heavy crash as the steamer
struck a glancing blow with the bluff of her bow about our fore-rigging.
There was a moment of confusion, yelling, and running about. Steam
roared. Then somebody was heard saying, 'All clear, sir.' . . . 'Are you
all right?' asked the gruff voice. I had jumped forward to see the
damage, and hailed back, 'I think so.' 'Easy astern,' said the gruff voice.
A bell jingled. 'What steamer is that?' screamed Mahon. By that time
she was no more to us than a bulky shadow manœuvring a little way off.
They shouted at us some name—a woman's name, Miranda or Melissa—
or some such thing. 'This means another month in this beastly hole,'
said Mahon to me, as we peered with lamps about the splintered bulwarks
and broken braces. 'But where's the captain?'

"We had not heard or seen anything of him all that time. We went
aft to look. A doleful voice arose hailing somewhere in the middle of
the dock, *'Judea* ahoy!' . . . How the devil did he get there? . . .
'Hallo!' we shouted. 'I am adrift in our boat without oars,' he cried.

A belated water-man offered his services, and Mahon struck a bargain with him for half-a-crown to tow our skipper alongside; but it was Mrs. Beard that came up the ladder first. They had been floating about the dock in that mizzly cold rain for nearly an hour. I was never so surprised in my life.

"It appears that when he heard my shout 'Come up' he understood at once what was the matter, caught up his wife, ran on deck, and across, and down into our boat, which was fast to the ladder. Not bad for a sixty-year-old. Just imagine that old fellow saving heroically in his arms that old woman—the woman of his life. He set her down on a thwart, and was ready to climb back on board when the painter came adrift somehow, and away they went together. Of course in the confusion we did not hear him shouting. He looked abashed. She said cheerfully, 'I suppose it does not matter my losing the train now?' 'No, Jenny—you go below and get warm,' he growled. Then to us: 'A sailor has no business with a wife—I say. There I was, out of the ship. Well, no harm done this time. Let's go and look at what that fool of a steamer smashed.'

"It wasn't much, but it delayed us three weeks. At the end of that time, the captain being engaged with his agents, I carried Mrs. Beard's bag to the railway-station and put her all comfy into a third-class carriage. She lowered the window to say, 'You are a good young man. If you see John—Captain Beard—without his muffler at night, just remind him from me to keep his throat well wrapped up.' 'Certainly, Mrs. Beard,' I said. 'You are a good young man; I noticed how attentive you are to John—to Captain——' The train pulled out suddenly; I took my cap off to the old woman: I never saw her again. . . . Pass the bottle.

"We went to sea next day. When we made that start for Bankok we had been already three months out of London. We had expected to be a fortnight or so—at the outside.

"It was January, and the weather was beautiful—the beautiful sunny winter weather that has more charm than in the summer-time, because it is unexpected, and crisp, and you know it won't, it can't, last long. It's like a windfall, like a godsend, like an unexpected piece of luck.

"It lasted all down the North Sea, all down Channel; and it lasted till we were three hundred miles or so to the westward of the Lizards: then the wind went round to the sou'west and began to pipe up. In two days it blew a gale. The *Judea,* hove to, wallowed on the Atlantic like an old candle-box. It blew day after day: it blew with spite, without interval, without mercy, without rest. The world was nothing but an immensity of great foaming waves rushing at us, under a sky low enough to touch with the hand and dirty like a smoked ceiling. In the stormy space surrounding us there was as much flying spray as air. Day after day and night after night there was nothing round the ship but the howl of the wind, the tumult of the sea, the noise of water pouring over her deck. There was no rest for her and no rest for us. She tossed, she pitched, she stood on her head, she sat on her tail, she rolled, she groaned, and we had to hold on while on deck and cling to our bunks when below, in a constant effort of body and worry of mind.

"One night Mahon spoke through the small window of my berth. It opened right into my very bed, and I was lying there sleepless, in my boots, feeling as though I had not slept for years, and could not if I tried. He said excitedly—

"'You got the sounding-rod in here, Marlow? I can't get the pumps to suck. By God! it's no child's play.'

"I gave him the sounding-rod and lay down again, trying to think of various things—but I thought only of the pumps. When I came on deck they were still at it, and my watch relieved at the pumps. By the light of the lantern brought on deck to examine the sounding-rod I caught a glimpse of their weary, serious faces. We pumped all the four hours. We pumped all night, all day, all the week—watch and watch. She was working herself loose, and leaked badly—not enough to drown us at once, but enough to kill us with the work at the pumps. And while we pumped the ship was going from us piecemeal: the bulwarks went, the stanchions were torn out, the ventilators smashed, the cabin-door burst in. There was not a dry spot in the ship. She was being gutted bit by bit. The long-boat changed, as if by magic, into matchwood where she stood in her gripes. I had lashed her myself, and was rather proud of my handiwork, which had withstood so long the malice of the sea. And we pumped. And there was no break in the weather. The sea was white like a sheet of foam, like a caldron of boiling milk; there was not a break in the clouds, no—not the size of a man's hand—no, not for so much as ten seconds. There was for us no sky, there were for us no stars, no sun, no universe—nothing but angry clouds and an infuriated sea. We pumped watch and watch, for dear life; and it seemed to last for months, for years, for all eternity, as though we had been dead and gone to a hell for sailors. We forgot the day of the week, the name of the month, what year it was, and whether we had ever been ashore. The sails blew away, she lay broadside on under a weather-cloth, the ocean poured over her, and we did not care. We turned those handles, and had the eyes of idiots. As soon as we had crawled on deck I used to take a round turn with a rope about the men, the pumps, and the mainmast, and we turned, we turned incessantly, with the water to our waists, to our necks, over our heads. It was all one. We had forgotten how it felt to be dry.

"And there was somewhere in me the thought: By Jove! this is the deuce of an adventure—something you read about; and it is my first voyage as second mate—and I am only twenty—and here I am lasting it out as well as any of these men, and keeping my chaps up to the mark. I was pleased. I would not have given up the experience for worlds. I had moments of exultation. Whenever the old dismantled craft pitched heavily with her counter high in the air, she seemed to me to throw up, like an appeal, like a defiance, like a cry to the clouds without mercy, the words written on her stern: 'Judea, London. Do or Die.'

"O youth! The strength of it, the faith of it, the imagination of it! To me she was not an old rattletrap carting about the world a lot of coal for a freight—to me she was the endeavour, the test, the trial of life. I think of her with pleasure, with affection, with regret—as you would think of someone dead you have loved. I shall never forget her. . . . Pass the bottle.

"One night when tied to the mast, as I explained, we were pumping on, deafened with the wind, and without spirit enough in us to wish ourselves dead, a heavy sea crashed aboard and swept clean over us. As soon as I got my breath I shouted, as in duty bound, 'Keep on, boys!' when suddenly I felt something hard floating on deck strike the calf of my leg. I made a grab at it and missed. It was so dark we could not see each other's faces within a foot—you understand.

"After that thump the ship kept quiet for a while, and the thing, whatever it was, struck my leg again. This time I caught it—and it was a saucepan. At first, being stupid with fatigue and thinking of nothing but the pumps, I did not understand what I had in my hand. Suddenly it dawned upon me, and I shouted, 'Boys, the house on deck is gone. Leave this, and let's look for the cook.'

"There was a deck-house forward, which contained the galley, the cook's berth, and the quarters of the crew. As we had expected for days to see it swept away, the hands had been ordered to sleep in the cabin—the only safe place in the ship. The steward, Abraham, however, persisted in clinging to his berth, stupidly, like a mule—from sheer fright I believe, like an animal that won't leave a stable falling in an earthquake. So we went to look for him. It was chancing death, since once out of our lashings we were as exposed as if on a raft. But we went. The house was shattered as if a shell had exploded inside. Most of it had gone overboard—stove, men's quarters, and their property, all was gone;

but two posts, holding a portion of the bulkhead to which Abraham's bunk was attached, remained as if by a miracle. We groped in the ruins and came upon this, and there he was, sitting in his bunk, surrounded by foam and wreckage, jabbering cheerfully to himself. He was out of his mind; completely and for ever mad, with this sudden shock coming upon the fag-end of his endurance. We snatched him up, lugged him aft, and pitched him head-first down the cabin companion. You understand there was no time to carry him down with infinite precautions and wait to see how he got on. Those below would pick him up at the bottom of the stairs all right. We were in a hurry to go back to the pumps. That business could not wait. A bad leak is an inhuman thing.

"One would think that the sole purpose of that fiendish gale had been to make a lunatic of that poor devil of a mulatto. It eased before morning, and next day the sky cleared, and as the sea went down the leak took up. When it came to bending a fresh set of sails the crew demanded to put back—and really there was nothing else to do. Boats gone, decks swept clean, cabin gutted, men without a stitch but what they stood in, stores spoiled, ship strained. We put her head for home, and—would you believe it? The wind came east right in our teeth. It blew fresh, it blew continuously. We had to beat up every inch of the way, but she did not leak so badly, the water keeping comparatively smooth. Two hours' pumping in every four is no joke—but it kept her afloat as far as Falmouth.

"The good people there live on casualties of the sea, and no doubt were glad to see us. A hungry crowd of shipwrights sharpened their chisels at the sight of that carcass of a ship. And, by Jove! they had pretty pickings off us before they were done. I fancy the owner was already in a tight place. There were delays. Then it was decided to take part of the cargo out and caulk her topsides. This was done, the repairs finished, cargo reshipped; a new crew came on board, and we went out—for Bankok. At the end of a week we were back again. The crew said they weren't going to Bankok—a hundred and fifty days' passage—in a something hooker that wanted pumping eight hours out of the twenty-four; and the nautical papers inserted again the little paragraph: 'Judea. Barque. Tyne to Bankok; coal; put back to Falmouth leaky and with crew refusing duty.'

"There were more delays—more tinkering. The owner came down for a day, and said she was as right as a little fiddle. Poor old Captain Beard looked like the ghost of a Geordie skipper—through the worry and humiliation of it. Remember he was sixty, and it was his first command. Mahon said it was a foolish business, and would end badly.

I loved the ship more than ever, and wanted awfully to get to Bankok. To Bankok! Magic name, blessed name. Mesopotamia wasn't a patch on it. Remember I was twenty, and it was my first second-mate's billet, and the East was waiting for me.

"We went out and anchored in the outer roads with a fresh crew—the third. She leaked worse than ever. It was as if those confounded shipwrights had actually made a hole in her. This time we did not even go outside. The crew simply refused to man the windlass.

"They towed us back to the inner harbour, and we became a fixture, a feature, an institution of the place. People pointed us out to visitors as 'That 'ere barque that's going to Bankok—has been here six months—put back three times.' On holidays the small boys pulling about in boats would hail, '*Judea,* ahoy!' and if a head showed above the rail shouted, 'Where you bound to?—Bankok?' and jeered. We were only three on board. The poor old skipper mooned in the cabin. Mahon undertook the cooking, and unexpectedly developed all a Frenchman's genius for preparing nice little messes. I looked languidly after the rigging. We became citizens of Falmouth. Every shopkeeper knew us. At the barber's or tobacconist's they asked familiarly, 'Do you think you will ever get to Bankok?' Meantime the owner, the underwriters, and the charterers squabbled amongst themselves in London, and our pay went on. . . . Pass the bottle.

"It was horrid. Morally it was worse than pumping for life. It seemed as though we had been forgotten by the world, belonged to nobody, would get nowhere; it seemed that, as if bewitched, we would have to live for ever and ever in that inner harbour, a derision and a byword to generations of long-shore loafers and dishonest boatmen. I obtained three months' pay and a five days' leave, and made a rush for London. It took me a day to get there and pretty well another to come back—but three months' pay went all the same. I don't know what I did with it. I went to a music-hall, I believe, lunched, dined, and supped in a swell place in Regent Street, and was back to time, with nothing but a complete set of Byron's works and a new railway rug to show for three months' work. The boat-man who pulled me off to the ship said: 'Hallo! I thought you had left the old thing. *She* will never get to Bankok.' 'That's all *you* know about it,' I said scornfully—but I didn't like that prophecy at all.

"Suddenly a man, some kind of agent to somebody, appeared with full powers. He had grog-blossoms all over his face, an indomitable energy, and was a jolly soul. We leaped into life again. A hulk came alongside, took our cargo, and then we went into dry dock to get our copper stripped. No wonder she leaked. The poor thing, strained beyond endurance by the gale, had, as if in disgust, spat out all the oakum of her lower seams. She was recaulked, new coppered and made as tight as a bottle. We went back to the hulk and reshipped our cargo.

"Then, on a fine moonlight night, all the rats left the ship.

"We had been infested with them. They had destroyed our sails, consumed more stores than the crew, affably shared our beds and our dangers, and now, when the ship was made seaworthy, concluded to clear out. I called Mahon to enjoy the spectacle. Rat after rat appeared on our rail, took a last look over his shoulder, and leaped with a hollow thud into the empty hulk. We tried to count them, but soon lost the tale. Mahon said: 'Well, well! don't talk to me about the intelligence of rats. They ought to have left before, when we had that narrow squeak from foundering. There you have the proof how silly is the superstition about them. They leave a good ship for an old rotten hulk, where there is nothing to eat, too, the fools! . . . I don't believe they know what is safe or what is good for them, any more than you or I.'

"And after some more talk we agreed that the wisdom of rats had been grossly overrated, being in fact no greater than that of men.

"The story of the ship was known, by this, all up the Channel from Land's End to the Forelands, and we could get no crew on the south coast. They sent us one all complete from Liverpool, and we left once more—for Bankok.

"We had fair breezes, smooth water right into the tropics, and the old *Judea* lumbered along in the sunshine. When she went eight knots everything cracked aloft, and we tied our caps to our heads; but mostly she strolled on at the rate of three miles an hour. What could you expect? She was tired—that old ship. Her youth was where mine is— where yours is—you fellows who listen to this yarn; and what friend would throw your years and your weariness in your face? We didn't grumble at her. To us aft, at least, it seemed as though we had been born in her, reared in her, had lived in her for ages, had never known any other ship. I would just as soon have abused the old village church at home for not being a cathedral.

"And for me there was also my youth to make me patient. There was all the East before me, and all life, and the thought that I had been tried in that ship and had come out pretty well. And I thought of men of old who, centuries ago, went that road in ships that sailed no better, to the land of palms, and spices, and yellow sands, and of brown nations ruled by kings more cruel than Nero the Roman, and more splendid than Solomon the Jew. The old bark lumbered on, heavy with her age and the burden of her cargo, while I lived the life of youth in ignorance and hope. She lumbered on through an interminable procession of days; and the fresh gilding flashed back at the setting sun, seemed to cry out over the darkening sea the words painted on her stern, '*Judea*, London. Do or Die.'

"Then we entered the Indian Ocean and steered northerly for Java Head. The winds were light. Weeks slipped by. She crawled on, do or die, and people at home began to think of posting us as overdue.

"One Saturday evening, I being off duty, the men asked me to give them an extra bucket of water or so—for washing clothes. As I did not wish to screw on the fresh-water pump so late, I went forward whistling, and with a key in my hand to unlock the forepeak scuttle, intending to serve the water out of a spare tank we kept there.

"The smell down below was as unexpected as it was frightful. One would have thought hundreds of paraffin-lamps had been flaring and smoking in that hole for days. I was glad to get out. The man with me coughed and said, 'Funny smell, sir.' I answered negligently, 'It's good for the health they say,' and walked aft.

"The first thing I did was to put my head down the square of the midship ventilator. As I lifted the lid a visible breath, something like a thin fog, a puff of faint haze, rose from the opening. The ascending air was hot, and had a heavy, sooty, paraffiny smell. I gave one sniff, and put down the lid gently. It was no use choking myself. The cargo was on fire.

"Next day she began to smoke in earnest. You see it was to be expected, for though the coal was of a safe kind, that cargo had been so handled, so broken up with handling, that it looked more like smithy coal than anything else. Then it had been wetted—more than once. It rained all the time we were taking it back from the hulk, and now with this long passage it got heated, and there was another case of spontaneous combustion.

"The captain called us into the cabin. He had a chart spread on the table, and looked unhappy. He said, 'The coast of West Australia is near, but I mean to proceed to our destination. It is the hurricane month, too; but we will just keep her head for Bankok, and fight the fire. No more putting back anywhere, if we all get roasted. We will try first to stifle this 'ere damned combustion by want of air.'

"We tried. We battened down everything, and still she smoked. The smoke kept coming out through imperceptible crevices; it forced itself through bulkheads and covers; it oozed here and there and everywhere in slender threads, in an invisible film, in an incomprehensible manner. It made its way into the cabin, into the forecastle; it poisoned the sheltered places on the deck, it could be sniffed as high as the main-yard. It was clear that if the smoke came out the air came in. This was disheartening. This combustion refused to be stifled.

"We resolved to try water, and took the hatches off. Enormous volumes of smoke, whitish, yellowish, thick, greasy, misty, choking, ascended as high as the trucks. All hands cleared out aft. Then the poisonous cloud blew away, and we went back to work in a smoke that was no thicker now than that of an ordinary factory chimney.

"We rigged the force-pump, got the hose along, and by and by it burst. Well, it was as old as the ship—a prehistoric hose, and past repair. Then we pumped with the feeble head-pump, drew water with buckets, and in this way managed in time to pour lots of Indian Ocean into the main hatch. The bright stream flashed in sunshine, fell into a layer of white crawling smoke, and vanished on the black surface of coal. Steam ascended mingling with the smoke. We poured salt water as into a barrel without a bottom. It was our fate to pump in that ship, to pump out of her, to pump into her; and after keeping water out of her to save our-selves from being drowned, we frantically poured water into her to save ourselves from being burnt.

"And she crawled on, do or die, in the serene weather. The sky was a miracle of purity, a miracle of azure. The sea was polished, was blue, was pellucid, was sparkling like a precious stone; extending on all sides, all round to the horizon—as if the whole terrestrial globe had been one jewel, one colossal sapphire, a single gem fashioned into a planet. And on the lustre of the great calm waters the *Judea* glided imperceptibly, enveloped in languid and unclean vapours, in a lazy cloud that drifted to leeward, light and slow; a pestiferous cloud defiling the splendour of sea and sky.

"All this time of course we saw no fire. The cargo smouldered at the bottom somewhere. Once Mahon, as we were working side by side, said to me with a queer smile: 'Now, if she only would spring a tidy leak—like that time when we first left the Channel—it would put a stopper on this fire. Wouldn't it?' I remarked irrelevantly, 'Do you remember the rats?'

"We fought the fire and sailed the ship too as carefully as though nothing had been the matter. The steward cooked and attended on us. Of the other twelve men, eight worked while four rested. Everyone took his turn, captain included. There was equality, and if not exactly fraternity, then a deal of good feeling. Sometimes a man, as he dashed bucketful of water down the hatchway, would yell out, 'Hurrah for

Bankok!' and the rest laughed. But generally we were taciturn and serious—and thirsty. Oh! how thirsty! And we had to be careful with the water. Strict allowance. The ship smoked, the sun blazed. . . . Pass the bottle.

"We tried everything. We even made an attempt to dig down to the fire. No good, of course. No man could remain more than a minute below. Mahon, who went first, fainted there, and the man who went to fetch him out did likewise. We lugged them out on deck. Then I leaped down to show how easily it could be done. They had learned wisdom by that time, and contented themselves by fishing for me with a chainhook tied to a broom-handle, I believe. I did not offer to go and fetch up my shovel, which was left down below.

"Things began to look bad. We put the long-boat into the water. The second boat was ready to swing out. We had also another, a 14-foot thing, on davits aft, where it was quite safe.

"Then, behold, the smoke suddenly decreased. We redoubled our efforts to flood the bottom of the ship. In two days there was no smoke at all. Everybody was on the broad grin. This was on a Friday. On Saturday no work, but sailing the ship of course, was done. The men washed their clothes and their faces for the first time in a fortnight, and had a special dinner given them. They spoke of spontaneous combustion with contempt, and implied *they* were the boys to put out combustions. Somehow we all felt as though we each had inherited a large fortune. But a beastly smell of burning hung about the ship. Captain Beard had hollow eyes and sunken cheeks. I had never noticed so much before how twisted and bowed he was. He and Mahon prowled soberly about hatches and ventilators, sniffing. It struck me suddenly poor Mahon was a very, very old chap. As to me, I was as pleased and proud as though I had helped to win a great naval battle. O! Youth!

"The night was fine. In the morning a homeward-bound ship passed us hull down—the first we had seen for months; but we were nearing the land at last, Java Head being about 190 miles off, and nearly due north.

"Next day it was my watch on deck from eight to twelve. At breakfast the captain observed, 'It's wonderful how that smell hangs about the cabin.' About ten, the mate being on the poop, I stepped down on the main-deck for a moment. The carpenter's bench stood abaft the main-mast: I leaned against it sucking at my pipe, and the carpenter, a young chap, came to talk to me. He remarked, 'I think we have done very well, haven't we?' and then I perceived with annoyance the fool was trying to tilt the bench. I said curtly, 'Don't, Chips,' and immediately became aware of a queer sensation, of an absurd delusion,—I seemed somehow to be in the air. I heard all round me like a pent-up breath released—as if a thousand giants simultaneously had said Phoo!—and felt a dull concussion which made my ribs ache suddenly. No doubt about it—I was in the air, and my body was describing a short parabola. But short as it was, I had the time to think several thoughts in, as far as I can remember, the following order: 'This can't be the carpenter—What is it?—Some accident—Submarine volcano?—Coals, gas!—By Jove! we are being blown up—Everybody's dead—I am falling into the after-hatch—I see fire in it.'

"The coal-dust suspended in the air of the hold had glowed dull-red at the moment of the explosion. In the twinkling of an eye, in an infinitesimal fraction of a second since the first tilt of the bench, I was sprawling full length on the cargo. I picked myself up and scrambled out. It was quick like a rebound. The deck was a wilderness of smashed timber, lying crosswise like trees in a wood after a hurricane; an immense curtain of soiled rags waved gently before me—it was the mainsail blown to strips. I thought, The masts will be toppling over directly; and to get out of the way bolted on all-fours towards the poop-ladder. The first person I saw was Mahon, with eyes like saucers, his mouth open, and the long white hair standing straight on end round his head like a silver halo. He was just about to go down when the sight of the main-deck stirring, heaving up, and changing into splinters before his eyes, petrified him on the top step. I stared at him in unbelief, and he stared at me with a queer kind of shocked curiosity. I did not know that I had no hair, no eyebrows, no eyelashes, that my young moustache was burnt off, that my face was black, one cheek laid open, my nose cut, and my chin bleeding. I had lost my cap, one of my slippers, and my shirt was torn to rags. Of all this I was not aware. I was amazed to see the ship still afloat, the poop-deck whole—and, most of all, to see anybody alive. Also the peace of the sky and the serenity of the sea were distinctly surprising. I suppose I expected to see them convulsed with horror. . . . Pass the bottle.

"There was a voice hailing the ship from somewhere—in the air, in the sky—I couldn't tell. Presently I saw the captain—and he was mad. He asked me eagerly, 'Where's the cabin-table?' and to hear such a question was a frightful shock. I had just been blown up, you understand, and vibrated with that experience,—I wasn't quite sure whether I was alive. Mahon began to stamp with both feet and yelled at him, 'Good God! don't you see the deck's blown out of her?' I found my voice, and stammered out as if conscious of some gross neglect of duty, 'I don't know where the cabin-table is.' It was like an absurd dream.

"Do you know what he wanted next? Well, he wanted to trim the yards. Very placidly, and as if lost in thought, he insisted on having the foreyard squared. 'I don't know if there's anybody alive,' said Mahon, almost tearfully. 'Surely,' he said, gently, 'there will be enough left to square the foreyard.'

"The old chap, it seems, was in his own berth winding up the chronometers, when the shock sent him spinning. Immediately it occurred to him—as he said afterwards—that the ship had struck something, and he ran out into the cabin. There, he saw, the cabin-table had vanished somewhere. The deck being blown up, it had fallen down into the lazarette of course. Where we had our breakfast that morning he saw only a great hole in the floor. This appeared to him so awfully mysterious, and impressed him so immensely, that what he saw and heard after he got on deck were mere trifles in comparison. And, mark, he noticed directly the wheel deserted and his barque off her course—and his only thought was to get that miserable, stripped, undecked, smouldering shell of a ship back again with her head pointing at her port of destination. Bankok! That's what he was after. I tell you this quiet, bowed, bandy-legged, almost deformed little man was immense in the singleness of his idea and in his placid ignorance of our agitation. He motioned us forward with a commanding gesture, and went to take the wheel himself.

"Yes; that was the first thing we did—trim the yards of that wreck! No one was killed, or even disabled, but everyone was more or less hurt. You should have seen them! Some were in rags, with black faces, like coal-heavers, like sweeps, and had bullet heads that seemed closely cropped, but were in fact singed to the skin. Others, of the watch below, awakened by being shot out from their collapsing bunks, shivered incessantly, and kept on groaning even as we went about our work. But they all worked. That crew of Liverpool hard cases had in them the right stuff. It's my experience they always have. It is the sea that gives it—the vastness, the loneliness surrounding their dark stolid souls. Ah! Well! we stumbled, we crept, we fell, we barked our shins on the wreckage, we hauled. The masts stood, but we did not know how much they might be charred down below. It was nearly calm, but a long swell ran from the west and made her roll. They might go at any moment. We looked at them with apprehension. One could not foresee which way they would fall.

"Then we retreated aft and looked about us. The deck was a tangle of planks on edge, of planks on end, of splinters, of ruined woodwork. The masts rose from that chaos like big trees above a matted undergrowth. The interstices of that mass of wreckage were full of something whitish, sluggish, stirring—of something that was like a greasy fog. The smoke of the invisible fire was coming up again, was trailing, like a poisonous thick mist in some valley choked with dead wood. Already lazy wisps were beginning to curl upwards amongst the mass of splinters. Here and there a piece of timber, stuck upright, resembled a post. Half of a fife-rail had been shot through the foresail, and the sky made a patch of glorious blue in the ignobly soiled canvas. A portion of several boards holding together had fallen across the rail, and one end protruded overboard, like a gangway leading upon nothing, like a gangway leading over the deep sea, leading to death—as if inviting us to walk the plank at once and be done with our ridiculous troubles. And still the air, the sky—a ghost, something invisible was hailing the ship.

"Someone had the sense to look over, and there was the helmsman, who had impulsively jumped overboard, anxious to come back. He yelled and swam lustily like a merman, keeping up with the ship. We threw him a rope, and presently he stood amongst us streaming with water and very crestfallen. The captain had surrendered the wheel, and apart, elbow on rail and chin in hand, gazed at the sea wistfully. We asked ourselves, What next? I thought, Now, this is something like. This is great. I wonder what will happen. O youth!

"Suddenly Mahon sighted a steamer far astern. Captain Beard said, 'We may do something with her yet.' We hoisted two flags, which said in the international language of the sea, 'On fire. Want immediate assistance.' The steamer grew bigger rapidly, and by and by spoke with two flags on her foremast, 'I am coming to your assistance.'

"In half an hour she was abreast, to windward, within hail, and rolling slightly, with her engines stopped. We lost our composure, and yelled all together with excitement, 'We've been blown up'. A man in a white helmet, on the bridge, cried, 'Yes! All right! all right!' and he nodded his head, and smiled, and made soothing motions with his hand as though at a lot of frightened children. One of the boats dropped in the water, and walked towards us upon the sea with her long oars. Four Calashes pulled a swinging stroke. This was my first sight of Malay seamen. I've known them since, but what struck me then was their unconcern: they came alongside, and even the bowman standing up and holding to our main-chains with the book-hook did not deign to lift his head for a glance. I thought people who had been blown up deserved more attention.

"A little man, dry like a chip and agile like a monkey, clambered up. It was the mate of the steamer. He gave one look, and cried, 'O boys— you had better quit.'

"We were silent. He talked apart with the captain for a time,—seemed to argue with him. Then they went away together to the steamer.

"When our skipper came back we learned that the steamer was the *Somerville,* Captain Nash, from West Australia to Singapore *via* Batavia with mails, and that the agreement was she should tow us to Anjer or Batavia, if possible, where we could extinguish the fire by scuttling, and then proceed on our voyage—to Bankok! The old man seemed excited. 'We will do it yet,' he said to Mahon, fiercely. He shook his fist at the sky. Nobody else said a word.

"At noon the steamer began to tow. She went ahead slim and high, and what was left of the *Judea* followed at the end of seventy fathom of tow-rope,—followed her swiftly like a cloud of smoke with mast-heads protruding above. We went aloft to furl the sails. We coughed on the yards, and were careful about the bunts. Do you see the lot of us there, putting a neat furl on the sails of that ship doomed to arrive nowhere? There was not a man who didn't think that at any moment the masts would topple over. From aloft we could not see the ship for smoke, and they worked carefully, passing the gaskets with even turns. 'Harbour furl—aloft there!' cried Mahon from below.

"You understand this? I don't think one of those chaps expected to get down in the usual way. When we did I heard them saying to each other, 'Well, I thought we would come down overboard, in a lump—sticks and all—blame me if I didn't.' 'That's what I was thinking to myself,' would answer wearily another battered and bandaged scarecrow. And, mind, these were men without the drilled-in habit of obedience. To an onlooker they would be a lot of profane scallywags without a redeeming point. What made them do it—what made them obey me when I, thinking consciously how fine it was, made them drop the bunt of the foresail twice to try and do it better? What? They had no professional reputation—no examples, no praise. It wasn't a sense of duty; they all knew well enough how to shirk, and laze, and dodge—when they had a mind to it—and mostly they had. Was it the two pounds ten a-month that sent them there? They didn't think their pay half good enough. No, it was something in them, something inborn and subtle and everlasting. I don't say positively that the crew of a French or German merchantman wouldn't have done it, but I doubt whether it would have been done in the same way. There was a completeness in it, something solid like a principle, and masterful like an instinct—a disclosure of something secret—of that hidden something, that gift of good or evil that makes racial difference, that shapes the fate of nations.

"It was that night at ten that, for the first time since we had been fighting it, we saw the fire. The speed of the towing had fanned the smouldering destruction. A blue gleam appeared forward, shining below the wreck of the deck. It wavered in patches, it seemed to stir and creep like the light of a glowworm. I saw it first, and told Mahon. 'Then the game's up,' he said. 'We had better stop this towing, or she will burst out suddenly fore and aft before we can clear out.' We set up a yell; rang bells to attract their attention; they towed on. At last Mahon and I had to crawl forward and cut the rope with an axe. There was no time to cast off the lashings. Red tongues could be seen licking the wilderness of splinters under our feet as we made our way back to the poop.

"Of course they very soon found out in the steamer that the rope was gone. She gave a loud blast of her whistle, her lights were seen sweeping in a wide circle, she came up ranging close alongside, and stopped. We were all in a tight group on the poop looking at her. Every man had saved a little bundle or a bag. Suddenly a conical flame with a twisted top shot up forward and threw upon the black sea a circle of light, with the two vessels side by side and heaving gently in its centre. Captain Beard had been sitting on the gratings still and mute for hours, but now he rose slowly and advanced in front of us, to the mizzen-shrouds. Captain Nash hailed: 'Come along! Look sharp. I have mail-bags on board. I will take you and your boats to Singapore.'

" 'Thank you! No!' said our skipper. 'We must see the last of the ship.'

" 'I can't stand by any longer,' shouted the other. 'Mails—you know.'

" 'Ay! ay! We are all right.'

" 'Very well! I'll report you in Singapore. . . . Good-bye!'

"He waved his hand. Our men dropped their bundles quietly. The steamer moved ahead, and passing out of the circle of light, vanished at once from our sight, dazzled by the fire which burned fiercely. And then I knew that I would see the East first as commander of a small boat. I thought it fine; and the fidelity to the old ship was fine. We should see the last of her. Oh, the glamour of youth! Oh, the fire of it, more dazzling than the flames of the burning ship, throwing a magic light on the wide earth, leaping audaciously to the sky, presently to be quenched by time, more cruel, more pitiless, more bitter than the sea—and like the flames of the burning ship surrounded by an impenetrable night.

    *   *   *   *   *   *   *

"The old man warned us in his gentle and inflexible way that it was part of our duty to save for the underwriters as much as we could of the ship's gear. Accordingly we went to work aft, while she blazed forward to give us plenty of light. We lugged out a lot of rubbish. What didn't we save? An old barometer fixed with an absurd quantity of screws nearly cost me my life: a sudden rush of smoke came upon me, and I just got away in time. There were various stores, bolts of canvas, coils of rope; the poop looked like a marine bazaar, and the boats were lumbered to the gunwales. One would have thought the old man wanted to take as much as he could of his first command with him. He was very, very quiet, but off his balance evidently. Would you believe it? He wanted to take a length of old stream-cable and a kedge-anchor with him in the long-boat. We said, 'Ay, ay, sir,' deferentially, and on the quiet let the things slip overboard. The heavy medicine-chest went that way, two bags of green coffee, tins of paint—fancy, paint!—a whole lot of things. Then I was ordered with two hands into the boats to make a stowage and get them ready against the time it would be proper for us to leave the ship.

"We put everything straight, stepped the long-boat's mast for our skipper, who was to take charge of her, and I was not sorry to sit down for a moment. My face felt raw, every limb ached as if broken, I was aware of all my ribs, and would have sworn to a twist in the backbone. The boats, fast astern, lay in a deep shadow, and all around I could see the circle of the sea lighted by the fire. A gigantic flame arose forward straight and clear. It flared fierce, with noises like the whirr of wings, with rumbles as of thunder. There were cracks, detonations, and from the cone of flame the sparks flew upwards, as man is born to trouble, to leaky ships, and to ships that burn.

"What bothered me was that the ship, lying broadside to the swell and to such a wind as there was—a mere breath—the boats would not keep astern where they were safe, but persisted, in a pig-headed way boats have, in getting under the counter and then swinging alongside. They were knocking about dangerously and coming near the flame, while the ship rolled on them, and, of course, there was always the danger of the masts going over the side at any moment. I and my two boat-keepers kept them off as best we could, with oars and boat-hooks; but to be constantly at it became exasperating, since there was no reason why we should not leave at once. We could not see those on board, nor could we imagine what caused the delay. The boat-keepers were swearing feebly, and I had not only my share of the work but also had to keep at it two men who showed a constant inclination to lay themselves down and let things slide.

"At last I hailed, 'On deck there,' and someone looked over. 'We're ready here,' I said. The head disappeared, and very soon popped up again. 'The captain says, All right, sir, and to keep the boats well clear of the ship.'

"Half an hour passed. Suddenly there was a frightful racket, rattle, clanking of chain, hiss of water, and millions of sparks flew up into the shivering column of smoke that stood leaning slightly above the ship. The cat-heads had burned away, and the two red-hot anchors had gone to the bottom, tearing out after them two hundred fathom of red-hot chain. The ship trembled, the mass of flame swayed as if ready to collapse, and the fore top-gallant-mast fell. It darted down like an arrow of fire, shot under, and instantly leaping up within an oar's-length of the boats, floated quietly, very black on the luminous sea. I hailed the deck again. After some time a man in an unexpectedly cheerful but also muffled tone, as though he had been trying to speak with his mouth shut, informed me, 'Coming directly, sir,' and vanished. For a long time I heard nothing but the whirr and roar of the fire. There were also whistling sounds. The boats jumped, tugged at the painters, ran at each other playfully, knocked their sides together, or, do what we would, swung in a bunch against the ship's side. I couldn't stand it any longer, and swarming up a rope, clambered aboard over the stern.

"It was as bright as day. Coming up like this, the sheet of fire facing me was a terrifying sight, and the heat seemed hardly bearable at first. On a settee cushion dragged out of the cabin Captain Beard, his legs drawn up and one arm under his head, slept with the light playing on him. Do you know what the rest were busy about? They were sitting on deck right aft, round an open case, eating bread and cheese and drinking bottled stout.

"On the background of flames twisting in fierce tongues above their heads they seemed at home like salamanders, and looked like a band of desperate pirates. The fire sparkled in the whites of their eyes, gleamed on patches of white skin seen through the torn shirts. Each had the marks as of a battle about him—bandaged heads, tied-up arms, a strip of dirty rag round a knee—and each man had a bottle between his legs and a chunk of cheese in his hand. Mahon got up. With his handsome and disreputable head, his hooked profile, his long white beard, and with an uncorked bottle in his hand, he resembled one of those reckless sea-robbers of old making merry amidst violence and disaster. 'The last meal on board,' he explained solemnly. 'We had nothing to eat all day, and it was no use leaving all this.' He flourished the bottle and indicated the sleeping skipper. 'He said he couldn't swallow anything, so I got him to lie down,' he went on; and as I stared, 'I don't know whether you are aware, young fellow, the man had no sleep to speak of for days—and there will be dam' little sleep in the boats.' 'There will be no boats by-and-by if you fool about much longer,' I said, indignantly. I walked up to the skipper and shook him by the shoulder. At last he opened his eyes, but did not move. 'Time to leave her, sir,' I said quietly.

"He got up painfully, looked at the flames, at the sea sparkling round the ship, and black, black as ink farther away; he looked at the stars shining dim through a thin veil of smoke in a sky black, black as Erebus.

" 'Youngest first,' he said.

"And the ordinary seaman, wiping his mouth with the back of his hand, got up, clambered over the taffrail, and vanished. Others followed. One, on the point of going over, stopped short to drain his bottle, and with a great swing of his arm flung it at the fire. 'Take this!' he cried.

"The skipper lingered disconsolately, and we left him to commune alone for a while with his first command. Then I went up again and brought him away at last. It was time. The ironwork on the poop was hot to the touch.

"Then the painter of the long-boat was cut, and the three boats, tied together, drifted clear of the ship. It was just sixteen hours after the explosion when we abandoned her. Mahon had charge of the second boat, and I had the smallest—the 14-foot thing. The long-boat would have taken the lot of us; but the skipper said we must save as much property as we could—for the underwriters—and so I got my first command. I had two men with me, a bag of biscuits, a few tins of meat, and a breaker of water. I was ordered to keep close to the long-boat, that in case of bad weather we might be taken into her.

"And do you know what I thought? I thought I would part company as soon as I could. I wanted to have my first command all to myself. I wasn't going to sail in a squadron if there were a chance for independent cruising. I would make land by myself. I would beat the other boats. Youth! All youth! The silly, charming, beautiful youth.

"But we did not make a start at once. We must see the last of the ship. And so the boats drifted about that night, heaving and setting on the swell. The men dozed, waked, sighed, groaned. I looked at the burning ship.

"Between the darkness of earth and heaven she was burning fiercely upon a disc of purple sea shot by the blood-red play of gleams; upon a disc of water glittering and sinister. A high, clear flame, an immense and lonely flame, ascended from the ocean, and from its summit the black smoke poured continuously at the sky. She burned furiously; mournful and imposing like a funeral pile kindled in the night, surrounded by the sea, watched over by the stars. A magnificent death had come like a grace, like a gift, like a reward to that old ship at the end of her laborious days. The surrender of her weary ghost to the keeping of stars and sea was stirring like the sight of a glorious triumph. The masts fell just before daybreak, and for a moment there was a burst and turmoil of sparks that seemed to fill with flying fire the night patient and watchful, the vast night lying silent upon the sea. At daylight she was only a charred shell, floating still under a cloud of smoke and bearing a glowing mass of coal within.

"Then the oars were got out, and the boats forming in a line moved round her remains as if in procession—the long-boat leading. As we pulled across her stern a slim dart of fire shot out viciously at us, and suddenly she went down, head first, in a great hiss of steam. The unconsumed stern was the last to sink; but the paint had gone, had cracked, had peeled off, and there were no letters, there was no word, no stubborn device that was like her soul, to flash at the rising sun her creed and her name.

"We made our way north. A breeze sprang up, and about noon all the boats came together for the last time. I had no mast or sail in mine, but I made a mast out of a spare oar and hoisted a boat-awning for a sail, with a boat-hook for a yard. She was certainly over-masted, but I had the satisfaction of knowing that with the wind aft I could beat the other two. I had to wait for them. Then we all had a look at the captain's chart, and, after a sociable meal of hard bread and water, got our last instructions. These were simple: steer north, and keep together as much as possible. 'Be careful with that jury-rig, Marlow,' said the captain; and Mahon, as I sailed proudly past his boat, wrinkled his curved nose and hailed, 'You will sail that ship of yours under water, if you don't look out, young fellow.' He was a malicious old man—and may the deep sea where he sleeps now rock him gently, rock him tenderly to the end of time!

"Before sunset a thick rain-squall passed over the two boats, which were far astern, and that was the last I saw of them for a time. Next day I sat steering my cockle-shell—my first command—with nothing but water and sky around me. I did sight in the afternoon the upper sails of a ship far away, but said nothing, and my men did not notice her. You see I was afraid she might be homeward bound, and I had no mind to turn back from the portals of the East. I was steering for Java—another blessed name—like Bankok, you know. I steered many days.

"I need not tell you what it is to be knocking about in an open boat. I remember nights and days of calm, when we pulled, we pulled, and the boat seemed to stand still, as if bewitched within the circle of the sea horizon. I remember the heat, the deluge of rain-squalls that kept us baling for dear life (but filled our water-cask), and I remember sixteen hours on end with a mouth dry as a cinder and a steering-oar over the stern to keep my first command head on to a breaking sea. I did not know how good a man I was till then. I remember the drawn faces, the dejected figures of my two men, and I remember my youth and the feeling that will never come back any more—the feeling that I could last for ever, outlast the sea, the earth, and all men; the deceitful feeling that lures us on to joys, to perils, to love, to vain effort—to death; the triumphant conviction of strength, the heat of life in the handful of dust, the glow in the heart that with every year grows dim, grows cold, grows small, and expires—and expires, too soon, too soon—before life itself.

"And this is how I see the East. I have seen its secret places and have looked into its very soul; but now I see it always from a small boat, a high outline of mountains, blue and afar in the morning; like faint mist at noon; a jagged wall of purple at sunset. I have the feel of the oar in my hand, the vision of a scorching blue sea in my eyes. And I see a bay, a wide bay, smooth as glass and polished like ice, shimmering in the dark. A red light burns far off upon the gloom of the land, and the night is soft and warm. We drag at the oars with aching arms, and suddenly a puff of wind, a puff faint and tepid and laden with strange odours of blossoms, of aromatic wood, comes out of the still night—the first sigh of the East on my face. That I can never forget. It was impalpable and enslaving, like a charm, like a whispered promise of mysterious delight.

"We had been pulling this finishing spell for eleven hours. Two pulled, and he whose turn it was to rest sat at the tiller. We had made out the red light in that bay and steered for it, guessing it must mark some small coasting port. We passed two vessels, outlandish and high-sterned, sleeping at anchor, and, approaching the light, now very dim, ran the boat's nose against the end of a jutting wharf. We were blind with fatigue. My men dropped the oars and fell off the thwarts as if dead. I made fast to a pile. A current rippled softly. The scented obscurity of the shore was grouped into vast masses, a density of colossal clumps of vegetation, probably—mute and fantastic shapes. And at their foot the semicircle of a beach gleamed faintly, like an illusion. There was not a light, not a stir, not a sound. The mysterious East faced me, perfumed like a flower, silent like death, dark like a grave.

"And I sat weary beyond expression, exulting like a conqueror, sleepless and entranced as if before a profound, a fateful enigma.

"A splashing of oars, a measured dip reverberating on the level of water, intensified by the silence of the shore into loud claps, made me jump up. A boat, a European boat, was coming in. I invoked the name of the dead; I hailed: *Judea* ahoy! A thin shout answered.

"It was the captain. I had beaten the flagship by three hours, and I was glad to hear the old man's voice again, tremulous and tired. 'Is it you, Marlow?' 'Mind the end of that jetty, sir,' I cried.

"He approached cautiously, and brought up with the deep-sea lead-line which we had saved—for the underwriters. I eased my painter and fell alongside. He sat, a broken figure at the stern, wet with dew, his hands clasped in his lap. His men were asleep already. 'I had a terrible time of it,' he murmured. 'Mahon is behind—not very far.' We conversed in whispers, in low whispers, as if afraid to wake up the land. Guns, thunder, earthquakes would not have awakened the men just then.

"Looking round as we talked, I saw away at sea a bright light travelling in the night. 'There's a steamer passing the bay,' I said. She was not passing, she was entering, and she even came close and anchored. 'I wish,' said the old man, 'you would find out whether she is English. Perhaps they could give us a passage somewhere.' He seemed nervously anxious. So by dint of punching and kicking I started one of my men into a state of somnambulism, and giving him an oar, took another and pulled towards the lights of the steamer.

"There was a murmur of voices in her, metallic hollow clangs of the engine-room, footsteps on the deck. Her ports shone, round like dilated eyes. Shapes moved about, and there was a shadowy man high up on the bridge. He heard my oars.

"And then, before I could open my lips, the East spoke to me, but it was in a Western voice. A torrent of words was poured into the enigmatical, the fateful silence; outlandish, angry words, mixed with words and even whole sentences of good English, less strange but even more surprising. The voice swore and cursed violently; it riddled the solemn peace of the bay by a volley of abuse. It began by calling me Pig, and from that went crescendo into unmentionable adjectives—in English. The man up there raged aloud in two languages, and with a sincerity in his fury that almost convinced me I had, in some way, sinned against the harmony of the universe. I could hardly see him, but began to think he would work himself into a fit.

"Suddenly he ceased, and I could hear him snorting and blowing like a porpoise. I said—

" 'What steamer is this, pray?'

" 'Eh? What's this? And who are you?'

" 'Castaway crew of an English barque burnt at sea. We came here to-night. I am the second mate. The captain is in the long-boat, and wishes to know if you would give us a passage somewhere.'

" 'Oh, my goodness! I say. . . . This is the *Celestial* from Singapore on her return trip. I'll arrange with your captain in the morning, . . . and, . . . I say, . . . did you hear me just now?'

" 'I should think the whole bay heard you.'

" 'I thought you were a shore-boat. Now, look here—this infernal lazy scoundrel of a caretaker has gone to sleep again—curse him. The light is out, and I nearly ran foul of the end of this damned jetty. This is the third time he plays me this trick. Now, I ask you, can anybody stand this kind of thing? It's enough to drive a man out of his mind. I'll report him. . . . I'll get the Assistant Resident to give him the sack, by . . . ! See—there's no light. It's out, isn't it? I take you to witness the light's out. There should be a light, you know. A red light on the——'

" 'There was a light,' I said, mildly.

" 'But it's out, man! What's the use of talking like this? You can see for yourself it's out—don't you? If you had to take a valuable steamer along this God-forsaken coast you would want a light, too. I'll kick him from end to end of his miserable wharf. You'll see if I don't, I will——'

" 'So I may tell my captain you'll take us?' I broke in.

" 'Yes, I'll take you. Good-night,' he said, brusquely.

"I pulled back, made fast again to the jetty, and then went to sleep at last. I had faced the silence of the East. I had heard some of its language. But when I opened my eyes again the silence was as complete as though it had never been broken. I was lying in a flood of light, and the sky had never looked so far, so high, before. I opened my eyes and lay without moving.

"And then I saw the men of the East—they were looking at me. The whole length of the jetty was full of people. I saw brown, bronze, yellow faces, the black eyes, the glitter, the colour of an Eastern crowd. And all these beings stared without a murmur, without a sigh, without a movement. They stared down at the boats, at the sleeping men who at night had come to them from the sea. Nothing moved. The fronds of palms stood still against the sky. Not a branch stirred along the shore, and the brown roofs of hidden houses peeped through the green foliage, through the big leaves that hung shining and still like leaves forged of

heavy metal. This was the East of the ancient navigators, so old, so
mysterious, resplendent and sombre, living and unchanged, full of danger
and promise. And these were the men. I sat up suddenly. A wave of
movement passed through the crowd from end to end, passed along the
heads, swayed the bodies, ran along the jetty like a ripple on the water,
like a breath of wind on a field—and all was still again. I see it now—
the wide sweep of the bay, the glittering sands, the wealth of green
infinite and varied, the sea blue like the sea of a dream, the crowd of
attentive faces, the blaze of vivid colour—the water reflecting it all, the
curve of the shore, the jetty, the high-sterned outlandish craft floating still,
and the three boats with the tired men from the West sleeping, unconscious of the land and the people and of the violence of sunshine.
They slept thrown across the thwarts, curled on bottom-boards, in the
careless attitudes of death. The head of the old skipper, leaning back
in the stern of the long-boat, had fallen on his breast, and he looked as
though he would never wake. Farther out old Mahon's face was upturned
to the sky, with the long white beard spread out on his breast, as though
he had been shot where he sat at the tiller; and a man, all in a heap in
the bows of the boat, slept with both arms embracing the stem-head and
with his cheek laid on the gunwale. The East looked at them without
a sound.

"I have known its fascination since; I have seen the mysterious
shores, the still water, the lands of brown nations, where a stealthy
Nemesis lies in wait, pursues, overtakes so many of the conquering race,
who are proud of their wisdom, of their knowledge, of their strength.
But for me all the East is contained in that vision of my youth. It is
all in that moment when I opened my young eyes on it. I came upon it
from a tussle with the sea—and I was young—and I saw it looking at
me. And this is all that is left of it! Only a moment; a moment of
strength, of romance, of glamour—of youth! . . . A flick of sunshine
upon a strange shore, the time to remember, the time for a sigh, and—
good-bye!—Night—Good-bye . . . !"

He drank.

"Ah! The good old time—the good old time. Youth and the sea.
Glamour and the sea! The good, strong sea, the salt, bitter sea, that
could whisper to you and roar at you and knock your breath out of
you."

He drank again.

"By all that's wonderful it is the sea, I believe, the sea itself—or
is it youth alone? Who can tell? But you here—you all had something
out of life: money, love—whatever one gets on shore—and, tell me,

wasn't that the best time, that time when we were young at sea; young
and had nothing, on the sea that gives nothing, except hard knocks—
and sometimes a chance to feel your strength—that only—what you all
regret?"

And we all nodded at him: the man of finance, the man of accounts,
the man of law, we all nodded at him over the polished table that like a
still sheet of brown water reflected our faces, lined, wrinkled; our faces
marked by toil, by deceptions, by success, by love; our weary eyes looking still, looking always, looking anxiously for something out of life,
that while it is expected is already gone—has passed unseen, in a sigh, in
a flash—together with the youth, with the strength, with the romance of
illusions.

SIR WILLIAM WATSON

Wordsworth's Grave

I

THE old rude church, with bare, bald
    tower, is here;
    Beneath its shadow high-born Rotha
      flows;
Rotha, remembering well who slumbers
    near,
    And with cool murmur lulling his re-
      pose.

Rotha, remembering well who slumbers
    near,
    His hills, his lakes, his streams are with
      him yet.
Surely the heart that read her own heart
    clear
    Nature forgets not soon: 'tis we forget.

We that with vagrant soul his fixity
    Have slighted; faithless, done his deep
      faith wrong;
Left him for poorer loves, and bowed the
    knee
    To misbegotten strange new gods of
      song.

Yet, led by hollow ghost or beckoning elf
    Far from her homestead to the desert
      bourn,

The vagrant soul returning to herself,
    Wearily wise, must needs to him re-
      turn.

To him and to the powers that with him
    dwell:—
    Inflowings that divulged not whence
      they came;
And that secluded Spirit unknowable,
    The mystery we make darker with a
      name;

The Somewhat which we name but can-
    not know,
    Ev'n as we name a star and only see
His quenchless flashings forth, which ever
    show
    And ever hide him, and which are not
      he.

II

Poet who sleepest by this wandering
    wave!
    When thou wast born, what birth-gift
      hadst thou then?
To thee what wealth was that the Im-
    mortals gave,
    The wealth thou gavest in thy turn to
      men?

Not Milton's keen, translunar music
    thine;
    Not Shakespeare's cloudless, boundless
      human view;

Not Shelley's flush of rose on peaks
    divine;
Nor yet the wizard twilight Coleridge
    knew.

What hadst thou that could make so large
    amends
    For all thou hadst not and thy peers
      possessed,
Motion and fire, swift means to radiant
    ends?—
    Thou hadst, for weary feet, the gift of
      rest.

From Shelley's dazzling glow or thun-
    derous haze,
    From Byron's tempest-anger, tempest-
      mirth,
Men turned to thee and found—not blast
    and blaze,
    Tumult of tottering heavens, but peace
      on earth.

Nor peace that grows by Lethe, scentless
    flower,
    There in white languors to decline and
      cease;
But peace whose names are also rapture,
    power,
    Clear sight, and love: for these are
      parts of peace.

III

I hear it vouched the Muse is with us
    still;—
    If less divinely frenzied than of yore,
In lieu of feelings she has wondrous skill
    To simulate emotion felt no more.

Not such the authentic Presence pure,
    that made
    This valley vocal in the great days
      gone!—
In *his* great days, while yet the spring-
    time played
    About him, and the mighty morning
      shone.

No word-mosaic artificer, he sang
    A lofty song of lowly weal and dole.

Right from the heart, right to the heart
    it sprang,
    Or from the soul leapt instant to the
      soul.

He felt the charm of childhood, grace of
    youth,
    Grandeur of age, insisting to be sung.
The impassioned argument was simple
    truth
    Half-wondering at its own melodious
      tongue.

Impassioned? ay, to the song's ecstatic
    core!
    But far removed were clangour, storm
      and feud;
For plenteous health was his, exceeding
    store
    Of joy, and an impassioned quietude.

IV

A hundred years ere he to manhood came,
    Song from celestial heights had wan-
      dered down,
Put off her robe of sunlight, dew and
    flame,
    And donned a modish dress to charm
      the Town.

Thenceforth she but festooned the porch
    of things;
    Apt at life's lore, incurious what life
      meant.
Dextrous of hand, she struck her lute's
    few strings;
    Ignobly perfect, barrenly content.

Unflushed with ardour and unblanched
    with awe,
    Her lips in profitless derision curled,
She saw with dull emotion—if she saw—
    The vision of the glory of the world.

The human masque she watched, with
    dreamless eyes
    In whose clear shallows lurked no
      trembling shade:

The stars, unkenned by her, might set and
    rise,
    Unmarked by her, the daisies bloom
      and fade.

The age grew sated with her sterile wit.
    Herself waxed weary on her loveless
      throne.
Men felt life's tide, the sweep and surge
    of it,
    And craved a living voice, a natural
      tone.

For none the less, though song was but
    half true,
    The world lay common, one abounding
      theme.
Man joyed and wept, and fate was ever
    new,
    And love was sweet, life real, death no
      dream.

In sad, stern verse the rugged scholar-
    sage
    Bemoaned his toil unvalued, youth un-
      cheered.
His numbers wore the vesture of the age,
    But, 'neath it beating, the great heart
      was heard.

From dewy pastures, uplands sweet with
    thyme,
    A virgin breeze freshened the jaded day.
It wafted Collins' lonely vesper-chime,
    It breathed abroad the frugal note of
      Gray.

It fluttered here and there, nor swept in
    vain
    The dusty haunts where futile echoes
      dwell,—
Then, in a cadence soft as summer rain,
    And sad from Auburn voiceless,
      drooped and fell.

It drooped and fell, and one 'neath north-
    ern skies,
    With southern heart, who tilled his
      father's field,

Found Poesy a-dying, bade her rise
    And touch quick Nature's hem and go
      forth healed.

On life's broad plain the ploughman's con-
    quering share
    Upturned the fallow lands of truth
      anew,
And o'er the formal garden's trim par-
    terre
    The peasant's team a ruthless furrow
      drew.

Bright was his going forth, but clouds
    ere long
    Whelmed him; in gloom his radiance
      set, and those
Twin morning stars of the new century's
    song,
    Those morning stars that sang to-
      gether, rose.

In elvish speech the *Dreamer* told his tale
    Of marvellous oceans swept by fateful
      wings.—
The *Seër* strayed not from earth's human
    pale,
    But the mysterious face of common
      things

He mirrored as the moon in Rydal Mere
    Is mirrored, when the breathless night
      hangs blue:
Strangely remote she seems and wondrous
    near,
    And by some nameless difference born
      anew.

V

Peace—peace—and rest! Ah, how the
    lyre is loth,
    Or powerless now, to give what all men
      seek!
Either it deadens with ignoble sloth
    Or deafens with shrill tumult, loudly
      weak.

Where is the singer whose large notes
    and clear
    Can heal, and arm, and plenish, and
      sustain?

Lo, one with empty music floods the ear,
  And one, the heart refreshing, tires the
    brain.

And idly tuneful, the loquacious throng
  Flutter and twitter, prodigal of time,
And little masters make a toy of song
  Till grave men weary of the sound of
    rhyme.

And some go prankt in faded antique
    dress,
  Abhorring to be hale and glad and free;
And some parade a conscious naturalness,
  The scholar's not the child's simplicity.

Enough;—and wisest who from words
    forbear.
  The gentle river rails not as it glides;
And suave and charitable, the winsome air
  Chides not at all, or only him who
    chides.

VI

Nature! we storm thine ear with choric
    notes.
  Thou answerest through the calm great
    nights and days,
"Laud me who will: not tuneless are your
    throats;
  Yet if ye paused I should not miss the
    praise."

We falter, half-rebuked, and sing again.
  We chant thy desertness and haggard
    gloom,
Or with thy splendid wrath inflate the
    strain,
  Or touch it with thy colour and per-
    fume.

One, his melodious blood aflame for thee,
  Wooed with fierce lust, his hot heart
    world-defiled.
One, with the upward eye of infancy,
  Looked in thy face, and felt himself thy
    child.

Thee he approached without distrust or
    dread—
  Beheld thee throned, an awesome
    queen, above—
Climbed to thy lap and merely laid his
    head
  Against thy warm wild heart of
    mother-love.

He heard that vast heart beating—thou
    didst press
  Thy child so close, and lov'dst him un-
    aware.
Thy beauty gladdened him; yet he scarce
    less
  Had loved thee, had he never found
    thee fair!

For thou wast not as legendary lands
  To which with curious eyes and ears we
    roam.
Nor wast thou as a fane 'mid solemn
    sands,
  Where palmers halt at evening. Thou
    wast home.

And here, at home, still bides he; but he
    sleeps;
  Not to be wakened even at thy word;
Though we, vague dreamers, dream he
    somewhere keeps
  An ear still open to thy voice still
    heard,—

Thy voice, as heretofore, about him
    blown,
  For ever blown about his silence now;
Thy voice, though deeper, yet so like his
    own
  That almost, when he sang, we deemed
    'twas thou!

VII

Behind Helm Crag and Silver Howe the
    sheen
  Of the retreating day is less and less.
Soon will the lordlier summits, here un-
    seen,
  Gather the night about their nakedness.

The half-heard bleat of sheep comes from
the hill.
Faint sounds of childish play are in the
air.
The river murmurs past. All else is
still.
The very graves seem stiller than they
were.

Afar though nation be on nation hurled,
And life with toil and ancient pain depressed,

Here one may scarce believe the whole
wide world
Is not at peace, and all man's heart at
rest.

Rest! 'twas the gift *he* gave; and peace!
the shade
He spread, for spirits fevered with the
sun.
To him his bounties are come back—here
laid
In rest, in peace, his labour nobly done.

KENNETH GRAHAME

From THE GOLDEN AGE

The Roman Road

ALL the roads of our neighbourhood were cheerful and friendly, having each of them pleasant qualities of their own; but this one seemed different from the others in its masterful suggestion of a serious purpose, speeding you along with a strange uplifting of the heart. The others tempted chiefly with their treasures of hedge and ditch; the rapt surprise of the first lords-and-ladies, the rustle of a field-mouse, the splash of a frog; while cool noses of brother-beasts were pushed at you through gate or gap. A loiterer you had need to be, did you choose one of them; so many were the tiny hands thrust out to detain you, from this side and that. But this one was of a sterner sort, and even in its shedding off of bank and hedgerow as it marched straight and full for the open downs, it seemed to declare its contempt for adventitious trappings to catch the shallow-pated. When the sense of injustice or disappointment was heavy on me, and things were very black within, as on this particular day, the road of character was my choice for that solitary ramble when I turned my back for an afternoon on a world that had unaccountably declared itself against me.

"The Knights' Road" we children had named it, from a sort of feeling that, if from any quarter at all, it would be down this track we might some day see Lancelot and his peers come pacing on their great war-horses; supposing that any of the stout band still survived, in nooks and unexplored places. Grown-up people sometimes spoke of it as the "Pilgrims' Way"; but I didn't know much about pilgrims—except Walter in the Horselberg story. Him I sometimes saw, breaking with haggard eyes out of yonder copse; and calling to the pilgrims as they hurried along on their desperate march to the Holy City, where peace and pardon were awaiting them. "All roads lead to Rome," I had once heard somebody say; and I had taken the remark very seriously, of course, and puzzled over it many days. There must have been some mistake, I concluded at last; but of one road at least I intuitively felt it to be true. And my belief was clinched by something that fell from Miss Smedley during a history-lesson, about a strange road that ran right down the middle of England till it reached the coast, and then began again in France, just opposite, and so on undeviating, through city and vineyard, right from the misty Highlands to the Eternal City. Uncorroborated, any statement of Miss Smedley's usually fell on incredulous ears; but here, with the road itself in evidence, she seemed, once in a way, to have strayed into truth.

Rome! It was fascinating to think that it lay at the other end of this white ribbon that rolled itself off from my feet over the distant downs. I was not quite so uninstructed as to imagine I could reach it that afternoon; but some day, I thought, if things went on being as unpleasant as they were now—some day, when Aunt Eliza had gone on a visit,—some day, we would see.

I tried to imagine what it would be like when I got there. The Coliseum I knew, of course, from a woodcut in the history-book: so to begin with I plumped that down in the middle. The rest had to be patched up from the little grey market-town where twice a year we went to have our hair cut; hence, in the result, Vespasian's amphitheatre was approached by muddy little streets, wherein the Red Lion and the Blue Boar, with Somebody's Entire along their front, and "Commercial Room" on their windows; the doctor's house, of substantial red-brick; and the façade of the New Wesleyan chapel, which we thought very fine, were the chief architectural ornaments: while the Roman populace pottered about in smocks and corduroys, twisting the tails of Roman calves and inviting each other to beer in musical Wessex. From Rome I drifted on to other cities, faintly heard of—Damascus, Brighton (Aunt Eliza's ideal), Athens, and Glasgow, whose glories the gardener sang; but there was a certain sameness in my conception of all of them: that Wesleyan chapel would keep cropping up everywhere. It was easier to go a-building among those dream-cities where no limitations were imposed, and one was sole architect, with a free hand. Down a delectable street of cloud-built palaces I was mentally pacing, when I happened upon the Artist.

He was seated at work by the roadside, at a point whence the cool large spaces of the downs, juniper-studded, swept grandly westwards.

His attributes proclaimed him of the artist tribe: besides, he wore knickerbockers like myself,—a garb confined, I was aware, to boys and artists. I knew I was not to bother him with questions, nor look over his shoulder and breathe in his ear—they didn't like it, this *genus irritabile*. But there was nothing about staring in my code of instructions, the point having somehow been overlooked: so, squatting down on the grass, I devoted myself to the passionate absorbing of every detail. At the end of five minutes there was not a button on him that I could not have passed an examination in; and the wearer himself of that homespun suit was probably less familiar with its pattern and texture than I was. Once he looked up, nodded, half held out his tobacco pouch, mechanically as it were, then, returning it to his pocket, resumed his work, and I my mental photography.

After another five minutes or so had passed, he remarked, without looking my way: "Fine afternoon we're having: going far to-day?"

"No, I'm not going any farther than this," I replied; "I *was* thinking of going on to Rome: but I've put it off."

"Pleasant place, Rome," he murmured: "you'll like it." It was some minutes later that he added: "But I wouldn't go just now, if I were you: too jolly hot."

"*You* haven't been to Rome, have you?" I inquired.

"Rather," he replied briefly. "I live there."

This was too much, and my jaw dropped as I struggled to grasp the fact that I was sitting there talking to a fellow who lived in Rome. Speech was out of the question: besides I had other things to do. Ten solid minutes had I already spent in an examination of him as a mere stranger and artist; and now the whole thing had to be done over again, from the changed point of view. So I began afresh, at the crown of his soft hat, and worked down to his solid British shoes, this time investing everything with the new Roman halo; and at last I managed to get out: "But you don't really live there, do you?" never doubting the fact, but wanting to hear it repeated.

"Well," he said, good-naturedly overlooking the slight rudeness of my query, "I live there as much as I live anywhere. About half the year sometimes. I've got a sort of shanty there. You must come and see it some day."

"But do you live anywhere else as well?" I went on, feeling the forbidden tide of questions surging up within me.

"O yes, all over the place," was his vague reply. "And I've got a diggings somewhere off Piccadilly."

"Where's that?" I inquired.

"Where's what?" said he. "O, Piccadilly! It's in London."

"Have you a large garden?" I asked; "and how many pigs have you got?"

"I've no garden at all," he replied sadly, "and they don't allow me to keep pigs, though I'd like to, awfully. It's very hard."

"But what do you do all day, then," I cried, "and where do you go and play, without any garden, or pigs, or things?"

"When I want to play," he said gravely, "I have to go and play in the street; but it's poor fun, I grant you. There's a goat, though, not far off, and sometimes I talk to him when I'm feeling lonely; but he's very proud."

"Goats *are* proud," I admitted. "There's one lives near here, and if you say anything to him at all, he hits you in the wind with his head. You know what it feels like when a fellow hits you in the wind?"

"I do, well," he replied, in a tone of proper melancholy, and painted on.

"And have you been to any other places," I began again presently, "besides Rome and Piccy-what's-his-name?"

"Heaps," he said. "I'm a sort of Ulysses—seen men and cities, you know. In fact, about the only place I never got to was the Fortunate Island."

I began to like this man. He answered your questions briefly and to the point, and never tried to be funny. I felt I could be confidential with him.

"Wouldn't you like," I inquired, "to find a city without any people in it at all?"

He looked puzzled. "I'm afraid I don't quite understand," said he.

"I mean," I went on eagerly, "a city where you walk in at the gates, and the shops are all full of beautiful things, and the houses furnished as grand as can be, and there isn't anybody there whatever! And you go into the shops, and take anything you want—chocolates and magic-lanterns and injirubber balls—and there's nothing to pay; and you choose your own house and live there and do just as you like, and never go to bed unless you want to!"

The artist laid down his brush. "That *would* be a nice city," he said. "Better than Rome. You can't do that sort of thing in Rome—or in Piccadilly either. But I fear it's one of the places I've never been to."

"And you'd ask your friends," I went on, warming to my subject; "only those you really like, of course; and they'd each have a house to themselves—there'd be lots of houses,—and there wouldn't be any relations at all, unless they promised they'd be pleasant; and if they weren't they'd have to go."

"So you wouldn't have any relations?" said the artist. "Well, perhaps you're right. We have tastes in common, I see."

"I'd have Harold," I said reflectively, "and Charlotte. They'd like it awfully. The others are getting too old. O, and Martha—I'd have Martha to cook and wash up and do things. You'd like Martha. She's ever so much nicer than Aunt Eliza. She's my idea of a real lady."

"Then I'm sure I should like her," he replied heartily, "and when I come to—what do you call this city of yours? Nephelo—something, did you say?"

"I—I don't know," I replied timidly. "I'm afraid it hasn't got a name—yet."

The artist gazed out over the downs. " 'The poet says, dear city of Cecrops,' " he said softly to himself, " 'and wilt not thou say, dear city of Zeus?' That's from Marcus Aurelius," he went on, turning again to his work. "You don't know him, I suppose; you will some day."

"Who's he?" I inquired.

"O, just another fellow who lived in Rome," he replied, dabbing away.

"O dear!" I cried disconsolately. "What a lot of people seem to live at Rome, and I've never even been there! But I think I'd like *my* city best."

"And so would I," he replied with unction. "But Marcus Aurelius wouldn't, you know."

"Then we won't invite him," I said; "will we?"

"*I* won't if you won't," said he. And that point being settled, we were silent for a while.

"Do you know," he said presently, "I've met one or two fellows from time to time, who have been to a city like yours—perhaps it was the same one. They won't talk much about it—only broken hints, now and then; but they've been there sure enough. They don't seem to care about anything in particular—and everything's the same to them, rough or smooth, and sooner or later they slip off and disappear; and you never see them again. Gone back, I suppose."

"Of course," said I. "Don't see what they ever came away for; *I* wouldn't. To be told you've broken things when you haven't, and stopped having tea with the servants in the kitchen, and not allowed to have a dog to sleep with you. But *I've* known people, too, who've gone there."

The artist stared, but without incivility.

"Well, there's Lancelot," I went on. "The book says he died, but it never seemed to read right, somehow. He just went away, like Arthur. And Crusoe, when he got tired of wearing clothes and being respectable. And all the nice men in the stories who don't marry the Princess, 'cos only one man ever gets married in a book, you know. They'll be there!"

"And the men who never come off," he said, "who try like the rest, but get knocked out, or somehow miss—or break down or get bowled over in the melée—and get no Princess, nor even a second-class kingdom —some of them'll be there, I hope?"

"Yes, if you like," I replied, not quite understanding him; "if they're friends of yours, we'll ask 'em, of course."

"What a time we shall have!" said the artist reflectively; "and how shocked old Marcus Aurelius will be!"

The shadows had lengthened uncannily, a tide of golden haze was flooding the grey-green surface of the downs, and the artist began to put his traps together, preparatory to a move. I felt very low: we would have to part, it seemed, just as we were getting on so well together. Then he stood up, and he was very straight and tall, and the sunset was in his hair and beard as he stood there, high over me. He took my hand like an equal. "I've enjoyed our conversation very much," he said. "That was an interesting subject you started, and we haven't half exhausted it. We shall meet again, I hope?"

"Of course we shall," I replied, surprised that there should be any doubt about it.

"In Rome perhaps?" said he.

"Yes, in Rome," I answered; "or Piccy-the-other-place, or somewhere."

"Or else," said he, "in that other city—when we've found the way there. And I'll look out for you, and you'll sing out as soon as you see me. And we'll go down the street arm-in-arm, and into all the shops, and then I'll choose my house, and you'll choose your house, and we'll live there like princes and good-fellows."

"O, but you'll stay in my house, won't you?" I cried; "I wouldn't ask everybody; but I'll ask you."

He affected to consider a moment; then "Right!" he said: "I believe you mean it, and I will come and stay with you. I won't go to anybody else, if they ask me ever so much. And I'll stay quite a long time, too, and I won't be any trouble."

Upon this compact we parted, and I went down-heartedly from the man who understood me, back to the house where I never could do anything right. How was it that everything seemed natural and sensible to him, which these uncles, vicars, and other grown-up men took for the merest tomfoolery? Well, he would explain this, and many another thing, when we met again. The Knights' Road! How it always brought consolation! Was he possibly one of those vanished knights I had been looking for so long? Perhaps he would be in armour next time—why not? He would look well in armour, I thought. And I would take care to get there first, and see the sunlight flash and play on his helmet and shield, as he rode up the High Street of the Golden City.

Meantime, there only remained the finding it. An easy matter.

The Burglars

It was much too fine a night to think of going to bed at once, and so, although the witching hour of nine P. M. had struck, Edward and I were still leaning out of the open window in our nightshirts, watching the play of the cedar-branch shadows on the moonlit lawn, and planning schemes of fresh devilry for the sunshiny morrow. From below, strains of the jocund piano declared that the Olympians were enjoying themselves in their listless impotent way; for the new curate had been bidden to dinner that night, and was at the moment unclerically proclaiming to all the world that he feared no foe. His discordant vociferations doubtless started a train of thought in Edward's mind, for he presently remarked, à propos of nothing whatever that had been said before, "I believe the new curate's rather gone on Aunt Maria."

I scouted the notion; "Why, she's quite old," I said. (She must have seen some five-and-twenty summers.)

"Of course she is," replied Edward scornfully. "It's not her, it's her money he's after, you bet!"

"Didn't know she had any money," I observed timidly.

"Sure to have," said my brother with confidence. "Heaps and heaps."

Silence ensued, both our minds being busy with the new situation thus presented: mine, in wonderment at this flaw that so often declared itself in enviable natures of fullest endowment,—in a grown-up man and a good cricketer, for instance, even as this curate; Edward's (apparently) in the consideration of how such a state of things, supposing it existed, could be best turned to his own advantage.

"Bobby Ferris told me," began Edward in due course, "that there was a fellow spooning his sister once——"

"What's spooning?" I asked meekly.

"O I dunno," said Edward indifferently. "It's—it's—it's just a thing they do, you know. And he used to carry notes and messages and things between 'em, and he got a shilling almost every time."

"What, from each of 'em?" I innocently inquired.

Edward looked at me with scornful pity. "Girls never have any money," he briefly explained. "But she did his exercises, and got him out of rows, and told stories for him when he needed it—and much better ones than he could have made up for himself. Girls are useful in some ways. So he was living in clover, when unfortunately they went and quarrelled about something."

"Don't see what that's got to do with it," I said.

"Nor don't I," rejoined Edward. "But anyhow the notes and things stopped, and so did the shillings. Bobby was fairly cornered, for he had bought two ferrets on tick, and promised to pay a shilling a week, thinking the shillings were going on for ever, the silly young ass. So when the week was up, and he was being dunned for the shilling, he went off to the fellow and said: 'Your broken-hearted Bella implores you to meet her at sundown. By the hollow oak as of old, be it only for a moment. Do not fail!' He got all that out of some rotten book, of course. The fellow looked puzzled and said:

" 'What hollow oak? I don't know any hollow oak.'

" 'Perhaps it was the Royal Oak?' said Bobby promptly, 'cos he saw he had made a slip, through trusting too much to the rotten book; but this didn't seem to make the fellow any happier."

"Should think not," I said, "the Royal Oak's an awful low sort of pub."

"I know," said Edward. "Well, at last the fellow said, 'I think I know what she means: the hollow tree in your father's paddock. It happens to be an elm, but she wouldn't know the difference. All right: say I'll be there.' Bobby hung about a bit, for he hadn't got his money. 'She was crying awfully,' he said. Then he got his shilling."

"And wasn't the fellow riled," I inquired, "when he got to the place and found nothing?"

"He found Bobby," said Edward indignantly. "Young Ferris was a gentleman, every inch of him. He brought the fellow another message from Bella: 'I dare not leave the house. My cruel parents immure me closely. If you only knew what I suffer. Your broken-hearted Bella.' Out of the same rotten book. This made the fellow a little suspicious, 'cos it was the old Ferrises who had been keem about the thing all through. The fellow, you see, had tin."

"But what's that got to——" I began again.

"O *I* dunno," said Edward impatiently. "I'm telling you just what Bobby told me. He got suspicious, anyhow, but he couldn't exactly call Bella's brother a liar, so Bobby escaped for the time. But when he was in a hole next week, over a stiff French exercise, and tried the same sort of game on his sister, she was too sharp for him, and he got caught out. Somehow women seem more mistrustful than men. They're so beastly suspicious by nature, you know."

"*I* know," said I. "But did the two—the fellow and the sister— make it up afterwards?"

"I don't remember about that," replied Edward indifferently; "but Bobby got packed off to school a whole year earlier than his people meant to send him. Which was just what he wanted. So you see it all came right in the end!"

I was trying to puzzle out the moral of this story—it was evidently meant to contain one somewhere—when a flood of golden lamplight mingled with the moon-rays on the lawn, and Aunt Maria and the new curate strolled out on the grass below us, and took the direction of a garden-seat which was backed by a dense laurel shrubbery reaching round in a half-circle to the house. Edward meditated moodily. "If we only knew what they were talking about," said he, "you'd soon see whether I was right or not. Look here! Let's send the kid down by the porch to reconnoitre!"

"Harold's asleep," I said; "it seems rather a shame——"

"O rot!" said my brother; "he's the youngest, and he's got to do as he's told!"

So the luckless Harold was hauled out of bed and given his sailing-orders. He was naturally rather vexed at being stood up suddenly on the cold floor, and the job had no particular interest for him; but he was both staunch and well disciplined. The means of exit were simple enough. A porch of iron trellis came up to within easy reach of the window, and was habitually used by all three of us, when modestly anxious to avoid public notice. Harold climbed deftly down the porch like a white rat, and his night-gown glimmered a moment on the gravel walk ere he was lost to sight in the darkness of the shrubbery. A brief interval of silence ensued; broken suddenly by a sound of scuffle, and then a shrill long-drawn squeal, as of metallic surfaces in friction. Our scout had fallen into the hands of the enemy!

Indolence alone had made us devolve the task of investigation on

KENNETH GRAHAME   319

our younger brother. Now that danger had declared itself, there was no hesitation. In a second we were down the side of the porch, and crawling Cherokee-wise through the laurels to the back of the garden seat. Piteous was the sight that greeted us. Aunt Maria was on the seat, in a white evening frock, looking—for an aunt—really quite nice. On the lawn stood an incensed curate, grasping our small brother by a large ear, which—judging from the row he was making—seemed on the point of parting company with the head it completed and adorned. The gruesome noise he was emitting did not really affect us otherwise than æsthetically. To one who has tried both, the wail of genuine physical anguish is easily distinguishable from the pumped-up *ad miseri-cordiam* blubber. Harold's could clearly be recognised as belonging to the latter class. "Now you young—" (whelp, *I* think it was, but Edward stoutly maintains it was devil), said the curate sternly; "tell us what you mean by it!"

"Well leggo of my ear then!" shrilled Harold, "and I'll tell you the solemn truth!"

"Very well," agreed the curate, releasing him, "now go ahead, and don't lie more than you can help."

We abode the promised disclosure without the least misgiving; but even we had hardly given Harold due credit for his fertility of resource and powers of imagination.

"I had just finished saying my prayers," began that young gentleman slowly, "when I happened to look out of the window, and on the lawn I saw a sight which froze the marrow in my veins! A burglar was approaching the house with snake-like tread! He had a scowl and a dark lantern, and he was armed to the teeth!"

We listened with interest. The style, though unlike Harold's native notes, seemed strangely familiar.

"Go on," said the curate grimly.

"Pausing in his stealthy career," continued Harold, "he gave a low whistle. Instantly the signal was responded to, and from the adjacent shadows two more figures glided forth. The miscreants were both armed to the teeth."

"Excellent," said the curate; "proceed."

"The robber chief," pursued Harold, warming to his work, "joined his nefarious comrades, and conversed with them in silent tones. His expression was truly ferocious, and I ought to have said that he was armed to the t——"

"There, never mind his teeth," interrupted the curate rudely; "there's too much jaw about you altogether. Hurry up and have done."

"I was in a frightful funk," continued the narrator, warily guarding his ear with his hand, "but just then the drawing-room window opened, and you and Aunt Maria came out—I mean emerged. The burglars vanished silently into the laurels, with horrid implications!"

The curate looked slightly puzzled. The tale was well sustained, and certainly circumstantial. After all, the boy might really have seen something. How was the poor man to know—though the chaste and lofty diction might have supplied a hint—that the whole yarn was a free adaptation from the last Penny Dreadful lent us by the knife-and-boot boy?

"Why did you not alarm the house?" he asked.

"'Cos I was afraid," said Harold sweetly, "that p'raps they mightn't believe me!"

"But how did you get down here, you naughty little boy?" put in Aunt Maria.

Harold was hard pressed—by his own flesh and blood, too!

At that moment Edward touched me on the shoulder and glided off through the laurels. When some ten yards away he gave a low whistle. I replied with another. The effect was magical. Aunt Maria started up with a shriek. Harold gave one startled glance around, and then fled like a hare, made straight for the back-door, burst in upon the servants at supper, and buried himself in the broad bosom of the cook, his special ally. The curate faced the laurels—hesitatingly. But Aunt Maria flung herself on him. "O Mr. Hodgitts!" I heard her cry, "you are brave! for my sake do not be rash!" He was not rash. When I peeped out a second later, the coast was entirely clear.

By this time there were sounds of a household timidly emerging; and Edward remarked to me that perhaps we had better be off. Retreat was an easy matter. A stunted laurel gave a leg-up on to the garden wall, which led in its turn to the roof of an out-house, up which, at a dubious angle, we could crawl to the window of the box-room. This overland route had been revealed to us one day by the domestic cat, when hard pressed in the course of an otter-hunt, in which the cat—somewhat unwillingly—was filling the title *rôle;* and it had proved distinctly useful on occasions like the present. We were snug in bed—minus some cuticle from knees and elbows—and Harold, sleepily chewing something sticky, had been carried up in the arms of the friendly cook, ere the clamour of the burglar-hunters had died away.

The curate's undaunted demeanour, as reported by Aunt Maria, was generally supposed to have terrified the burglars into flight, and much kudos accrued to him thereby. Some days later, however, when he had dropped in to afternoon tea, and was making a mild curatorial joke about the moral courage required for taking the last piece of bread-and-butter, I felt constrained to remark dreamily, and as it were to the universe at large: "Mr. Hodgitts! you are brave! for my sake, do not be rash!"

Fortunately for me, the vicar also was a caller on that day; and it was always a comparatively easy matter to dodge my long-coated friend in the open.

SIR JAMES MATTHEW BARRIE

From MY LADY NICOTINE

Matrimony and Smoking Compared

THE circumstances in which I gave up smoking were these.

I was a mere bachelor, drifting toward what I now see to be a tragic middle age. I had become so accustomed to smoke issuing from my mouth that I felt incomplete without it; indeed the time came when I could refrain from smoking if doing nothing else, but hardly during the hours of toil. To lay aside my pipe was to find myself soon afterwards wandering restlessly round my table. No blind beggar was ever more abjectly led by his dog, or more loth to cut the string.

I am much better without tobacco, and already have difficulty in sympathizing with the man I used to be. Even to call him up, as it were, and regard him without prejudice is a difficult task, for we forget the old selves on whom we have turned our backs as we forget a street that has been reconstructed. Does the freed slave always shiver at the crack of a whip? I fancy not, for I recall but dimly, and without acute suffering, the horrors of my smoking days. There were nights when I woke with a pain at my heart that made me hold my breath. I did not dare move. After perhaps ten minutes of dread, I would shift my position an inch at a time. Less frequently I felt this sting in the daytime, and believed I was dying while my friends were talking to me. I never mentioned these experiences to a human being; indeed, though a medical man was among my companions, I cunningly deceived him on the rare occasions when he questioned me about the amount of tobacco I was consuming weekly. Often in the dark I not only vowed to give up smoking, but wondered why I cared for it. Next morning I went straight from breakfast to my pipe, without the smallest struggle with myself. Latterly I knew, while resolving to break myself of the habit, that I would be better employed trying to sleep. I had elaborate ways of cheating myself, for it became disagreeable to me to know how many ounces of tobacco I was smoking weekly. Often I smoked cigarettes to reduce the number of my cigars.

On the other hand, if these sharp pains be excepted, I felt quite well. My appetite was as good as it is now, and I worked as cheerfully and certainly harder. To some slight extent, I believe, I experienced the same pains in my boyhood, before I smoked, and I am not an absolute stranger to them yet. They were most frequent in my smoking days, but I have no other reason for charging them to tobacco. Possibly a doctor who smoked himself would have pooh-poohed them. Nevertheless, I have lit my pipe, and then, as I may say, hearkened for them. At the first intimation that they were coming I laid the pipe down and ceased to smoke—until they had passed.

I will not admit that, once sure it was doing me harm, I could not, unaided, have given up tobacco. But I was reluctant to make sure. I should like to say that I left off smoking because I considered it a mean form of slavery, to be condemned for moral as well as physical reasons; but though I see the folly of smoking clearly now, I was blind to it for some months after I had smoked my last pipe. I gave up my most delightful solace, as I regarded it, for no other reason than that the lady who was willing to fling herself away on me said that I must choose between it and her. This deferred our marriage for six months.

I have now come, as those who read will see, to look upon smoking with my wife's eyes. My old bachelor friends complain because I do not allow smoking in the house, but I am always ready to explain my position, and I have not an atom of pity for them. If I cannot smoke here neither shall they. When I visit them in the old Inn they take a poor revenge by blowing rings of smoke almost in my face. This ambition to blow rings is the most ignoble known to man. Once I was a member of a club for smokers, where we practised blowing rings. The most successful got a box of cigars as a prize at the end of the year. Those were days! Often I think wistfully of them. We met in a cosey room off the Strand. How well I can picture it still; timetables lying everywhere, with which we could light our pipes. Some smoked clays, but for the Arcadia Mixture give me a briar. My briar was the sweetest ever known. It is strange now to recall a time when a pipe seemed to be my best friend.

My present state is so happy that I can only look back with wonder at my hesitation to enter upon it. Our house was taken while I was still arguing that it would be dangerous to break myself of smoking all at once. At that time my ideal of married life was not what it is now, and I remember Jimmy's persuading me to fix on this house because the large room upstairs with the three windows was a smoker's dream. He pictured himself and me there in the summer-time blowing rings, with our coats off and our feet out at the windows; and he said that the closet at the back, looking on to a blank wall, would make a charming drawing-room for my wife. For the moment his enthusiasm carried me away, but I see now how selfish it was, and I have before me the face of Jimmy when he paid us his first visit and found that the closet was not the drawing-room. Jimmy is a fair specimen of a man, not without parts, destroyed by devotion to his pipe. To this day he thinks that mantelpiece vases are meant for holding pipe-lights in. We are almost certain that when he stays with us he smokes in his bedroom—a detestable practice that I cannot permit.

Two cigars a day at ninepence apiece come to £27 7s. 6d. yearly, and four ounces of tobacco a week at nine shillings a pound come to £5 17s. yearly. That makes £33 4s. 6d. When we calculate the yearly expense of tobacco in this way we are naturally taken aback, and our extravagance shocks us the more after we have considered how much more satisfactorily the money might have been spent. With £33 4s. 6d. you can buy new Oriental rugs for the drawing-room, as well as a spring bonnet and a nice dress. These are things that give permanent pleasure, whereas you have no interest in a cigar after flinging away the stump. Judging by myself, I should say that it is want of thought rather than selfishness that makes heavy smokers of so many bachelors. Once a man marries his eyes are opened to many things that he was quite unaware of previously, among them being the delight of adding an article of furniture to the drawing-room every month and having a bedroom in pink and gold, the door of which is always kept locked. If men would only consider that every cigar they smoke would buy part of a new piano-stool in terra-cotta plush, and that for every pound tin of tobacco purchased away goes a vase for growing dead geraniums in, they would surely hesitate. They do not consider, however, until they marry, and then they are forced to it. For my own part, I fail to see why bachelors should be allowed to smoke as much as they like when we are debarred from it.

The very smell of tobacco is abominable, for one cannot get it out of the curtains, and there is little pleasure in existence unless the curtains are all right. As for a cigar after dinner, it only makes you dull and sleepy and disinclined for ladies' society. A far more delightful way of spending the evening is to go straight from dinner to the drawing-room and have a little music. It calms the mind to listen to your wife's niece singing "Oh, that we two were maying." Even if you are not musical, as is the case with me, there is a great deal in the drawing-room to refresh you. There are the Japanese fans on the wall, which are things of beauty, though your artistic taste may not be sufficiently educated to let you know it except by hearsay; and it is pleasant to feel that they were bought with money which, in the foolish old days, would have been squandered on a box of cigars. In like manner every pretty trifle in the room reminds you how much wiser you are now than you used to be. It is even gratifying to stand in summer at the drawing-room window and watch the very cabbies passing with cigars in their mouths. At the same time, if I had the making of the laws I would prohibit people's smoking in the street. If they are married men, they are smoking drawing-room fire-screens and mantelpiece borders for the pink and gold room. If they are bachelors, it is a scandal that bachelors should get the best of everything.

Nothing is more pitiable than the way some men of my acquaintance enslave themselves to tobacco. Nay, worse, they make an idol of some one particular tobacco. I know a man who considers a certain mixture so superior to all others that he will walk three miles for it. Surely every one will admit that this is lamentable. It is not even a good mixture, for I used to try it occasionally; and if there is one man in London who knows tobaccos, it is myself. There is only one mixture in London deserving the adjective superb. I will not say where it is to be got, for the result would certainly be that many foolish men would smoke more than ever; but I never knew anything to compare to it. It is deliciously mild yet of full fragrance, and it never burns the tongue. If you try it once you smoke it ever afterwards. It clears the brain and soothes the temper. When I went away for a holiday anywhere I took as much of that exquisite health-giving mixture as I thought would last me the whole time, but I always ran out of it. Then I telegraphed to London for more, and was miserable until it arrived. How I tore the lid off the canister! That is a tobacco to live for. But I am better without it.

Occasionally I feel a little depressed after dinner still, without being able to say why, and if my wife has left me I wander about the room restlessly, like one who misses something. Usually, however, she takes me with her to the drawing-room, and reads aloud her delightfully long home letters or plays soft music to me. If the music be sweet and sad it takes me away to a stair in an Inn, which I climb gaily and shake open a heavy door on the top floor, and turn up the gas. It is a little room I am in once again, and very dusty. A pile of papers and magazines stands as high as a table in the corner furthest from the door. The cane-chair shows the exact shape of Marriot's back. What is left (after lighting the fire) of a framed picture lies on the hearthrug. Gilray walks in uninvited. He has left word that his visitors are to be sent on to me. The room fills. My hand feels along the mantelpiece for a brown jar. The jar is between my knees, I fill my pipe. . . .

After a time the music ceases, and my wife puts her hand on my shoulder. Perhaps I start a little, and then she says I have been asleep. This is the book of my dreams.

My First Cigar

It was not in my chambers, but three hundred miles further north that I learned to smoke. I think I may say with confidence that a first cigar was never smoked in such circumstances before.

At that time I was a schoolboy, living with my brother who was a man. People mistook our relations, and thought I was his son. They would ask me how my father was, and when he heard of this he scowled at me. Even to this day I look so young that people who remember me as a boy, now think I must be that boy's younger brother. I shall tell presently of a strange mistake of this kind, but at present I am thinking of the evening when my brother's eldest daughter was born—perhaps the most trying evening he and I ever passed together. So far as I knew the affair was very sudden, and I felt sorry for my brother as well as for myself.

We sat together in the study, he on an armchair drawn near the fire and I on the couch. I cannot say now at what time I began to have an inkling that there was something wrong. It came upon me gradually and made me very uncomfortable, though of course I did not show this. I heard people going up and down stairs, but I was not at that time naturally suspicious. Comparatively early in the evening I felt that my brother had something on his mind. As a rule, when we were left together, he yawned or drummed with his fingers on the arm of his chair to show that he did not feel uncomfortable, or I made a pretence of being at ease by playing with the dog or saying that the room was close. Then one of us would rise, remark that he had left his book in the dining-room, and go away to look for it, taking care not to come back till the other had gone. In this crafty way we helped each other. On that occasion, however, he did not adopt any of the usual methods; and though I went up to my bedroom several times and listened through the wall, I heard nothing. At last some one told me not to go upstairs, and I returned to the study, feeling that I now knew the worst. He was still in the armchair, and I again took the couch. I could see by the way he looked at me over his pipe that he was wondering whether I knew anything. I don't think I ever liked my brother better than on that night; and I wanted him to understand that, whatever happened, it would make no difference between us. But the affair upstairs was too delicate to talk of, and all I could do was to try to keep his mind from brooding on it by making him tell me things about politics. This is the kind of man my brother is. He is an astonishing master of facts, and I suppose he never read a book yet, from a Blue Book to a volume of verse, without catching the author in error about something. He reads books for that purpose. As a rule, I avoided argument with him, because he was disappointed if I was right and stormed if I was wrong. It was therefore a dangerous thing to begin on politics, but I thought the circumstances warranted it. To my surprise he answered me in a rambling manner, occasionally breaking off in the middle of a sentence and seeming to listen for something. I tried him on history, and mentioned 1822 as the date of the Battle of Waterloo merely to give him his opportunity. But he let it pass. After that there was silence. By and by he rose from his chair, apparently to leave the room, and then sat down again, as if he had thought better of it. He did this several times, always eyeing me narrowly. Wondering how I could make it easier for him, I took up a book and pretended to read with deep attention, meaning to show him that he could go away if he liked without my noticing it. At last he jumped up, and, looking at me boldly, as if to show that the house was his and he could do what he liked in it, went heavily from the room. As soon as he was gone I laid down my book. I was now in a state of nervous excitement, though outwardly I was quite calm. I took a look at him as he went up the stairs, and noticed that he had slipped off his shoes on the bottom step. All haughtiness had left him now.

In a little while he came back. He found me reading. He lit his pipe and pretended to read too. I shall never forget that my book was "Anne Judge, Spinster," while his was a volume of "Blackwood." Every five minutes his pipe went out, and sometimes the book lay neglected on his knee as he stared at the fire. Then he would go out for five minutes and come back again. It was late now, and I felt that I should like to go to my bedroom and lock myself in. That, however, would have been selfish; so we sat on defiantly. At last he started from his chair, as some one knocked at the door. I heard several people talking, and then loud above their voices a younger one.

When I came to myself, the first thing I thought was that they would ask me to hold it. Then I remembered, with another sinking at the heart, that they might want to call it after me. These, of course, were selfish reflections; but my position was a trying one. The question was, what was the proper thing for me to do? I told myself that my brother might come back at any moment, and all I thought of after that was what I should say to him. I had an idea that I ought to congratulate him, but it seemed a brutal thing to do. I had not made up my mind when I heard him coming down. He was laughing and joking in what seemed to me a flippant kind of way, considering the circumstances. When his hand touched the door I snatched at my book and read as hard as I could. He was swaggering a little as he entered, but the swagger went out of him as soon as his eye fell on me. I fancy he had come down to tell me, and now he did not know how to begin. He walked up and down the room restlessly, looking at me as he walked the one way while I looked at him as he walked the other way. At length he sat down again and took up his book. He did not try to smoke. The silence was something terrible; nothing was to be heard but an occasional cinder falling from the grate. This lasted I should say for twenty minutes, and then he closed his book and flung it on the table. I saw that the game was up, and closed "Anne Judge, Spinster." Then he said, with affected jocularity, "Well, young man, do you know that you are an uncle?" There was silence again, for I was still trying to think out some appropriate remark. After a time I said, in a weak voice, "Boy or girl?" "Girl," he answered. Then I thought hard again, and all at once remembered something. "Both doing well?" I whispered. "Yes," he said, sternly. I felt that something great was expected of me, but I could not jump up and wring his hand. I was an uncle. I stretched out my arm toward the cigar-box, and firmly lit my first cigar.

The Arcadia Mixture

DARKNESS comes, and with it the porter to light our stair gas. He vanishes into his box. Already the Inn is so quiet that the tap of a pipe on a windowsill startles all the sparrows in the quadrangle. The men on my stair emerge from their holes. Scrymgeour, in a dressing-gown, pushes open the door of the boudoir on the first floor, and climbs lazily. The sentimental face and the clay with a crack in it are Marriot's. Gilray, who has been rehearsing his part in the new original comedy from the Icelandic, ceases muttering and feels his way along his dark lobby.

Jimmy pins a notice on his door "Called away on Business," and crosses to me. Soon we are all in the old room again, Jimmy on the hearthrug, Marriot in the cane-chair; the curtains are pinned together with a pennib, and the five of us are smoking the Arcadia Mixture.

Pettigrew will be welcomed if he comes, but he is a married man, and we seldom see him nowadays. Others will be regarded as intruders. If they are smoking common tobaccos, they must either be allowed to try ours or requested to withdraw. One need only put his head in at my door to realize that tobaccos are of two kinds, the Arcadia and others. No one who smokes the Arcadia would ever attempt to describe its delights, for his pipe would be certain to go out. When he was at school, Jimmy Moggridge smoked a cane-chair, and he has since said that from cane to ordinary mixtures was not so noticeable as the change from ordinary mixtures to the Arcadia. I ask no one to believe this, for the confirmed smoker in Arcadia detests arguing with anybody about anything. Were I anxious to prove Jimmy's statement, I would merely give you the only address at which the Arcadia is to be had. But that I will not do. It would be as rash as proposing a man with whom I am unacquainted for my club. You may not be worthy to smoke the Arcadia Mixture.

Even though I became attached to you, I might not like to take the responsibility of introducing you to the Arcadia. This mixture has an extraordinary effect upon character, and probably you want to remain as you are. Before I discovered the Arcadia, and communicated it to the other five—including Pettigrew—we had all distinct individualities, but now, except in appearance—and the Arcadia even tells on that— we are as like as holly-leaves. We have the same habits, the same ways of looking at things, the same satisfaction in each other. No doubt we are not yet absolutely alike, indeed I intend to prove this, but in given circumstances we would probably do the same thing, and, furthermore, it would be what other people would not do. Thus when we are together we are only to be distinguished by our pipes; but any one of us in the company of persons who smoke other tobaccos would be considered highly original. He would be a pigtail in Europe.

If you meet in company a man who has ideas and is not shy, yet refuses absolutely to be drawn into talk, you may set him down as one of us. Among the first effects of the Arcadia is to put an end to jabber. Gilray had at one time the reputation of being such a brilliant talker that Arcadians locked their doors on him, but now he is a man who can be invited anywhere. The Arcadia is entirely responsible for the change. Perhaps I myself am the most silent of our company, and hostesses usually think me shy. They ask ladies to draw me out, and when the ladies find me as hopeless as a sulky drawer they call me stupid. The charge may be true, but I do not resent it, for I smoke the Arcadia Mixture, and am consequently indifferent to abuse.

I willingly gibbet myself to show how reticent the Arcadia makes us. It happens that I have a connection with Nottingham, and whenever a man mentions Nottingham to me, with a certain gleam in his eye, I know that he wants to discuss the lace trade. But it is a curious fact that the aggressive talker constantly mixes up Nottingham and Northampton. "Oh, you know Nottingham," he says interestedly; "and how do you like Labouchere for a member?" Do you think I put him right? Do you imagine me thirsting to tell that Mr. Labouchere is the Christian member for Northampton? Do you suppose me swift to explain that Mr. Broadhurst is one of the Nottingham members and that the "Nottingham lambs" are notorious in the history of political elections? Do you fancy me explaining that he is quite right in saying that Nottingham has a large market-place? Do you see me drawn into half an hour's talk about Robin Hood? That is not my way. I merely reply that we like Mr. Labouchere pretty well. It may be said that I gain nothing by this; that the talker will be as curious about Northampton as he would have been about Nottingham, and that Bradlaugh and Labouchere and boots will serve his turn quite as well as Broadhurst and lace and Robin Hood. But that is not so. Beginning on Northampton in the most confident manner, it suddenly flashes across him that he has mistaken Northampton for Nottingham. "How foolish of me!" he says. I maintain a severe silence. He is annoyed. My experience of talkers tells me that nothing annoys them so much as a blunder of this kind. From the coldly polite way in which I have taken the talker's remarks he discovers the value I put upon them, and after that, if he has a neighbor on the other side, he leaves me alone.

Enough has been said to show that the Arcadian's golden rule is to be careful about what he says. This does not mean that he is to say nothing. As society is at present constituted you are bound to make an occasional remark. But you need not make it rashly. It has been said somewhere that it would be well for talkative persons to count twenty, or to go over the alphabet, before they let fall the observation that trembles on their lips. The non-talker has no taste for such an unintellectual exercise. At the same time he must not hesitate too long, for, of course, it is to his advantage to introduce the subject. He ought to think out a topic of which his neighbor will not be able to make very much. To begin on the fall of snow or the number of tons of turkeys consumed on Christmas Day as stated in the *Daily Telegraph,* is to deserve your fate. If you are at a dinner-party of men only, take your host aside, and in a few well-considered sentences find out from him what kind of men you are to sit between during dinner. Perhaps one of them is an African traveller. A knowledge of this prevents your playing into his hands by remarking that the papers are full of the relief of Emin Pasha. These private inquiries will also save you from talking about Mr. Chamberlain to a neighbor who turns out to be the son of a Birmingham elector. Allow that man his chance, and he will not only give you the Birmingham gossip, but what individual electors said about Mr. Chamberlain to the banker or the tailor, and what the grocer did the moment the poll was declared, with particulars about the antiquity of Birmingham and the fishing to be had in the neighborhood. What you ought to do is to talk about Emin Pasha to this man, and to the traveller about Mr. Chamberlain, taking care, of course, to speak in a low voice. In that way you may have comparative peace. Everything, however, depends on the calibre of your neighbors. If they agree to look upon you as an honorable antagonist, and so to fight fair, the victory will be to him who deserves it; that is to say, to the craftier man of the two. But talkers, as a rule, do not fight fair. They consider silent men their prey. It will thus be seen that I distinguish between talkers, admitting that some of them are worse than others. The lowest in the social scale is he who stabs you in the back, as it were, instead of crossing swords. If one of the gentlemen introduced to you is of that type, he will not be ashamed to say, "Speaking of Emin Pasha, I wonder if Mr. Chamberlain is interested in the relief expedition. I don't know if I told you that my father"—and there he is, fairly on horseback. It is seldom of any use to tempt him into other channels. Better turn to your traveller and let him describe the different routes to the Egyptian Equatorial Provinces, with his own views thereon. Allow him even to draw a map of Africa with a fork on the table-cloth. A talker of this kind is too full of his subject to insist upon your answering questions, so that he does not trouble you much. It is his own dinner that is spoilt rather than yours. Treat in the same way as the Chamberlain talker the man who sits down beside you and begins, "Remarkable man, Mr. Gladstone."

There was a ventilator in my room, which sometimes said "Crik-Crik!" reminding us that no one had spoken for half an hour. Occasionally, however, we had lapses of speech, when Gilray might tell over again—though not quite as I mean to tell it—the story of his first pipeful of the Arcadia, or Scrymgeour, the travelled man, would give us the list of famous places in Europe where he had smoked. But, as a rule, none of us paid much attention to what the others said, and after the last pipe, the room emptied—unless Marriot insisted on staying behind to bore me with his scruples—by first one and then another putting his pipe into his pocket and walking silently out of the room.

From SENTIMENTAL TOMMY

The Essay-Writing Contest

Hugh Blackadder, a Thrums man, had made his fortune in America, and bequeathed the interest of three hundred pounds to be competed for yearly by the youth of his native place. The prize was for the best essay in the Scots tongue.

Mr. Cathro, the dominie of the school in Thrums, had not intended to enter Master Thomas Sandys. Though he knew only too well Tommy's ability with the pen, he had thought that Tommy's failure in the bursary examinations ended the posssibility of Mr. McLean's aiding Tommy to go to the university. This obstacle, however, Grizel succeeded in removing; and Mr. Cathro was more than delighted to enter Tommy and thus, he was sure, avenge his pride on Mr. Ogilvy of the Glenquharity school, who for years had carried the Blackadder, and who this year had made by far the better showing with his boys in the bursary examinations.

The only competitor against Tommy was Laughlan McLaughlan of Mr. Ogilvy's school. The contest took place in the Thrums school. Besides some of Tommy's friends, outside, there were present, within, "the Rev. Mr. Duthie, the Rev. Mr. Dishart, the Rev. Mr. Gloag of Noran Side, the Rev. Mr. Lorrimer of Glenquharity (these on hair-bottomed chairs), and Mr. Cathro and Mr. Ogilvy (cane)." The subject assigned for the essay was "A Day in Church." Tommy began at once with a confident smirk that presently gave way to a most holy expression; while Laughlan gaped at him and at last got started also. Mr. Cathro sat smiling with the ministers, and Mr. Ogilvy dolefully paced the floor.

Before an hour had passed, the door of the little room in which the boys were writing was closed, to spare the feelings of Mr. Ogilvy, who had been unhappily peeping through at Tommy and poor Laughlan. But before the end of the two hours, Mr. Ogilvy, still hovering about the door, was quite unhappy. "'I'm an old fool,' the Dominie admitted, 'but I can't help being cast down. The fact is that—I have only heard the scrape of one pen for nearly an hour.'"

Presently Mr. Cathro winked at Mr. Ogilvy.

He winked a great deal more after a moment.

FOR after all—how to tell it! Tommy was ignominiously beaten, making such a beggarly show that the judges thought it unnecessary to take the essays home with them for leisurely consideration before pronouncing Mr. Lauchlan McLauchlan winner. There was quite a commotion in the school-room. At the end of the allotted time the two competitors had been told to hand in their essays, and how Mr. McLauchlan was sniggering is not worth recording, so dumfounded, confused and raging was Tommy. He clung to his papers, crying fiercely that the two hours could not be up yet, and Lauchlan having tried to keep the laugh in too long it exploded in his mouth, whereupon, said he, with a guffaw, "He hasna written a word for near an hour!"

"What! It was you I heard!" cried Mr. Ogilvy, gleaming, while the unhappy Cathro tore the essay from Tommy's hands. Essay! It was no more an essay than a twig is a tree, for the gowk had stuck in the middle of his second page. Yes, stuck is the right expression, as his chagrined teacher had to admit when the boy was cross-examined. He had not been "up to some of his tricks," he had stuck, and his explanations, as you will admit, merely emphasized his incapacity.

He had brought himself to public scorn for lack of a word. What word? they asked testily, but even now he could not tell. He had wanted a Scotch word that would signify how many people were in church, and it was on the tip of his tongue but would come no farther. Puckle was nearly the word, but it did not mean so many people as he meant. The hour had gone by just like winking; he had forgotten all about time while searching his mind for the word.

When Mr. Ogilvy heard this he seemed to be much impressed, repeatedly he nodded his head as some beat time to music, and he muttered to himself, "The right word—yes, that's everything," and "'the time went by like winking'—exactly, precisely," and he would have liked to examine Tommy's bumps, but did not, nor said a word aloud, for was he not there in McLauchlan's interest?

The other five were furious; even Mr. Lorrimer, though his man had won, could not smile in face of such imbecility. "You little tattie-doolie," Cathro roared, "were there not a dozen words to wile from if you had an ill-will to puckle? What ailed you at manzy, or——"

"I thought of manzy," replied Tommy woefully, for he was ashamed of himself, "but—but a manzy's a swarm. It would mean that the folk in the kirk were buzzing thegither like bees, instead of sitting still."

"Even if it does mean that," said Mr. Duthie, with impatience, "what was the need of being so particular? Surely the art of essay-writing consists in using the first word that comes and hurrying on."

"That's how I did," said the proud McLauchlan, who is now leader of a party in the church, and a figure in Edinburgh during the month of May.

"I see," interposed Mr. Gloag, "that McLauchlan speaks of there being a mask of people in the church. Mask is a fine Scotch word."

"Admirable," assented Mr. Dishart.

"I thought of mask," whimpered Tommy, "but that would mean the kirk was crammed, and I just meant it to be middling full."

"Flow would have done," suggested Mr. Lorrimer.

"Flow's but a handful," said Tommy.

"Curran, then, you jackanapes!"

"Curran's no enough."

Mr. Lorrimer flung up his hands in despair.

"I wanted something between curran and mask," said Tommy, dogged, yet almost at the crying.

Mr. Ogilvy, who had been hiding his admiration with difficulty, spread a net for him. "You said you wanted a word that meant middling full. Well, why did you not say middling full—or fell mask?"

"Yes, why not?" demanded the ministers, unconsciously caught in the net.

"I wanted one word," replied Tommy unconsciously avoiding it.

"You jewel!" muttered Mr. Ogilvy under his breath, but Mr. Cathro would have banged the boy's head had not the ministers interfered.

"It is so easy, too, to find the right word," said Mr. Gloag.

"It's no; it's as difficult as to hit a squirrel," cried Tommy, and again Mr. Ogilvy nodded approval.

But the ministers were only pained.

"The lad is merely a numskull," said Mr. Dishart, kindly.

"And no teacher could have turned him into anything else," said Mr. Duthie.

"And so, Cathro, you need not feel sore over your defeat," added Mr. Gloag; but nevertheless Cathro took Tommy by the neck and ran him out of the parish school of Thrums. When he returned to the others he found the ministers congratulating McLauchlan, whose nose was in the air, and complimenting Mr. Ogilvy, who listened to their formal phrases solemnly and accepted their hand-shakes with a dry chuckle.

"Ay, grin away, sir," the mortified dominie of Thrums said to him sourly, "the joke is on your side."

"You are right, sir," replied Mr. Ogilvy, mysteriously, "the joke is on my side, and the best of it is that not one of you knows what the joke is!"

And then an odd thing happened. As they were preparing to leave the school, the door opened a little and there appeared in the aperture the face of Tommy, tear-stained but excited. "I ken the word now," he cried, "it came to me a' at once; it is hantle!"

From Margaret Ogilvy

My Heroine

When it was known that I had begun another story my mother might ask what it was to be about this time.

"Fine we can guess who it is about," my sister would say pointedly.

"Maybe you can guess, but it is beyond me," says my mother, with the meekness of one who knows that she is a dull person.

My sister scorned her at such times. "What woman is in all his books?" she would demand.

"I'm sure I canna say," replies my mother determinedly. "I thought the women were different every time."

"Mother, I wonder you can be so audacious! Fine you know what woman I mean."

"How can I know? What woman is it? You should bear in mind that I hinna your cleverness" (they were constantly giving each other little knocks).

"I won't give you the satisfaction of saying her name. But this I will say, it is high time he was keeping her out of his books."

And then as usual my mother would give herself away unconsciously.

"That is what I tell him," she says chuckling, "and he tries to keep me out, but he canna; it's more than he can do!"

On an evening after my mother had gone to bed, the first chapter would be brought upstairs, and I read, sitting at the foot of the bed, while my sister watched to make my mother behave herself, and my father cried H'sh! when there were interruptions. All would go well at the start, the reflections were accepted with a little nod of the head, the descriptions of scenery as ruts on the road that must be got over at a walking pace (my mother did not care for scenery, and that is why there is so little of it in my books). But now I am reading too quickly, a little apprehensively, because I know that the next paragraph begins with—let us say with, "Along this path came a woman": I had intended to rush on here in a loud bullying voice, but "Along this path came a woman" I read, and stop. Did I hear a faint sound from the other end of the bed? Perhaps I did not; I may only have been listening for it, but I falter and look up. My sister and I look sternly at my mother. She bites her under-lip and clutches the bed with both hands, really she is doing her best for me, but first comes a smothered gurgling sound, then her hold on herself relaxes and she shakes with mirth.

"That's a way to behave!" cries my sister.

"I cannot help it," my mother gasps.

"And there's nothing to laugh at."

"It's that woman," my mother explains unnecessarily.

"Maybe she's not the woman you think her," I say, crushed.

"Maybe not," says my mother doubtfully. "What was her name?"

"Her name," I answer with triumph, "was not Margaret"; but this makes her ripple again. "I have so many names nowadays," she mutters.

"H'sh!" says my father, and the reading is resumed.

Perhaps the woman who came along the path was of tall and majestic figure, which should have shown my mother that I had contrived to start my train without her this time. But it did not.

"What are you laughing at now?" says my sister severely. "Do you not hear that she was a tall, majestic woman?"

"It's the first time I ever heard it said of her," replies my mother.

"But she is."

"Ke fy, havers!"

"The book says it."

"There will be a many queer things in the book. What was she wearing?"

I have not described her clothes. "That's a mistake," says my mother. "When I come upon a woman in a book, the first thing I want to know about her is whether she was good-looking, and the second, how she was put on."

The woman on the path was eighteen years of age, and of remarkable beauty.

"That settles you," says my sister.

"I was no beauty at eighteen," my mother admits, but here my father interferes unexpectedly. "There wasna your like in this countryside at eighteen," says he stoutly.

"Pooh!" says she, well-pleased.

"Were you plain, then?" we ask.

"Sal," she replies briskly, "I was far from plain."

"H'sh!"

Perhaps in the next chapter this lady (or another) appears in a carriage.

"I assure you we're mounting in the world," I hear my mother murmur, but I hurry on without looking up. The lady lives in a house where there are footmen—but the footmen have come on the scene too hurriedly. "This is more than I can stand," gasps my mother, and just as she is getting the better of a fit of laughter, "Footman, give me a drink of water," she cries, and this sets her off again. Often the readings had to end abruptly because her mirth brought on violent fits of coughing.

Sometimes I read to my sister alone, and she assured me that she could not see my mother among the women this time. This she said to humor me. Presently she would slip upstairs to announce triumphantly, "You are in again!"

Or in the small hours I might make a confidant of my father, and when I had finished reading he would say thoughtfully, "That lassie is very natural. Some of the ways you say she had—your mother had them just the same. Did you ever notice what an extraordinary woman your mother is?"

Then would I seek my mother for comfort. She was the more ready to give it because of her profound conviction that if I was found out—that is, if readers discovered how frequently and in how many guises she appeared in my books—the affair would become a public scandal.

"You see Jess is not really you," I begin inquiringly.

"Oh, no, she is another kind of woman altogether," my mother says, and then spoils the compliment by adding naïvely, "She had but two rooms and I have six."

I sigh. "Without counting the pantry, and it's a great big pantry," she mutters.

This was not the sort of difference I could greatly plume myself upon, and honesty would force me to say, "As far as that goes, there was a time when you had but two rooms yourself——"

"That's long since," she breaks in. "I began with an up-the-stair, but I always had it in my mind—I never mentioned it, but there it was—to have the down-the-stair as well. Ay, and I've had it this many a year."

"Still, there is no denying that Jess had the same ambition."

"She had, but to her two-roomed house she had to stick all her born days. Was that like me?"

"No, but she wanted——"

"She wanted, and I wanted, but I got and she didna. That's the difference betwixt her and me."

"If that is all the difference, it is little credit I can claim for having created her."

My mother sees that I need soothing. "That is far from being all the difference," she would say eagerly. "There's my silk, for instance.

Though I say it mysel, there's not a better silk in the valley of Strath-more. Had Jess a silk of any kind—not to speak of a silk like that?"

"Well, she had no silk, but you remember how she got that cloak with beads."

"An eleven and a bit! Hoots, what was that to boast of! I tell you, every single yard of my silk cost——"

"Mother, that is the very way Jess spoke about her cloak!"

She lets this pass, perhaps without hearing it, for solicitude about her silk has hurried her to the wardrobe where it hangs.

"Ah, mother, I am afraid that was very like Jess!"

"How could it be like her when she didna even have a wardrobe? I tell you what, if there had been a real Jess and she had boasted to me about her cloak with beads, I would have said to her in a careless sort of voice, 'Step across with me, Jess, and I'll let you see something that is hanging in my wardrobe.' That would have lowered her pride!"

"I don't believe that is what you would have done, mother."

Then a sweeter expression would come into her face. "No," she would say reflectively, "it's not."

"What would you have done? I think I know."

"You canna know But I'm thinking I would have called to mind that she was a poor woman, and ailing, and terrible windy about her cloak, and I would just have said it was a beauty and that I wished I had one like it."

"Yes, I am certain that is what you would have done. But oh, mother, that is just how Jess would have acted if some poorer woman than she had shown her a new shawl."

"Maybe, but though I hadna boasted about my silk I would have wanted to do it."

"Just as Jess would have been fidgeting to show off her eleven and a bit!"

It seems advisable to jump to another book; not to my first, because—well, as it was my first there would naturally be something of my mother in it, and not to the second, as it was my first novel and not much esteemed even in our family. (But the little touches of my mother in it are not so bad.) Let us try the story about the minister.

My mother's first remark is decidedly damping. "Many a time in my young days," she says, "I played about the Auld Licht manse, but I little thought I should live to be the mistress of it!"

"But Margaret is not you."

"N—no, oh no. She had a very different life from mine. I never let on to a soul that she is me!"

"She was not meant to be you when I began. Mother, what a way you have of coming creeping in!"

"You should keep better watch on yourself."

"Perhaps if I had called Margaret by some other name——"

"I should have seen through her just the same. As soon as I heard she was the mother I began to laugh. In some ways, though, she's no so very like me. She was long in finding out about Babbie. I'se uphaud I should have been quicker."

"Babbie, you see, kept close to the garden-wall."

"It's not the wall up at the manse that would have hidden her from me."

"She came out in the dark."

"I'm thinking she would have found me looking for her with a candle."

"And Gavin was secretive."

"That would have put me on my mettle."

"She never suspected anything."

"I wonder at her."

But my new heroine is to be a child. What has madam to say to that?

A child! Yes, she has something to say even to that. "This beats all!" are the words.

"Come, come, mother, I see what you are thinking, but I assure you that this time——"

"Of course not," she said soothingly, "oh, no, she canna be me"; but anon her real thoughts are revealed by the artless remark, "I doubt, though, this is a tough job you have on hand—it is so long since I was a bairn."

We came very close to each other in those talks. "It is a queer thing," she would say softly, "that near everything you write is about this bit place. You little expected that when you began. I mind well the time when it never entered your head, any more than mine, that you could write a page about our squares and wynds. I wonder how it has come about?"

There was a time when I could not have answered that question, but that time had long passed. "I suppose, mother, it was because you were most at home in your own town, and there was never much pleasure to me in writing of people who could not have known you, nor of squares and wynds you never passed through, nor of a countryside where you never carried your father's dinner in a flaggon. There is scarce a house in all my books where I have not seemed to see you a thousand times, bending over the fireplace or winding up the clock."

"And yet you used to be in such a quandary because you knew nobody you could make your women-folk out of! Do you mind that, and how we both laughed at the notion of your having to make them out of me?"

"I remember."

"And now you've gone back to my father's time. It's more than sixty years since I carried his dinner in a flaggon through the long parks of Kinnordy."

"I often go into the long parks, mother, and sit on the stile at the edge of the wood till I fancy I see a little girl coming toward me with a flaggon in her hand."

"Jumping the burn (I was once so proud of my jumps!) and swinging the flaggon round so quick that what was inside hadna time to fall out. I used to wear a magenta frock and a white pinafore. Did I ever tell you that?"

"Mother, the little girl in my story wears a magenta frock and a white pinafore."

"You minded that! But I'm thinking it wasna a lassie in a pinafore you saw in the long parks of Kinnordy, it was just a gey done auld woman."

"It was a lassie in a pinafore, mother, when she was far away, but when she came near it was a gey done auld woman."

"And a fell ugly one!"

"The most beautiful one I shall ever see."

"I wonder to hear you say it. Look at my wrinkled auld face."

"It is the sweetest face in all the world."

"See how the rings drop off my poor wasted finger."

"There will always be some one nigh, mother, to put them on again."

"Ay, will there! Well I know it. Do you mind how when you were but a bairn you used to say, 'Wait till I'm a man, and you'll never have a reason for greeting again'?"

I remember.

"You used to come running into the house to say, 'There's a proud dame going down the Marywellbrae in a cloak that is black on one side and white on the other; wait till I'm a man, and you'll have one the very same.' And when I lay on gey hard beds you said, 'When I'm a man you'll lie on feathers.' You saw nothing bonny, you never heard of my setting my heart on anything, but what you flung up your head and cried, 'Wait till I'm a man.' You fair shamed me before the neighbors, and yet I was windy, too. And now it has all come true like a dream. I can call to mind not one little thing I ettled for in my lusty days that hasna been put into my hands in my auld age; I sit here useless, surrounded by the gratification of all my wishes and all my ambitions, and at times I'm near terrified, for it's as if God had mista'en me for some other woman."

"Your hopes and ambitions were so simple," I would say, but she did not like that. "They werna that simple," she would answer, flushing.

I am reluctant to leave those happy days, but the end must be faced, and as I write I seem to see my mother growing smaller and her face more wistful, and still she lingers with us, as if God had said, "Child of mine, your time has come, be not afraid," and she was not afraid, but still she lingered, and He waited, smiling. I never read any of that last book to her; when it was finished she was too heavy with years to follow a story. To me this was as if my book must go out cold into the world (like all that may come after it from me), and my sister, who took more thought for others and less for herself than any other human being I have known, saw this, and by some means unfathomable to a man coaxed my mother into being once again the woman she had been. On a day but three weeks before she died my father and I were called softly upstairs. My mother was sitting bolt upright, as she loved to sit, in her old chair by the window, with a manuscript in her hands. But she was looking about her without much understanding. "Just to please him," my sister whispered, and then in a low, trembling voice my mother began to read. I looked at my sister. Tears of woe were stealing down her face. Soon the reading became very slow and stopped. After a pause, "There was something you were to say to him," my sister reminded her. "Luck," muttered a voice as from the dead, "luck." And then the old smile came running to her face like a lamp-lighter, and she said to me, "I am ower far gone to read, but I'm thinking I am in it again!" My father put her Testament in her hands, and it fell open—as it always does—at the Fourteenth of John. She made an effort to read but could not. Suddenly she stooped and kissed the broad page. "Will that do instead?" she asked.

R. L. S.

THESE familiar initials are, I suppose, the best beloved in recent literature, certainly they are the sweetest to me, but there was a time when my mother could not abide them. She said "That Stevenson man" with a sneer, and it was never easy to her to sneer. At thought of him her face would become almost hard, which seems incredible, and she would knit her lips and fold her arms, and reply with a stiff "oh" if you mentioned his aggravating name. In the novels we have a way of writing of our heroine, "she drew herself up haughtily," and when mine draw themselves up haughtily I see my mother thinking of Robert Louis Stevenson. He knew her opinion of him, and would write, "My ears tingled yesterday; I sair doubt she has been miscalling me again." But the more she miscalled him the more he delighted in her, and she was informed of this, and at once said "The scoundrel!" If you would know what was his unpardonable crime, it was this, he wrote better books than mine.

I remember the day she found it out, which was not, however, the day she admitted it. That day, when I should have been at my work, she came upon me in the kitchen, "The Master of Ballantrae" beside me, but I was not reading: my head lay heavy on the table and to her anxious eyes, I doubt not, I was the picture of woe. "Not writing!" I echoed, no, I was not writing, I saw no use in ever trying to write again. And down, I suppose, went my head once more. She misunderstood, and thought the blow had fallen; I had awakened to the discovery, always dreaded by her, that I had written myself dry; I was no better than an empty ink-bottle. She wrung her hands, but indignation came to her with my explanation, which was that while R. L. S. was at it we others were only 'prentices cutting our fingers on his tools. "I could never thole his books," said my mother immediately, and indeed vindictively.

"You have not read any of them," I reminded her.

"And never will," said she, with spirit.

And I have no doubt that she called him a dark character that very day. For weeks too, if not for months, she adhered to her determination not to read him, though I, having come to my senses and seen that there is a place for the 'prentice, was taking a pleasure, almost malicious, in putting "The Master of Ballantrae" in her way. I would place it on her table so that it said good-morning to her when she rose. She would frown, and carrying it downstairs, as if she had it in the tongs, replace it on its book-shelf. I would wrap it up in the cover she had made for the latest Carlyle: she would skin it contemptuously and again bring it down. I would hide her spectacles in it, and lay it on top of the clothes-basket and prop it up invitingly open against her tea-pot. And at last I got her, though I forget by which of many contrivances. What I recall vividly is a key-hole view, to which another member of the family invited me. Then I saw my mother wrapped up in "The Master of Ballantrae" and muttering the music to herself, nodding her head in approval, and taking a stealthy glance at the foot of each page before she began at the top. Nevertheless she had an ear for the door, for when I bounced in she had been too clever for me; there was no book to be seen, only an apron on her lap and she was gazing out at the window. Some such conversation as this followed:

"You have been sitting very quietly, mother."

"I always sit quietly, I never do anything, I'm just a finished stocking."

"Have you been reading?"

"Do I ever read at this time of day?"

"What is that in your lap?"

"Just my apron."

"Is that a book beneath the apron?"

"It might be a book."

"Let me see."

"Go away with you to your work."

But I lifted the apron. "Why, it's 'The Master of Ballantrae!'" I exclaimed, shocked.

"So it is!" said my mother, equally surprised. But I looked sternly at her, and perhaps she blushed.

"Well what do you think: not nearly equal to mine?" said I with humor.

"Nothing like them," she said determinedly.

"Not a bit," said I, though whether with a smile or a groan is immaterial; they would have meant the same thing. Should I put the book back on its shelf? I asked, and she replied that I could put it wherever I liked for all she cared, so long as I took it out of her sight (the implication was that it had stolen on to her lap while she was looking out at the window). My behavior may seem small, but I gave her a last chance, for I said that some people found it a book there was no putting down until they reached the last page.

"I'm no that kind," replied my mother.

Nevertheless our old game with the haver of a thing, as she called it, was continued, with this difference, that it was now she who carried the book covertly upstairs, and I who replaced it on the shelf, and several times we caught each other in the act, but not a word said either of us; we were grown self-conscious. Much of the play no doubt I forget, but one incident I remember clearly. She had come down to sit beside me while I wrote, and sometimes, when I looked up, her eye was not on me, but on the shelf where 'The Master of Ballantrae' stood inviting her. Mr. Stevenson's books are not for the shelf, they are for the hand;

even when you lay them down, let it be on the table for the next comer. Being the most sociable that man has penned in our time, they feel very lonely up there in a stately row. I think their eye is on you the moment you enter the room, and so you are drawn to look at them, and you take a volume down with the impulse that induces one to unchain the dog. And the result is not dissimilar, for in another moment you two are at play. Is there any other modern writer who gets round you in this way? Well, he had given my mother the look which in the ball-room means, "Ask me for this waltz," and she ettled to do it, but felt that her more dutiful course was to sit out the dance with this other less entertaining partner. I wrote on doggedly, but could hear the whispering.

"Am I to be a wall-flower?" asked James Durie reproachfully. (It must have been leap-year.)

"Speak lower," replied my mother, with an uneasy look at me.

"Pooh!" said James contemptuously, "that kail-runtle!"

"I winna have him miscalled," said my mother, frowning.

"I am done with him," said James (wiping his cane with his cambric handkerchief), and his sword clattered deliciously (I cannot think this was accidental), which made my mother sigh. Like the man he was, he followed up his advantage with a comparison that made me dip viciously.

"A prettier sound that," said he, clanking his sword again, "than the clack-clack of your young friend's shuttle."

"Whist!" cried my mother, who had seen me dip.

"Then give me your arm," said James, lowering his voice.

"I dare not," answered my mother. "He's so touchy about you."

"Come, come," he pressed her, "you are certain to do it sooner or later, so why not now?"

"Wait till he has gone for his walk," said my mother; "and, forby that, I'm ower old to dance with you."

"How old are you?" he inquired.

"You're gey an' pert!" cried my mother.

"Are you seventy?"

"Off and on," she admitted.

"Pooh!" he said, "a mere girl!"

She replied instantly, "I'm no to be catched with chaff"; but she smiled and rose as if he had stretched out his hand and got her by the finger-tip.

After that they whispered so low (which they could do as they were now much nearer each other) that I could catch only one remark. It came from James, and seems to show the tenor of their whisperings, for his words were, "Easily enough, if you slip me beneath your shawl."

That is what she did, and furthermore she left the room guiltily, muttering something about redding up the drawers. I suppose I smiled wanly to myself, or conscience must have been nibbling at my mother, for in less than five minutes she was back, carrying her accomplice openly, and she thrust him with positive viciousness into the place where my Stevenson had lost a tooth (as the writer whom he most resembled would have said). And then like a good mother she took up one of her son's books and read it most determinedly. It had become a touching incident to me, and I remember how we there and then agreed upon a compromise: she was to read the enticing thing just to convince herself of its inferiority.

"The Master of Ballantrae" is not the best. Conceive the glory, which was my mother's, of knowing from a trustworthy source that there are at least three better awaiting you on the same shelf. She did not know Alan Breck yet, and he was as anxious to step down as Mr. Bally himself. John Silver was there, getting into his leg, so that she should not have to wait a moment, and roaring, "I'll lay to that!" when she told me consolingly that she could not thole pirate stories. Not to know these gentlemen, what is it like? It is like never having been in love. But they are in the house! That is like knowing that you will fall in love to-morrow morning. With one word, by drawing one mournful face, I could have got my mother to adjure the jam-shelf—nay, I might have managed it by merely saying that she had enjoyed "The Master of Ballantrae." For you must remember that she only read it to persuade herself (and me) of its unworthiness, and that the reason she wanted to read the others was to get further proof. All this she made plain to me, eyeing me a little anxiously the while, and of course I accepted the explanation. Alan is the biggest child of them all, and I doubt not that she thought so, but curiously enough her views of him are among the things I have forgotten. But how enamored she was of "Treasure Island," and how faithful she tried to be to me all the time she was reading it! I had to put my hands over her eyes to let her know that I had entered the room, and even then she might try to read between my fingers, coming to herself presently, however, to say "It's a haver of a book."

"Those pirate stories are so uninteresting," I would reply without fear, for she was too engrossed to see through me. "Do you think you will finish this one?"

"I may as well go on with it since I have begun it," my mother says, so slily that my sister and I shake our heads at each other to imply, "Was there ever such a woman!"

"There are none of those one-legged scoundrels in my books," I say.

"Better without them," she replies promptly.

"I wonder, mother, what it is about the man that so infatuates the public?"

"He takes no hold of me," she insists. "I would a hantle rather read your books."

I offer obligingly to bring one of them to her, and now she looks at me suspiciously. "You surely believe I like yours best," she says with instant anxiety, and I soothe her by assurances, and retire advising her to read on, just to see if she can find out how he misleads the public. "Oh, I may take a look at it again by and by," she says indifferently, but nevertheless the probability is that as the door shuts the book opens, as if by some mechanical contrivance. I remember how she read "Treasure Island," holding it close to the ribs of the fire (because she could not spare a moment to rise and light the gas), and how, when bed-time came, and we coaxed, remonstrated, scolded, she said quite fiercely, clinging to the book, "I dinna lay my head on a pillow this night till I see how that laddie got out of the barrel."

After this, I think, he was as bewitching as the laddie in the barrel to her—Was he not always a laddie in the barrel himself, climbing in for apples while we all stood around, like gamins, waiting for a bite? He was the spirit of boyhood tugging at the skirts of this old world of ours and compelling it to come back and play. And I suppose my mother felt this, as so many have felt it : like others she was a little scared at first to find herself skipping again, with this masterful child at the rope, but soon she gave him her hand and set off with him for the meadow, not an apology between the two of them for the author left behind. But never to the end did she admit (in words) that he had a way with him which was beyond her son. "Silk and sacking, that is what we are," she was informed, to which she would reply obstinately, "Well, then, I prefer sacking."

"But if he had been your son?"

"But he is not!"

"You wish he were?"

"I dinna deny but what I could have found room for him."

And still at times she would smear him with the name of black (to his delight when he learned the reason). That was when some podgy red-sealed blue-crossed letter arrived from Vailima, inviting me to journey thither. (His directions were, "You take the boat at San Francisco, and then my place is the second to the left.") Even London seemed to her to carry me so far away that I often took a week to the journey (the first six days in getting her used to the idea), and these letters terrified her. It was not the finger of Jim Hawkins she now saw beckoning me across the seas, it was John Silver, waving a crutch. Seldom, I believe, did I read straight through one of these Vailima letters; when in the middle I suddenly remembered who was upstairs and what she was probably doing, and I ran to her, three steps at a jump, to find her, lips pursed, hands folded, a picture of gloom.

"I have a letter from——"

"So I have heard."

"Would you like to hear it?"

"No."

"Can you not abide him?"

"I canna thole him."

"Is he a black?"

"He is all that."

Well, Vailima was the one spot on earth I had any great craving to visit, but I think she always knew I would never leave her. Sometime, she said, she should like me to go, but not until she was laid away. "And how small I have grown this last winter. Look at my wrists. It canna be long now." No, I never thought of going, was never absent for a day from her without reluctance, and never walked so quickly as when I was going back. In the meantime that happened which put an end for ever to my scheme of travel. I shall never go up the Road of Loving Hearts now, on "a wonderful clear night of stars," to meet the man coming toward me on a horse. It is still a wonderful clear night of stars, but the road is empty. So I never saw the dear king of us all. But before he had written books he was in my part of the country with a fishing wand in his hand, and I like to think that I was the boy who met him that day by Queen Margaret's burn, where the rowans are, and busked a fly for him, and stood watching, while his lithe figure rose and fell as he cast and hinted back from the crystal waters of Noran-side.

From THE LITTLE WHITE BIRD

The Inconsiderate Waiter

THEY were the family of William, one of our club waiters who had been disappointing me grievously of late. Many a time have I deferred dining several minutes that I might have the attendance of this ingrate. His efforts to reserve the window-table for me were satisfactory, and I used to allow him privileges, as to suggest dishes; I have given him information, as that some one had startled me in the reading-room by slamming a door; I have shown him how I cut my finger with a piece of string. William was none of your assertive waiters. We could have plotted a murder safely before him. It was one member who said to him that Saucy Sarah would win the Derby and another who said that Saucy Sarah had no chance, but it was William who agreed with both. The excellent fellow (as I thought him) was like a cheroot which may be smoked from either end.

I date his lapse from one evening when I was dining by the window. I had to repeat my order "Devilled kidney," and instead of answering brightly, "Yes, sir," as if my selection of devilled kidney was a personal gratification to him, which is the manner one expects of a waiter, he gazed eagerly out at the window, and then, starting, asked, "Did you say devilled kidney, sir?" A few minutes afterward I became aware that some one was leaning over the back of my chair, and you may conceive my indignation on discovering that this rude person was William. Let me tell, in the measured words of one describing a past incident, what next took place. To get nearer the window he pressed heavily on my shoulder. "William," I said, "you are not attending to me!"

To be fair to him, he shook, but never shall I forget his audacious apology, "Beg pardon, sir, but I was thinking of something else."

And immediately his eyes resought the window, and this burst from him passionately, "For God's sake, sir, as we are man and man, tell me if you have seen a little girl looking up at the club-windows."

Man and man! But he had been a good waiter once, so I pointed out the girl to him. As soon as she saw William she ran into the middle of Pall Mall, regardless of hansoms (many of which seemed to pass over her), nodded her head significantly three times and then disappeared (probably on a stretcher). She was the tawdriest little Arab of about ten years, but seemed to have brought relief to William. "Thank God!" said he fervently, and in the worst taste.

I was as much horrified as if he had dropped a plate on my toes. "Bread, William," I said sharply.

"You are not vexed with me, sir?" he had the hardihood to whisper.

"It was a liberty," I said.

"I know, sir, but I was beside myself."

"That was a liberty again."

"It is my wife, sir, she—"

So William, whom I had favored in so many ways, was a married man. I felt that this was the greatest liberty of all.

I gathered that the troublesome woman was ailing, and as one who likes after dinner to believe that there is no distress in the world, I desired to be told by William that the signals meant her return to health. He answered inconsiderately, however, that the doctor feared the worst.

"Bah, the doctor," I said in a rage.

"Yes, sir," said William.

"What is her confounded ailment?"

"She was allus one of the delicate kind, but full of spirit, and you see, sir, she has had a baby-girl lately—"

"William, how dare you," I said, but in the same moment I saw that this father might be useful to me. "How does your baby sleep, William?" I asked in a low voice, "how does she wake up? what do you put in her bath?"

I saw surprise in his face, so I hurried on without waiting for an answer. "That little girl comes here with a message from your wife?"

"Yes, sir, every evening; she's my eldest, and three nods from her means that the missus is a little better."

"There were three nods to-day?"

"Yes, sir."

"I suppose you live in some low part, William?"

The impudent fellow looked as if he could have struck me. "Off Drury Lane," he said, flushing, "but it isn't low. And now," he groaned, "she's afeared she will die without my being there to hold her hand."

"She should not say such things."

"She never says them, sir. She allus pretends to be feeling stronger. But I knows what is in her mind when I am leaving the house in the morning, for then she looks at me from her bed, and I looks at her from the door—oh, my God, sir!"

"William!"

At last he saw that I was angry, and it was characteristic of him to beg my pardon and withdraw his wife as if she were some unsuccessful dish. I tried to forget his vulgar story in billiards, but he had spoiled my game, and next day to punish him I gave my orders through another waiter. As I had the window-seat, however, I could not but see that the little girl was late, and though this mattered nothing to me and I had finished my dinner, I lingered till she came. She not only nodded three times but waved her hat, and I arose, having now finished my dinner.

William came stealthily toward me. "Her temperature has gone down, sir," he said, rubbing his hands together.

"To whom are you referring?" I asked coldly, and retired to the billiard-room, where I played a capital game.

I took pains to show William that I had forgotten his maunderings, but I observed the girl nightly, and once, instead of nodding, she shook her head, and that evening I could not get into a pocket. Next evening there was no William in the dining-room, and I thought I knew what had happened. But, chancing to enter the library rather miserably, I was surprised to see him on a ladder dusting books. We had the room practically to ourselves, for though several members sat on chairs holding books in their hands they were all asleep, and William descended the ladder to tell me his blasting tale. He had sworn at a member!

"I hardly knew what I was doing all day, sir, for I had left her so weakly that——"

I stamped my foot.

"I beg your pardon for speaking of her," he had the grace to say. "But Irene had promised to come every two hours; and when she came about four o'clock and I saw she was crying, it sort of blinded me, sir, and I stumbled against a member, Mr. B——, and he said, 'Damn you!' Well, sir, I had but touched him after all, and I was so broken it sort of stung me to be treated so, and I lost my senses, and I said, 'Damn you!'"

His shamed head sank on his chest, and I think some of the readers shuddered in their sleep.

"I was turned out of the dining-room at once, and sent here until the committee have decided what to do with me. Oh, sir, I am willing to go on my knees to Mr. B——"

How could I but despise a fellow who would be thus abject for a pound a week?

"For if I have to tell her I have lost my place she will just fall back and die."

"I forbid your speaking to me of that woman," I cried wryly, "unless you can speak pleasantly," and I left him to his fate and went off to look for B——. "What is this story about your swearing at one of the waiters?" I asked him.

"You mean about his swearing at me," said B——, reddening.

"I am glad that was it," I said, "for I could not believe you guilty of such bad form. The version which reached me was that you swore at each other, and that he was to be dismissed and you reprimanded."

"Who told you that?" asked B——, who is a timid man.

"I am on the committee," I replied lightly, and proceeded to talk of other matters, but presently B——, who had been reflecting, said: "Do you know I fancy I was wrong in thinking that the waiter swore at me, and I shall withdraw the charge to-morrow."

I was pleased to find that William's troubles were near an end without my having to interfere in his behalf, and I then remembered that he would not be able to see the girl Irene from the library windows, which are at the back of the club. I was looking down at her, but she refrained from signalling because she could not see William, and irritated by her stupidity I went out and asked her how her mother was.

"My," she ejaculated after a long scrutiny of me, "I b'lieve you are one of them!" and she gazed at me with delighted awe. I suppose William tells them of our splendid doings.

The invalid, it appeared, was a bit better, and this annoying child wanted to inform William that she had took all the tapiocar. She was to indicate this by licking an imaginary plate in the middle of Pall Mall. I gave the little vulgarian a shilling, and returned to the club disgusted.

"By the way, William," I said, "Mr. B—— is to inform the committee that he was mistaken in thinking you used improper language to him, so you will doubtless be restored to the dining-room to-morrow."

I had to add immediately, "Remember your place, William."

"But Mr. B—— knows I swore," he insisted.

"A gentleman," I replied stiffly, "cannot remember for many hours what a waiter has said to him."

"No, sir, but——"

To stop him I had to say, "And—ah—William, your wife is decidedly better. She has eaten the tapioca—all of it."

"How can you know, sir?"

"By an accident."

"Irene signed to the window?"

"No."

"Then you saw her and went out and——"

"How dare you, William?"

"Oh, sir, to do that for me! May God bl——"

"William."

He was reinstated in the dining-room, but often when I looked at him I seemed to see a dying wife in his face, and so the relations between us were still strained. But I watched the girl, and her pantomime was so illuminating that I knew the sufferer had again cleaned the platter on Tuesday, had attempted a boiled egg on Wednesday (you should have seen Irene chipping it in Pall Mall, and putting in the salt), but was in a woful state of relapse on Thursday.

"Is your mother very ill to-day, Miss Irene?" I asked, as soon as I had drawn her out of range of the club-windows.

"My!" she exclaimed again, and I saw an ecstatic look pass between her and a still smaller girl with her, whom she referred to as a neighbor.

I waited coldly. William's wife, I was informed, had looked like nothing but a dead one till she got the brandy.

"Hush, child," I said, shocked. "You don't know how the dead look."

"Bless yer!" she replied.

Assisted by her friend, who was evidently enormously impressed by Irene's intimacy with me, she gave me a good deal of miscellaneous information, as that William's real name was Mr. Hicking, but that he was known in their street, because of the number of his shirts, as Toff Hicking. That the street held he should get away from the club before two in the morning, for his missus needed him more than the club needed him. That William replied (very sensibly) that if the club was short of waiters at supper-time some of the gentlemen might be kept waiting for their marrow-bone. That he sat up with his missus most of the night, and pretended to her that he got some nice long naps at the club. That what she talked to him about mostly was the kid. That the kid was in another part of London (in charge of a person called the old woman), because there was an epidemic in Irene's street.

"And what does the doctor say about your mother?"

"He sometimes says she would have a chance if she could get her kid back."

"Nonsense."

"And if she was took to the country."

"Then why does not William take her?"

"My! And if she drank porty wine."

"Doesn't she?"

"No. But father, he tells her 'bout how the gentlemen drinks it."

I turned from her with relief, but she came after me.

"Ain't yer going to do it this time?" she demanded with a falling face. "You done it last time. I tell her you done it"—she pointed to her friend who was looking wistfully at me—"ain't you to let her see you doing of it?"

For a moment I thought that her desire was another shilling, but by a piece of pantomime she showed that she wanted me to lift my hat to her. So I lifted it, and when I looked behind she had her head in the air and her neighbor was gazing at her awestruck. These little creatures are really not without merit.

About a week afterward I was in a hired landau, holding a newspaper before my face lest any one should see me in company of a waiter and his wife. William was taking her into Surrey to stay with an old nurse of mine, and Irene was with us, wearing the most outrageous bonnet.

I formed a mean opinion of Mrs. Hicking's intelligence from her pride in the baby, which was a very ordinary one. She created a regrettable scene when it was brought to her, because "she had been feared it would not know her again." I could have told her that they know no one for years had I not been in terror of Irene, who dandled the child on her knees and talked to it all the way. I have never known a bolder little hussy than this Irene. She asked the infant improper questions, such as "Oo know who gave me this bonnet?" and answered them herself. "It was the pretty gentleman there," and several times I had to affect sleep, because she announced, "Kiddy wants to kiss the pretty gentleman."

Irksome as all this necessarily was to a man of taste, I suffered still more acutely when we reached our destination, where disagreeable circumstances compelled me to drink tea with a waiter's family. William knew that I regarded thanks from persons of his class as an outrage, yet he looked them though he dared not speak them. Hardly had he sat down at the table by my orders than he remembered that I was a member of the club and jumped up. Nothing is in worse form than whispering, yet again and again he whispered to his poor, foolish wife, "How are you now? You don't feel faint?" and when she said she felt like another woman already, his face charged me with the change. I could not but conclude from the way she let the baby pound her that she was stronger than she pretended.

I remained longer than was necessary because I had something to say to William which I feared he would misunderstand, but when he announced that it was time for him to catch a train back to London, at which his wife paled, I delivered the message.

"William," I said, backing away from him, "the head-waiter asked me to say that you could take a fortnight's holiday. Your wages will be paid as usual."

Confound him.

"William," I cried furiously, "go away."

Then I saw his wife signing to him, and I knew she wanted to be left alone with me.

"William," I cried in a panic, "stay where you are."

But he was gone, and I was alone with a woman whose eyes were filmy. Her class are fond of scenes. "If you please, ma'am!" I said imploringly.

But she kissed my hand; she was like a little dog.

"It can be only the memory of some woman," said she, "that makes you so kind to me and mine."

Memory was the word she used, as if all my youth were fled. I suppose I really am quite elderly.

"I should like to know her name, sir," she said, "that I may mention her with loving respect in my prayers."

I raised the woman and told her the name. It was not Mary. "But she has a home," I said, "as you have, and I have none. Perhaps, ma'am, it would be better worth your while to mention me."

It was this woman, now in health, whom I intrusted with the purchase of the outfits, "one for a boy of six months," I explained to her, "and one for a boy of a year," for the painter had boasted to me of David's rapid growth. I think she was a little surprised to find that both outfits were for the same house; and she certainly betrayed an ignoble curiosity about the mother's Christian name, but she was much easier to brow-beat than a fine lady would have been, and I am sure she and her daughter enjoyed themselves hugely in the shops, from one of which I shall never forget Irene emerging proudly with a commissionaire, who conducted her under an umbrella to the cab where I was lying in wait. I think that was the most celestial walk of Irene's life.

I told Mrs. Hicking to give the articles a little active ill-treatment that they might not look quite new, at which she exclaimed, not being in my secret, and then to forward them to me. I then sent them to Mary and rejoiced in my devilish cunning all the evening, but chagrin came in the morning with a letter from her which showed she knew all, that I was her Mr. Anon, and that there never had been a Timothy. I think I was never so gravelled. Even now I don't know how she had contrived it.

Her cleverness raised such a demon in me that I locked away her letter at once and have seldom read it since. No married lady should have indited such an epistle to a single man. It said, with other things which I decline to repeat, that I was her good fairy. As a sample of the deliberate falsehoods in it, I may mention that she said David loved me already. She hoped that I would come in often to see her husband, who was very proud of my friendship, and suggested that I should pay him my first visit to-day at three o'clock, an hour at which, as I happened to know, he is always away giving a painting lesson. In short, she wanted first to meet me alone, so that she might draw the delicious, respectful romance out of me, and afterward repeat it to him, with sighs and little peeps at him over her pocket handkerchief.

She had dropped what were meant to look like two tears for me upon the paper, but I should not wonder though they were only artful drops of water.

I sent her a stiff and tart reply, declining to hold any communication with her.

FRANCIS THOMPSON (1860-1907)

Daisy

WHERE the thistle lifts a purple crown
　Six foot out of the turf,
And the harebell shakes on the windy
　　hill—
　O breath of the distant surf!—

The hills look over on the South,
　And southward dreams the sea;
And with the sea-breeze hand in hand
　Came innocence and she.

Where 'mid the gorse the raspberry
　Red for the gatherer springs,
Two children did we stray and talk
　Wise, idle, childish things.

She listened with big-lipped surprise,
　Breast-deep 'mid flower and spine:
Her skin was like a grape whose veins
　Run snow instead of wine.

She knew not those sweet words she
　　spake,
　Nor knew her own sweet way;
But there's never a bird, so sweet a song
　Thronged in whose throat that day.

Oh, there were flowers in Storrington
　On the turf and on the spray;
But the sweetest flower on Sussex hills
　Was the Daisy-flower that day!

Her beauty smoothed earth's furrowed
　　face.
　She gave me tokens three:—
A look, a word of her winsome mouth,
　And a wild raspberry.

A berry red, a guileless look,
　A still word,—strings of sand!
And yet they made my wild, wild heart
　Fly down to her little hand.

For standing artless as the air,
　And candid as the skies,
She took the berries with her hand,
　And the love with her sweet eyes.

The fairest things have fleetest end,
　Their scent survives their close:
But the rose's scent is bitterness
　To him that loved the rose.

She looked a little wistfully,
　Then went her sunshine way:—
The sea's eye had a mist on it,
　And the leaves fell from the day.

She went her unremembering way,
　She went and left in me
The pang of all the partings gone,
　And partings yet to be.

She left me marvelling why my soul
　Was sad that she was glad;
At all the sadness in the sweet,
　The sweetness in the sad.

Still, still I seemed to see her, still
　Look up with soft replies,
And take the berries with her hand,
　And the love with her lovely eyes.

Nothing begins, and nothing ends,
　That is not paid with moan;
For we are born in other's pain,
　And perish in our own.

The Poppy

SUMMER set lip to earth's bosom bare,
And left the flushed print in a poppy
　　there:
Like a yawn of fire from the grass it
　　came,
And the fanning wind puffed it to flapping
　　flame.

With burnt mouth, red like a lion's, it
    drank
The blood of the sun as he slaughtered
    sank,
And dipped its cup in the purpurate shine
When the Eastern conduits ran with wine.

Till it grew lethargied with fierce bliss,
And hot as a swinked gipsy is,
And drowsed in sleepy savageries,
With mouth wide a-pout for a sultry kiss.

A child and man paced side by side,
Treading the skirts of eventide;
But between the clasp of his hand and
    hers
Lay, felt not, twenty withered years.

She turned, with the rout of her dusk
    South hair,
And saw the sleeping gipsy there:
And snatched and snapped it in swift
    child's whim,
With—"Keep it, long as you live!"—to
    him.

And his smile, as nymphs from their
    laving meres,
Trembled up from a bath of tears;
And joy, like a mew sea-rocked apart,
Tossed on the waves of his troubled heart.

For *he* saw what she did not see,
That—as kindled by its own fervency—
The verge shrivelled inward smoulder-
    ingly:
And suddenly 'twixt his hand and hers
He knew the twenty withered years—
No flower, but twenty shrivelled years.

"Was never such thing until this hour,"
Low to his heart he said; "the flower
Of sleep brings wakening to me,
And of oblivion, memory."

"Was never this thing to me," he said,
"Though with bruisèd poppies my feet
    are red!"
And again to his own heart very low:
"Oh child! I love, for I love and know;

"But you, who love nor know at all
The diverse chambers in Love's guest-
    hall,
Where some rise early, few sit long:
In how differing accents hear the throng
His great Pentecostal tongue;

"Who know not love from amity,
Nor my reported self from me;
A fair fit gift is this, meseems,
You give—this withering flower of
    dreams.

"O frankly fickle, and fickly true,
Do you know what the days will do to
    you?
To your love and you what the days will
    do,
O frankly fickle, and fickly true?

"You have loved me, Fair, three lives—or
    days:
'Twill pass with the passing of my face.
But where *I* go, your face goes too,
To watch lest I play false to you.

"I am but, my sweet, your foster-lover,
Knowing well when certain years are over
You vanish from me to another;
Yet I know, and love, like the foster-
    mother.

"So, frankly fickle, and fickly true!
For my brief life-while I take from you
This token, fair and fit, meseems,
For me—this withering flower of
    dreams."

The sleep-flower sways in the wheat its
    head,
Heavy with dreams, as that with bread:
The goodly grain and the sun-flushed
    sleeper
The reaper reaps, and Time the reaper.

I hang 'mid men my needless head,
And my fruit is dreams, as theirs is bread:
The goodly men and the sun-hazed sleeper
Time shall reap, but after the reaper
The world shall glean of me, me the
    sleeper.

Love, love! your flower of withered
dream
In leavèd rhyme lies safe, I deem,
Sheltered and shut in a nook of rhyme,
From the reaper man, and his reaper
Time.

Love! *I* fall into the claws of Time:
But lasts within a leavèd rhyme
All that the world of me esteems—
My withered dreams, my withered
dreams.

The Hound of Heaven

I FLED Him, down the nights and down
the days;
I fled Him, down the arches of the
years;
I fled Him, down the labyrinthine ways
Of my own mind; and in the mist of
tears
I hid from Him, and under running
laughter.
Up vistaed hopes I sped;
And shot, precipitated,
Adown Titanic glooms of chasmèd fears,
From those strong Feet that followed,
followed after.
But with unhurrying chase,
And unperturbèd pace,
Deliberate speed, majestic instancy,
They beat—and a Voice beat
More instant than the Feet—
"All things betray thee, who be-
trayest Me."

I pleaded, outlaw-wise,
By many a hearted casement, curtained
red,
Trellised with intertwining charities;
(For, though I knew His love Who fol-
lowèd,
Yet was I sore adread
Lest, having Him, I must have naught
beside.)
But, if one little casement parted wide,
The gust of His approach would clash
it to:

Fear wist not to evade, as Love wist to
pursue.
Across the margent of the world I fled,
And troubled the gold gateways of the
stars,
Smiting for shelter on their clangèd
bars;
Fretted to dulcet jars
And silvern chatter the pale ports o' the
moon.
I said to Dawn: Be sudden—to Eve: Be
soon;
With thy young skiey blossoms heap me
over
From this tremendous Lover—
Float thy vague veil about me, lest He
see!
I tempted all His servitors, but to
find!
My own betrayal in their constancy,
In faith to Him their fickleness to me,
Their traitorous trueness, and their
loyal deceit.
To all swift things for swiftness did I
sue;
Clung to the whistling mane of every
wind.
But whether they swept, smoothly
fleet,
The long savannahs of the blue;
Or whether, Thunder-driven,
They clanged his chariot 'thwart a
heaven,
Plashy with flying lightnings round the
spurn o' their feet:—
Fear wist not to evade as Love wist to
pursue.
Still with unhurrying chase,
And unperturbèd pace,
Deliberate speed, majestic instancy,
Came on the following Feet,
And a Voice above their beat—
"Naught shelters thee, who wilt not
shelter Me."

I sought no more that after which I
strayed
In face of man or maid;

But still within the little children's eyes
   Seems something, something that re-
     plies,
They at least are for me, surely for me!
I turned me to them very wistfully;
But just as their young eyes grew sudden
   fair
     With dawning answers there,
Their angel plucked them from me by the
   hair.
"Come then, ye other children, Nature's
   —share
With me" (said I) "your delicate fellow-
   ship;
     Let me greet you lip to lip,
     Let me twine with you caresses,
       Wantoning
     With our Lady-Mother's vagrant
       tresses,
       Banqueting
With her in her wind-walled palace,
Underneath her azured daïs,
Quaffing, as your taintless way is,
     From a chalice
Lucent-weeping out of the dayspring."
     So it was done:
I in their delicate fellowship was one—
Drew the bolt of Nature's secrecies.
   I knew all the swift importings
   On the wilful face of skies;
   I knew how the clouds arise
   Spumèd of the wild sea-snortings;
     All that's born or dies
   Rose and drooped with; made them
     shapers
Of mine own moods, or wailful or divine;
   With them joyed and was bereaven.
   I was heavy with the even,
   When she lit her glimmering tapers
   Round the day's dead sanctities.
   I laughed in the morning's eyes.
I triumphed and I saddened with all
   weather,
   Heaven and I wept together,
And its sweet tears were salt with mortal
   mine;
Against the red throb of its sunset-heart
   I laid my own to beat,
   And share commingling heat;

But not by that, by that, was eased my
   human smart.
In vain my tears were wet on Heaven's
   grey cheek.
For ah! we know not what each other
   says,
   These things and I; in sound I
     speak—
Their sound is but their stir, they speak
   by silences.
Nature, poor stepdame, cannot slake my
   drouth;
   Let her, if she would owe me,
Drop yon blue bosom-veil of sky, and
   show me
   The breasts o' her tenderness:
Never did any milk of hers once bless
   My thirsting mouth.
     Nigh and nigh draws the chase,
     With unperturbèd pace,
   Deliberate speed, majestic instancy;
     And past those noisèd Feet
     A voice comes yet more fleet—
   "Lo! naught contents thee, who con-
     tent'st not Me."

Naked I wait Thy love's uplifted stroke!
My harness piece by piece Thou hast
   hewn from me,
   And smitten me to my knee;
   I am defenceless utterly.
   I slept, methinks, and woke,
And, slowly gazing, find me stripped in
   sleep.
In the rash lustihead of my young
   powers,
   I shook the pillaring hours
And pulled my life upon me; grimed with
   smears,
I stand amid the dust o' the mounded
   years—
My mangled youth lies dead beneath the
   heap.
My days have crackled and gone up in
   smoke,
Have puffed and burst as sun-starts on a
   stream.
   Yea, faileth now even dream
The dreamer, and the lute the lutanist;

Even the linked fantasies, in whose blos-
somy twist
I swung the earth a trinket at my wrist,
Are yielding; cords of all too weak ac-
count
For earth with heavy griefs so over-
plussed.
Ah! is Thy love indeed
A weed, albeit an amaranthine weed,
Suffering no flowers except its own to
mount?
Ah! must—
Designer infinite!—
Ah! must Thou char the wood ere Thou
canst limn with it?
My freshness spent its wavering shower
i' the dust;
And now my heart is as a broken fount,
Wherein tear-drippings stagnate, spilt
down ever
From the dank thoughts that shiver
Upon the sighful branches of my mind.
Such is; what is to be?
The pulp so bitter, how shall taste the
rind?
I dimly guess what Time in mists con-
founds;
Yet ever and anon a trumpet sounds
From the hid battlements of Eternity;
Those shaken mists a space unsettle, then
Round the half-glimpsèd turrets slowly
wash again.
But not ere him who summoneth
first have seen, enwound
With glooming robes purpureal, cypress-
crowned;
His name I know, and what his trumpet
saith.
Whether man's heart or life it be which
yields
Thee harvest, must Thy harvest-
fields
Be dunged with rotten death?

Now of that long pursuit
Comes on at hand the bruit;
That Voice is round me like a burst-
ing sea:
"And is thy earth so marred,

Shattered in shard on shard?
Lo, all things fly thee, for thou fliest
Me!
Strange, piteous, futile thing!
Wherefore should any set thee love
apart?
Seeing none but I makes much of naught"
(He said),
"And human love needs human merit-
ing:
How hast thou merited—
Of all man's clotted clay the dingiest
clot?
Alack, thou knowest not
How little worthy of any love thou
art!
Whom wilt thou find to love ignoble
thee,
Save Me, save only Me?
All which I took from thee I did but
take,
Not for thy harms,
But just that thou might'st seek it in My
arms.
All which thy child's mistake
Fancies as lost, I have stored for thee at
home:
Rise, clasp My hand, and come!"
Halts by me that footfall:
Is my gloom, after all,
Shade of His hand, outstretched caress-
ingly?
"Ah, fondest, blindest, weakest,
I am He Whom thou seekest!
Thou dravest love from thee, who dravest
Me."

WILLIAM BUTLER YEATS

The Lake Isle of Innisfree

I WILL arise and go now, and go to
Innisfree,
And a small cabin build there, of clay
and wattles made;
Nine bean rows will I have there, a
hive for the honey bee,
And live alone in the bee-loud glade.

And I shall have some peace there, for
    peace comes dropping slow,
Dropping from the veils of the morning
    to where the cricket sings;
There midnight's all a glimmer, and noon
    a purple glow,
And evening full of the linnets' wings.

I will arise and go now, for always night
    and day
I hear lake water lapping with low
    sounds by the shore;
While I stand on the roadway, or on the
    pavements gray,
I hear it in the deep heart's core.

From CATHLEEN NI HOOLIHAN

One day in 1798, in a cottage close to Killala, Peter Gillane and his wife Bridget were busy with thoughts of the approaching wedding of their elder son Michael to Delia Cahel. The younger son, Patrick, a lad of twelve, saw an old woman wandering along the road, and watched her from the window. First she turned into the gap that went down to where Murteen and his sons were shearing their sheep. Patrick recalled a story of a strange woman that goes through the country whatever time there is war or trouble coming. Michael had just come in with Delia's marriage portion, a hundred pounds, and sent Patrick down to the town to see what might be causing the cheering they had heard, and Peter was glorying in the hundred pounds that Michael had brought home, when the poor old woman came to their own door.

PERSONS

PETER GILLANE
MICHAEL GILLANE.—*His son, going to be married*
PATRICK GILLANE.—*A lad of twelve,* MICHAEL'S *brother*
BRIDGET GILLANE.—*Peter's wife*
DELIA CAHEL.—*Engaged to* MICHAEL
THE POOR OLD WOMAN
NEIGHBOURS

SCENE: *Interior of a cottage close to Killala, in* 1798.

MICHAEL. They're not done cheering yet. [*He goes over to the door and stands there for a moment, putting up his hand to shade his eyes.*]

BRIDGET. Do you see anything?

MICHAEL. I see an old woman coming up the path.

BRIDGET. Who is it, I wonder?

MICHAEL. I don't think it's one of the neighbours, but she has her cloak over her face.

BRIDGET. Maybe it's the same woman Patrick saw a while ago. It might be some poor woman heard we were making ready for the wedding, and came to look for her share.

PETER. I may as well put the money out of sight. There's no use leaving it out for every stranger to look at. [*He goes over to a large box by the wall, opens it and puts the bag in, and fumbles with the lock.*]

MICHAEL. There she is, father! [*An* OLD WOMAN *passes the window slowly. She looks at* MICHAEL *as she passes.*] I'd sooner a stranger not to come to the house the night before the wedding.

BRIDGET. Open the door, Michael; don't keep the poor woman waiting. [*The* OLD WOMAN *comes in;* MICHAEL *stands aside to make way for her.*]

THE POOR OLD WOMAN. God save all here!

PETER. God save you kindly.

THE POOR OLD WOMAN. You have good shelter here.

PETER. You are welcome to whatever shelter we have.

BRIDGET. Sit down there by the fire and welcome.

THE POOR OLD WOMAN [*warming her hands*]. There's a hard wind outside.

MICHAEL *watches her curiously from the door.* PETER *comes over to the table.*

PETER. Have you travelled far to-day?

THE POOR OLD WOMAN. I have travelled far, very far; there are few have travelled so far as myself.

PETER. It is a pity, indeed, for any person to have no place of their own.

THE POOR OLD WOMAN. That is true for you indeed, and it is long I am on the road since I first went wandering. It is seldom I have any rest.

BRIDGET. It is a wonder you are not worn out with so much wandering.

THE POOR OLD WOMAN. Sometimes my feet are tired and my hands are quiet, but there is no quiet in my heart. When the people see me quiet, they think old age has come on me, and that all the stir has gone out of me.

BRIDGET. What was it put you astray?

THE POOR OLD WOMAN. Too many strangers in the house.

BRIDGET. Indeed you look as if you had had your share of trouble.

THE POOR OLD WOMAN. I have had trouble indeed.

BRIDGET. What was it put the trouble on you?

THE POOR OLD WOMAN. My land that was taken from me.

PETER. Was it much land they took from you?

THE POOR OLD WOMAN. My four beautiful green fields.

PETER. [*aside to* BRIDGET]. Do you think could she be the Widow Casey that was put out of her holding at Kilglas a while ago?

BRIDGET. She is not. I saw the Widow Casey one time at the market in Ballina, a stout, fresh woman.

PETER [*to* OLD WOMAN]. Did you hear a noise of cheering, and you coming up the hill?

THE POOR OLD WOMAN. I thought I heard the noise I used to hear when my friends came to visit me. [*She begins singing half to herself*]

> I will go cry with the woman,
> For yellow-haired Donough is dead;
> With a hempen rope for a neckcloth
> And a white cloth on his head.

10

MICHAEL [*coming from the door*]. What is that you are singing, ma'am?

THE POOR OLD WOMAN. Singing I am about a man I knew one time, yellow-haired Donough, that was hanged in Galway. [*She goes on singing much louder*]

> I am come to cry with you, woman,
> My hair is unwound and unbound;
> I remember him ploughing his field,
> Turning up the red side of the ground.
>
> And building his barn on the hill
> With the good mortared stone;
> O! we'd have pulled down the gallows
> Had it happened in Enniscrone!

MICHAEL. What was it brought him to his death?

THE POOR OLD WOMAN. He died for love of me; many a man has died for love of me.

PETER [*aside to* BRIDGET]. Her trouble has put her wits astray.

MICHAEL. Is it long since that song was made? Is it long since he got his death?

THE POOR OLD WOMAN. Not long, not long. But there were others that died for love of me a long time ago.

MICHAEL. Were they neighbours of your own, ma'am?

THE POOR OLD WOMAN. Come here beside me and I'll tell you about them. [MICHAEL *sits down beside her at the hearth.*] There was a red man of the O'Donells from the North, and a man of the O'Sullivans from the South, and there was one Brian that lost his life at Clontarf, by the sea, and there were a great many in the West, some that died hundreds of years ago, and there are some that will die to-morrow.

MICHAEL. Is it in the West that men will die to-morrow?

THE POOR OLD WOMAN. Come nearer, nearer to me.

BRIDGET. Is she right, do you think? or is she a woman from the North?

PETER. She doesn't know well what she's talking about, with the want and the trouble she has gone through.

BRIDGET. The poor thing, we should treat her well.

PETER. Give her a drink of milk and a bit of the oaten cake.

BRIDGET. Maybe we should give her something along with that to bring her on her way—a few pence, or a shilling itself, and we with so much money in the house.

PETER. Indeed, I'd not begrudge it to her if we had it to spare; but if we go running through what we have, we'll soon have to break the hundred pounds, and that would be a pity.

BRIDGET. Shame on you, Peter. Give her the shilling and your blessing with it, or our own luck will go from us.

PETER *goes to the box and takes out a shilling.*

BRIDGET [*to the* OLD WOMAN]. Will you have a drink of milk?

THE POOR OLD WOMAN. It is not food or drink that I want.

PETER [*offering the shilling*]. Here is something for you.

THE POOR OLD WOMAN. That is not what I want. It is not silver I want.

PETER. What is it you would be asking for?

THE POOR OLD WOMAN. If anyone would give me help he must give me himself, he must give me all. [PETER *goes over to the table, staring at the shilling in his hand in a bewildered way and stands whispering to* BRIDGET.]

MICHAEL. Have you no man of your own, ma'am?

THE POOR OLD WOMAN. I have not. With all the lovers that brought me their love, I never set out the bed for any.

MICHAEL. Are you lonely going the roads, ma'am?

THE POOR OLD WOMAN. I have my thoughts and I have my hopes.

MICHAEL. What hopes have you to hold to?

THE POOR OLD WOMAN. The hope of getting my beautiful fields back again; the hope of putting the strangers out of my house.

MICHAEL. What way will you do that, ma'am?

THE POOR OLD WOMAN. I have good friends that will help me. They are gathering to help me now. I am not afraid. If they are put down to-day, they will get the upper hand to-morrow. [*She gets up.*] I must be going to meet my friends. They are coming to help me, and I must be there to welcome them. I must call the neighbours together to welcome them.

MICHAEL. I will go with you.

BRIDGET. It is not her friends you have to go and welcome, Michael; it is the girl coming into the house you have to welcome. You have plenty to do; it is food and drink you have to bring to the house. The woman that is coming is not coming with empty hands; you would not have an empty house before her. [*To the* OLD WOMAN] Maybe you don't know, ma'am, that my son is going to be married to-morrow.

THE POOR OLD WOMAN. It is not a man going to his marriage that I look to for help.

PETER [*to* BRIDGET]. Who is she, do you think, at all?

BRIDGET. You did not tell us your name yet, ma'am.

THE POOR OLD WOMAN. Some call me the Poor Old Woman, and there are some that call me Cathleen the daughter of Hoolihan.

PETER. I think I knew some one of that name once. Who was it, I wonder? It must have been some one I knew when I was a boy. No, no, I remember I heard it in a song.

THE POOR OLD WOMAN [*who is standing in the doorway*]. They are wondering that there were songs made for me; there have been many songs made for me. I heard one on the wind this morning. [*She sings*]

> Do not make a great keening
> When the graves have been dug to-morrow.
> Do not call the white-scarfed riders
> To the burying that shall be to-morrow.
> Do not spread food to call strangers
> To the wakes that shall be to-morrow.
> Do not give money for prayers
> For the dead that shall die to-morrow.
> They will have no need of prayers, they will
>   have no need of prayers.

MICHAEL. I do not know what that song means; but tell me something I can do for you.

PETER. Come over to me, Michael.

MICHAEL. Hush, father; listen to her.

THE POOR OLD WOMAN. It is a hard service they take that help me. Many that are red-cheeked now will be pale-cheeked; many that have been free to walk the hills and the bogs and the rushes will be sent to walk hard streets in far countries; many a good plan will be broken; many that have gathered money will not stay to spend it; many a child will be born and there will be no father at its christening to give it a name. They that had red cheeks will have pale cheeks for my sake; and for all that they will think they are well paid. [*She goes out. Her voice is heard outside singing*]

> They shall be remembered for ever
> They shall be alive for ever
> They shall be speaking for ever
> The people shall hear them for ever.

BRIDGET [*to* PETER]. Look at him, Peter; he has the look of a man that has got the touch. [*Raising her voice*] Look here, Michael, at the wedding clothes [*taking clothes from dresser*]. You have a right to fit them on now. It would be a pity to-morrow if they did not fit; the boys would be laughing at you. Take them, Michael, and go into the room and fit them on. [*She puts them on his arm.*]

MICHAEL. What wedding are you talking of? What clothes will I be wearing to-morrow?

BRIDGET. These are the clothes you are going to wear when you marry Delia Cahel to-morrow.

MICHAEL. I had forgotten that. [*He looks at the clothes and turns toward the inner room, but stops at the sound of cheering outside.*]

PETER. There is the shouting come to our own door. What is it has happened?

Neighbours come crowding in, PATRICK *and* DELIA *with them.*

PATRICK. There are ships in the bay; the French are landing at Killala.

PETER *takes his pipe from his mouth and his hat off and stands up. The clothes slip from* MICHAEL'S *arm.*

DELIA. Michael! [*He takes no notice.*] Michael! [*He turns towards her.*] Why do you look at me like a stranger? [*She drops his arm.* BRIDGET *goes over toward her.*]

PATRICK. The boys are all hurrying down the hillsides to meet the French.

DELIA. Michael won't be going to join the French.

BRIDGET [*to* PETER]. Tell him not to go, Peter.

PETER. It's no use. He doesn't hear a word we're saying.

BRIDGET. Try, Delia, and coax him over to the fire.

DELIA. Michael, Michael, you won't leave me! You won't join the French and we going to be married to-morrow! [*She puts her arms about him. He turns to her as if about to yield.*]

OLD WOMAN'S *voice outside*—

> They shall be remembered for ever
> The people shall hear them for ever.

MICHAEL *breaks away from* DELIA *and goes out.*

BRIDGET [*laying her hand on* PATRICK'S *arm*]. Did you see an old woman going down the path?

PATRICK. I did not, but I saw a young girl and she had the walk of a queen.

RUDYARD KIPLING

The Last Chantey

"And there was no more sea"

THUS said the Lord in the Vault above
  the Cherubim,
  Calling to the Angels and the Souls in
    their degree:
  "Lo! Earth has passed away
  On the smoke of Judgment Day.
  That Our word may be established
    shall We gather up the sea?"

Loud sang the souls of the jolly, jolly
    mariners:
  "Plague upon the hurricane that made
    us furl and flee!
  But the war is done between us,
  In the deep the Lord hath seen us—
  Our bones we'll leave the barracout',
    and God may sink the sea!"

Then said the soul of Judas that betrayèd
    Him:
  "Lord, hast Thou forgotten Thy cove-
    nant with me?
  How once a year I go
  To cool me on the floe?
  And Ye take my day of mercy if Ye
    take away the sea."

Then said the soul of the Angel of the
    Off-shore Wind:
  (He that bits the thunder when the
    bull-mouthed breakers flee):
  "I have watch and ward to keep
  O'er Thy wonders on the deep,
  And Ye take mine honour from me if
    Ye take away the sea!"

Loud sang the souls of the jolly, jolly
    mariners:
  "Nay, but we were angry, and a hasty
    folk are we.
  If we worked the ship together
  Till she foundered in foul weather,
  Are we babes that we should clamour
    for a vengeance on the sea?"

Then said the souls of the slaves that men
    threw overboard:
  "Kennelled in the picaroon a weary
    band were we;
  But Thy arm was strong to save,
  And it touched us on the wave,
  And we drowsed the long tides idle till
    Thy Trumpets tore the sea."

Then cried the soul of the stout Apostle
    Paul to God:
  "Once we frapped a ship, and she
    laboured woundily.
  There were fourteen score of these,
  And they blessed Thee on their knees,
  When they learned Thy Grace and
    Glory under Malta by the sea!"

Loud sang the souls of the jolly, jolly
    mariners,
  Plucking at their harps, and they
    plucked unhandily:
  "Our thumbs are rough and tarred,
  And the tune is something hard—
  May we lift a Deepsea Chantey such as
    seamen use at sea?"

Then said the souls of the gentlemen-
    adventurers—
  Fettered wrist to bar all for red in-
    iquity:
  "Ho, we revel in our chains
  O'er the sorrow that was Spain's;
  Heave or sink it, leave or drink it, we
    were masters of the sea!"

Up spake the soul of a grey Gothavn
    'speckshioner—
  (He that led the flenching in the fleets
    of fair Dundee):
  "Oh, the ice-blink white and near,
  And the bowhead breaching clear!
  Will Ye whelm them all for wanton-
    ness that wallow in the sea?"

Loud sang the souls of the jolly, jolly
    mariners,
  Crying: "Under Heaven, here is neither
    lead nor lee!

Must we sing for evermore
On the windless, glassy floor?
Take back your golden fiddles and we'll
beat to open sea!"

Then stooped the Lord, and He called the
good sea up to Him,
And 'stablishèd its borders unto all
eternity,
That such as have no pleasure
For to praise the Lord by measure,
They may enter into galleons and serve
Him on the sea.

*Sun, Wind, and Cloud shall fail not from
the face of it,*
*Stinging, ringing spindrift, nor the ful-
mar flying free;*
And the ships shall go abroad
To the Glory of the Lord
*Who heard the silly sailor-folk and
gave them back their sea!*

The Truce of the Bear

Yearly, with tent and rifle, our careless
white men go
By the pass called Muttianee, to shoot in
the vale below.
Yearly by Muttianee he follows our white
men in—
Matun, the old blind beggar, bandaged
from brow to chin.

Eyeless, noseless, and lipless—toothless,
broken of speech,
Seeking a dole at the doorway he mum-
bles his tale to each;
Over and over the story, ending as he
began:
"Make ye no truce with Adam-zad—the
Bear that walks like a Man!

"There was a flint in my musket—pricked
and primed was the pan,
When I went hunting Adam-zad—the
Bear that stands like a Man.

I looked my last on the timber, I looked
my last on the snow,
When I went hunting Adam-zad fifty
summers ago!

"I knew his times and his seasons, as he
knew mine, that fed
By night in the ripened maizefield and
robbed my house of bread.
I knew his strength and cunning, as he
knew mine, that crept
At dawn to the crowded goat-pens and
plundered while I slept.

"Up from his stony playground—down
from his well-digged lair—
Out on the naked ridges ran Adam-zad
the Bear;
Groaning, grunting, and roaring, heavy
with stolen meals,
Two long marches to northward, and I
was at his heels!

"Two long marches to northward, at the
fall of the second night,
I came on mine enemy Adam-zad all
panting from his flight.
There was a charge in the musket—
pricked and primed was the pan—
My finger crooked on the trigger—when
he reared up like a man.

"Horrible, hairy, human, with paws like
hands in prayer,
Making his supplication rose Adam-zad
the Bear!
I looked at the swaying shoulders, at the
paunch's swag and swing,
And my heart was touched with pity for
the monstrous, pleading thing.

"Touched with pity and wonder, I did
not fire then . . .
I have looked no more on women—I have
walked no more with men.
Nearer he tottered and nearer, with paws
like hands that pray—
From brow to jaw that steel-shod paw, it
ripped my face away!

"Sudden, silent, and savage, searing as
flame the blow—
Faceless I fell before his feet, fifty summers ago.
I heard him grunt and chuckle—I heard
him pass to his den.
He left me blind to the darkened years
and the little mercy of men.

"Now ye go down in the morning with
guns of the newer style,
That load (I have felt) in the middle and
range (I have heard) a mile!
Luck to the white man's rifle, that shoots
so fast and true,
But—pay, and I lift my bandage and
show what the Bear can do!"

"(Flesh like slag in the furnace, knobbed
and withered and grey—
Matun, the old blind beggar, he gives
good worth for his pay.)
"Rouse him at noon in the bushes, follow
and press him hard—
Not for his ragings and roarings flinch ye
from Adam-zad.

"But (pay, and I put back the bandage)
this is the time to fear,
When he stands up like a tired man, tottering near and near;
When he stands up as pleading, in wavering, man-brute guise,
When he veils the hate and cunning of his
little, swinish eyes;

"When he shows as seeking quarter, with
paws like hands in prayer,
That is the time of peril—the time of the
Truce of the Bear!"

Eyeless, noseless, and lipless, asking a dole
at the door,
Matun, the old blind beggar, he tells it
o'er and o'er;
Fumbling and feeling the rifles, warming
his hands at the flame,
Hearing our careless white men talk of
the morrow's game;

Over and over the story, ending as he
began:—
*"There is no truce with Adam-zad, the
Bear that looks like a Man!"*

The Bell Buoy

THEY christened my brother of old—
And a saintly name he bears—
They gave him his place to hold
At the head of the belfry-stairs,
Where the minster-towers stand
And the breeding kestrels cry.
Would I change with my brother a
league inland?
(*Shoal! 'Ware shoal!*) Not I!

In the flush of the hot June prime,
O'er sleek flood-tides afire,
I hear him hurry the chime
To the bidding of checked Desire;
Till the sweated ringers tire
And the wild bob-majors die.
Could I wait for my turn in the godly
choir?
(*Shoal! 'Ware shoal!*) Not I!

When the smoking scud is blown—
When the greasy wind-rack lowers—
Apart and at peace and alone,
He counts the changeless hours.
He wars with darkling Powers
(I war with a darkling sea);
Would he stoop to my work in the
gusty mirk?
(*Shoal! 'Ware shoal!*) Not he!

There was never a priest to pray,
There was never a hand to toll,
When they made me guard of the bay,
And moored me over the shoal.
I rock, I reel, and I roll—
My four great hammers ply—
Could I speak or be still at the Church's
will?
(*Shoal! 'Ware shoal!*) Not I!

The landward marks have failed,
The fog-bank glides unguessed,

The seaward lights are veiled,
　The spent deep feigns her rest:
　But my ear is laid to her breast,
I lift to the swell—I cry!
　　Could I wait in sloth on the Church's
　　　oath?
(*Shoal! 'Ware shoal!*)　Not I!

At the careless end of night
　I thrill to the nearing screw;
I turn in the clearing light
　And I call to the drowsy crew;
　And the mud boils foul and blue
As the blind bow backs away.
　　Will they give me their thanks if they
　　　clear the banks?
(*Shoal! 'Ware shoal!*)　Not they!

The beach-pools cake and skim,
　The bursting spray-heads freeze,
I gather on crown and rim
　The grey, grained ice of the seas,
　Where, sheathed from bitt to trees,
The plunging colliers lie.
　　Would I barter my place for the
　　　Church's grace?
(*Shoal! 'Ware shoal!*)　Not I!

Through the blur of the whirling snow,
　Or the black of the inky sleet,
The lanterns gather and grow,
　And I look for the homeward fleet.
　Rattle of block and sheet—
"Ready about—stand by!"
　　Shall I ask them a fee ere they fetch
　　　the quay?
(*Shoal! 'Ware shoal!*)　Not I!

I dip and I surge and I swing
　In the rip of the racing tide,
By the gates of doom I sing,
　On the horns of death I ride.
　A ship-length overside,
Between the course and the sand,
　Fretted and bound I bide
　　Peril whereof I cry.
　　Would I change with my brother a
　　　league inland?
(*Shoal! 'Ware shoal!*)　Not I!

Mandalay

By the old Moulmein Pagoda, lookin'
　　eastward to the sea,
There's a Burma girl a-settin', and I
　　know she thinks o' me;
For the wind is in the palm-trees, and the
　　temple-bells they say:
"Come you back, you British soldier;
　　come you back to Mandalay!"
　　Come you back to Mandalay,
　　Where the old Flotilla lay:
　　Can't you 'ear their paddles chunkin'
　　　from Rangoon to Mandalay?
　　On the road to Mandalay,
　　Where the flyin'-fishes play,
　　An' the dawn comes up like thunder
　　　outer China 'crost the Bay!

'Er petticoat was yaller an' 'er little cap
　　was green,
An' 'er name was Supi-yaw-lat—jes' the
　　same as Theebaw's Queen,
An' I seed her first a-smokin' of a
　　whackin' white cheroot,
An' a-wastin' Christian kisses on an
　　'eathen idol's foot:
　　Bloomin' idol made o' mud—
　　Wot they called the Great Gawd
　　　Budd—
　　Plucky lot she cared for idols when
　　　I kissed 'er where she stud!
　　On the road to Mandalay . . .

When the mist was on the rice-fields an
　　the sun was droppin' slow,
She'd git 'er little banjo an' she'd sing
　　"*Kulla-lo-lo!*"
With 'er arm upon my shoulder an' 'er
　　cheek agin my cheek
We useter watch the steamers an' the
　　hathis pilin' teak.
　　Elephints a-pilin' teak
　　In the sludgy, squdgy creek,
　　Where the silence 'ung that 'eavy you
　　　was 'arf afraid to speak!
　　On the road to Mandalay . . .

But that's all shove be'ind me—long ago
an' fur away,
An' there ain't no 'busses runnin' from the
Bank to Mandalay;
An' I'm learnin' 'ere in London what the
ten-year soldier tells:
"If you've 'eard the East a-callin', you
won't never 'eed naught else."
No! you won't 'eed nothin' else
But them spicy garlic smells,
An' the sunshine an' the palm-trees
an' the tinkly temple-bells;
On the road to Mandalay . . .

I am sick o' wastin' leather on these gritty
pavin'-stones,
An' the blasted Henglish drizzle wakes
the fever in my bones;
'Tho' I walks with fifty 'ousemaids outer
Chelsea to the Strand,
An' they talks a lot o' lovin', but wot do
they understand?
Beefy face an' grubby 'and—
Law! wot do they understand?
I've a neater, sweeter maiden in a
cleaner, greener land!
On the road to Mandalay . . .

Ship me somewheres east of Suez, where
the best is like the worst,
Where there aren't no Ten Command-
ments an' a man can raise a
thirst;
For the temple-bells are callin', an' it's
there that I would be—
By the old Moulmein Pagoda, looking
lazy at the sea;
On the road to Mandalay,
Where the old Flotilla lay,
With our sick beneath the awnings
when we went to Mandalay!
O the road to Mandalay,
Where the flyin'-fishes play,
An' the dawn comes up like thunder
outer China 'crost the Bay!

The 'Eathen

THE 'eathen in 'is blindness bows down
to wood an' stone;
'E don't obey no orders unless they is 'is
own;
'E keeps 'is side-arms awful: 'e leaves 'em
all about,
An' then comes up the Regiment an' pokes
the 'eathen out.

All along o' dirtiness, all along o' mess,
All along o' doin' things rather-more-or-
less,
All along of abby-nay, kul, an' hazar-ho,
Mind you keep your rifle an' yourself jus'
so!

The young recruit is 'aughty—'e draf's
from Gawd knows where;
They bid 'im show 'is stockin's an' lay 'is
mattress square;
'E calls it bloomin' nonsense—'e doesn't
know, no more—
An' then up comes 'is Company an' kicks
'im round the floor!

The young recruit is 'ammered—'e takes
it very hard;
'E 'angs 'is 'ead an' mutters—'e sulks
about the yard;
'E talks o' "cruel tyrants" which 'e'll
swing for by-an'-by,
An' the others 'ears an' mocks 'im, an' the
boy goes orf to cry.

The young recruit is silly—'e thinks o'
suicide;
'E's lost 'is gutter-devil; 'e 'asn't got 'is
pride;
But day by day they kicks 'im, which 'elps
'im on a bit,
Till 'e finds 'isself one mornin' with a full
an' proper kit.

Gettin' clear o' dirtiness, gettin' done with
mess,
Gettin' shut o' doin' things rather-more-
or-less;

Not so fond of abby-nay, kul, nor hazar-
ho,
Learns to keep 'is rifle an' 'issell jus' so!

The young recruit is 'appy—'e throws a
chest to suit;
You see 'im grow mustaches; you 'ear 'im
slap 'is boot;
'E learns to drop the "bloodies" from
every word 'e slings,
An' 'e shows an 'ealthy brisket when 'e
strips for bars an' rings.

The cruel-tyrant-sergeants they watch
'im 'arf a year;
They watch 'im with 'is comrades, they
watch 'im with 'is beer;
They watch 'im with the women at the
regimental dance,
And the cruel-tyrant-sergeants send 'is
name along for "Lance."

'An' now 'e's 'arf o' nothin', an' all a private yet,
'Is room they up an' rags 'im to see what
they will get.
They rags 'im low an' cunnin', each dirty
trick they can,
But 'e learns to sweat 'is temper an' 'e
learns to sweat 'is man.

An', last, a Colour-Sergeant, as such to
be obeyed,
'E schools 'is men at cricket, 'e tells 'em
on parade;
They sees 'im quick an' 'andy, uncommon
set an' smart,
An' so 'e talks to orficers which 'ave the
Core at 'eart.

'E learns to do 'is watchin' without it
showin' plain;
'E learns to save a dummy, an' shove 'im
straight again;
'E learns to check a ranker that's buyin'
leave to shirk;
An' 'e learns to make men like 'im so
they'll learn to like their work.

An' when it comes to marchin' he'll see
their socks are right,
An' when it comes to action 'e shows 'em
how to sight.
'E knows their ways of thinkin' and just
what's in their mind;
'E knows when they are takin' on an'
when they've fell be'ind.

'E knows each talkin' corpril that leads
a squad astray;
'E feels 'is innards 'eavin', 'is bowels givin'
way;
'E sees the blue-white faces all tryin' 'ard
to grin,
An' 'e stands an' waits an' suffers till it's
time to cap 'em in.

An' now the hugly bullets come peckin'
through the dust,
An' no one wants to face 'em, but every
beggar must;
So, like a man in irons, which isn't glad
to go,
They moves 'em off by companies uncommon stiff an' slow.

Of all 'is five years' schoolin' they don't
remember much
Excep' the not retreatin', the step an'
keepin' touch.
It looks like teachin' wasted when they
duck an' spread an' 'op—
But if 'e 'adn't learned 'em they'd be all
about the shop.

An' now it's " 'Oo goes backward?" an'
now it's " 'Oo comes on?"
An' now it's "Get the doolies, an' now
the Captain's gone;
An' now it's bloody murder, but all the
while they 'ear
'Is voice, the same as barrick-drill,
a-shepherdin' the rear.

'E's just as sick as they are, 'is 'eart is
like to split,
But 'e works 'em, works 'em, works 'em
till he feels 'em take the bit;

The rest is 'oldin' steady till the watchful bugles play,
An' 'e lifts 'em, lifts 'em, lifts 'em through
the charge that wins the day!

*The 'eathen in 'is blindness bows down to
wood an' stone;*
*'E don't obey no orders unless they is 'is
own.*
*The 'eathen in 'is blindness must end
where 'e began,*
*But the backbone of the Army is the Non-
commissioned Man!*

*Keep away from dirtiness—keep away
from mess,*
*Don't get into doin' things rather-more-
or-less!*
*Let's ha' done with abby-nay, kul, and
hazar-ho;*
*Mind you keep your rifle an' yourself jus'
so!*

Chant-Pagan

ME that 'ave been what I've been—
Me that 'ave gone where I've gone—
Me that 'ave seen what I've seen—
'Ow can I ever take on
With awful old England again,
An' 'ouses both sides of the street,
And 'edges two sides of the lane,
And the parson an' gentry between,
An' touchin' my 'at when we meet—
Me that 'ave been what I've been?

Me that 'ave watched 'arf a world
'Eave up all shiny with dew,
Kopje on kop to the sun,
An' as soon as the mist let 'em through
Our 'elios winkin' like fun—
Three sides of a ninety-mile square,
Over valleys as big as a shire—
*Are ye there? Are ye there? Are ye
there?*
An' then the blind drum of our fire . . .
An' I'm rollin' 'is lawns for the Squire,
Me!

Me that 'ave rode through the dark
Forty mile, often, on end,
Along the Ma'ollisberg Range,
With only the stars for my mark
An' only the night for my friend,
An' things runnin' off as you pass,
An' things jumpin' up in the grass,
An' the silence, the shine an' the size
Of the 'igh, unexpressible skies—
I am takin' some letters almost
As much as a mile to the post,
An' "mind you come back with the
change"!
Me!

Me that saw Barberton took
When we dropped through the clouds on
their 'ead,
An' they 'ove the guns over and fled—
Me that was through Di'mond 'Ill,
An' Pieters an' Springs an' Belfast—
From Dundee to Vereeniging all—
Me that stuck out to the last
(An' five bloomin' bars on my chest)—
I am doin' my Sunday-school best,
By the 'elp of the Squire an' 'is wife
(Not to mention the 'ousemaid an'
cook),
To come in an' 'ands up an' be still,
An' honestly work for my bread,
My livin' in that state of life
To which it shall please God to call
Me!

Me that 'ave followed my trade
In the place where the Lightnin's are
made,
'Twixt the Rains and the Sun and the
Moon—
Me that lay down an' got up
Three years with the sky for my roof—
That 'ave ridden my 'unger an' thirst
Six thousand raw mile on the hoof
With the Vaal and the Orange for cup,
An' the Brandwater Basin for dish,—
Oh! it's 'ard to be'ave as they wish
(Too 'ard, an' a little too soon),
I'll 'ave to think over it first—
Me!

I will arise an' get 'ence;—
I will trek South and make sure
If it's only my fancy or not
That the sunshine of England is pale,
And the breezes of England are stale,
An' there's somethin' gone small with the
    lot;
For *I* know of a sun an' a wind,
An' some plains and a mountain be'ind,
An' some graves by a barb-wire fence;
An' a Dutchman I've fought 'oo might
    give
Me a job were I ever inclined,
To look in an' offsaddle an' live
Where there's neither a road nor a tree—
But only my Maker an' me,
And I think it will kill me or cure,
So *I* think I will go there an' see.
                    Me!

LIONEL JOHNSON (1867-1902)

By the Statue of King Charles at Charing Cross

Sombre and rich, the skies;
Great glooms, and starry plains.
Gently the night wind sighs;
Else a vast silence reigns.

The splendid silence clings
Around me: and around
The saddest of all kings
Crowned, and again discrowned.

Comely and calm, he rides
Hard by his own Whitehall:
Only the night wind glides:
No crowds, nor rebels, brawl.

Gone, too, his Court; and yet,
The stars his courtiers are:
Stars in their stations set;
And every wandering star.

Alone he rides, alone,
The fair and fatal king:
Dark night is all his own,
That strange and solemn thing.

Which are more full of fate:
The stars; or those sad eyes?
Which are more still and great:
Those brows; or the dark skies?

Although his whole heart yearn
In passionate tragedy:
Never was face so stern
With sweet austerity.

Vanquished in life, his death
By beauty made amends:
The passing of his breath
Won his defeated ends.

Brief life, and hapless? Nay:
Through death, life grew sublime.
Speak after sentence? Yea:
And to the end of time.

Armoured he rides, his head
Bare to the stars of doom:
He triumphs now, the dead,
Beholding London's gloom.

Our wearier spirit faints,
Vexed in the world's employ:
His soul was of the saints;
And art to him was joy.

King, tried in fires of woe!
Men hunger for thy grace:
And through the night I go,
Loving thy mournful face.

Yet, when the city sleeps;
When all the cries are still:
The stars and heavenly deeps
Work out a perfect will.